A Year with Swollen

Brian Eno – musician, producer, visual artist and activist – first came to international prominence in the early seventies as a founding member of British band Roxy Music. His visionary production includes albums with Talking Heads, Devo, U2, Laurie Anderson and Coldplay, while his long list of collaborations include recordings with David Bowie, David Byrne, Grace Jones, Karl Hyde and James Blake, among many others. His visual experiments with light and video continue to parallel his musical career, with exhibitions all over the globe.

To date he has released over thirty albums of his own music and exhibited extensively, as far afield as the Venice Biennale and the sails of the Sydney Opera House. He is a founding member of the Long Now Foundation, a trustee of ClientEarth and patron of Videre est Credere. His latest album, *ForeverAndEverNoMore*, was released on UMC in October 2022.

Further praise for *A Year with Swollen Appendices*:

'What's striking is how perpetually busy Eno is, as he flits between his overwhelming personal life and the four music projects he undertook that year (with James, U2, David Bowie, and the War Child Help album). The diary format is ideal for reflecting that ebb and flow.' *Pitchfork*

'Brian Eno is famously a man of many ideas . . . *A Year with Swollen Appendices* is full of them.' Alexis Petridis, *Guardian*

'[An] insight into the mind of the enigmatic musician, record-producer and artist . . . Heroically indiscreet . . . a compelling mishmash of random aphorisms ("cooking is a way of listening to the radio", "saying that cultural objects have value is like saying that telephones have conversations"), impassioned meditations on the Bosnian situation, and whimsical musings.' *Independent*

'Eno is not your average person, which makes the diary as invigorating and enthralling a read as you could possibly wish for . . . Eno appears to have mastered the art of intellectual juggling . . . Inevitably, he writes extremely well and cogently on all manner of diverse subjects . . . this diary mutates from wilful self-absorption into a form drifting self-expression that anyone with an open mind can partake of and enjoy. It's all very astute and genuinely clever . . . If you're looking for stoicism and humdrum with a major difference, look towards *A Year with Swollen Appendices* . . . throughout is an almost hypnotic passing of time and a person in full engagement with it.' *Irish Times*

'*A Year with Swollen Appendices* is by turns fascinating, engaging and wonderfully mundane. Our world has changed in profound ways, but Eno's ideas are remarkably durable, his perspectives still feel fresh with possibility. This writing hasn't lost any of its power to entertain, persuade and inspire.' *The Wire*

'A cranium tour of one of the most creative minds of our age . . . [Eno] delivers razor-sharp commentary with devilish snarkiness and brutal honesty.' *Wired*

'Fun facts about Eno that have never once come across in an interview jump out readily from his own writing . . . Reading Eno's diary gives me a lot to think about . . . it looks beautiful . . . I mean, you could do worse than escaping into the world of a sexy genius who travels the world making art and dining with legends. At the same time, if you're looking to make something with this time, the essays on culture and creativity will prompt new ways of thinking about your craft.' *Medium*

A Year with Swollen Appendices

Brian Eno's Diary 1995

25th
Anniversary
Edition

First published in the UK in 1996
This anniversary edition first published in the UK and the USA in 2020
by Faber & Faber Ltd,
Bloomsbury House,
74–77 Great Russell Street,
London WC1B 3DA

This paperback edition published in 2023

Typeset by Faber & Faber Ltd
Printed in Italy by Graphicom

A CIP record for this book
is available from the British Library

ISBN 978–0–571–37462–5

2 4 6 8 10 9 7 5 3 1

CONTENTS

INTRODUCTION
TO THE ANNIVERSARY EDITION

This book was first published twenty-five years ago. What has happened in those twenty-five years?

I started out by making a list of new words – ideas that either didn't exist or weren't in the air when I wrote the diary. What astonished me is how many of them there are. Some of these words – and the ideas and activities they relate to – have become so normal that we forget they're only a few years old.

A friend told me a story that captures how quickly things become taken for granted – indispensable parts of our lives. He was on a flight and, after take-off, the pilot announced that the airline had just introduced Wi-Fi to its fleet of jets, so everybody could now use their phones on the plane. There was delighted applause and many of the passengers immediately took out their devices and began doing all the things we do with them. After about thirty minutes the Wi-Fi stopped working, for some technical reason. Within seconds, people were complaining angrily about the 'terrible service': it had gone from miracle to expectation in half an hour.

Looking at this list of words makes me realize that we live in a profoundly different reality now than we did in 1995. I assume new language evolves when there are new things that need to be talked about – so the faster those new things are coming at us, the more new language we need for them. Perhaps we would expect there to be lots of new words to do with the Internet and social media, but what's noticeable about the list is that there are some areas of human activity that hardly figure in it at all: for example, art, religion and philosophy. Does this mean that we aren't so interested in those things any more and have stopped talking about them? Could it mean that they just aren't changing so quickly to need new language? Or does it mean that they're changing so much that we no longer recognize them in their new forms? For example, is *QAnon* actually an emerging religion? Is *CRISPR* gene-editing technology possibly a new form of art? Is *decluttering*, à la Marie Kondo, a sort of spiritual discipline that operates in the space where religion operated? Is *TikTok* a new mass art form that we aren't taking seriously? (Will we, in another twenty-five years, reverently scroll through old TikTok videos, recognizing them as the beginnings of a truly universal, democratic art form?) Is *binge-watching* Netflix the future of art, as galleries and public spaces become more dangerous?

Completely missing from the diary is any mention of climate change, populism, pandemics or China, just to mention a few of the things that occupy a lot of our thoughts now.

Looking at any item on the list I ask myself: 'In which category of human experience does this particular phenomenon belong?' It turns out that a large fraction of the new words are, perhaps unsurprisingly, to do with interpersonal relationships – how we relate and present ourselves to each other.

Body-shaming, cancel culture, chatlines, Chaturbate, cisgender, Creative Commons licence, crowdfund, crowdsource, distance learning, DM, dox, emoji, emoticon, follow/unfollow, friend/unfriend, and then all the new language around social media. This category is where there seems to have been most activity. Are humans communicating more than they ever did in the past? Is this process of 'community forming' now in hyperdrive because our old ways of making communities (i.e., by growing up and living and working with other people, or by engaging with them in common causes) are no longer working? Or do we just need more forms of community? And from whence arises this insatiable appetite for constant conversation? Is it a case of, in Eric Hoffer's words, you can never get enough of what you don't really want?

And what are we *not* doing when we're doing all this chatting?

Novelty in the world isn't the only thing that spurs new language. New people want new language because it's a way of distinguishing themselves from old people. This driver of linguistic evolution has to do with another kind of communication. It's often not about saying new things but about saying the same things differently and, in doing so, indicating which tribe you belong to (and which ones you don't). Language is a badge of membership or affiliation, and sometimes that's most of what it's saying. Language of that kind is designed to tell you more about the speaker than of what is being spoken.

One of the things that seems to have happened in the last twenty-five years is that the distinction between these two kinds of language has blurred in the public sphere. This era has been called post-truth because language is increasingly intended to be instrumental – that is, intended to bring about an effect – rather than accurate. There's a difference between shouting 'FIRE' in a crowded theatre that is actually on fire as opposed to doing so in one that isn't. Increasingly the role of the media – particularly in England, Australia and America; the Murdoch constellation – has become to trigger volatile public response by shouting 'FIRE' almost all the time. When it's all about clickbait – grabbing attention – it turns out you don't actually need much news. Just a flood of red flags will do the job.

This confusion – between language as the articulation of meaning and language as *trigger* or *mood music* – has now penetrated thoroughly into public discourse. *Twenty-four-hour rolling news* and the Internet have created a demand for content that apparently can't be met with actual news and has to be augmented by *opinion columnists, shock jocks, influencers* and *Twitterati. Churnalists*, freed of the need to actually conduct research and fact-checking, trade in *recycled* 'news' about as substantial as smoke. But if you know that people are inclined to believe there's no smoke without a fire, then all you have to do is keep producing more smoke.

Many of these new words suggest the dissolution of a certain quality of public discourse that we have taken for granted since the Enlightenment, which hinged on the possibility of reaching evidence-based consensus – albeit even temporarily – about what constitutes reality. The post-modern scepticism of any distinction between ideologically derived value systems and evidence-driven science is now grasped at gratefully by libertarians, populists, identitarians and tax evaders the world over: 'Why shouldn't there be a special reality just for me?' they demand. An early warning sign of this attitude creeping into politics was when a member of Dubya's entourage, questioned about the veracity of some claims he'd made in support of the Iraq war, said: 'We're an empire now, and when we act, we create our own reality.'

It's interesting to watch that kind of hubris crash up against a little strand of RNA – and conspicuously lose the battle. As I write this, we're five months into the Covid pandemic, and it turns out that even an empire can't change biological reality. I wonder if it will make any difference to how we view the role of leadership in the future, when we evaluate the various national responses to Covid and notice that the people who dealt with it more successfully were not the macho braggarts, not the 'we-make-our-own-reality' brigade, not the 'man-up' populists, not the Panglossian libertarians, but the people who had the humility to listen to the science and the humanity to care enough to act upon it.

3D printer
4chan
9/11
AI (artificial intelligence)
Airbnb
Alexa
algorithm
alt-right
alternative facts
Amazon
Anonymous
Anthropocene
anti-natalism
Antifa
apps
Arab Spring

ASMR
augmented reality
avatar
B2B (business-to-business)
bank bailout
Bank of Mum and Dad
barista
Belt and Road
bendy bus
bestie
big data
billionaires
binge-watch
biodiversity
biosphere
birtherism
bitcoin
black hat
Black Lives Matter
bling
blockchain
blog
Blu-ray
Bluetooth
body-shaming
boogaloo
boomer
Border Force (UK)
Botox
bots
box set
Brexit

BRICS, the
bromance
butt lift
buzzy
cancel culture
cannabis stores
carbon footprint
carbon-neutral
CBT (cognitive behavioural therapy)
CDO (collateralized debt obligations)
CDS (credit default swap)
chatlines
Chaturbate
chav
China
chip and PIN
churnalism
cisgender
Citizens United
cli-fi
clickbait
climate crisis
climate refugee
cloud, the
command and control
conflict minerals
contactless
content farm
cookies
Corbynista
Covid
Creative Commons licence

CRISPR
crowdfund
crowdsource
cultural appropriation
cyber attack
cyber crime
cyber warfare
daisy-cutter
dark money
dark web
data-driven
data harvesting
data point
data set
Davos
day trader
declutter
deep state
deepfake
denialism
derivatives
digital audio
dirty bomb
disaster capitalism
disinformation
distance learning
DM (direct message, Instagram)
DMT (drug)
doomscrolling
dot com bubble
dox
drone warfare

drones
dubstep
e-bike
e-cigarettes
eBay
ecocide
egg donor
electric cars
embedded (journalists)
emo
emoji
emoticon
end of days
end times
end-to-end encryption
enhanced interrogation
entitled
essential worker
ETF (exchange-traded fund)
facial recognition
factoid
fake news
false flag (attack)
fat finger
fat studies
first responders
fit (attractive)
flash crash
flash mob
flat-earther
follow/unfollow
followers

FOMO (fear of missing out)
foodie
football mum
friend/unfriend
garage (music)
gaslighting
gated community
gender-neutral
gender studies
Generation Z
generative
ghost (as a verb)
gig economy
glamping
global warming
globalization
gluten-free
goji berries
goldilocks
GPS
graphene
Great Awakening
grime
ground-source heating
grunge
hacking
hands-free
hashtag
helicopter parenting
hive mind
Homeland Security
hooking up

hotdesking
hotspot
housing bubble
ICE (Immigration and Customs Enforcement, USA)
iconic
identity theft
ifpology
impostor syndrome
inbox
incel
influencer
information warfare
Instagram
intersectionality
iPod
Islamophobia
isolation
Jägerbomb
'jump on a call'
Jungle (refugee camp), the
Karen
ketamine
Kindle
lab meat
labradoodle
laptop
Leaver (*cf* Remainer)
LGBTQA+
libtard
LinkedIn
localization (*cf* globalization)
location services

lockdown
LOL
machine learning
malware
mansplain
Matrix, The
MeToo
Melissa worm, the
MERS
microaggression
microdosing
milk substitutes
millennial
mindfulness
Minecraft
minger/minging
mission creep
mood music
MSM (mainstream media)
muted
nanotechnology
Napster
Netflix
news threads
NLP (neuro-linguistic programming)
non-binary
nose to tail
noughties
Occupy
oligarch
OMG
one-click shopping

one per cent, the
online banking
online shopping
open-source
opinion columnist
optics
Oyster card
page view
palimony
pandemics
parkour
PayPal
paywall
peng
Pepe the Frog
Periscope
phishing
photobomb
Photoshopped
'ping me'
Pizzagate
platform
pocket call
podcast
pop-up
portrait mode
post-Internet
post-truth
POV
PPE (personal protective equipment)
preprint
privately owned spacecraft

pronouns
QAnon
QR code
quantified self
quantum computing
quarantini
queen bee
ransomware
rapture
reality TV
reboot
recycling
red-pilled
reddit
Remainer (*cf* Leaver)
Remoaner
renewables
retweet
rewilding
robotics
router
routine mass surveillance
SARS
satnav
screen time
Second Life
Segway
self-isolate
selfie
selfie stick
server
sexting

Shazam
shielding
shock jocks
shrooms
SIM card
singular they
Siri
SJW (social justice warrior)
Skype
slacktivism
smartphones
SMS
snowflake
social capital
social distancing
social media
sockpuppet accounts
Soundcloud
spam
spear phishing
speed dating
spice
stan
Stans, the
starchitect
staycation
streaming
Stuxnet
subprime mortgages
sudoku
super PACs
superfoods

surrogate parenting
sustainable
swipe left/right
tablet
targeted killing
teabagging
teardown culture
telemedicine
Tesla
texting
Three Percenters, the
TikTok
Tinder
top-down/bottom-up
trans
trending
triggering
trillion-dollar companies
tripcode
Trojan horse
troll
truthiness
tweeting
twenty-four-hour rolling news
twerking
Twitter
Twitterati
Twittersphere
two-factor identification
Uber
uncanny valley
universal basic income

universal credit
unplug
upcycling
upload (to the cloud)
USB
vape/vaping
viral
vlog
vulture capitalism
waterboarding
wealth management
web surfing
WeChat
wellness
WFH (work from home)
whole face transplants
Wi-Fi
WikiLeaks
Wikipedia
woke
women's studies
workstation
Y2K
zero-hours contract
zero-tolerance
Zooming
zoonotic

Thanks to Kevin Kelly, Peter, Ben and Cathleen Schwartz, Karl Hyde, Dom Theobald, Leo Abrahams, Roger Eno, Mary Evers, Leon Sealey-Huggins, Rick Holland, Stewart Brand and Danny Hillis, who contributed to this list.

ABOUT THIS DIARY

I've never kept a diary past about 6 January (so I know a lot about the early Januaries of my life), but at the end of 1994 I made a resolution to keep one for 1995. I did it because I wanted to schedule in advance some of the things that Anthea and I don't get round to doing often enough – going to the cinema, the theatre, galleries and so on.

So I started this diary – an A5 page-a-day type – by ambitiously writing in all the things we were going to do, on the days we were going to do them (cinema every first Tuesday of the month, for example). As a sideline, I thought I might as well try to keep a record of the year. The preplanning idea failed within weeks, but, surprisingly, I kept up the diary.

When I started I had no intention at all of publishing it. It wasn't until mid-October that I began to think that an expanded, addended form of this diary, with its mishmash of ideas, observations, admirations, speculations and grumbles, could become the book for which Matthew Evans of Faber so trustingly gave me a £100,000,000 advance several years ago. I'd put a lot of thought into that, and never found the form I wanted. One day Stewart Brand said to me in an e-mail, 'Why don't you assume you've written your book already – and all you have to do now is find it?', and several weeks later this way of doing exactly that dawned on me.

From October onwards the diary becomes more self-conscious – I knew from that date that I was probably going to publish. Also from that time I switched from writing in the diary itself to writing directly on to the word processor – since I'd had everything to date transcribed into it anyway. These two things changed the nature of the writing: I became both more diplomatic and more prolix. I write much faster at the WP, and I was not limited by the single-page format. I haven't tried to match up the two sections of the diary.

The diary covers four recording projects. I'm very aware of the possibility of there being a breach of confidence in reporting these: working situations are intimate, and what goes on within them is assumed to be private. Accordingly, I've spoken to the people who are frequently mentioned, and sent them the relevant parts of the manuscript to read. The fact that this is published with their permission doesn't necessarily mean that they agree with the emphasis of my descriptions: it just means that they're magnanimous enough to let a one-sided story be told. And it really is one-sided: this is just my day-by-day perception of what was happening. I could have rewritten it so that they all came out looking serious and saintly and I came out looking measured and gracious and non-judgmental, but I'm very glad to say that none of them asked for that. I removed some things that were actually untrue or gave such a slanted emphasis that they were as good as untrue. In the end what you read here is still very reactive and often biased, but what is perhaps harder to pick up is the warmth of the long-standing, friendly and productive relationships that persist behind all this.

The recording projects are caught at different times in their evolution. The project with JAMES (whose *Laid* and *Wah Wah* albums I'd produced two years earlier) is seen here in its earliest days – the period when the first sparks are being kindled. The David Bowie project, which became *Outside*, started in Switzerland in March 1994 and is moving towards its closing stages when it first appears in this book. The *Passengers* record – a collaboration between the members of U2 and myself and some occasional visitors – was somewhere in the early middle. We'd done two weeks of recording in November 1994 which had yielded a lot of material and a strong sense of direction. It was released in October 1995, as was the last project, *Spinner*, which was based on a soundtrack I'd made for Derek Jarman's last film two years earlier, and was finished by Jah Wobble in mid-1995.

Two particularly important conversations thread through this diary. One is with my wife Anthea (see page xxvi: About Anthea, Opal and me) and continues almost daily, mostly over dinner, but also in the premises where we both work. The second is with Stewart Brand (see the note on page 6), and happens mainly over the Internet, a few times a week. In the course of my conversations with these two companions I exchange reports and discuss the events of the moment. The evening conversations with Anthea can cover anything from talking about children, work, home, people, ideas, impressions and politics to what's in *New Scientist* this week. It's here that most of our projects get going.

My conversation with Stewart Brand is primarily a written one – in the form of e-mail that I routinely save, and which in 1995 alone came to about 100,000 words. Often I discuss things with him in much greater detail than I would write about them for my own benefit in the diary, and occasionally I've excerpted from that correspondence. I've also used bits from current notebooks and letters when they were similarly diary-like.

I left out (at Anthea's request) some details of our private life. I added a few words here and there to make sense of some things that would have been meaningless to a reader otherwise. And of course all the footnotes and appendices were added.

Thankyous: To my four sweethearts: Anthea, Hannah, Irial and Darla; to David Bowie, to the members of U2, to the members of JAMES, and to all others whose lives have inadvertently become the stuff of this diary; to Stewart Brand, whose comments and conversations were always inspiring and whose encouragement was invaluable; to Matthew Evans, who created the right atmosphere and stayed on my case; to James Topham for reading and re-reading this.

ABOUT ANTHEA, OPAL AND ME

I have a wonderful life. I do pretty much what I want, and the only real problem I ever have is wondering what that is. But I divide my time, arbitrarily, between working as a musician, a visual artist and a record producer, and one of the reasons I am capable of running three careers in parallel is because I married my manager.

Anthea runs our business. That means, for example, that I never pay bills. I usually don't even know about them. Anthea, James Topham ('Jameos' in this book) and Lin Barkass look after me. I have a vague idea of what's going on, but essentially I enjoy the great luxury of hardly having to worry about it at all. This may be an extreme kind of ivory-towerism, or a really lucky accident, or a very smart idea.

Anthea looks after something else as well. In military terms it would be called Grand Strategy. Whereas in details she's fairly methodical and careful, in big things she's much more ambitiously improvisational than me. It's because of her that we live in a nice house (I didn't want to move), that I have a great studio in a great area of London (ditto), and that we got involved with War Child, among many other things.

We often refer to ourselves as Wide Angle and Zoom. I'm Zoom – good at intense and exclusive concentration on something until I get somewhere with it. She's Wide Angle – able to keep a lot of different things in the picture and pay attention to them all and adjust the balance between them. These are good interlocking talents.

We started Opal in 1983 (five years before we married) as the company by which my various activities could be managed, and also as a management and publishing company for a small group of like-minded artists and musicians.

For eight years (until 1991, when our second child was born) Opal looked after me, Daniel Lanois, Jon Hassell, Harold Budd, Michael Brook, Roger Eno (my brother) and, for a time, John Paul Jones. After perestroika

Anthea became a frequent visitor to Russia and Opal helped an array of Russian musicians. In England we had our own 'indie' record label ('Land'). For the rest of the world, we ran a label funded by Warner Bros and released a string of eclectic, interesting, often lovely and nearly always not-very-profitable records. During this time I was making records and sound, light and video installations around the world, and was active as a record producer.

Anthea looked after all this business, helped by her old friend Jane Geerts and her brother Dominic.

Having children changed things. It became more difficult for her to be in the office, and, because much of our business was with the West Coast (via Warner Bros), she'd receive long business calls late into (our) night, or just when the kids needed a bath or their evening meal. So we slimmed things down, concentrating only on music publishing and my own work. At the present time the office is run mainly by Jameos and Lin, with Anthea still overseeing things.

The quantity of stuff that can pour into a small business is amazing. Every day the postman turns up with a four- or six-inch heap of mail, requests, demos, invitations, bills, payments, questions, proposals, etc. Every day there are six or ten requests for participation in something or other – press, radio or TV interviews; requests to speak at art schools or universities, to take part in seminars about new media or the future of this or that, to mount installations, and so on. None of these pays very much and in fact they are subsidized through my other, paying, work – such as producing or collaborating with other artists. Fortunately I do enough of this for the balancing act to work. But it all has to be dealt with, and, by and large and to my amazement, is.

Publishing music, for example, involves not just registering compositions with the various collection societies round the world but also checking label credits, corresponding with all the overseas publishers, and taking decisions about requests to license the pieces. Then, of course, there is all the accounting work: royalty statements are insanely complicated, their complexity usually increasing exponentially with the size of the company issuing them.

Then there are the big projects. These generate huge files of correspondence and receipts and invoices and faxes, and of course everything always requires immediate attention. *Passengers*, as an example, aside from being a CD, is also a four-inch file of documents in our office (and this after just a few months of its life).

Anthea also deals with nearly all of our legal work. She's been in this business for 20 years, and is good at writing simple, clear and exemplary contracts. She can also deal with the (much more labyrinthine) contracts we get sent. But there's always quite a few of these things sitting in a neat pile to be dealt with.

Then there are all the normal things businesses do – bills, accounts, bank balances, etc. We have a part-time bookkeeper (Grazyna Goworek – a sunny Polish lady), and she and Anthea look after those things. I rarely know what we have in the bank, let alone get involved with chasing late payments or wire transfers.

Aside from all this, Anthea also 'manages' our family. From 1991 until September 1995 we had a daytime nanny (Titi – a West Indian grandmother who the children love but who returned to Saint Lucia after 40 years here), but Anthea has always done most of the things mothers do – shopping, cooking, clothing, ferrying the kids around, organizing holidays and parties and friends' visits, making sure that school homework gets done, getting sports bags ready, dealing with coughs and cuts, and remembering things.

In the last year and a half Anthea has become increasingly involved with War Child, and Opal has become a sort of unofficial second office for the organization. There's never a dull moment.

PEOPLE

A	My wife, Anthea, mother of Irial and Darla (see also page xxvi: About Anthea, Opal and me)
Andrée	My mother-in-law (aka 'Nonna')
Anton	Anton Corbijn, photographer friend
Arlette	My younger sister, art therapist
Art	Artyom Troitsky, Muscovite friend
Arto	Arto Lindsay, New York musician
Ben	Ben Fenner, recording engineer and producer
Bill	Andrée's husband, my father-in-law
David (or D.B.)	David Bowie
David and Bill	David Wilson and Bill Leeson, film-makers and founders of War Child (see page 424)
Diego	Diego Cortez, New York curator
Dominic	Dominic Norman-Taylor, All Saints Records
Drew	Andrew Burdon, my technical assistant from March 1995
The girls	My daughters, Irial and Darla (aged nearly 5 and 3½ at the start of 1995)
Hannah	My 28-year-old daughter from my first marriage
Jameos	James Topham, our office manager (pronounced 'Hamayos')
JAMES	The band: Tim Booth, Larry Gott, Mark Hunter, David Baynton-Power, Saul Davies, Jim Glennie
Joan	Joan Harvey, my first wife's mother, Hannah's grandmother
Laurie	Laurie Anderson, recording and performance artist
Lin	Lin Barkass, Anthea's assistant at work
Michael	Michael Morris, of Artangel, organizers of Self-Storage (see note on page 7)

Petra	Petra Blaisse, Dutch friend
Rem	Rem Koolhaas, architect
Rita and Paul	My older sister and her husband, living in Seattle, USA
Roger	My younger brother – composer and music therapist (married to Bee)
Rolf	Rolf Engel of Atelier Markgraph, Frankfurt, organizer of most of my overseas installations and friend
Stewart	Stewart Brand, friend and e-mailer
U2	The band: Larry Mullen, Adam Clayton, Bono, The Edge
Wingy	My sister-in-law, Charmian

DIARY

1 JANUARY

Cold clear morning. Beautiful low peach winter sun. Thinking today (after seeing pictures of the ten Greats and Goods – five of them ex-Oxford – on the Millennium Commission) how to present the idea of the Kensington Campus.* It satisfies art and science, leisure and education, learning and practice, tourism, heritage and research. Seems irresistible, and is clearly much too sensible an idea for them to countenance – plus it would mean diverting vehicles, which is naturally out of the question (they'll somehow find a way to spend most of the money on opera).

Put up bird-feeder. Called Rita and Paul, Roger and Bee.

Afternoon to Bron† with both girls. Trying to get them both working separately but in the same room is like trying to balance two buckets of water on your head. We made the invitations for Irial's birthday, using stencils and sprays on a big sheet of heavy paper and cutting up the results into small cards. Simple rule — choose the right four colours in the first place and everything looks fine. Same as Ambient Music. [See page 293: Ambient Music] Darla starts playing with the computer (doing Fripples in Thinking Things). We watched the *Red Shoes* on TV. How do kids sort out fantasy from fact so easily? Do we tell them all those stories about witches and monsters and princes and fairies in order to make them distrust us, so they'll realize

* This was a proposal to unify the 'museum area' of Kensington into a cultural area and pedestrian zone for the millennium. It would have included The British Museum, the V&A, the Natural History Museum, the National Sound Archive, Imperial College, the Science Museum, the Royal College of Music, the Royal College of Art, the Geographical Society, the Royal Albert Hall and other institutions. The proposal was to join it to the southern end of Hyde Park, and to make Kensington Road subterranean at that point. The idea was to stimulate the area as a new cultural centre in London, with cafés and 'whole family day out' schemes.

† Brondesbury Villas, my studio in Kilburn until July 1995, when we moved both studio and office to Notting Hill Gate.

3

that what grown-ups say is largely suspect?

Right ribs hurt from bunk-climbing accident. Cooked two poussins for dinner.

Spoke to Rita (while cooking).

One cigarette, two glasses of wine.

Just remembered my father's diaries – his attempt to counter his senility – full of things like 'Shopping and walk to Rotary Club fete. Bought waffle-maker: 45p.'

Idea for a story: 'How the other half of me lives'.

2 JANUARY

Cold bright day. No one about at 8.15 as I go to Bron. I like taking the bus (getting on at Great Western Road, after a walk of about half a mile). One of the unsung benefits of public transport: people relate to each other and have a chance to be nice to each other. It's a mobile version of the village well. Cars are the equivalent of private plumbing.

On arrival at studio (after being so anxious to get there) nothing much. Played with Bliss [see page 308: Bliss and screensavers], wrote some letters, created some novel pornography in Photoshop – modifying back views of women to expand their bottoms to cosmic proportions, creating she-males by collage. Strange that one remains gripped by the same fantasies throughout life. Perhaps stranger that new ones keep getting added (my old maxim: 'Old ideas don't go away – new ones just get added') to make an ever-increasing possibility set. What dramas are being enacted and re-enacted? Why?

Decided to buy a computer for the girls after watching them playing on mine yesterday.

WHEN IN DOUBT, TIDY UP. I didn't, and left studio about 1.00. Dazzlingly strong low sun.

Took Irial to park and then cooked some own-recipe mince pies. (Watched *Hamar Trilogy* and *Beelsdorp* from VPRO. Nice phrase from Paul Saffo: 'releasing culture from the accident of ancestry'.) Dancing with kids, then told Irial the *Red Shoes* story again – which she says is her favourite.

Suggested to Jean Tantra that he markets a 'kit' like Greg Jalbert's Bliss, various 'growing machines' and some 'packets of seeds'. If I knew how to write code I could do this myself.

3 JANUARY

Noticing the overwhelming relief – almost joy – that some people feel when it transpires that they are 'really' ill, and so can at last relax and become inert without feeling guilty any more. My dad was a good example – after a life of cruel working hours, the relief of resignation.

The nice gay guy at Kilburn Bookshop got me hundreds of leaflets on talking books. My new criterion for choice of work: do only those things that allow me to listen to talking books at the same time.

Good day's work: four new interlude pieces using samples of David's voice. Took buses both ways.

At home alone listened to radio: *The Implausible Spy*, Bernard Durrant. But what about the woman? Did he never contact her again? Him 17, her 29. Watched *Kavanagh* on TV (John Thaw). New form of story: the good guy wins but is on the wrong side. Or is this a classic form?

4 JANUARY

Good night's sleep. No doubt result of (1) rehashed Indian meal, (2) painful rib giving excuse to stay in bed, (3) drink and painkillers, (4) empty house. Dazed this morning.

Still thinking about those Hamar whippings. What reasons? Conspicuous health display (proven by ability to bear pain)? The right balance of submission and pride? Basic S&M stuff built into courtship ritual? The origin of scarification?

Yesterday's work was good (on relistening). Did a sad 'Touchshriek' piece today. Renata cleaned. Set up my 'holiday'. A. and kids back at 3.00. We went for a walk together.

Took down Christmas cards and tree and then played a game of identifying people (country, occupation) from their photos in the new GBN book.*

I always admire people who marvel at things that anyone could have noticed before but didn't.

My taxi-driver (the Eritrean man who vehemently hates Arabs) told me there's no hash in Eritrea, but lots of alcohol – which people call 'Liar's Tears'. Why do Muslims prefer marijuana and Christians alcohol? Do the drugs arise from the culture or the culture from the drugs?

5 JANUARY

Left home at 5.30 after bad, short sleep. Back to work on more vocal support structures for David's voice samples – picture frames. Michael Morris came over to discuss Self-Storage.† Such a good person to develop ideas with – clever, lateral, with a good sense of both what is actually worth doing and what is worth cheating about. Played him some songs, which sounded really crisp and clear through his ears. *Value the ears that things sound good through.* Amazing I've done so much so quickly.

* GBN-Global Business Network is a futures scenario development group founded by Peter Schwartz and Stewart Brand. It seeks to advise on economic, social and cultural developments. Peter Schwartz is author of *The Art of the Long View*. Stewart Brand is an inventor/designer, and my frequent correspondent through out this diary. He studied biology with Gregory Bateson, was an army officer, a multimedia artist, a member of Ken Kesey's Merry Pranksters, the inventor of the *Whole Earth Catalog*, the originator of The Well (the first public network in what subsequently became the Internet) and a trustee of the Santa Fe Institute; he is is now the curator of the Clock Library. His most recent book is *How Buildings Learn: What Happens After They're Built*.

GBN has a permanent conference on The Well, which is open to GBN members and their sponsor companies. It undertakes scenario-building programmes and seminars for those sponsors. Stewart tells me that the criteria for deciding what GBN should do are as follows: will it be fun? will we learn anything from it? will it make the world a >>

6

Went to Chinese Circus at the Roundhouse in the afternoon. Freezing cold – and almost identical to the one I saw in Vienna with Heller.‡ Back to studio to finish piece – also new one: 'Ramona Was So Cold'.

Back home, doo-wop dancing with girls (Irial always cries at 'Daddy's Home'). Their favourites: 'Remember Then', 'Duke of Earl' (which Darla always sings in the car), 'Blue Moon', 'I Love How You Love Me'. Plus their current number one: Robert Wyatt's version of 'The Internationale' ('The International Arlay' as Irial calls it).

Cooked chicken and polenta. Chicken legs sautéed in chopped garlic, stock, mustard powder and onion. Spot of turmeric.

6 JANUARY

Logged in early. Stewart asks, 'Why are Wildean wits so miserable in real life?' Perhaps cynicism is not a containable talent – and ends up extending to oneself.

To Stewart:

True, the only person I ever knew with a 'Wildean' wit was deeply miserable and a serious alcoholic. But what is this connection? Is it that they are not just acting out the cynicism that forms the basis of wit, but showing how they really feel – totally cynical? What makes for good humorists is an ability to slide between frames of reference unexpectedly, and to misapportion value to them. One assumes that

>> better place? and will it earn enough money to pay for the first three?

† Under the auspices of Artangel, an organization which sponsors site-specific works, Michael Morris and I developed the idea of making a series of installations in a self-storage depot. I wanted to do this work in collaboration with Laurie Anderson and my students at the Royal College of Art.

Thanks to William Palmer, an Artangel supporter, we were able to use the large Acorn Storage depot at Wembley. There were a total of 640 rooms in the depot, of all sizes – endless metal corridors. We used about 40 rooms for the show, ranging from broom-closet size to about 2,000 sq. ft. Altogether about 30 people, most of them students from the RCA, were involved in the final show, which ran for five weeks.

‡ An Austrian artist specialising in circuses, theatre and other large-scale presentations.

7

this is something people choose to do, but perhaps there are people who can't help doing it, and who really can't make any convincing decisions about the relative value of their different possible reference frames.

Just had three great days' work – starting at 4.30 a.m. (when the whole of London is pitch dark and completely silent) and getting three hours' work done before even having a break for a dawn breakfast. I did so much work – listening back yesterday I was astonished at its confidence and quality as well as its sheer abundance. Sometimes I know I just can't put a foot (finger?) wrong, or rather, if I do, I'll take advantage of it. Great start to the year. I might continue this early-working habit. Interestingly, I don't seem to have to go to bed much earlier to be able to do this – five hours' sleep (lately) seems quite fine to me. And the other thing about having such long days is that I really luxuriate in the breaks in the day – so breakfast is allowed to be a long, slow business with newspapers and magazines (because I've already done a good slice of work, so I 'deserve' it).

Actually, it's even less than five hours' sleep – more like four. Now that doesn't sound enough.

Off to Brussels on Eurostar. God, I need more exercise. My body is singing with energy and nearly everything I do has me sitting down. On the train a man is in my seat and explains that he wants a window view. I say, 'So do I.' He apologetically moves to the next seat. Ten minutes later a lady arrives. Repeat. I realize he's a bit simple: 'train-spotter type', I think. He reaches up into the luggage and takes down an anorak. Train-spotting: the desire to be able to understand just a little part of the world, a manifestly controllable part. There are train-spotters everywhere.

Reading Oliver Sacks's piece in the *New Yorker* about Stephen Wiltshire – disconnection between autism and sense of humour. Are there degrees of national autism (the extent to which a people is capable of empathizing with other peoples)?

Wandering round Brussels – the 'big city' of my mother's childhood – grey and cold and thinking, 'Now why exactly am I here?' I guess it will become clear, as usual. Everything in Brussels is in neat sections – the restaurant section, the furniture section, etc. This is a characteristic of cooperative, guild- or clan-based societies (i.e. very un-American – there you only see it among immigrant groups such as the Chinese and the Orthodox Jews in the diamond district).

Jamie Lee Byars's exhibition – a shop-front gallery, large window on to street, completely covered internally with gold leaf, applied so as to leave little corners shimmering in the air currents. On the golden floor, a coffin, also gilded. Beneath the window frame a concealed light, so the whole room shimmering gold.

Had a bath and then walked for a long time (past the gorgeously lit church), finally settling in Aux Armes de Bruxelles – cheap meal with expensive wine (good dining formula). Finding it hard to read my smaller writing these days: must think about reading-glasses (chance for a general face rethink). Also considering removal of part of my second chin, which has slowly appeared over the last few years.

Women here give me very curious and invitational looks – Hey!

Hold that chin!

On the hotel TV: *The Day Today* – British humour at its sharpest. Take back all I said about Armando Iannucci (after a too-clever article in the *Guardian*). What's most interesting is when the show is almost identical to reality — when the tiniest twist is hilarious. I admire this economy. What fails is when they try to 'be funny', which by comparison seems like the crassest slapstick.

Oliver Sacks on Stephen Wiltshire. Is the clarity of autism due precisely to the inability to conceptualize the world in any other way? I mean, is 'mediated vision' the price of imagination? When non-autists look at things, they see all their concepts about those things – in fact they 'see' less, but categorize and generalize and classify more. An extreme autist just sees and relays, and apparently is left with little trace of the process – doesn't fit the experience into a bigger picture.

Strange, having noted the other day how certain fancies and predilections shadow one (are one) for the whole of one's life, to notice that my traditional (i.e. from age seven) *National Geographic*-inspired sexual preferences (i.e. dusky exotic) are now less strong.

Acknowledging that a computer is actually a place for sticking Post-it notes (mine is surrounded by them), make the frame much bigger – give the conceit 'desktop' some real meaning. The problem with computers is that they exist too exclusively in the electronic domain: what you need is a transitional area round the edge.

7 JANUARY

Up very late (10.15!). Reading Popper at breakfast. I keep hoping that one day it'll make some sense to me. I read it because it makes so much sense to Joan, and she makes so much sense to me, but it is dry.

Bought some shirts at a store called Alizari from a lady with a big, soft bottom and lips to match. Very interesting shape – almost diagrammatic: a very deeply formed bow. Can't recall lower lip – probably not adequate to extreme aesthetic demands of top lip. No lipstick (assumed ideological reasons). Claims to hate banks – which is why she doesn't take Visa.

Spent a long time at the Musée de l'Armée. Exhibition called 'J'avais 20 à '45' – about the war but including extraordinary reconstructions of whole rooms and streets: you turn a corner and suddenly you're looking through a shattered Berlin tenement out on to the bombed street, or you're in a subway train in a London station on a night during the Blitz. Of course what makes these things so strange is that they are totally unpopulated and still – as if in fact everyone had somehow been killed and cleanly removed. Very moving – tears in many eyes, including mine.

Many photographs in WW2 'atrocity' high contrast. The strong images: two Yugoslav hostages on their way to be shot in a German reprisal execution. Their eyes. Naked Polish Jewesses standing beside the pit they are about to fall into when they have been shot. One feels a freezing wind. A naked, beautiful young girl thrown down on to cobbles, trying to cover herself with her hands. Behind her, cropped by the picture, the legs of two or three men, in smart uniforms, leather coats, jackboots.

Other reconstructions: a room precisely (to my memory) like my grandmother's kitchen in Buggenhout (visited when I was five), a North Sea concrete bunker with a cold sea wind blowing in through the gunslot, the sound of a barking dog, a dressing-room with 'Judensau' scrawled across the wall.

I notice two things about Belgians. First, they only get wild with their spectacle frames   Belgian spectacles are spectacular – second, they seem almost universally tainted (blessed?) with personal, regional and national self-doubt – reservation, detachment, melancholy. *Almost universally*, because the woman in the museum (mid 30s, looked a little like Jill Phillips) had the most genuine and deep smile for all her children (dozens of them) – a smile that only issues from complete sweetness and confidence. What a person to have as a mother. I bet Belgians have very complicated affairs and tortuous, heart-searching marriage breakups.

But all the same I enjoy these spuddy, craggy, torn-by-conflicting-emotions Flemish faces. When they smile it's like sun in a cold country – so welcome, so sweet. Some fabulous noses. Proposal: A Book of Flemish Noses – coffee-table type, like Roadside Shrines of India.

The subway here is so civilized, so sensible and boring. If you could keep everything else the same but then import some NY graffiti artists . . . I keep wondering, can you have this degree of security and civilization without cutting away the sensuality and colour and experimentation of say New York? Is there anywhere that doesn't happen? (Barcelona? Dublin?)

The woman in the restaurant – pretty, decadent, with dog and husband (or affair) – turns to me and smiles that complicated Belgian smile, an affair-inviting smile. No: an 'in another life we could have been an item – couldn't we? – but we are trapped where we are' type of smile – offering less but evoking so much more. So complex, so indirect, so sublimated, we Northern Europeans. Then she reaches down into her sweater to adjust her bra strap – as if to say, 'Oh, these great big breasts – what a problem.' (In fact her breasts are not really so large – but the allusion is to her femininity and the fact that there are actually breasts down there.) She glances back at me – conspiratorially wistful – to make sure I noticed? – and does another smile, differently complex but equally susceptible to a full University of Brussels thesis.

A man with gunmetal grey hair and the most fabulous Mr Potato Man battleship of a hooter is wrestling with his mussels. If Leonardo had seen that nose – anatomy and weaponry unified at last! He reminds me of that optical illusion where two profiles (figure) make a candlestick (ground). That strange, sad face – created only to define a negative candlestick. Makes me wish I really could draw. The bulbosity! The fissuration! The redness! The NOSINESS!

As I got up to leave the restaurant, the crêpe chef in the middle of the room gestured urgently to warn me of something. I assumed, 'Careful – this stuff is flambé', and waved to acknowledge. I moved between the tables around him. He cried out again. I realized he was saying 'Serviette!' and that I had it hanging neatly from below my now buttoned jacket – a large, white, triangular codpiece. Everyone looked at me with the patronizing admiration the Europeans show to the absent-minded and/or obsessed.

The hotel elevator is decorated with bookshelves – the spines of books pasted on to the wall. The best elevator I've ever been in, especially since the books are all invented: *Notes of a Retired Gardener* (six volumes, enormous).

Earlier I was thinking 'What the fuck am I here for?', but now it gets clearer. 'What the fuck am I here for?' is a very modern question, only available at a certain level of luxury and self-importance. Most people, most of the time, are just where they end up. (Robert Wyatt: 'You end up committing yourself to what you're left with.')

If you could classify TV shows on a scale of 'good for future attitudes', *Star Trek* would score well.

Watching a Holocaust programme. Why doesn't anyone ask old Germans exactly how great it felt to be a Nazi? What were they getting from it? We know, at last, the victims' stories. What about the perpetrators? 'I really hated those fucking Jews. Kicking them about was a game for us.' Or 'I was in it for the sex. There's nothing like a frightened Jew – plus you can just get rid of them when you've finished.' That's the abyss . . .

8 JANUARY

Spending lots of money is often an admission of lack of research, preparation and imagination. First class on Eurostar, for example – to be placed with boring and ugly people stinking of ill-chosen colognes rather than with the smart and lively people in 'standard accommodation'. Or the hotel – in a dull part of Brussels and very expensive. We must be more careful about this sort of thing in future. How much more satisfying to make clever, original (cheap) choices.

The pain in my side starts to feel like a growth, an entity. Must go to a doctor.

When the various troops hit northern France, did they not think 'Why on earth are we fighting over this?'

In Popper's 'World 3' he includes art and literature etc., but is in no doubt that science is the important part. He also says, 'In the hierarchy of controls, the self is not the highest control centre since it is, in its turn, plastically controlled by World 3 theories. But the whole body of 'theories' which constitutes people's sense of what is morally and socially and personally acceptable is actually arrived at by a grindingly detailed process of consensus – not proof or disproof. The strong voices in this process may include philosophers and scientists but also artists and soap-opera directors and ideologues and advertisers. So what Popper seems to be saying is that the *valuable* (as opposed to the most effective) voices are those of science. But couldn't you invert this and say that, since the *most heard* voices are those of art and soap, then a sensible policy would be to improve their quality, to dignify them by serious critical attention (that's to say, with a type of criticism which tries to ask, 'What is the effect of this work?' – that asks questions outside art), to require that *they do better for us?*

Now, where would the vague idea of 'our feelings about things' belong? Surely World 3 needs at least one distinction – say 'land' and 'sea' – between that which is relatively solid, 'objective', and that which constitutes the fluid ocean of 'feelings about things' – and then there's all that marshland, coastal territory, polder, in between.

Nice to get home to the unqualified adoration of the girls. Anthea bought an Elvis compilation which we played and danced to – amazed I still know every song in its most intimate and secret details. Anthea, reading the cover notes, discovered that today would have been his 60th birthday

In the evening, another dose of *Shoah* on TV. The reason we remain fascinated is because we wonder where this barbarism comes from, and how much is in us, and what it would take to awaken it.

9 JANUARY

Day of bureaucracy: archiving Duo, copying stuff for NY sessions. Letter to JAMES – suggesting some new voice roles for Tim Booth. [See page 382: New ways of singing.]

In the evening A. and I to Nick Lacey's place for discussion about the War Child music centre in Mostar. [See page 380: Mostar Children's Music Centre.] What an extremely sweet man – slightly abstracted in a cheerful kind of way. Also liked his partner and the engineer. Good team.

Good ideas coming out of this session: three echelons of openness — isolated core rooms for severely traumatized youngsters, shared and changeable group rooms (into which musical and recording facilities could be wheeled), then some places deliberately opening out to the outside world – a large hall reception room that can become a performance space and also can open on to the 'garden' and extend itself out there. Also like the idea of the 'workshop' being a facility for visitors (as in the Exploratorium). We think we'll add a top floor with alluring living accommodation – since one of the biggest (covert) functions of the place is to make it irresistible to visitors and thus get the social circulation going again. Also a public coffee-shop, of course, and a 'motorbike room' – for real loudness.

After that we went to Whiteleys for *Pulp Fiction*, which I found disappointing. Very slow, surprisingly, and much too archly retro (I was there first time round). How do others, particularly young others, regard this type of violence? Is it just kitsch for them – have they become ironic enough about media not to be particularly affected by it? Or is it a sort of self-testing peer into the abyss? What would it be like if the perps were not so engaging in their decadence? Somehow I feel it buys one type of 'realism' by selling out another – the activities are cocooned by their cultural setting, made romantically safe. In that sense it has a funny relationship with *Rambo* and *Terminator*. We didn't stay for the whole movie. Uma Thurman does not give me the horn she seems to give everyone else. Too self-consciously *femme fatale* in a Californian (therefore basically non-threatening) sort of way for me. Californians are *femmes vitales*, not *fatales*.

10 JANUARY

Peter Cook died yesterday and of course today is the funniest man who ever lived. He may almost have been. (Dud: 'So would you say you've learned from your mistakes?' Pete: 'Oh yes, I'm certain I could repeat them exactly.')

15

This morning, after dark thoughts about my life, I picked up *Whole Earth Review* and read the interview with Annie Nearing, now 94 years old. She said something that struck me right in the heart – though it seems very minor: 'People give so much attention to food.' This struck a chord because last night we left the Lacey meeting prematurely primarily so we could have a proper sit-down meal. A snack would have done me fine, and I was slightly discomfited that eating had come to occupy such a major position in our lives. Then I thought about all the evenings that evaporate in the long haze of preparing, eating, drinking, smoking. Lately when cooking (unless I'm really in the mood) I find myself thinking, 'This is taking an absurdly long time.'

Generally my feeling is towards less: less shopping, less eating, less drinking, less wasting, less playing by the rules and recipes. All of that I want in favour of more thinking on the feet, more improvising, more surprises, more laughs.

I took the 52 bus into the Royal College and saw on it an attractive woman I thought I recognized. As usual I was circumspect – nervous of the corny 'Don't I know you?' pick-up. But it turned out to be Helen from Winchester, Dave Hallows's girlfriend. She is again a student, having had a career as an actress and four children. She was as full of sparkle as ever, and very beautiful – her eyes have a Siamese-cat quality, and her nose is very pert. I cannot for the life of me remember her surname, and felt embarrassed to ask.

At the college, a very good meeting (Dan Fern and Michael Morris there) with several students to discuss their Self-Storage projects. Spoke with Dan Levy and his friend Simon Waterfall (very interesting couple – Dan ex-Israeli army, burly, bearlike, darkly handsome; Simon beanpole English art student with spiky hair and a skirt, who's very lovingly condescending to Dan – 'Oh, he's just a big softie.'), Michael Callan, several others. Looking forward to this collaboration.

Then on to Bron to tidy up and finish JAMES and Robert Wyatt letter. Home to play with the girls for a few hours before leaving for NY. I hate going anywhere, and hardly ever look forward to it.

On the plane I got sucked right into Rebecca West's *Black Lamb and Grey Falcon*. Such incandescent writing — you find yourself wanting to mark every sentence in order to go back and relish it again. Her voice reminds me of Joan – which makes me realize a lot about the origins of Joan's voice: I shall never be able to separate them from now on. I'm sure she pronounced 'girl' as 'gel'.

11 JANUARY

Sent A. a fax ('Happy Wooden Anniversary') from Essex House Hotel when I got there. One back from her ('Sweet of you to remember! Miss you already!!') this morning.

Big room – view of vast, windowless brick wall and intriguing plumbing fixtures (very non-European looking).

David called (at 7.50 a.m.) full of tangential ideas – the kind of ideas people usually have when their lyrics aren't ready. But no, these were genuine enthusiasms – a soundtrack for this, a title song for something else, a fashion show in Venice, Camille Paglia on lead vocals, etc. No mention of actually finishing the album, for which I'm ostensibly here. Should I be pushing this? I just don't know. But I want to leave here with some kind of result – not just more promising bits and pieces, all half-finished.

Snow falling as I left for a delightful walk to the studio.

(Evening) Good day's work, but only on Johnny Mnemonic (a.k.a. 'Dummy' a.k.a. 'I'm Afraid of Americans') proposed title music for same (though I must say the film sounds a bit virtuously Virtual and consequently rather dull). David on phone with director in studio and generally in very good spirits. Later he's discussing Schnabel with me, suggesting we go over to his house tomorrow. Reported conversation:

Julian Schnabel: 'Oh! you're working with Eno again! I love his music!'
David: 'He doesn't like your paintings!'
At least it's a candid basis for a meeting.

Also listened today to our other songs to date. All very underdisciplined in my opinion – rambling, murky, over-and-overdubbed – things just left where they happened to fall. I suppose it's an evolutionary approach – just setting up procedures that are semi-coherent and seeing what survives at the end of the evening. Unfortunately, since we're working on 48-track (I hate that), far too much can survive. It's a structural thing: when things are good, their structure – the balance of tension and release, light and dark, heaviness and lightness, earth and air, all those things – is obvious to me. If I'm not seeing that kind of structure, something's wrong.

On TV this morning a woman reported fired as Newt Gingrich's chronicler for saying, in an academic report eight years ago, that a college course about the Holocaust should also show what were the views of the Nazis and the Klan. American censorship – if you want a career don't stick your moral neck out. English censorship – if you want a career don't rise above your social station.

12 JANUARY
To Stewart:
More and more I find I work better with quite strict structures around me. What I was doing last week in those early mornings was working up some new material for these Bowie sessions. I only had a few days – and the effect of this is to focus attention. Less exploring of all the possible journeys you could make; more determination to take one journey (even if the choice of it is initially rather arbitrary) and make it take you somewhere. The big surprise for me when I work like that is discovering myself capable of an almost 'automatic writing' way of working. I cease to evaluate much, instead just letting something carry me along. Listening back later, I think, 'How on earth did I get an idea like that?'

Working with greater leisure, my ideas become much more 'reasonable' and surprise me less. The other thing is that I've been developing a new way of working – with a computer. In the past I had a 24-track studio, which tends to make you divide your activity into 'playing' and 'mixing' – as though the piece does not truly exist until the mix is finished. Now I'm working, via the computer, direct to stereo DAT, which means I'm making things knowing I won't go back to 'fix them up'. They have to be right now. This is a regression I've found very thrilling. In the studio here we're doing just about the exact opposite. My brows wrinkle frequently, and I become the sculptor to David's tendency to paint. I keep trying to cut things back, strip them to something tense and taut, while he keeps throwing new colours on the canvas. It's a good duet.

In New York you often look at people working for an honest minimum wage in mind-numbingly awful jobs and think, 'They are the suckers, the poor suckers.' The Mexican guys in the pizza place – sweet, kind and friendly lads sweeping up under drab light at 10.30 in the evening while the obese cunt who owns the place mistreats them – what can life promise them? Why on earth don't they turn to crime?

In the studio today David was recording an idea on my microcassette. I said to Dave Richards,* 'Watch out – he'll have you sampling it off to use it for real.' David said, 'Ah yes – it'll end in Art.' Later, listening to something very rhythmic I'd played earlier, I said, 'How on earth did I get so funky?' He said, 'Whites try harder' – quoting, he said, Iman.

* Engineer on the Bowie record.

David on phone to a director about soundtrack. Very long call, it seemed. I set up a new mix of 'Dummy', but David thought it sounded linear and flat and played me a mix that Dave Richards had done. He was right – it was better. But I fear this messiness and density and cloudedness. It sounds great on big speakers after a day's work – an all-engrossing world – but totally baffling otherwise.

13 JANUARY

Took a long walk this morning – down 7th Avenue to 42nd Street. Such nostalgic air – cool but clear, straight up Manhattan fresh off the Atlantic, having crossed the Sargasso Sea, then accented with all those residual traces of faint fishiness, cinnamon muffins, subway urine, women's perfumes, bacon, coffee, newsprint.

Art in the community: on 42nd Street the now redundant sex cinemas have hoardings with those movable letters, carrying texts by poets, in the form of movie titles. Very clever idea, yielding things like 'HER RED PURSE' 'FOREVER OPEN' 'OH MY MOTHER'. Further uptown, on 7th Avenue, a series of little ceramic boxes in scruffy glazed bays on the outside of a sixties building. 'For Jesse Long, died of cancer', or 'For Uncle Seymour, died of coronary arrest'. The things had the look of very homemade shrines, but exhibited to the public in a grotty part of 7th Avenue.

At the studio, a bureaucratic day. We finished the mix of 'Dummy' but then had to spend hours doing the mono version and the four-channel version and the version without vocals and the four-channel version without vocals and the etc., etc., etc. This is why I hate working for film – the clerical work is overwhelming. Always I have the feeling if the budgets were drastically cut (and if there weren't all those people employed having to justify their positions by covering every remote possibility) everything would improve overnight. Interesting people, for example, might be attracted to the idea of making films. Film is modern opera, with all its conceit and self-importance.

We didn't do anything interesting until about 3.30. Then I started a new track based on my drums from 'Dummy'. It's a beginning, though the current vocal ('We fuck you, we fuck you') leaves something to be desired.

The problem with making records is that you can't listen to the radio while you're doing it, so you never know what's going on. David's solution: he gets 20 or 30 current releases and sticks them on one after the other, seeing what's around. If we aren't impressed by the first few bars, off it goes.

Ruthless – hope they never find out. Most of it was *déjà vu,* but we enjoyed the Dust Brothers.

In the evening, to dinner with Arto, Diego, Philip Taaffe, Daniella and an extraordinarily interesting-looking, very tall woman with great dominatrix potential and some others. Indian vegetarian restaurant – food so-so (after the Kilburn Sharma, not so so-so). Diego telling me how he now has another bed for sex because his sleeping bed is too squeaky. Philip Taaffe's eyebrows are demonic. We were wearing identical violet check shirts.

Very, very warm today. I was sweating in the restaurant. Why does human contact have to be based round eating? Like Moscow, there is no acknowledgement of the change in temperature: the calendar says it's winter, so the heating stays on. (Add to list 'Similarities between US and USSR'.)

I feel sure that the old improvisational problem – grooves versus chords – is an analogy of a basic social/political dilemma: the attempt to strike an interesting and fruitful balance between the security of steady states and the thrill of progressive, evolving structures. Solving this in a musical context should be a carefully watched experiment (cf. *The Great Learning*: see page 339).

14 JANUARY

The acceptability of various solutions depends on our tolerance of strange collisions, emotional mixtures we didn't expect ever to see. Perhaps post-modernism is a good rehearsal for this.

Visited Walter and Mary Chatham down in their new place in Crosby Street (right next to where the only other Walter I knew – de Maria – used to live). What a lovely couple (add to the very short list 'Successful marriages'). They've always been 'Walter-and-Mary' to me. Their new loft is in what could be called an evolutionary condition – Walter's always in the process of building, imagining foolishly that one day he'll be finished. Now there are kids everywhere, like insects.

But what a wonderful day – such a glorious weather – soft and warm and with a sheeny mist on the highest peaks (such as 666 5th, which was just fading away into the cloud). Then a fabulous day in the studio doing 'We Prick You', which fell together faultlessly. Whatever strange thing it is that the two of us are good at (three including Dave Richards) is so well manifest here. The deal is simple: I start on a musical landscape to develop a sense of emotional place; D. B. does all the singing and thus discovers the voice in the wilderness. Meanwhile D. R. pays attention and facilitates. The result sounds like something no one else would have done.

In the evening to Indochine with Arto and talked at length to his brother Duncan. Strange seeing this variant of Arto. Nice chap – and with that odd way of seeing things quite unavailable to me (perhaps an inevitable product of being offspring to missionaries in Brazil). He described, for example, how English trees were different – because just by looking at them you could know what was behind them. I have no idea what he meant, but it stuck in my mind like a tune you can't get out – a brainworm.

Going home, I saw a newly married couple being photographed leaving the Essex House (at 11.15). I managed to get in the picture.

15 JANUARY
Walked all morning. Bought books – Stewart Davis, E. Annie Proulx. Up to Diego's place. (He actually owns, or has custody of, that beautiful Lari Pitman painting whose tiny reproduction I have on the studio wall. It's huge – maybe 12 ft tall.) David and Iman and Arto came over. David admired my very 6H 1985 self-portrait – the one that Diego, hindleg-off-a-donkey style, talked me out of. Remarking on the lightness of the pencil, David explained in his 'Basingstoke Man' voice, 'You see, Brian's basically a 6H man, whereas I, on the other hand, am a quintessentially 5 or 6B man. That is intrinsically the basic difference between us, and that is why we are known as the Gilbert and George of rock.' His delivery of lines like that is so perfect in tone and timing that I weep with laughter. It's inter-

esting that he and Bono are both such remarkable comedians – but with David it's a side that is only recently beginning to be seen, especially as the characterizations in the music we're doing allow humour and irony.

After we went to DIA gallery for the Boetti/Bouabré show. Lunch in the Empire Diner (David, Iman, myself) and then I went on to the studio where Arto was working, to throw a few ideas about. I like the record – eccentric and dreamy and passionate in a slightly bent way. After to dinner.

In the bookshop this morning, a book about the Holocaust and a couple of pictures that stick in the mind. An old rabbi standing in a cart, drawn by eight other Jews, harnessed to it in place of horses. Another: several elderly Jewish men on hands and knees scrubbing the street. On the back on one of the pictures is handwritten, 'Putting the Jews to work'. But the worst thing is that beside each scene are German soldiers, smirking at their clever ideas.

16 JANUARY

Gripped by the Annie Proulx book, but slightly ashamed of my infidelity to Rebecca West. Ah! it began with such bright hopes, but it is 1,100 pages long. Surprising similarities between the two in their appreciation of human detail and the texture of events.

At work we pretty well finished 'Robot Punk' – or whatever we'll finally call it – thanks to Carlos's amazing contribution. He plays like a kind of liquid – always making lovely melodies within his rhythm lines, and rhythms within his melody lines. What a good team we three make. Joey Baron's idea: to charge such a lot for sessions that you don't get booked too often. That way you get to do your own work.

I feel bad because I told Andy Grassi, the very helpful assistant, to shut up when he started asking David technical questions about bloody film transfers while we were sorting something out.

23

Called Quine, but Alice answered and said he was shut in his studio – miserable because the Matthew Sweet record on which he played is badly mixed. Poor Bob, this seems to be the case every time.

Walked round in the light evening rain – in the 50s, very deserted. Outside a huge building, seven trees each clad in several thousand tiny lights following their shapes perfectly, and among them a huge red metal '9' sitting on the pavement – perhaps 8 ft high, 2 ft thick. Absolutely lovely, and infected with that shameless enthusiasm for flash that I so love in America.

Crappy Chinese meal in huge restaurant, completely empty.

17 JANUARY

This day started out a pig, and got piggier and piggier. David had hired Carlos and Joey, and I assumed that he'd planned what they might work on. They arrived, but he didn't turn up till 11.30. Meanwhile I tried with them to get some kind of result on 'I'm Deranged' – a poorly organized song with no meaningful structure. It goes something like ABBBBBBBB-BCBBBBBBBB, but the hook is A. I've had relationships like that, where the bit you liked never happens again. It was driving me absolutely fucking mad, the laissez-fairiness of it all, the lack of rigour. I gave up on it, and we broke for lunch.

After lunch I suggested not trying to throw more overdubs at half-formed songs in the hope they'd be rescued by sheer firepower, but instead start a new piece. So after that, and with total chaos in the studio (Carlos, David, myself, Dave Richards, Andy Grassi all in the control room; Joey smiling moonlike in the drum booth next door; loose cables everywhere; technical hitches; D. impatient to get going; me scribbling out structures and chord patterns; film directors calling) we went on to 'Moondust' – by stripping it right down to almost nothing. I wrote some lightning chords and spaces (knowing I wouldn't get long to do it), and suddenly, miraculously, we had something, Carlos and Joey at their shining best. Instantly D came up with a really great vocal strategy (something about a Spaceboy), delivered with total confidence and certainty. When he's on, he's really on. Perhaps I should accept that he's the hunter to my pastoralist – he hangs round for a long time and then springs for the kill, whereas I get results by slower, semi-agricultural, processes. It seems to work every time when we use these rules. Sometimes I wish he'd leave my side of things completely to me – that way we could end up with sharp, clear structures that could support the orgies of evocative chaos that he deals in so successfully (i.e. 6B on 6H).

Tearjerking fax from Irial (her first ever to me): *I hope you come home soon. Love from Irial and Darla.*

18 JANUARY

I love this National Debt clock on 6th Avenue clicking up $10,000 a second. What a great piece of public art! I'd love to make clocks like that for everything – good news and bad: increase in world population, deaths due to wars, deaths due to Aids, growth in numbers of cars, forested acreage of the world, defence expenditure, social security expenditure, etc., etc. And then a whole range of other displays, showing changing demographics such as the age distribution in the population. A whole art made of information . . .

Walked to MoMA for Rem's show (it was closed) and then bought some beads for the girls in the garment district; then on to Unusual Books on 37th. Bought a copy of *Splosh* – filled cover to cover with pictures of people having baked beans emptied over them, or falling into puddles or muddy ditches. They have the funniest film reviews, where they discuss films entirely in relation to the number of scenes where people get wet.

We started today on the new song – 'Spaceboy' – and I added a bass sax thing. Wanted to do more, but when David's around bristling with ideas, advice and 'Don't change anything' the atmosphere isn't right for finessing. Once he hears something he likes, he never wants to change anything – he'll make do with what's there. I sympathize – there are a billion variations and we'll never be able to check them all, so why not make do with this one? But sometimes I'm certain that a tiny structural adjustment early on will make life better for everyone later. I made a great bass part: very African, with wide, bouncing intervals – pygmy anarchism with Lagos Mack-truck weight.

After he'd gone (mid-afternoon) I worked on the new thing I started in desperation with Carlos and Joey yesterday – currently called 'Trio'. That came out well: swampy and viscous, something you might find in Unusual Books – 'Erect Man in Mud', or 'Semi-naked Woman in Dense Syrup'. Very weird.

Evening to visit Quine at his loft. He was quite tipsy and gossipy. Seems a bit down at the moment, wondering what it's all for (every man's question to himself). He's 52 and has (at least) a guitar for every year. I like him – he's a one-of-a-kind crusty bastard, and a great music listener.

After that to Philip Taaffe's for his birthday party. Arto there and a film-maker called Ari, plus Brice Marden, Ryuichi Sakamoto, Clemente and others. An annoying bloke whose name I forget – the 'I'm not at all impressed by the fact that you're famous, and to prove it I'll be rude and intrusive' kind. Taaffe's paintings are fabulous: huge, arabesque, spidery, opulent.

The old picture of the art-process had God at the top, and He inspired the Artist, who then made the Work. The work was seen as a shrine for, and a transmitter of, Value. There were supposed to be objective ways of measuring this Value. It was independent of you and what you thought about it. Of course God has gone now, which is why artists get paid so much more than they used to.

19 JANUARY

Spoke to Anthea this morning. Getting homesick, though I really enjoy my studious Essex House breakfasts here. I've nearly finished the Proulx book, entirely at breakfast! I sense it drawing to a Japanese end – tragic, everyone equally dead. Anthea said that Jane's unwell and off work – very rare – and I feel sorry for A. having to try to deal with everything. There's such a lot of traffic through our little office. But perhaps Jane's sabbatical is a rehearsal for a possible future – life without an office.

Suddenly occurred to me last night that Arto may be someone to whom I could address my writing. I think he'd get it, and I don't care much whether he actually responds or not.

The thing I started last night really burst into life today when David heard it. Bizarre: he sat down and started writing the song on the first hearing, listened once more and said, 'I'll need five tracks.' Then he went into the vocal booth and sang the most obscure thing imaginable – long spaces; little, incomplete lines. On track 2 he sang a companion part to that, on track 3 a 'question' to which tracks 1 and 2 had been the 'answers', and then, on the other two tracks, the lead lines! So he unfolded the whole thing in reverse, keeping us in suspense for the main song. Within half an hour he'd substantially finished what may be the most infectious song we've ever written together – currently called 'Toll the Bell'. What's fascinating is that he has glided over my careful structure, rambled around it in a fantastic way – so that you have two structures floating together, but not locked in an obvious way. This makes me think of two things: first, my recent evangelical buzzword, 'unlocked',* and, second, those Peter Eisenman buildings (of which I have been very

* This idea recurs in various forms. More and more I want experiences which oscillate between 'locked' and 'unlocked' – between the elements of an experience being closely tied together or, at the other end of this axis, independently drifting, just happening to be in the same space together. Zooming out to cultural scale, these are two different visions of society and cooperation: the rigidly structured and the completely amorphous. I don't make a pitch for either, but for the ability to use the whole palette.

suspicious) which utilize two different grid systems intersecting. There's something lovely about the almost accidental relationship between these two strata – music and song – which share the same sonic space. The song had everyone going – including Arto, who called by. What's fascinating about him is complete lack of either arrogance or deference – he seems simply straightforward with everyone. People who don't seem to care whether or not they're liked are nearly always in some way likeable.

After everyone had gone I started a new piece for tomorrow with Dave R. Promising.

D. so excited about his idea for a staging of 'Leon': a conflation of the original Leon things and what we're doing now. He's tempted both by the prospect itself and by the vaguely offered financial backing. Fascinating how he so productively mixes Muse with Mammon and sometimes makes them increase each other. Perhaps Robert Wilson is a bit like that – though for him the bait isn't Mammon but Massive Social Kudos. (I remember him saying to me, 'I want my work performed in the best opera houses', which struck me as snobbish at the time, but which I now see the point of: it's the frame against which his pictures resonate best.)

In the evening we visited Schnabel's extraordinary place. The biggest lift ever (designed to carry six horses – for this was a multi-storey stable for the NY police horses), 16-ft-high ceilings and deep-crimson paintings to match, and him saying he wanted to convert me because so many of his pictures were done listening to *Music for Airports* etc. The most incredible bedroom I've ever seen (a 2,500 sq. ft altar to his lovely Basque wife, complete with a beautiful late Picasso, a Picabia, and a gigantic Schnabel which looked interestingly sombre). Funny conversation about films. Listening to Julian it's obvious that he has no doubts at all about his status in the pantheon of great artists: he talks about them as his peers and equals. I rather admired the confidence of that – and in fact I liked him too: he's charming, funny and bright, and one of the world's great interior designers – the palace is innovatively grand. But his painting still leaves me puzzled, in general.

28

Home in limo with D. and a French stylist called Sylvie. Broad shoulders, attractive poise and different coloured eyes (so I was the only passenger with identical eyes). David gave me an exercise kit.

After all other talents have been shown to be irrelevant to whether someone makes 'important' paintings or not – drawing, colour theory, compositional skills, an ideology, an eye, etc., etc. – the one thing that is left is confidence – just like with paper money. The question of intrinsic value is not even in it (though art critics still write as though it is). All the value, as with any piece of paper currency, is that which has been conferred by artist and viewer. The artist's job becomes that of getting the viewer to agree to co-confer value – which is to say, to extend confidence. That is what is being sold. Is it conceivable that this last rule could be broken, that there could be an artist whose lack of confidence was part of the story? The eighties was really the era of confidence-art: think of Basquiat, Salle, Schnabel, and more recently Damien Hirst (who I think of as a kind of eighties artist).

20 JANUARY

Another remarkable day. Woke very early (after late bed) and packed to leave. Visited Egghead Software to get some games for the girls and me – I plan to get Irial a computer for her fifth birthday. Into the studio to work further on last night's beginning – and added a lovely descending bell line.

David appeared and on first hearing had the body of a great song. It was effectively finished in the hour, making five bull's-eyes in five days. The song 'No Control' – gorgeous, mature. There's a stunning section in it where he alludes to that style of singing you get in Broadway musicals, when the hero looks up into the sun, one arm extended to the future, and sings in this gloriously open-throated, honest, touchingly trusting way. It's a style of singing that belongs to the middle of this century, the time of great dreams for the future. It manifested itself in totalitarian theatre (e.g. Chinese revolutionary opera) and Broadway musicals. Watching him tune it to just the right pitch of sincerity and parody was one of the most fascinating things I've ever seen in a studio. I wonder if he realizes how good an artist he is at that kind of thing. People often take their own talents for granted. It's funny that the song is called 'No Control', because this performance by him is a paradigm of control.

I felt a little sad leaving NY – though of course happy to go home. There's such a lively and friendly feeling here, lots of culture and life going on in its usual extravagant and monumental pace. But it's the drop-in-ability of the scene that is so exciting – dropping into Arto's studio to help on his record; dropping in to Philip Taaffe's. It's a village, with all the good and bad sides of that:

Good sides: osmotic learning/cooperation/informality/support/intense hybridization/shared assumptions;

Bad sides: malicious gossip/exclusivity/taking people for granted/lack of focus/small-mindedness/overscrutiny/forgetting that this is not the whole world/backscratching/shared assumptions unquestioned.

At the Virgin lounge – Tom Stoppard. So I introduced myself (as a co-patron of War Child) and we had supper together. Just as pleasant as you could imagine – we talked about recording, doing interviews, theatres, etc. The flight, though short, was very tedious. No sleep as usual, and Stoppard, in the smoking section, took sleeping pills, but we had another very friendly conversation in the morning. We joked that both of us knew nothing whatsoever about the other's medium. I didn't mention that I'm seeing *Arcadia* next Tuesday.

21 JANUARY

A very short day. Got home at 12.00. Went to sleep at 1.00 p.m. Woke at 3.00 to visit the market for some fruit (how stylish – how *committed to style* – English kids are compared to Americans!). And then went to bed with both girls (one each side of me) at 7.00 or so.

Back home, as usual I feel like a displaced person – nowhere for me here. Still imagine a time when home and studio can be integrated again.

22 JANUARY

Up early (6.10) but after nearly 12 hours' sleep to make a fruit-face for Irial and Darla. Breakfast takes so long to do – I so came to enjoy those very expensive Essex House breakfasts with heaps of fresh berries, croissants and cottage cheese chosen from the buffet. Half an hour of good thinking and reading time before a nice morning walk creates a good basis for the day's work.

Took the girls to the studio in the morning to play with some CD-Rom stories (typically disappointing) and then a maths program.

All lacking something – and Darla finds it hard to understand how to use the mouse. The maths program is very minimal for 4.1 megs – four floppies and only six quite simple games.

Trying to tidy up. So much unclassifiable crap. I hate to throw away cassettes and CDs, but there are so many – and I know I'll never listen to them. Every day more arrive. The visits to Bron with the kids are very tiring. They drain attention. Slept again in the afternoon. Dreamed I was a song. Disappointing to wake and find myself a man in a hole.

In the evening Rolf came over and showed us pics of Goa. He gave me two Tibetan singing bowls and ate (Indian) dinner with us. The delivery boy gave me three Bombay Jungle tapes to borrow. Mum called – bills, boilers, etc. Arlette called re place to stay while in London.

23 JANUARY

Sudden panic this morning to remember that I was due at RCA today. Rushed down there – very early. Chat with Dan, saw Helen, then a long sequence of students. I felt a lack of verve among them. Michael looked uninterested too. Exhausting. Worried about making the show good.

To Bron in a hurry. Tidied; saw Rolf about Swarovski.* Stewart came over. Nice conversation, hastily curtailed by kids feeling ill.

* The Austrian glass-making company Swarovski, which is based at Wattens, near Innsbruck, commissioned André Heller to design a museum/showroom to celebrate the company's centenary. Heller in turn asked me if I would make a permanent installation – a complete room – in the >>

31

Back home watching André Heller's *Jag Mandir* with both girls in my arms. A. out.

Invited to become Visiting Prof at Royal College of Music.

>> museum. I made the room with the help of Rolf Engel and a team from Atelier Markgraph. It uses 13 slide projectors controlled by a digital programming system.

24 JANUARY

Stewart over at 9.15 for Big Ben visit. Visit almost aborted by both of us wearing Russian hats, which set the guards off – they were quite snippy about it (Cold War flashbacks obviously). Chaperoned by someone called Brian (a real, genuine, Brian-ish Brian), we ascended the 294 steps with 14 Argentinians. Stewart much more knowledgeable about the whole lot than Brian-the-guide – pointing out clock escapements etc. We stood in the belfry for the 11.00 a.m. chimes. Looked at fine gilded detail on finials at clock face – wondering if they were visible at ground level. They were – as subliminal detail. Stewart explained theory of 'least distinguishable detail' (Christopher Alexander has it too), and we discussed the idea of working beyond perceptible ranges of detail – the idea that the mind registers detail without necessarily being able to distinguish it.

Walked round Westminster and had lunch in a pub. Then back for Prime Minister's Questions at the House of Commons. Noisy, riotous, adolescent – Stewart said 'compressed'. All staff very cheeky, like Ealing Comedy army privates. Occurred to me that where rank is totally secure and unquestioned, cheekiness is more tolerated (because it isn't a threat, just a game).

In evening to *Arcadia* by Stoppard. Magnificent, intricate, complete and intellectual piece of work. Would it ever be possible to achieve such multi-layeredness in music? One of the advantages of having a group of people working on something is that they are all polishing their detail – and the concentration of all of it is impressive. Andrew Logan and Anthea loved it too. Interesting mirror: as the future is unpredictable, so the past is unguessable. Both history-thinking and future-thinking are forms of scenario-building.

25 JANUARY

Irial's birthday.

5.50 a.m.: Irial stroking my back, saying, 'Are you awake yet, Dad?' Me: 'Please sleep a little longer.' 5.51: 'Is it time to get up yet, Dad?'

Out *en masse* to Acorn Storage with no special expectations. In fact an exciting visit – saw 59 rooms, all shapes and sizes, and now think it better to do lots of rooms – some one-liners – rather than just a few. Wet old day.

On to my studio, where I discovered (great embarrassment) that you can record grids and rows in Bliss – as well as many other parameters such as blend, invert. Must confess to Greg Jalbert.

After to Irial's party at the church hall – incredible noise. Astonishingly greedy little boy who hardly played but compulsively sat determinedly jamming food into his mouth – probably the future Lord Hanson. Walked home with girls.

Stewart called and gave me the new Chris Alexander (*The Foreshadowing of 21st Century Art*) and Anthea the script for *Arcadia*. After to L'Altro (too-low seats) for dinner with John and Roz Preston.

26 JANUARY

To British Museum with Stewart to meet James Putnam, who curated the art show in the Egyptian Department. What on earth can artists usefully do in such a place? Should they even bother? Perhaps they could work as non-archaeologists – people who think of different ways of arranging things, for different reasons. Cf. Paolozzi's show at the Museum of Mankind. James took us into the backrooms of the museum, the storerooms.

Long letter to Petra. [See page 359: Letter to Petra.]

On to the RCA, to lunch with Michael Brook in the SCR, and to see the Interval Research musical instruments. Same question: 'Is this something worth spending time on?' It all depends on the idea that everyone wants to make music – to 'interact' – rather than just listen.

On to Channel 4 – a glass building with an appeal, apparently, to everyone but me. The producers kept Stewart waiting, pissing around with lighting and talking him out in the dressing-room till eventually I left. Saw Yoko Ono and Sean Lennon, Anthony Fawcett and Waldemar Januszczak on way out.

To studio for two hours. Letter to Peter Norton re Oblique Strategies.*

Home alone (Anthea out War Child-ing); Irial asleep on couch. Nice dinner of scampi (fried in garlic and Woh Hup lemon sauce) and rice and greens and turnip tops. Watched a little TV and went to bed early.

27 JANUARY

Took Irial to school. On to studio, fiddling around with Bliss and Photoshop (enlarging bottoms mostly). Andrew Logan over, working on the head of me that he's doing, while I did my Spanish (first four lessons). We talked about Egypt, with which I'm still abuzz.

At 5.30 on to the V&A to meet Carol (McNicoll), Richard Slee, Stewart and Paul Greenhalgh (from the museum). I'm not sure what any of this has to do with artists – at least in the terms proposed: placing 'radical 20th-century artworks' in context with old stuff. But the journey round the museum at night – with no people and very

* The Oblique Strategies are a series of cards – about the size of playing-cards – to be used in creative and problem-solving situations. They come in a black box. Each card carries a single phrase or sentence: the first was 'Honour thy error as a hidden intention' The original set was assembled by the painter Peter Schmidt and myself, and arose out of observations of our working processes.

The purpose of the cards is to try to derail normal thinking habits when they've proven ineffective, and to suggest new ways of approaching problems The original box, which we published in 1975, contained 113 cards, but since then some have been omitted and new ones have been added.

Peter Schmidt died in early 1980, and since then I've been the curator of the Oblique Strategies. They have been published three times in English, and also in French and Japanese. They have also been produced as a floppy disc No two releases are exactly identical – cards come and go Each year Peter and Eileen Norton of California commission and produce an artwork in an edition of >>

few lights – was incredibly dramatic. Standouts: Trajan's column, the old Gothic gate (with intertwined serpents), the millefiore dishes (Nero paid for one of them what he paid a whole legion in a month). Cool to this project at present – hate the idea of wasting their money on something that doesn't make much difference.

In evening, A. and I to Emma's party. She's so spry and alive – very attractive woman. Talked to Sam, a financier doing maths, John and Claudia Brown, Eddy (Emma's bro). Nice cake.

>> 5,000 which they send to their friends and associates. They approached me in 1995 to ask if they could republish the Oblique Strategies as part of this programme. I agreed, and made several changes and updates to the pack. Some of the new additions are mentioned in this diary.

28 JANUARY

I'm finding myself increasingly coming to resent artists and their daft conceits, Internetters and their stupid gadgetry. Dear Juan (Arzubialde) invited me to Bilbao, and A. arranged for Stewart to go too. The idea was to look at some sites for an installation. Picked up at Bilbao by deputation of sweet Spanish men with strong breath. One of them laid straight into S. (as Godfather of The Well) with tortuous accounts of baud rates and net-surfing. Anyway, to truly fantastic restaurant (Marinaro) in Laredo – where the proprietor very kindly gave me a 1954 Viña Real out of goodness of his heart (I had asked how much such a bottle might cost). Huge meal: wine and all (at 3.30 p.m.).

On to Santander, discussing Real World* with Juan, and then a mysterious journey round harbour facilities. 'Why am I here?' says a voice deep in my limbic system. The same voice began

* A proposal for a future theme park instigated by Peter Gabriel.

positively screaming upon our arrival at the oil refinery (turned out to be an olive oil refinery!), when we were thrust into a room of mayors and lawyers and PR men and architects and asked to help design the proposed 'Data Centre' on the promenade. This was interspersed by a largely incomprehensible presentation (projected from a laptop, of course) and booklet (all Photoshop-designed – overlays, fades, etc. – and the only thing you really needed, the maps, unreadably minute) – both astonishing triumphs of form over content.

Taken somewhat by surprise, we started by saying that data, as such, is not that interesting. Stewart said that installations that depend on cutting-edge technology are fine the first year, out of date the second, and embarrassing for ever afterwards, and that, on a promenade, people would prefer to walk. S. and I pushed the theme 'Improve the promenade', while I silently fumed at poor Juan for being dropped into this. Still, they seemed pleased that we'd come down 'for the people'. Later discovered that there had been a big rift within the council between the Internetters and the architects, and that we – hired in by the Internetters – had inadvertently supported the architects.

Another enormous and delicious meal. Must improve my Spanish. To bed at 1.30.

29 JANUARY

The view from the hotel on this overcast, strange day was like a biblical picture, or the background on a Leonardo painting. Talked to Juan at breakfast about Ainhoa Arteta, soprano. His idea is that perhaps I can think of a hybrid project for her, but nothing yet springs to mind – and probably never will.

On to the lighthouse above the rocks on to which Republicans and Fascists flung each other. Stewart in heaven at such beautifully functional architecture. 300 Hz foghorn powered by 2,000 W resonating metal-plate membrane. Think about such simple oscillators. Biscay so powerful.

On to the visually fabulous but functionally disastrous theatre. Air conditioning in each seat – at neck level, just where you need it least. Nonworking entrance. But really glorious colours – gold-leaf walls, deep-red pillars, lapis, deep rose, flash pink. The windows are small openings through deep walls, and the insides of the openings are painted deep red, so that the light coming in is pink.

To Palacete, proposed site for my installation, where I sketched an idea for something. Nice to be right on that promenade.

Hannah at home – all my daughters in one place. Stewart over for dinner – guinea-fowl – and complete Spain report to Anthea. Sitting outside smoking, Anthea saw 'burglar' on roof opposite. Police here in seconds. Turned out to be man mending roof in torrential rain.

30 JANUARY

Darla came into our bed this morning and stretched out on me – then put both arms round my neck. Lovely way to start the day.

Lovely sunny morning. Walked to Stewart's hotel to take him to studio-to-be at Pembridge. Measured up, looked around. After for a coffee and talking ideas. Bade him goodbye. To the record shop to buy Cranberries record (very strong, but too long) and saw Christine Lear there. To studio in 28 bus. Faffed around meaninglessly. Rolf's Tibetan bowl tape very nice.

That weird feeling again. I ran, quite slowly, up the hill at Brondesbury. Stopped long before exhaustion, but after a few minutes my heart started feeling like it would drop out. Aches in my arms; dizzy and slightly nauseous. A dangerous feeling (connected with the congestion of last two days?). Horrible.

Home at 4.00 to play with Darla, who made me up with lipstick. ('Can you put some musit on?') She is so charming and charmed. Andrée here. Later cooked dinner (braised onion, potato, fennel, pecan nuts, garlic, chopped tomatoes, carrots with chicken-stock rice). Chatting about Wingy and womanhood today.

Watching *World at War* about relief of Brussels and destruction of Warsaw. Another let-down by us.

Generally wasted day.

31 JANUARY

Holger Czukay letter / Miyajima at Queen's House, Greenwich / Measure for Swarovski/Haircut.

Dreamed last night of Mum and Dad going for a drive in a tiny plywood Vauxhall sports car; of our (A. and I) house somehow attached to the new studio and lots of space for us to share out to each other. Nice dream.

To studio for another semi-chaotic and half-assed day. Wrote Bono, Rolf and Holger Czukay. Had some ideas for Self-Storage project and made some music for it. Too long playing with Photoshop – lethal time-waster – like chronic alcoholism. Should schedule it in the diary and not use it otherwise.

Left all machines running recording two-hour-long Self-Storage piece making itself.

Home, shower, then on to Greenwich (A. driving). I always enjoy just the two of us in the car – like old times. Greenwich is an oasis of middle-class civilization in the increasing squalor of South London. Saw the Tatsuo Miyajima at Queen's House – very hypnotic and gentle, but slightly ruined by some twit making all the little cars go the 'right' way.

Huge attendance – wads of acquaintances. Doris Saatchi, Karen Wright, Jeremy King (a real gentleman), Piers Gough, etc. – and of course the Boyle family, whose mammoth house we went to afterwards. Every wall had their huge pieces – giving a strangely sombre black, white and tan effect. Gorgeous pieces, very starkly displayed. Wish they'd let me do some for them. They seemed very pleased to see me. It struck me what an interesting type of knowledge they must have acquired in that project.

38

1 FEBRUARY

To Acorn again. Met Michael at Marylebone at 9.00. Looking round again, choosing rooms. May do symmetrical room with Rachel Hale. Some students still weak – must be spoken to. Students getting on with it at the moment: Mark Gaved, Bettine and Patrizia, Dan and Simon, Chris Jones. These students must all be far more conscious than I ever was of the precise cost and duration of their education.

Exhausting. Back to studio at 4.15, Netting for an hour. Listened to yesterday's piece. Good – better than I thought at the time.

Evening: *World at War* (fall of Berlin and death of Hitler), O. J. Simpson trial. David phoned – talked to A.

2 FEBRUARY

To RCA early. Coffee with Dan Fern and Joan Ashworth, then watched Quay Bros film. Dan cycles in (from Muswell Hill) each morning. To animation dept till Liz called me and said six students waiting to see me. Rushed over, up stairs, suddenly thought I was having a heart attack. Spoke to M. Callan, Lauren Goode, Michelle and Louise Lattimore as a group, then to Rachel and Richard Levy separately. After looked at Michelle's work – but I felt completely rough. To lunch with Dan and Jake Tilson and David Blarney.

Suddenly had the strongest urge to get out into the bright sun, and did. Walked across Hyde Park to Queensway and then to Kilburn by cab. Faxed David – he phoned at once. Long enthusiastic description of record – 'the best thing I've done in 15 years', all things to all men, etc. Hard to argue such bliss. Petra phoned and we had a nice long chat (she's called her company Inside/Outside).

Took home tools and made a sort of Indian caravan for Darla, who used it to do a series of very short puppet shows (about 20 seconds long each). Fixed door. Cooked with Irial. Watched Coco Chanel deconstruction with Anthea. Discussed placement of toilet at office – she said, 'There's nothing

39

worse than standing in the kitchen and hearing someone doing a great PLOD next to you.' Aching sides.

Kitaj article seen at the college, very sad. Poor bastard. 'They went for me, but got her instead.'

3 FEBRUARY

To studio early (after long walk carrying electric drill and dry cleaning, then very sluggish bus ride). With great appetite into Kevin Kelly* interview until Andrew came   * Editor of *Wired*. over to work on the head. Spanish and posing. Nice visit. Did record mat for him – then signed it really badly. Received tape from Laurie. Good stuff.

Andy Gill came over – interview about producing for *MOJO*.

Back into the Kevin Kelly piece. Sent it off to him. Listening a lot to Cranberries songs.

Back home: bought some fish and made a marinade of garlic and garam masala (dubious recipe), then A. returned with the girls – carrying more fish! Dancing, playing, sorting records.

Any Questions: Jonathon Porritt and David Starkey. Porritt has history on his side, Starkey has hysteria on his.

4 FEBRUARY

Beautiful sunny morning. To studio with girls. Irial watching *Tortoise and Hare* CD-Rom. Darla in a house I made her from the overturned sofa. Later both drawing beautifully. The morning passed quickly. In the newsagent Irial squatted fascinated before an almost nude pic on the front of the *Daily Sport*. Darla said she had some Chinese food at school. It was made with noogles and gagetti and two rices and crisps. 'And I did love it.'

Back for a nice salad lunch, then I returned alone to the studio – worked more on Kevin Kelly and Photoshop.

40

In the evening to *Towering Inferno* at QEll with John and Roz Preston, Rolf and Nicky (his latest flame – 'what she don't know yet'). Although I maintained enthusiasm (since I was on the posters endorsing them), they made several mistakes. The film work (65 projectors) was mostly disappointing – arbitrary and too pointed. It worked when there were lots of films, but just one made you focus too much. The music is very original in parts but lacks a voice – a narrative element (whoever thought I'd be saying that!). Saw Michael Morris in the interval and he was negative, but I said they deserved encouragement. Basic set was good, but nothing hard enough or frightening enough. Lack of dynamic range – the 'loud' bits weren't loud enough. Anthea said they were playing as though their whole family was in the audience and they didn't want to frighten them. This turned out to be true (one of my students from RCA was talking to his boyfriend about the band and the mother of that particular band member leaned over from the seat behind and said something like, 'Yes, he was always very interested in music'). But I have complete faith in them.

Afterwards all home (Rolf, Nicky, A. and me) to smoke and drink on the balcony. Alan Yentob at front gate – asking me if I could do some emergency music for the Nigel Finch film, which now has to be finished without him.

5 FEBRUARY

Rolf's party.

Up at 6.15 – back to bed at 8.45! (Up again 9.30.) Worked in garden all morning. Anthea installed microwave. Met Alan Yentob at back gate (is this more than coincidence?). Irial helping in garden. I said, 'It's nice to have you helping. You're good company.' Irial, after due consideration: 'You are good company too.'

School-dinner lunch, Alice and Kuniko came over after. Alice likes me – and she's a really sweet and individual little person. Bouncing on bunk bed, throwing ball.

To studio, working on Kevin Kelly interview. Enjoying this way of writing – sending something off as though finally and then getting to correct it afterwards.

To Rolf's place. Mark Johnston (Russian, Irish, Mohawk and something else), Mark Baldwin (dancer: English, Fijian, Tongan, French), Carol Beckwith (Russian, Lithuanian and two other things), Rolf, Wingy, Christina, A. and me. Conversations about NGOs'* inheritance – Nigeria, Masai, etc.

* Non-Governmental Organisations.

Funny crowd – out-worldly-ing each other. A. fed up that this was called a 'party' when in fact it was a dinner – a distinction slightly too subtle for me.

'Armed incident' at nearby flats; roads closed off.

A. annoyed to discover that I'd decided to go to photog's studio tomorrow rather than have him come to me (Lin and A. having apparently spent ages getting him to agree to that).

6 FEBRUARY

Nice letter from Hannah. Yentob rang doorbell and, when I answered, walked straight in! As though he'd dropped in hundreds of times before.

Over to photog's. A. was right: it cost me several hours. What really gets me is that everyone except me gets paid. Told Kevin the same. Now he tells me that we've hit the deadline. So much for the exchange, and it was just starting to get somewhere. Disappointing that people always say, 'Thanks. Enough. Lovely', just when it's due to get really good. Haircut and head massage at photographer's from someone called Kate. Nice girl but unfortunately into astrology and Year of the Pig.

Back to studio – Bliss, Photoshop, getting things ready for sending to Self-Storage. Good way of offloading.

Rolf to new studio. Home. Bochum park project. Looks good and will happen. Nice dinner. Pasta with mushrooms and zucchini; salad.

To Stewart:

I've been thinking of a project for my new studio – an amusement really. I want to make a long chart on the longest wall – like a frieze – which would be a logarithmic journey through the last 10,000 years. So the first 5,000 of that would occupy, say, the first 25% of the line, the detail increasing as we come to the modern era. Then, whenever I pick up some interesting titbit – like that Egyptian chair, or like a picture of a beautiful old Korean pot I just saw – I'll stick it on the chart in its correct position. So I'll build up a text-and-image history. Just for fun, but it has something to do with keeping a diary (still going strong!) and Clock Library and the British Museum. [See page 315: Clock Library.]

Thanks for your suggestions about the *Wired* article. I'm very interested to hear that you paid for interviews (at *Whole Earth Review*). This makes such sense to me (not just because I stand to gain from it). If you really want someone to perform well and put their intelligence into it, why shouldn't you pay them? And if you offer to pay them surely they will in turn respect the professionalism of the situation. I would be quite happy to negotiate rates with small mags, or work for free, but I figure if there is money being made from one's contribution (and if they want to put me on the cover they clearly feel this is likely) then why shouldn't the 'primary producer' get a share?

It's not good enough to say, 'Well, it's good promotion for you.' I feel some resonance with the Esther Dyson* article: what I'm selling in an article is the 'services' that follow the product – not the other way round. This is why I've never particularly linked doing interviews to record releases – which most people do. I'm not promoting the record: the records are promoting the ideas.

* Fellow GBN member.

7 FEBRUARY

Call Dan Fern re performance space / 11.30 Storage collection (David S.) / War Child letter / Call Roger re Finch film (Pete Burgess) / 5.00 LIFT,* 19/20 Great Sutton St, EC1 / 8.15 Garden Committee.

* London International Festival of Theatre.

To studio at 8.00. Wrote invitation for Pagan Fun Wear [see page 387] and note for Anthea's Croatia visit. Practically emptied studio into David Scholfield's van. Suddenly thought of a good theme for storage show – shrines to neglected (disregarded? unacceptable? ephemeral?) gods.

A box is a deep frame. A room is a deep box.

Happy day working. Called Pete Burgess and Roger about music for Nigel Finch and then did some myself! Very good too. My rhythm touch is good. (I'm a bit drunk right now.)

Then to LIFT meeting – Arie de Geus, Ian Wigston (gave me some cards like Oblique Strategies), Charles Handy, Rose Fenton, Will Hutton, Julia Rowntree and Judy Neale. Then home – put a spud-to-be-liked in the microwave, and on to Blenheim/Elgin committee meeting, where I was elected member of the Garden Committee. After to the Pattons to eat my spud. Several neighbours there. That's where I got a bit drunk.

Talked to Quine on phone: he has a fuzzbox for me – 'You might like this one: it's just got the *nastiest* little sound.' He understood this whole retro historical thing – the ambience of *Pulp Fiction* etc. – long before anyone else.

8 FEBRUARY

To storage / RCA with David? 9.00, 2.30 / Dinner with Joan 7.00 / Organize a discussion about self-organization? Where would it be? / Tod Machover.

'What do you say to a man who's killed a lion with his bare hands and is sleeping with your wife?' – Derek Mason, when asked about his wife's affair with a Masai warrior.

Exciting visit to Wembley. Pissing rain (as always), but select (filtered) group of students. Discussion about shrines, getting situations where visitors make the show themselves, led into ideas of voice collection-booths at the entry where you are asked things and answer them, the results being broadcast to far-away rooms elsewhere in the space, so you get disembodied voices floating sporadically out of concealed speakers. Michael's

44

proposed question: 'How would you like to die?' Only the answers are broadcast. Then ideas of visual works with voice overlays. Mark Gaved's wine lake (glossed into lake with fluorescent cherubs floating) with spoken ghostly voice 'In my sleep' echoing out over it.

Faking the process – and making a confessional rap.

Afternoon to RCA, where met David and Alan Edwards. Joan Ashworth assembled good collection of animation stuff for us to watch – curious that David also picked out Adam and Alan, my original favourites. David suggested we do a precise copy of a Pete and Dud sketch at midsummer War Child dinner. Very stimulating day: talking ideas non-stop and absorbing.

Listening to new JAMES stuff – still muddled and looking for a direction, but something dimly emerging. The question: 'What is the vision?'

In evening I showed Irial a flicker book (horse jumping fence) and was thrilled that she was intrigued. A. off to Croatia meeting. Joan over – we talked about Bosnia, Ancient Egypt, children, Austria, Rebecca West, leisured intellectuals, D. H. Lawrence, Prozac, drugs, mortality, asparagus, tectonics, hunters and gatherers, NGOs. Anthea returned sweetly tipsy.

9 FEBRUARY

Find Artifical Intelligence essay / 11.00 Tim and Larry of JAMES / Flowers Gallery 25th anniversary.

Early to work again (pleasant bus ride (!) reading Negroponte's book) and then on to Well – Stewart and Kevin Kelly. Long discussion about the *Wired* piece and payment, etc. All gracefully resolved (Kevin volunteered $1,000).

Tidied studio, set up for JAMES visit. Who duly appeared – Tim, Larry and Jim. Played several things, but the nub was them asking me if I could work with them. They seemed to not want to record again until I would do it with them. Yet I'd so like to work on my own things – enjoying so much these last few high-action weeks. I guess I live for the adrenalin of fitting together new ideas.

Spoke to Pete Burgess re the ROC stuff for Finch. Ben came over to install new software, take H3000 progs and generally sort out the computer. I wish he lived closer. Home to adoring kids and Anthea, a bit harassed because travelling to Zagreb tomorrow. She's a bold one.

Dinner: lamb and garlic, greens and baked spuds.

Feel very happy this evening, full of beans and optimism.

10 FEBRUARY

A. off to Zagreb early; me up early. To studio at 8.30. Putting together Finch stuff. Good idea – reprocessing existing pieces (how often have I rediscovered this?). Sent off a bundle of things. No discussion whatsoever yet about whether I might get paid for this. Fiddled and Photoshopped until Philip (builder) came at 12.00. Enjoyed talking to him and showing him computery things. Worked on Bliss and tidied up a bit, then got Irial from school.

Went to market with I. and D. to choose our fish for dinner. Red mullet – I fried theirs and made spuds, carrots and cabbage. They really enjoyed it. Titi cleaned the fish and I made mine with chopped garlic and lemon stuffing. Crazy (i.e. psychotic) traffic tonight – a Friday syndrome.

Bathed with the girls – they both spent ages washing my back. Both in really high spirits, being very sweet and funny.

Reading *Being Digital*. Interesting connection between Negroponte's non-intrinsic value and mine. The Alexander book is precisely opposed to this idea, and supports the idea that there is *within things* a precise and codifiable grammar of value. Is it remotely possible that both these kinds of value exist?

To Stewart:

Reading the (fantastic) Negroponte book, I like very much the bit about 'the wink worth 100,000 bits'. That's the essence of rich conversation for me, when great blocks of assumptions are being traded and stuck together. Negroponte's style – concise, sharp, witty – is very similar to yours, I think. I really wish I knew how to write like that, which I guess is me saying I wish I knew how to think like that. I'm reading his book with the same mixture of headlong enthusiasm and punctuating gasps of enlightenment that I felt with *How Buildings Learn*. Especially interested in the (very post-modern and very my-territory) theme of the variable value of information – how the 'same' information changes value depending on where it appears to whom and when. Of course, what this means is that the 'information content' of something is not intrinsic to it: the wink to the wife triggers, not contains, information. This is exactly the argument I've been advancing about culture in general.

Which brings us to Chris Alexander's book, which proposes precisely the opposite idea – namely, that certain configurations are intrinsically, objectively, quantifiably 'deeper' or 'better' than others. I have never seen this argument, with which I profoundly disagree, more clearly advanced. It raises all sorts of interesting questions for me, and I'm thoroughly enjoying looking at the two books in tandem.

I have to do some serious writing about this theme. Essentially the problem is this: if I am saying that the 'value' of those Turkish carpets is a function of their ability to trigger 'value' in us, is that different from saying that they have intrinsic value?

11 FEBRUARY

Exhausting day with the girls – I think all men should be regularly compelled to spend days alone with their kids. But enjoyable. We went up to the studio, where Irial played with the science program and Darla played Fripples. Irial is easily able to pick this stuff up. And Darla now is also getting comfortable with it.

We had lunch (M&S sandwiches) and lots of biscuits, then hide-and-seek and house-building. Difficult doing anything else while they're around, and I didn't. Came back at about 4.30 and made baked spuds and quiche. After, we danced and they dressed up – using several thousand pairs of shoes.

They went to bed with an Ali Baba story and then crept down to my room. I videoed the two of them fast asleep. Watched Simpson trial in evening.

If all I'd ever wanted to do was make money, I'd probably be really poor by now.

Gardening with the girls in the morning. Built a little wall round one of the beds. I. and D. went back inside to draw. What a fantastic mess they can make in such a blink of the eye! I got really mad with them a couple of times this weekend about mess (and Darla losing my keys). Amazing how readily they forgive me.

We had a baked spud lunch again, and then went to Holland Park – just walked through, bought an ice-cream and on to the Natural History Museum. The Creepy Crawly room is the worst display I've ever seen in a museum – a meaningless confusion of scales and materials and 'interactive' things that don't work, or, even worse, do. The Shell BP display has a great feature – mirrored TV sets forming an enormous virtual globe. Incredibly clever use of a small space. Good idea for Self-Storage? The girls loved the old bird rooms – those lovely cases of stuffed birds – which are so much more beautiful and awe-inspiring than the crap interactive displays.

To Stewart (describing a Jeremy Beadle show):

An unsuspecting young man who works for a parcels delivery company is given a job to do taking a parcel out to an address in North London. He arrives and knocks on the door, which is opened by a young woman in a long white robe. This woman looks at him and is struck speechless. Her jaw drops and she just stares fixedly, unbelievingly, at him. She motions to him with her hand to wait there and hurries back into the house. Meanwhile he is still standing there with the parcel, wondering what is going on. She returns with two other similarly clad people who are similarly astonished and stare wide-eyed at him. He keeps trying to give them the parcel, but all three fall to their knees and begin praising him. By now others are crowding at the door, all chanting and praying to him. He is baffled and keeps trying to hand the parcel to one of them so he can get away.

They persuade him to come in, and then take him into a temple-like inner sanctum. On the wall there is a golden curtain. They draw his attention to it and then open it. Behind is a large, very Indianesque, gilded portrait – of him. He is their prophet, returned to earth. Now they induct him into a ceremony – him still protesting that he's just trying to deliver a parcel – and one by one these gorgeous skimpy-robe-clad virgins prostrate themselves before him. Suddenly you see a light go on in his head, and he switches, with incredible ease and panache, from fumbling delivery boy to full-fledged guru. They give him a prayer to read, which he does (this is very funny, because it is actually a phonetic list of dishes from an Indian restaurant menu). More virgins prostrate themselves, and he blesses them with Un Yun Buj Ee and Sag Paneers and Papadums while standing on one leg (he has been told this is how it is to be done).

More details, but you get the pic. What is incredible is seeing him assume the role when he suddenly starts to realize the possible benefits: so easy to see how someone can absorb conferred power like that and then amplify it and reflect it back larger. It's really something out of nothing. Of course this is one of the themes of *The Satanic Verses*.

13 FEBRUARY

Peter Greenaway 4.00.

In studio at 8.30. Dreadful crowded bus – trying to read *Being Digital* in very analogue conditions. Want to start getting some writing done, but worried that I also have to do the Storage press thing – really in the way. But, anyway, in I went to produce a typically stiff and tortuous five pages (double-spaced) which did however open up a few new ideas. Trouble is, as soon as I start thinking I go off into the back alleys and dirt tracks. I've found things up there before, and the habit stays.

Greenaway cancelled.

Renata came to clean, but I'd already wrecked the morning by resorting to Photoshop. Meanwhile office calling about 'Industrial Start Small Plot of Land', one of the D. B. mixes I'd done, which I couldn't find. Found another (forgotten) opening. I'm a bit remote from this project at the moment. Back to writing (title: 'Attention Creates Value'). Dull and pedantic, like a professor. Spoke to Michael re Storage.

Home at 5.30, playing with girls; defrosted sausages in microwave. Andrée came over and I made prawns and garlic.

Anthea returned at 7.30 from Zagreb, with lots of lists of bizarre and, she thought, rather suspicious 'aid' organizations, all with 'Freedom' or 'Democracy' or 'American' in their titles. War Child was apparently the only charity present that was actively doing something.

14 FEBRUARY

Beautiful sunny morning: early to studio (8.15). On the way in I saw Terry the greengrocer, the pleasantly weatherbeaten old jazzer who stands out all day on the corner. 'Lovely day,' I said. He agreed, and I said how I liked these cold bright days better than hot ones. 'Oh I love them all,' he said: 'I'm just happy to be alive.' I really think he's telling the truth.

Long note to Stewart on the Net. Tidying up for Greenaway visit (he cancelled). Called Bono and had a long and interesting chat about soundtracks and the return of 'big' (and the end of 'grey'). His feeling is towards making a positive, assertive, strong next record. Also talked about professorships and other accolades (he's just been nominated by some students for a poetry seat at Oxford!).

Worked on Photoshop (moiré grids) and a piece of music aptly called 'Cycle of Despair'. Desperate. Listening also to old microcassettes from many years ago (got that machine going). How strange to have these moments from so long ago – my Mum and Dad talking, a machine I liked the sound of in Long Island, a long-forgotten conversation with a taxi-driver.

Went for a bike ride up Kilburn High Road. Saw a lady with her nose smashed in, sitting dazed in a heap of bloody tissues with a policeman nearby. The scene had an African quality about it: the nonchalance of the passers-by contrasted with the woman's plight. Like that time at the festival in Ghana when the amputee was attacked by a swarm of bees and, after a few moments' helpless and hysterical bouncing round on the ground, he just settled down and let them cover him. Everyone was watching and laughing.

Bought a computer for the girls! Performa 630 plus with all sorts of kids' software.

Met with Barry Levine, music fixer for *Judge Dredd* at 192. Doesn't seem right for me. Hollywood usually makes me puke, I have to confess. If I were a little less snobbish I'd be cleverly ironic about it all and just take the money.

Home to dinner and rather fabulous Castillo Ygay '68 or '87 (not clear which! – tasted like '68). Anthea and I talked through JAMES, Bowie, U2, Greenaway. All this work with others. When will it stop?

To Stewart:

The contrast between America and Canada is for me that between an upper-case and lower-case culture. I can't imagine the Canadians talking about Good Government with capital letters, whereas in America even the Free Market gets that treatment. This might seem a pernickety point to make, but to capitalize is to hypostatize – to set in concrete, to dignify, to accord something a real and singular existence.

Of course with that goes the extraordinary and religiously fervent American feeling about Democracy, a feeling for which I used to have nothing but scorn but am now coming to respect. This is particularly in light of the Bosnia experience. Anthea went to Zagreb last weekend to attend a conference of organizations interested in the future of the Balkans. One of the purposes of this meeting was for groups that needed money to make contact with organizations disbursing it – almost all of which were American, as it turned out. They had very abstract titles, such as 'The Committee for Freedom' and 'The Alliance for Democracy' and so on. They all sounded like CIA fronts, and were rife with capital letters. But Anthea had high praise for them, and particularly the Jewish element (which is very heavily represented in these organizations, partly because Bosnia was a haven for exiled Jews for so long). Does it need capital letters to motivate people? And if it does, should one use them or should one recoil sheepishly in a Canadian or English way (as I tend to) to try to point out all the grey between the black and the white?

Must be the central problem of politics – do you paint simplistic pictures that make people act (and leave them with too simple a view of the world) or do you paint bafflingly shaded and contingent scenes that leave people paralysed by indecision?

Incidentally, one of the connections we've made is a guy called David Phillips, from an organization called The Congressional Human Rights Foundation, and he has proven extremely helpful: sort of taking Anthea and War Child under his wing, introducing her to all sorts of useful contacts.

15 FEBRUARY

Into the RCA for a really tough day pushing a boulder up the hill of no response. Fuck! It was exhausting. A lack of sensuality and enthusiasm. At one point I just wanted to dump the whole thing, feeling overwhelmed by this and all the other bits and pieces and watching another year being blocked out. Felt very ill and tired – bad chest pains and general dizziness. Said to Anthea, 'Those who don't have nervous breakdowns have physical ones.' Feels like where I'm heading. Desperate, sluggish feeling. Home to lovely Darla's caresses – when I sit on the steps to take off my shoes, she climbs up behind me and leans on me and puts her arms round my neck.

Fell asleep on the carpet.

Irial told me a story 'I heared on the news' about a baby suffocated by a dog.

Book from Roger: *The Evolution of Consciousness*. Also read Esther Dyson piece about copyright.

A. and I sat outside discussing Jews and Bosnia, euthanasia, capital punishment, Jane, big heads (I love hers – and her), computers for children (she's suspicious. Secretly so am I, but I defend them to see if they can be defended).

16 FEBRUARY

Write Roger / Shoes / Mark Baldwin 2.00 / Peter Schwartz / Call James Putnam / Laurie stuff.

Nightmare about falling off a cliff, screaming into the wind, clinging on to a tiny ledge with elbows and fingertips, knowing no one above – including Anton Corbijn – would hear me, knowing I must soon fall and crash on the rocks below.

Wasn't looking forward to today, but it turned out OK. Tons of annoying little jobs to do but I managed to work on some of Laurie's stuff, which turned out so well I suddenly had the idea to suggest each Self-Storage project use one of Laurie's pieces as its 'content' – ready-made content. Faxed and talked to David Blarney about this, and he liked it. It solves a lot of problems, giving the students the choice of making 'frames' rather than 'content' if they want to. I always prefer making frames: making context rather than content.

In the evening to the Browns' for dinner. Emma said all she wanted to do when she grew up was have children – and write a book at the age of 50.

17 FEBRUARY

To Berlin.

Saw A. and kids off to Geneva. Poor Irial so hates any separation, as if she fears it will be for ever. To studio, did a bit more work on Laurie pieces. It starts to make sense. Imagining the dog piece: either a single large dog in Anish Kapoor fluorescent blue under black light, or a field of identical found different made plaster dogs. Saw a strobe light in Portobello (where I'd gone to buy plaster dogs) and couldn't convince myself to get it (£50), but then thought of almost nothing else all day. It was such a glorious day. I left the studio early to walk up Portobello in the sun. Then home; walked round the garden, packed, and made ready to leave. Titi came with J. D., a lovely little girl, so amazed at everything.

Surprised to discover that Space Command tracks 7,000 objects in space from 10 cm up, that Uri Geller believes his attendance at Reading FC games helps them win, that Will Hutton's book is a best-seller.

At Berlin Tegel, Maria Vedder was waiting, in her fake leopard coat and big boots, holding up a big sheet of paper saying 'PROF. ENO', with a hole in the first 'O' through which she was looking. I burst out laughing – haven't felt so happy for days. She's going to Egypt on Thursday! Me go too?

18 FEBRUARY

Berlin.

Re counterfeiting of goods, CDs, etc.: all products gradually assume the status of paper money (i.e. all products become objects in which confidence is the biggest source of value)?

Fabulous reluctantly-ended breakfast (after swim) at Kempinski Hotel. Then brief walk into sun and met Sigi, who took me on a tour of new Berlin. Everything being built, and practically every name architect: Nouvel (glass wedding cake), Philip Johnson (an enlarged cut-out of him, not the proposed building, at the site), Aldo Rossi, Renzo Piano, Richard Rogers, etc. The usual suspects. FAR TOO MUCH GLASS! Architects believe in glass. I don't.

Then to Sigi's studio, where within 20 secs of viewing the tortuously produced computer model of my room-to-be at the Swarovski museum I knew my initial design was quite wrong. So we went to flat panels and made the walls a bit more complex. Looks a million times better.

We saw *Nico Icon* film by Susanne Ofteringer, one of Maria's students: very good, but strangely nostalgic – a feeling about music and the scene that won't come back. Then on to a restaurant – Abendmahl – very good, but miles away. Spoke to Bernard MacMahon about *Towering Inferno*, trying to tell him what I thought would improve the show.

On to *Glitterbug** just as marginally interesting as I recalled it, but my music sounded generally worse. In question time – in response to a question about Derek's use of time-lapse – I said we (the English) shot at that speed because we couldn't afford film.

* Derek Jarman's last film, for which I did the music.

19 FEBRUARY

How excitingly dominant these wealthy, healthy, modishly dressed and highly perfumed German ladies look! All German history – at least from Goethe to the Nazis – transmutes in them into a statement of sexual power.

Enormous breakfast! – fruit, meat, muesli, two pots of tea, papaya juice.

I feel like I had an ideal day today – it had fun, art, ideas and satisfactory work. Ever since I first met her I've had this great bond with Maria. Really a deep-fun friendship which I couldn't have with any man. I guess there's a kind of flirting in it – but ironic, a game, because I'm sure that in her mind as well as mine there's never been any thought of sexual contact. But the game of flirting is a fun game which we play – just for fun; and because it lets us talk about other things, serious things, in that just-for-fun way. I love her company – and so does Rolf. At dinner tonight I wanted to say, 'Will you please get married. Now!' because they both shine so much in each other's company.

At Pixelpark, home of the ROM-makers, I gave a speech [see page 309: CD-Roms] and really liked those people. I realize that what I'm talking about is a 'rule moiré': patterns of rule interactions created by overlays of probabilistic decision matrices. Of course I wouldn't say that to anyone.

At Sigi's MediaPool we put in birch trees – recalled from my show in Hanover. Well remembered, Rolf! In the evening we went to see Alan Wexler's show, which was full of thousands of good ideas. What a truly individual thinker. Then to CD-Rom fest, which was mildly yawnsome. BLINDROM was good.

Beautiful late TV show of pop?/classical?/Turkish?/Arabic? orchestra and singing. Extraordinarily ugly audience transformed to beauty by singing. What clothes the musicians were wearing! Style in an orchestra! What a good idea.

20 FEBRUARY

Farmyard.

A long swim this morning. When the pool was empty, I did a new kind of walking. Water height to chin, walking slowly on tiptoe from one end of the pool to the other, trying not to disturb the water. It was like dreaming – such grace and lightness and slow motion.

Breakfast with Rolf, talking about marriage etc. Funny seeing ladies walking about the hotel lobby looking chic and perfumed, when an hour before one sat naked with them – the collection of our sadly vulnerable little bodies – in the sauna.

Angus Deayton in hotel breakfast room (at next table) and then on same plane   next to me in the passport queue, then directly opposite in the departure lounge. We didn't talk – Englishly respecting privacy, I suppose. Also, Suzette, from all those years ago at Island.

The girls and Anthea arrived home squeaking about skiing and falling into deep snow. I heard the whole story in 52 seconds on the doorstep. How lucky they are to have such an adventurous mother. Slept in their room, at their request.

For Storage: fountain room? Would be good with real birds.

'To say Lord Hope is grey is being rude to porridge' – Nicholas Fairbairn, died yesterday.

Do all men leave this life feeling they've seen nowhere near enough nude people, played with far too few private parts, made a pitifully inadequate contribution to the honeyed chorus of bottom-slapping, tit-sucking, cock-pumping, belly-bulging lust issuing from the planet, and generally not fulfilled their once extremely promising sexperimental destiny?

Self-confidence – the last definable sine-qua-non artistic talent. The last place to ask questions.

21 FEBRUARY

Out to swim (8.20–8.45) in local pool, but a less lovely experience than Berlin. To studio early for tapes for RCA. Another difficult day. I thought Laurie's tapes would do the job, but the reaction was cautious. In the end, some good ideas.

Clemente show. Very uneven work – some really lovely things and some really incomprehensibly flat things. The pastels are beautiful – his medium for sure. The Upanishads! Eye-smashingly lovely. The kind of show that makes you think, 'Fuck me! What have I been doing with my life?' Saw Diego Cortez there! Felt oddly torn not to go to Groucho with Diego et al. Perhaps I was missing a possible future.

But a lovely dinner with Anthea. Her unthinkable future [see page 418: Unthinkable futures] = 'people of different signs go to war with each other' – from our delicious evening dinner at L'Altro. Conversation about cities, pragmatism *v.* ideology, NGOs, management.

Got home – message from Maria: she says I can go to Egypt (sleeping above the engine room). Now it's time to decide – things to move and change; Self-Storage project a problem. Anthea says everybody should visit Egypt and I should go (she went years ago).

22 FEBRUARY

Writing this sitting on the plane to Egypt – so one day later. It's so hard to remember a day after it's passed. In the morning I received final confirmation of the Egypt trip. Sudden panic of cancellation and rearrangements. Diego came over in the morning and we heard Arto's (lovely) album. Then Andrew Logan turned up to sculpt me; but it was a distracted session – tomorrow he's off to India. Anthea busily organized all tickets etc. (Probably the barrier of those tasks would have been sufficient to tip my balance to not going. My inertia.) When really confirmed, an attack of gnawing nerves at the thought of leaving my three ladies again. Somehow Andrew's story of being away for months made me think that I was also going to be, and I started buzzing around the studio wondering if I should be shutting things down more completely.

Home at 3.30 and then swimming (big pool) with the girls. Irial is a fish, squawking and splashing, while Darla sits dreamlike on the poolside, watching everything.

Spoke to David. He's going to South Africa tomorrow! Then talked to Danny Cannon, director of *Judge Dredd*. My Hollywood allergy again. How determined people seem to be to aim for exactly the same target again and again. A charitable interpretation: by doing so they evolve better tools for everyone else, creating vocabulary out of metaphor. Like those pathetic computer artists who are so thrilled when they've finally produced a picture of a daffodil with a drop of dew upon it – indistinguishable from a real photo. To me this would represent a total failure, but in fact it's probably those people who propel the evolution of tools.

Clare called (re Lucy's wedding on 14 March). Wrote to James Putnam at BM re storage and showing Egyptian stuff at Saatchi Gallery.

A future for air travel: inflight docking facilities above countries, so that 'Rome' – a huge Italian mall – hooks up as you fly over Italy. Aircraft and mall then move as a unit.

Bought three books about Egypt from the Travel Bookshop. Long flight – one whole book's worth. Bought a camera!

Getting off the plane – a hint of sewage in the air, but somehow exotic and alluring. My driver tells me it's Ramadan. We share a cigarette as we sit in Mercedes-rich traffic between beautiful orientalist buildings. Crowded, battered vehicles. Soft, cool air.

Apartments studded with air conditioners. It's nice arriving somewhere at night – night cloaks the mundane with intrigue. Solid traffic, people weaving in and out nonchalantly, drivers cursing very chalantly. A five- or six-year-old boy, arms full of cartons of cigarettes, dances thru five lanes of fast cars. Terrifying. The more wrecked the vehicle, the more shit stuck on it. People on mopeds – carrying kids, huge baskets, an oil-drum.

At the hotel, opening the curtains in my room and looking out into the night, I see, dimly, a dark amber against a hazy sky: the Great Pyramid of Cheops. Now there's a justifiable use of capital letters.

Ate dolmas, watched TV, listened to echoey laughing Arabs outside. Jay Leno, that stultifyingly unfunny man, on TV. The pyramids in the dim night outside. And yet I am watching Jay Leno (better reception).

24 FEBRUARY

Up early this morning (after a short night). Flung open the curtains to a wall of fog. No pyramid remotely visible. After breakfast I had my car take me to the closest point and gradually the fog cleared – but not enough for me to make any sense of the scale of it. I found two stones – a little waxy citrine and a larger triangular piece of shale, smoothed by time. The shale piece had a little cavity just right for the citrine. I kept them as my memento of the pyramids. Perhaps I'll mount them with the panoramic photos of mist that I took.

The drive into Cairo was fabulous – a special North African early-morning light and the type of cool air that you get only in hot countries. Lovely morning smells – I guess of fresh produce coming in from the delta. Markets. Mopeds. Lots of police. My plane has sand on the wings – a fine layer in which there are shoeless footprints.

Flying down the Nile as we left Cairo, I scanned the horizon with my bins, looking for the pyramids. Then I realized how big they are. This desert looks so permanent. What a wilderness it must have been! Imagine living on that narrow strip of land hundreds of miles long, with deep desert each side.

At Luxor, Maria met me (second time in one week) and we went to the boat – which you board by passing thru three other large ships moored in parallel. Lovely boat: the *Sudan* was built as the world's first tour-boat in 1890 by Thomas Cook, and is all of wood with lovely wide decks. King Farouk owned it later.

A nice lunch with my new German acquaintances, and then to Karnak. I try to imagine it with a roof – a forest of enormously thick, penile columns. Most impressive: writing everywhere – obviously no content problems. Bought some trinkets of poor quality, but was assured I'd saved several families by doing so.

In the evening (after tea on the top deck) we went to Luxor Temple. Wow! Going into such a place by night is completely different. Such stillness. Hard to imagine it all painted. I get the best deal by walking off alone (my excuse – the guide speaks German). For a moment I thought I felt what it might have been like visiting here 3,000 years ago. After, M. and I walked (coach gone without us) and took a horse and cart whose driver wanted baksheesh – for the horse.

Young boy riding by at high speed on a bicycle shouting repeatedly, 'I am here.' Perhaps the central and single message of humanity.

25 FEBRUARY

I keep singing 'Some Words', one of my better unreleased songs.

I seem to have been very lucky with my cabin – big, light and spacious. Up early, knocked on Maria's door, as she asked me to. Breathy voice from within: 'Ziss iss too urrly, Brian.' So I went for a walk alone, through dirt streets crowded with vegetable-sellers, smelling of dill and coriander. A very nice walk.

People hassle little or leave me alone – apparently rather baffled. I like watching people work, knowing their techniques and enjoying the dance of well-practised movements.

So much to write in one day. In the morning we crossed the river by ferry to visit the Valley of Kings. I saw four tombs: Rameses IX was deep and silent and I was able to be alone in there. Such bright and lively colour; such free drawing. Tuthmosis IV was down more deep steps. But at the bottom, where the big tomb had sat for 3,500 years, it was warm. Outside the tomb, among those wild, barren desert hills, I found some fossils. It didn't seem surprising. From there we drove on to Hatshepsut's huge symmetrical temple, against which the Nile had once lapped. Then to the most beautiful of all: Rameses II. The combination of almost frenetic intricacy and complete calm.

In the afternoon we began a long journey down-river to Esna. Beautiful journey. Night fell and I lay out alone on the top deck, watching stars, smelling burnt sugar cane and quassia, listening to amplified muezzins wailing from the banks, stray dogs, bullfrogs, distant car horns. After dinner we passed through two locks – the second only 8 inches wider than the boat (in fact it had been made that wide precisely to admit this boat). We broke a window going through. In Esna we walked – lots of tourists, police, the German gays trying on beautiful fabric stoles and hats.

26 FEBRUARY

What will we leave behind that future generations and races will be this impressed by? The only thing I can think of – the only comparable synergy of intellectual, artistic and technical talent – is our defence technology (for the pharaohs, what they were making was also a kind of defence system). If anyone had any idea how much time and money and energy and talent was being spent on that, they'd take it all very seriously. Perhaps a worthy artistic job in these times would be to 'curate' it all (cf. Chris Burden): to arrange that it is all carefully buried in underground hangars when it becomes redundant.

This morning I was first at breakfast and requested the music changed from Western slop to Arab pop – and got Om Kalsoum. I walked round early and engaged in a delightful and financially ruinous 'barter' with a charming woman with oil-dark eyes. I was happy to pay her even more than she asked, just to surprise her. In the Koran bookshop, the owner asked me to take his photo and send him a copy.

We sailed down to Edfu, the Nile becoming more wild and African – a decapitated black and white cow floating by, clumps of water-hyacinth, the occasional factory, kids calling, sullen barges full of stones. At Edfu (which we reached after lunch) we visited the most massive and beautifully preserved temple, a beautiful deep sand colour with giant figures cut into its slanting faces. I made a sketch there. There was a tiny tunnel cut through the front pylon – almost as if to show you how thick it really was. Lots of very dark stone steps inside the walls of the building – lit by very occasional tiny deep openings in the wall. Intense peach sunlight raking the walls, picking out the relief. We went in a horse and carriage through the most chaotic market-place. Vegetables everywhere, donkeys, kids, trucks, soldiers.

In the evening I went into the market alone. People were so friendly The boy on the bicycle, after our accidental collision, returned round the block to say, 'I'm very sorry.' The noodle-maker showed me how he makes noodles (on an enormous internally heated rotating drum above which a line of spouts dribbles thin streams of paste which harden on the drum).

Good Mustafa took me back to the ship, where I donned djellaba and fez and eye-shadow for the Egyptian evening. Everyone was similarly clad, with many Cleopatras among the various Rameses. I had such a great time – dancing and playing Murder – which was a complete scream. Rediscoveries: I like gays, and I like Germans. At least I can dance in their company. Everybody said how different I looked in my sheikh's outfit (black with gold trim), and indeed it felt that way.

27 FEBRUARY

Today was a real adventure. I got up very early to see the sun up, and soon decided to take a walk. Dusty early-morning streets, but again no baksheeshing so it was fine. Watching kids getting ready for school, taking pics of shopfronts (the style of ornament here is becoming more African, less Arabic), walking through alleys off backstreets, thinking I was heading for the temple. I wasn't, but I was out in fields of quizzical peasants and raised-eyebrow donkey boys before I realized. So I turned back, found the right road and, having negotiated two T-shirts for the girls, sat with a tea in the lovely semi-open café facing the back of the temple. It was delightfully calm and Protectorate-era-ish.

I casually asked the time of my neighbour, whose watch said AAAH! FIVE PAST EIGHT! And we're leaving for Kôm Ombo at 8.00. I jumped into a calash, and, sensing my urgency, the driver whipped the horse along at boneshaking speed. I was enjoying this – passing all the docile tourist calashes coming the other way; our driver shouting 'OWA! OWA!' at scattering confusions of people and donkeys and bikes and vegetables. My amusement faded as we approached the harbour, the *Sudan* conspicuous by its absence and then glimpsed on the far horizon: they'd left without me!

My calash driver immediately realized he was on to a winner, and took me to a taxi-stand, where there was much wheeling and dealing between the two of them – he'd sold me on to a taxi-driver. We sped off for Kôm Ombo and I managed a snap of what could have been the moment before

63

my death, but we somehow avoided crashing into any of the five parallel vehicles and survived.

In Kôm Ombo I went desolately to the temple (where I arrived at 9.00 a.m.) worried that the boat people would now be waking up and starting to notice my absence.

I walked out to get some water and some truly vile little maize puffs (I'd had no breakfast). I sat down by the Nile, so quiet and huge, and a young soldier with a 17th-century Kalashnikov approached me and looked down sneeringly (I fancied). Then he slowly walked off, looking back occasionally. It occurred to me that he might be after a little excitement and want to use me for target practice. For a few minutes I was nervous. I didn't know where he'd gone. There was no one else around. The maize puffs were dry in my mouth. A few minutes later he returned – with another young rifleman and a very large and grinningly chic-looking sergeant-major type. I explained that I was just having a bite to eat, and the sergeant-major chuckled menacingly and reminded me that it was Ramadan. Then, as I put away the putrid puffs, he burst out laughing, his fat belly rocking up and down, shook my hand, and clapped me on the shoulder. They all laughed and left, perhaps pleased to have mildly frightened me.

I went back to the completely empty temple and sat around for hours. I had a sleep on a big, warm stone carved 2,000 years ago. I rubbed my hands over my unshaven face, felt my tummy rumbling, and got up to find something to eat. That's when I met Ahmed Said Ahmed. Such a nice man – a handsome guide, not a hassler, who took me to the café and got me some tea and told me how he wanted to marry a European (or American or Asian) girl to 'improve his standing', told me about his work and family, and then took me into his office, where I met three of his friends: Abdul, the singing soldier; Shasly, the Nubian; and Fariman, the Japanese-speaking intellectual with thick glasses. Within five minutes we were all singing Farid el Atrache's 'Habina' together. They were fascinated that I knew the song, and in stitches at my phonetic version of the Arabic words.

It was a very easy and natural half-hour, and their hospitality was complete and unforced.

Finally, at two o'clock, the boat appeared in the distance, round the bend in the river. I waited on the bank with Abdul and Ahmed, and as the boat slowly closed I realized many of the passengers were on the decks waving at me. I was greeted like a prodigal son, and everyone was so sweet and relieved and pleased to see me (unlike I probably would have been).

In the evening I bought wine for them all, after a blissful hour lying out on the top deck in the dark silence. Maria and Bettina and Ulli and I went to the bazaar – the best yet – and bought scarves from Nubia. It was a great day, and I thought I would like all my days to be like this one.

Things people thought might have happened to me:
I got drunk and fell overboard;
I was kidnapped by fundamentalists;
I had found a quiet corner in the ship and got trapped there;
The mysterious stranger (Hindrich's date) had come for me and we'd gone off somewhere.

The people here are desert flowers – they can be completely dormant until conditions are right, and then frenzied with energy.

28 FEBRUARY

After a troubled night (engine repairs proceeding directly below my room long before dawn) I took breakfast alone and at 9.00 we left for the temple of Isis. On the way we stopped at the dams of Aswan – the smaller, older, one built by the British; the High Dam by the Russians. A huge technical achievement which feels quite naturally a successor of the tombs and temples we've seen. I wonder why the Egyptians used so little of their skills in the control of nature? Or did they? Amir says that the stones were held together by a vacuum created by the cooling of lead poured into the specially made grooves and cracks. The Nilometer of yesterday is evidence of at least a need to record nature, which is usually a first step to control. But

I have seen no evidence of dams or much other water-controlling – except for that channel to the priestesses' bath yesterday.

After Aswan we went on a small motorboat to the temple. This place had a very strong effect on me. As we approached it over the lake I felt moved almost to tears. I thought of all those lost generations of Nubians worshipping Isis. I want to know about her. I understand the attraction of having a (non-live) goddess in one's life. Her temple is covered with graffiti from all ages – some very carefully done with Italianate curves or Times Roman serifs. There's a memorial – obviously amateur – to '14 officers and 96 NCOs and men who were killed or died of disease' during Britain's Sudan campaign. Its not-quite-perfectness is touching. There's a small corner where all trace of Egyptian carving has been scraped away – this is where the early Christian priests tried to say mass. Somewhere in the temple is the last known hieroglyphic text – from AD 394. It is unfinished and in corrupt script, the final faint breath of a 3,000-year civilization.

But what's fascinating about the place is its unsquareness. The chief pylon is strangely aligned to the walls, and this slightly 'off' angle seems to echo the sides of the pylon themselves, with their facing side more upright than the back. The temple has a lightness and loveliness that sets it apart from the others I've seen.

On the bus Amir was saying that there was a revival of the Isis cult by an intellectual called Dr Hussein. Hussein sees it as the true and pure faith of Egypt. I suspect Amir has a more than passing interest in this.

Next we went to the unfinished obelisk – it was abandoned because it cracked. So powerful seeing this monstrous block still part of the rock, frozen in the process of breaking loose, emerging. Standing in that quarry, amid abandoned work in progress, created a strong feeling of what it might have been like to labour under that hot sun.

At lunch propounding a theory of Court TV and soaps, their value as moral/philosophical gossip.

After lunch, we took a felucca (small yacht) to the botanical gardens. The gardens were not remarkable except for their perfect positioning in the lake. The breeze was so soft and fresh. Tourists look so dreadful, and yet I am one. How not to look dreadful? Don't be predatory. Sit in one place and pay attention or surrender. What looks bad is constant tramping about, a greed for undigested experience. The photograph is digestion deferred: 'So that's where I was.'

Beside our boats little boys – six or seven – in miniature homemade boats, sing 'Alouette' and 'Row the Boat' in completely phonetic form. 'Raw raw raw ya bo jelly dower stree . . . ' How many generations of urchins has that been passed down to have mutated this far?

In the evening we wandered very slowly through the bazaar, having a great time and me buying coloured spices and things for Anthea and shoes for the girls. We sat in a café and drank Malven (hibiscus tea) and smoked hookah, leaving Karsten there looking glazed-eyed and stoned – he's really into the old hookah. Much good-natured banter with traders – me bidding them up, to their great amusement. Nubian music on the boat at night. Very accurate clapping styles, with completely open hands. Bed at 2.00 a.m.

Two totally vile Germans in shell-suits from another cruise grinningly humiliate a shoeshine boy – reminding me of that picture of Jews being forced to scrub the street. Ugly idiot laughter.

Wise old man with fluorescent-green rosary.

Just stop every 20 paces and take a photo in any direction.

Repair is what beautifies.

Do very hard things, just for the sake of it.*

1 MARCH

One of the revelations of this journey has been to see the kind of society that gay men, as opposed to the rest of us, make for themselves. It's very

* A way of doing something original is by trying something so painstaking that nobody else has ever bothered with it. Sixteen-foot-square black paintings made entirely with a very fine (6H) pencil would qualify (recently Jan Fabre has been covering castles and >>

kind and gentle – lots of non-sexual affection and touching, a sense of freedom, a blurring of identities. I've felt so loose here, enjoyed dressing up and being affectionate. There's a real tenderness – which is also characteristic of the mood of the market-places, where after all the furious haggling and arguing you suddenly break through into something close to love: a strange kind of friendship based entirely on respect for another person's style.

>> art galleries with Biro). Walking the Great Wall of China (Marina Abramović) isn't a bad try either.

Then the question arises in the mind: 'Why are they going to all this trouble?' I like this question. I like any question that makes you start thinking about the 'outside' of the experience – because it makes the experience bigger.

I did nothing much today – gave some of my supply of pethidine to Helmut, who had fallen from a camel; bazaared twice, and bought a lovely waistcoat and sat for a smoke with the charming Coptic man whose prices are marked (the only place this is done), got the Farid el Atrache tape and was ensnarled in a honeypot of ferocious waistcoat-selling. The things you get cheapest are the ones you really didn't want. Sunbathed and then bazaared at the end of the last fast of Ramadan. It was great being there in the market to watch people diving for their already stoked hookahs as the end-of-fast cannon fired, or large groups of men sitting down on the sidewalk together to eat elaborate dishes. I'm interested in this fasting thing, and bought a (very technical) Islam book about it which explains things like the circumstances under which you may vomit.

In the evening we had the final candlelight dinner, everyone by now gone native, in djellabas, turbans and fezzes. I wore my black fez and new striped waistcoat over the blue and gold Indian shirt. Alfred, the great host, looked amazing in his handmade djellaba and aba – and tonight saw the foundation of the Aberya cult (of which he is the high priest), which quickly degenerated into drinking and loose behaviour. Made photos of each boat member, Egypt-style.

2 MARCH

When did the idea of rhyming first appear?

Last night I heard from Karin Davison the true extent of the kerfuffle my absence from the boat caused – top-level meetings; discussions about whether to alert the government.

This morning everybody left, and I also decided to abandon ship in favour of the Isis Island Hotel. I thought it would be melancholy to be here alone after so much warmth and fun. Fond goodbyes to all, and some exchanges of addresses and numbers. Maria gave me the biggest hug imaginable – it was very sweet. I waved them off on the bus and went back to settle my bill and say goodbye to the ship. Dust is blowing in from the desert – you see it – like a haze on the horizon. Now everyone's gone I only want to be home with my family. I should have left too. What can I do with this day? Work on Self-Storage.

It was a rather flat day. I had a massage that zonked me out for about two hours. I had a fairly disgusting (compared to the *Sudan*) lunch, and a quite disgusting dinner. Between these bookend experiences, I went into the market and bought two more waistcoats. Then I sat in the shop of Fayez of the six languages and he told me how he liked the bodies of Nubian girls and got me some Malven tea and plied me with cigarettes. I told him that the harassment meted out to European bazaar-grazers actually frightened them away, and I decided to prove this by asking him to let me try out some new, revolutionary, very low-pressure techniques. I failed to make a single sale in 20 minutes: many stopped and lingered, but none bought. Nonetheless, I spent a further two pleasant hours watching market life drift by.

Thinking about this landscape made up of writing makes me feel differently about Jenny Holzer.

Once upon a time religion *was* politics, and the appearance of a new religion heralded a new set of possible relationships – between people, between peoples, between people and nature. New religions implicitly posed new ideas of government. Similarly moral philosophy has become dramatized – in soap operas; in Court TV.

I notice Japanese people are looking less Japanese these days.

3 MARCH

The long journey home. After an early rise and an Egyptian sun, and two hod-hod birds on a long overhanging stem, and a disgusting breakfast, to Aswan airport. The flight over Egypt was interesting and ended dramatically with us very close to the pyramids – actually my best view. Then from Cairo on to London – devouring newspapers senselessly, vaguely worrying about Self-Storage but unable to properly focus on it. I really don't quite know what I'm doing there. Stepped right back into the British class system with the awful 'cocky' driver who called me 'sir' (which I don't like) in a really nasty, sarcastic, way (subtext: 'Sir? You? What a fucking laugh!') which I hate even more.

Home, pulling out all the spoils of war, kids climbing all over me but A. looking a bit tired. Read my travel diary to A. Dinner, cigarettes, then bed.

Things to take everywhere:
    alarm clock
    Swiss Army knife (with scissors)
    mains-tester screwdriver
    single-edged razor blade
    mechanical pencil
    nail-clipper
    disposable razors
    measuring tape
    microcassette recorder
    Blu-tack
    torch
    toothpaste + brush

mint toothpicks
shampoo sachet
2 Powerbars
amber-tint sunglasses
foam earplugs
small pen
pethidine tablets
mini-can shaving foam
battery tester
passport
footcream

4 MARCH

Sunday morning. To studio with girls (in fez and scarf), both of them on computers, me tidying up. *Wired* pics sent on wrong disc-doubler format. Rik Poynor in afternoon. Hannah came over reading a ferociously difficult philosophy book (her course-work). Rorty looked good again.

Storage ideas:
Room full of rocks: maybe gobo-ed threads of light and mirror reflectors
Rock closet
Cone of henna and cone of indigo or four coloured cones
Dog show
Sand walk with altars
Back-of-door sounds – make music
– make trellises
– buy speakers and players
– TVs
– covered wall
– fans
Contemporary Data Lounge?
Clock room

Revolving animal squeakers
Cheap radios all tuned differently

Twenty years ago today I did my first public talk, at Trent Polytechnic (Michael Nyman invited me). Before the talk I was dying of fright, and the cup of tea in the common room seemed endless and nauseating. I just wanted to get the whole thing over with. Finally it was time to go out and do it. We walked out on to the stage, and I stayed back as Michael did what seemed like a six-hour introduction. I was close to blacking out. Finally it was time for me, and I walked up to the lectern. I then realized I'd forgotten to bring my notes up with me. I was too embarrassed to immediately turn round and go back to get them, so I just started speaking. To my surprise I was able to work through the whole two-hour talk in exactly the right order: it was all in my head. After that I always tried to prepare my talks in the same way – so that I knew the route I was going to take well enough to enjoy the journey.

* Some dates stick in my mind. This is one of them. I was so nervous about the whole thing that I'd written the complete talk out word for word – several times, until I was satisfied that the layout was just exactly as I wanted it.

5 MARCH

Irial came down (I was up early) looking all dozy and lovely and said she had 'a very nice dream' that Alexander picked her up and carried her all the way to the playground. In the morning Darla and Irial and I walked over to Westside, Darla singing away as happy as could be, and posted a note through the door. Then to Oxford in car with Rolf, A. driving. Terrible journey – a huge jam out of London and then arriving in Oxford to find the Pitt Rivers Museum closed. Lunch and to MoMA, where David Elliot and Chrissie were waiting. A vague and flaky meeting – still no sponsorship for anything and her asking lots of painfully detailed questions: this level of detail is not worth thinking about until the bigger questions (such as 'Do we actually have a show?') are answered. I thought, as I so often think nowadays, 'Why the fuck am I doing this?'

72

Other things I feel that about: *Judge Dredd,* Self-Storage, everything.

I don't know why, but there's just a general feeling of chaos around me. The kids' playroom is chaos – too many toys, bad organization. The house is chaos – tapes and letters and requests and receipts everywhere. My studio is chaos – the mess of a dabbler. And tomorrow I start JAMES, leaving this mess unresolved.

6 MARCH

Long day. To Brondesbury by 8.00. Severe dog-shit crisis.* Did some work and Welled Stewart after long Egyptian silence.

To Westside, setting up (tackling problems of hearing and visibility of seven players in one room) and, as band arrives, listening and making charts of song-starts in hand. Worked on 'Assembly' (new chord section) and 'Star' (ditto). Home at 11.00 p.m.

7 MARCH

To Bron early: Greg Jalbert and Blissing.

To studio for 11.45, but whole band not assembled till 1.00. We talked about making new vocal music over the instrumental discoveries of *Wah Wah* and after. We started working on a song in that mode – Ambient opening, song without changes over it. Promising – the song was. Also worked on 'Darling' and 'Make it All Right' (very nice new low-register singing).

* On the way to work one morning, manoeuvring past the usual several hundred piles of canine turd, I mentally formed the League Against Dog Shit. This would be a direct action group of bourgeois revolutionaries dedicated to ridding the world of crap.

LADS would operate in three main ways: by putting pressure on dog owners directly (for instance, scooping up the turds as they happen and 'returning' them to the owners), by putting pressure on the council (collecting unattended turds and filling rubbish sacks with them, then delivering them to the lord mayor), and by attacking the problem at source (this last depends on the development of a substance which can be liberally sprayed on trees and other public places, and which ignites or releases noxious fumes when contacted by dog crap).

Our sisters in revolution: LASSIE (League against Street Shit in England).

Things are going well but the poor band are tired (too much touring?). They need a lot of pushing. There are so many of us there, and therefore a tendency to submerge compositional problems in sheer density. Mark is brilliant but modest, so his contribution is always heard later (and therefore doesn't help in the jams). Tim asked the assistant (with flu) to take time off.

Home at 11.15. Darla sick. Slept in their room.

No thoughts of Wembley at all. My one-dimensional mind.

8 MARCH

Garden Committee meeting 8.30 / Wembley.

To Wembley on bright morning. (Met Jane Barnard on the street, who asked 'Do you really need those glasses?') Freezing there, but the sun helped. I explained my projects to Katy, David Schofield and Michael and they sounded good. Katy will research things for me. Also getting better vibe from students – looks like it'll be at least OK. Michael apologetic for coldness of room (heat was supposed to be on now).

On to studio. Today felt like pushing a rock up a hill. I was directing, in detail. That's fine – we get to try specific, controlled experiments; but it's hard. I have to get bossy or everything will dissolve. Like many of us intuitives, they have a great ability to start things 'by accident' but then it's hard to improve them 'by design'. I guess that's my – outsider – job. Dave gets frustrated because no one locks with him, so he's trying to make all the rhythm in the drums. With a big band, every beat tends to get filled, and, unless expressly prohibited, everyone tends to play all the time. That makes for an evenness of density. Nonetheless, we made 'Whiplash' come to rather triumphant life – a very beautiful, wistful song over a machine throb.

Ran non-stop from the studio to the Garden Committee meeting. How we English enjoy our eloquence! Lots of self-mocking brackets, complex contained clauses, elegant deferrals. Unfortunately no wine. The most important topic left till last, by which time I'd left from hunger.

9 MARCH

In the morning trying to do the Swarovski proposal (with 3D folds). Annoyed at doing this in a hurry. Looked through huge list of applicants for job as my assistant: 85 responses to one ad in *Loot*. Tragic – even people of my age, some enormously overqualified.

Some evenings I walk home from the studio feeling so happy. It's fine if you reach a summit after a day of hill-climbing, and we sometimes do. Worked today on 'Hedex', 'Waltzing Along' and 'Avalanche', for all of which I suggested new arrangements and sections. Things sounded really good. We tried to start at 11.00 but the band were not ready (I got bloody mad); but we did focus and stick to schedule after that, and it paid off. Came home for a brief child break at 6.30 while the guys were having dinner. Could I be as good-natured as them and still keep things moving?

10 MARCH

Hard day – photo session with Ireneusz Matusiak and his bro in morning. Set up camera for interviews. Called Rolf about Swarovski.

On to studio with fresh strawberries. 1½ hours on 'Honest Pleasure', but no result. Then a jam – really strong, good bass line and great drums and guitar – pure Larry. I suggested we graft 'Hey That Muscle' on to the jam, which seemed to work well, and we had a new, tougher thing. Later we attempted 'Whatever the Sound', but it's basically a dull song with a nice atmosphere. Everyone was tired by the evening – time for a day off.

Met Anthea on the way to L'Altro. We had a nice pre-Artyom sit down. Art came with his new bird. He's on the make, new-Russian style, but also has genuine and deep feelings for music. And he has a very kind nature, I think – almost despite himself. He'd probably like to be tougher. When we got home Aggy said Irial had been vomiting a lot.

Looks like the Sekhmet loan from the BM might be possible.

Night-time teeth-grinding – worrying.

11 MARCH

Beautiful day after bad night. Anthea also ill. Irial can't keep anything down. To chemist early for tummy things.

Made drawings for Self-Storage pieces. Suddenly I have millions of ideas.

12 MARCH

After a night of sickness – poor Irial not getting better – a beautiful morning. We went into the garden and played hide-and-seek. Irial very lackadaisical and curled up on the bench in the sun. Chatted with Emma and very well bred 11-year-old horse-rider with huge mouth. Such self-assurance would probably be called cheekiness in a kid with a cockney accent.

In the studio everyone was completely passed out. Tim asleep on the sofa, Jim on the worktop, Saul late. Dave had done some late mixes last night. Good old Dave, the grumbling, laughing leek, a dependable spirit. Some OK, some disappointing. Four or five standouts: 'Hedex', 'Avalanche', 'Assembly', 'Whiplash', 'Waltzing Along'. When I can listen without hearing the labour pains still echoing in the background it's good stuff. When I do, it's strong stuff. The other songs still conceptually smudgy. Playing on most things tired. Saul tending to noodliness.

Worked today on 'Home Boy or Girl' and 'All One to Me'. The first has some excitement, though not enough personality yet. The second ended up sounding proficiently poppish (and a bit pointless), so I suggested a completely different version – softer, more *a cappella,* melancholy – which was OK, but then started to think that the basic tune is too normal to do much with.

Interesting watching the dynamics here. Saul, whose sonic contributions are erratic, is essential to the social ecology of the band. He's the person (with Dave) most likely to say what's on his mind, but without any rancour (so it doesn't stir up bad feeling). This opens the door for other people to talk. These two, the most naturally undemocratic and un-polite, are the log-jam busters. Saul's lively and funny and explosive; Dave's a dry-witted Welsh sparkler. Both make for life and soul.

Now if a group existed only to make music you'd value everyone's contributions only in musical terms. But bands, like other entities, exist to perpetuate their own existence as a little subculture – and the qualities and talents for that are quite different. Remember that girl at Gwent College whose visual work was not that striking but who almost single-handedly kept the whole course alive – always getting things going.

Home at 9.30. Watched some O. J. trial.

What is the frame (package)? Where does it start? Where does it end?

13 MARCH

To studio – letter to Tim Cole at SSEYO [see page 335: Generative music].

At Westside, Tim ill and everyone hard to motivate. 'Orson' ground on with me singing a semi-crappy chorus vocal part, but a good instrumental/bridge idea evolved. I suggested the tag go on to the end. Tim suggested having the last chord of the sequence as bar 1. Weird, I said, but when played it sounded great, unsettling the sequence interestingly.

The difficulty is keeping all those different attentions in one place long enough for a process like that – a process of sculpting – to take place. Later on 'Strange Requests' I added a new bass part and some arrangement ideas. All these songs are either one-note-Joes or monocycles. Laissez-faire composing – which is not to deny the force of some of the ideas. But songs that don't depend on composition depend instead on performance – so the fire has to be there in the playing, which it isn't after several long days' work.

After that we went on to 'Waltzing Along', in which I yelled myself hoarse shouting new structure cues over the music. That's a great song – only they do songs like that. The emotional *mélange* in Tim's singing is hard to pin down: yearning/abandoned/intimate/warm/wide-eyed/ . . . It's interesting that he hardly ever sings in bluesy scales, so the result is very English – slightly nostalgic in a nice way. That Brazilian idea, 'Sodade'(?) – nostalgia for a future that didn't happen.

In afternoon Andrew Burdon for interview. My voice completely shot, me shattered.

An argument for equal splits whatever happens: that way people know they can contribute but don't feel they have to (dutiful contributions being worse than none at all).

14 MARCH

Lucy's wedding.

Interviewed Declan.

To studio early, sitting out in the sun; remembering other days sitting in city sun listening to traffic – at the Miyako in San Francisco one late afternoon in 1980; in the courtyard at Chelsea, Old Church St, in 1984. Memories like this – the essence of a feeling trapped in an experience of colour or light – deserve to be loved and nurtured, elaborated, evolved, exaggerated, falsified, turned into metaphor.

This morning my taxi passed a regiment of Household Cavalry crossing the Harrow Road – proud, snooty riders on beautiful horses, dragging out-of-date artillery. As defence it's totally laughable and wasteful. As art it's rather good value.

Worked on 'Whiplash', which shone with brave promise. Also 'Honest Pleasure' turned out well with Larry's new rhythm guitar part. I want Saul to think in terms of sections of strings (hard when you're only playing one), but he flits from idea to idea. Poorer musicians are so pleased to find just one thing that they can successfully play that they often contribute more to the architecture of the piece – because other people can then build on what they're holding in place.

Brief summing up of the work to date with the band and then on to the theatre with Lin and John and Roz Preston – Stoppard's *Indian Ink*. Formally a companion to *Arcadia:* less intellectual, but very funny and clever. Really enjoyable.

The value of serious illness? The chance to change one's life.

15 MARCH

To Wembley. Frantic but optimistic day. Setting up speakers: music sounds good there. Journalists came out, photogs also, so I got very little work done in fact. Sko wants precise specifications for everything; I don't yet know what's being made. My solution: work in reverse – buy the stuff (lots of cheap amps etc.) and then build something out of it. Cheaper, more improvisational. Perhaps you only need one good-quality element in all that – which we have with Laurie's voice.

During one of the photo sessions, Mark Borkowski told me that Declan Colgan's wife suddenly died. What a shock I felt. I kept my feelings at bay until evening, when, telling Anthea about it, I got very down. Also thinking about Lawrence Brennan. The age of deaths has begun. For our children, it will start earlier: born of older parents (like so many now), they will experience all this sooner than we did. Like in medieval times? So my generation was in a strange bubble: parents who had children early and yet themselves lived for much longer, which translates into having your parents round for a much longer part of your own life.

Graph: average age of first intimate death experience over the centuries.

16 MARCH

Awake half the night grinding and thinking about Wembley. Such a lot to do. Kept trying to sleep and then getting up to do more drawings.

At the studio (having left Declan in Wembley with the ziggurat job) we worked on 'Hedex', 'All One to Me' and 'Chunny Pop'. The shock of the day came when Larry produced the fax that Anthea had sent to Peter Rudge* referring to my nightly grumbles (to her) about the difficulties of the work. I was excruciatingly embarrassed. To grumble is one thing, but to have it in writing is another. They, however, were extremely gentlemanly about the whole thing, doing their best to make me feel better.

* Their manager.

No pyramid yet.

Idea for a novel: 'Biography of someone who didn't know they were being watched', in which the author follows and secretly documents the life of a complete stranger from birth. For fifty years.

17 MARCH

Mum's birthday.

Woke up several times in the night smarting with the embarrassment ensuing from A.'s letter. How can I ever talk normally to those guys again?

At Wembley – a dreadful, windswept place – we 'installed' the pyramid (cost £104 = two sheets each of 1 inch MDF, the largest 27 ft square, receding by 2 ft each time. Also five pieces for plinth) and also the speaker flowers, which do look gorgeous. Such an obvious idea – how come I haven't seen it done before?

Also we went into the worst café on earth. Should be awarded a blue plaque.

So now (later) I have to eat my words and several helpings of humble pie. I explained my feelings to Anthea, who then showed me her latest letter to Peter Rudge, which I thought not much better, so she immediately called Rudge to discuss it with him and smooth things. That was big of her – and a surprise to me.

We watched the tape of Prince at the Brits – single words only: 'Slave . . . Why . . . Money . . .' etc. Trust him to do the memorable thing. Elton John looked very down, and his claim that 'There's life in the old girl yet' made you think there wasn't much.

18 MARCH

To Woodbridge for Mum's birthday lunch. Nice to see Arlette and John with little Emile. Now we are all parents.

19 MARCH

No entry

20 MARCH

Back to London. At Wembley with David Blarney, recording the whistling windy window. Freezing.

21 MARCH

Ill all day. Went to meet James Putnam and looked at Victorian casts in the BM's warehouse, but then returned home to spend a day in bed. Ate nothing all day but a bowl of fruit salad later.

22 MARCH

Today felt better at first but worse as day moved on. Sometimes the students get on my nerves – I keep wanting to say, 'Just bloody improvise!' And this space – so problematic. All problems you'd rather not have. Stupid problems whose solutions are not interesting. And all this seems to be about nothing, or about dull things.

Home early. Cinema: *The Madness of King George* – between so-so and OK. Like most movies, I shall probably never think of it again.

23 MARCH

Interview with James Dellingpole from *Tatler*. Talking about conferred value – and if enough is conferred it comes to appear intrinsic. Perhaps this intrinsic/conferred distinction is actually an axis, a continuum. Perhaps all value starts as conferred and gradually settles into seeming intrinsic. What is the difference between something seeming and something being in this case?

Saying that cultural objects have value is like saying that telephones have conversations.

To Stewart:

I find I am capable of turning things down more easily when I receive the invitations in large bundles: accordingly Anthea now parcels them up so that, each week or so, I am faced with a great heap of flattering and usually time-wasting opportunities to put myself about – things with a diversity and irrelevance that few other people except you would probably understand. When I see them all together, and then imagine my year being chiselled away day by day and flight by flight, it gets much easier to just go through them with a sharp pencil – NO, NO, NO (well, maybe, if I'm in the area anyway), NO, NON, NIET, NEIN.

I saw you on TV the other night, on *Horizon*. A good programme with lots of rather unnecessary ambience (things intended to show the 'texture' of the future, I assume, but not too well done). You were very clear and guruesque, and it occurred to me that you should always pronounce with your hat and tinted spectacles on. The black coat helps too, but could be disposed of in hot weather. I felt proud to be associated with GBN, as a matter of fact, as you and Peter and Richard O'Brien and Kevin Kelly all appeared.

But something struck me quite forcefully. On the one hand there was Kevin eulogizing the technological revolution, and what it meant in terms of empowerment and freedom. Yet at 9.00, straight after the programme, was the news: that a small bunch of nutters in Tokyo had put 3,000 people in hospital. It struck me forcefully (again) that the more 'richly connected' we make our world the more vulnerable we make it. Empowerment cuts both ways: as the complexity of things increases, so does the ability of an increasingly minute number of people to destabilize it. This, it strikes me, is the real limit on development – that we will accept the threat of terrorism as a limit on how complex we make things. So the Utopian techie vision of a richly connected future will not happen – not because we can't (technically) do it, but because we will recognize its vulnerability and shy away from it.

So I expect a limit to be reached, a sense of pulling back from what is possible. And this will be followed by waves of nostalgia-for-the-future-that-could-have-been. Country songs that say, 'We could have had it all', etc., etc. A sense of disappointment with ourselves – perhaps like the sense that pervaded Europe on the failure of the League of Nations.

24 MARCH

Try some country songs from a future perspective.

Found-object-piece rules: objects must be small enough to fit in my pocket, free (discarded), and found on the morning walk between Wembley station and Acorn Storage.

Interview with Mick Brown (*Guardian*) at Wembley. Nice seeing him again after all these years. I thought he was probably thinking 'After all these years, he's still blabbing on . . .'

Darla protesting about school. I took her and enjoyed it. (We played snakes all the way, diversifying into wasps, beetles, turtles and jellyfish.)

Lovely day. Why am I spending it at Wembley? Anna Golitski and Jonathan Rutherfurd-Best on the train. I just get depressed thinking of all the money being spent on this – £5,000 to lay electrical cable alone, just for a month – because I feel ashamed to be a part of this end of the art world. All this money has been squeezed out of various committees on the pretext that something of high cultural value is being made for it. But whatever of value is made will not be the bit that cost all that money. I always want to work the other way round: 'Tell me what you can spare and I'll make something from it.'

I find myself surrendering everything I wanted to do in order to save money so that the students have more for their projects. The good result might be that I do something elegant with very little. I would so like to make things from almost nothing at all – to prove that this can be done, that you don't have to suck up resources like this. I hate waste.

Good side: we are employing a lot of electricians and builders . . .

I took *Face of the Gods* to inspire me in this. Two things impress: (1) use anything to hand; (2) if you don't call it art, you're likely to get a better result.

Discussion with Sko, cutting some of the expensive projects. My dictum: there must always be a positive relationship between what goes in and what comes out. Thrilling if little goes in and much comes out; OK when much goes in if much comes out; completely unacceptable if much goes in and little comes out. Classify all proposals on this continuum.

Ways of letting Africa into how we feel.

25 MARCH

Two sounds held.

Bought electric drill, long bits, hairdriers, etc. on Golborne Road. To studio with girls. Irial doing KidPix.

26 MARCH

To Clifton Nurseries. Buying random heaps of cheap second-hand audio and video equipment from second-hand shops. Two more drills at Music/Video.

    Dog Room (A209) 'I like that dog'
    Field of speakers (A347) 'Hiyah'
    Ballroom
    Steel Box 'Wedge Room' = 'Here come'
    Egyptian (C231)

Spice Room (A201) tracing-paper
Drill Room (E110) at Music Video
Sandshrines (Nl14-20) 'Plato'
Data Lounge 8 x 4 sheet and Anaglypta
Water drip?
Call? Indian corridor = Cree
corridor = walk on water
corridor = walking and falling
Record phone calls

27 MARCH

No entry.

28 MARCH

Wembley. Snowing. No heat. No one else here. Why am I doing this?

29 MARCH

Get vermiculite / Buy speakers and amp / Auto-reverse decks / Do It All –
tiles for room A201 / Take plaster home

30 MARCH

S.W. radio / Get auto-reverse players / Power supplies / Lay wires – big
speakers in H rooms?

31 MARCH

Opal plexiglas panel / Small tools / Blu-tack / Fishing-wire / Other small
radio

1 APRIL

Awful day: bought a lovely £5.00 projector and broke its bulb in the evening.
My Alessi vase (the one I designed) got broken. There are no others left.

2 APRIL

Amelanchier comes into blossom.

Things coming together. Dear students: I take it all back. Plan for hanging piece in the dark room under the stairs.

3 APRIL

Petra's birthday / Wembley opening.

Opening. Finally abandoned 'Wedge Room' piece – which looked best when just the red head revolved in the dim red light. Checked out speakers etc with Drew.

Laurie arrived from NY, full of beans (like she'd just taxied across town). Told me about the shoot with Annie Leibovitz, where she had to swim about in a tank of cold water for hours while Annie kept saying 'Just one more . . . ' Finally rescued by Lou.

The opening was crowded unbearably – though people seemed to enjoy the show. Anthea liked it for its humour. Everyone I've ever known there, and my throat completely shot. Awful shock of the evening – coming into my Plato's Cave and finding it crammed with people climbing over everything and knocking things about. Those huge humans made it look so small and fragile. I was shocked and furious and yelled at them to get out. One was poor Karen of *Modern Painters,* who emerged sheepishly, grinning apologetically. Put a more obvious barrier up. Queues of people everywhere – apparently all having quite a nice time. And the show looked good when I approached it as a visitor. Of course Michelle in her tank is an instant hit single: and it does look genuinely mysterious and dreamy. Will she keep it up?

Pleased too with the very discreet and subtle piece by the two photographers/graphic designers. Their clarity and purposeful-ness paid off well.

Tim Noble's video pieces are very funny, and the pool piece is captivating. Visually a big hit.

My Drill Room was juvenile – something I'd have abandoned if left to myself. Though it does have the value of making you slightly apprehensive about what might be behind all these doors. So perhaps it works as an attention-getter at the beginning of the story – as one might clap one's hands to command silence.

Plato's Cave (retreat) my favourite piece. Something new there – strange mixture of scales, spaces. And the text is just right (I spaced Laurie's sentences so that there are long, long gaps). I love this piece.

The dinner at the long table was nice. Probably 80 people. Nick Lacey with beautiful wife. I tried to call Petra from the dinner to have everyone sing 'Happy Birthday' to her over the phone, but she wasn't bloody-well home.

4 APRIL

To Stewart:

So here's the summary: the show turned out well in the end, after a lot of furious last-minute scrabbling about and me emptying my whole studio of equipment to be used there! Just about everything I own is now in that weird building, presumably safely stored at least. The opening was both awesome and dreadful – awesome because *tout Londres* appeared; dreadful because they crashed round the place like newly liberated rhinos. I really don't like openings and I was very against having one – expecially in a show like this, which has a lot to do with getting slightly lost in the strange, echoey blandness of the place. All the same, people seemed to really like it – not least, I think, because several of the works showed a certain humour and lightness of touch – i.e. it wasn't all dreadfully po-faced and arty.

Almost without exception the best works were the cheapest. There are so many good reasons why this should be so, but perhaps the best is that people who haven't invested much feel free to change their minds. So the cheap shows were the ones that suddenly changed quickly and for the better at the last moment. One show involved a rather flash computer (fortunately the only one that did) which of course failed on the opening night.

One of the best pieces was a 7 ft tall (and very fat) mummy – the Vizier of Memphis – loaned by James Putnam of the BM – which I placed in a tiny locker at the end of a corridor. It was a bit of a one-liner – great gasps when the door was opened – but certainly a good one-liner. Laurie Anderson (whose voice I threaded through the whole place in all sorts of different ways) came over for the opening on Concorde and was extremely thrilled. She'd sent me a tape of 19 short stories – from 12 seconds to 2 minutes long – which I then treated in different ways. At the press conference she said it was like sending someone a letter and having it turned into an opera.

Your suggestion about posting the price of each show outside its door would have been superb . . .

5 APRIL

To Rolf's at 1.00 for lunch with the ever-smoking duo, those Etnas of modern theatre, André Wilms and Elisabeth Schweeger, about doing music for the play in Munich. I proposed something more like an installation than a soundtrack. [See page 371: The Marstall proposal.] Good meeting, transferring to my studio and lasting all afternoon. Deadline 2 May.

6 APRIL

Gardening.

To Hannah's for dinner – superb food and a really nice evening. Talking about allotments, teaching and learning. My theory always: START HERE, START NOW!

In afternoon Tim Cole and Jon Pettigrew to studio to see some Bliss and to show Anthea the KOAN system.

Afternoon, a good interview with CBC.

The search for John Rowles's 'If I Only Had Time' continues.

To Clifton Nurseries for more bedding plants.

Rewatched mind-shifting programme about lesbian motherhood – a subject about which I've thought little and then probably with a slight, under-the-breath 'YUK'. I now feel that possibly the only people who shouldn't be questioned closely about their intentions when having children are lesbian couples. It made it clear to me that the biggest source of confusion in the whole gender topic is the assumption that the biological fact of one's body (whether you're physically 'male' or 'female') is 'hardwiring', whereas it has a very complex connection with the your behavioural and psychological style. So, though we divide physically into 'male' and female', we are distributed over a very complex space as regards behaviour. There are not just two possible conditions, but a different one for each of us.

In the documentary, people kept popping up to say that they considered children needed a man around to create the right sexual balance. This is clearly absurd. When has there ever been the 'right' sexual balance? Would we know it if we saw it? Some of those lesbians looked like they'd make much better fathers than a lot of guys I know.

Instead of thinking of people as male or female, think of a multi-axial field of possibilities running between these two poles. Then look at people as disposed throughout it – and capable of shifting when mood and circumstances require. Encourage exploration. Encourage new hybrids. [See page 298: Axis thinking.]

8 APRIL

To Sicily. Fancy going now, just when London looks its most beautiful and my garden is bursting into life. At Gatwick with billions of people. In Taormina the town is totally murdered by cars and the hotel is wrongly constructed. Fortunately the girls are having a great time.

9 APRIL

Do you know what I'd love to be doing? At home alone in London setting up the computer for the girls, going to my studio at night and working late, wandering round Holland Park in this lovely spring, looking after the garden, conditioning the grass, properly cataloguing the show at Wembley, writing letters to people (so many owed), working with SSEYO on the project.

My big toes have gone numb. The word 'trudge' keeps coming to mind.

10 APRIL

Down to Hotel Mazzaro in bubble cars. Sat by pool and beach all day, collecting green glass. Finally dived into *freezing* pool, but felt so glad I did. Bracing isn't quite the word.

A new kind of artist – one who turns abandoned industrial projects into useful (lovely) objects.
INTERACTIVE = UNFINISHED
Unfinished is a much better word than interactive – my tombstone:

†

'INTERACTIVE'

IS THE WRONG WORD.

IT SHOULD BE . . .

[See page 415: Unfinished.]

11 APRIL

A strange coincidence: walking with the kids in the botanical gardens here, I look up to see Angus Deayton – again. As in Berlin, I feign non-recognition. If he's noticed me at all, he must be starting to think I'm following him.

To Villa Imperiale at Casale (Piazza Armerina) to see the mosaics. So medieval – could have been from 850 or so (instead of fourth century). Freezing lunch in nearby café. Rain and clouds. Beautiful roadside flowers – deep red, bright yellow, soft mauve, very occasional trumpets of pink. Mysterious windmill-like towers: yellow plastic pipes with 'aid' (vertically) and 'POLY-GUARD' written on them, small blades. All over orange crops.

Fantastic spaghetti vongole and talking about the war; nice Regaleali wine and cigarettes.

Realize that possibly Scott Walker's record could occupy much of the territory of David's. If it does, David won't release those things and as time passes more will get chipped away, or submerged under later additions.

12 APRIL

Such changeable weather. Torrential rain and then very hot sun. Nice walk round Taormina with kids. Playing on fountain, buying ice-cream and gold shoes (for all of us!) and ceramics. My heel (right) aches tremendously. I've got this cold, and colds now translate into aches for me.

13 APRIL

Early-morning walk up hill, to little monastery right at the top. My heart pounding, pink light all around me. Such beautiful small flowers – especially a very soft nettle.

To Etna with Bill. Very cold – lava fields just like Lanzarote. Talking about Prozac and the possibility of Cosmetic Psychiatry. [See page 318: Cosmetic psychiatry]

Went walking with Irial in the evening and we had a picnic (cheese, olives, maize puffs and water) on a wall.

14 APRIL

Perfect Good Friday weather – dull, cold and miserable. I feel 20 times worse than when I came, plus I feel I've thrown away what would have been a productive and imaginative week. More trudging, while A., the kids and her parents go up to some boring-looking village even higher than this and undoubtedly even more stuffed with little cars. Reduced to the *Daily Telegraph* crossword.

Remembered song: 'All Gone, All Gone' (fast 3/4)

15 APRIL

Back to London. Horrible charter altercation with ugly, stuffy Brits at airport about queue-jumping. Bill lost his luggage. Oh – awfulness. So thrilled and relieved to get back. A. and girls stayed on in Kent with her parents. To studio to log on and wrote at length to Stewart about life and dying and installations.

16 APRIL

Jobs for Sunday:
    water garden
    scrub shower
    paint table
    correspondence
    washing-up and kitchen
    proposal to Tim Cole
    get milk
    write Michael Morris

Last night I dreamed of a beautiful installation using tree trunks (must get some from Woodbridge). Two nights ago I dreamed a piece of music that, naturally, had everything a piece of music could have. Dream experiences are like drug experiences – memorably impossible to remember or translate.

To cinema in evening – *Once Were Warriors:* a sort of Maori version of *Pulp Fiction* – but left after 30 minutes. Couldn't take it. Young lady at box office looked on me pityingly – 'Poor old sod.'

Reading Jay's book *Living Without a Goal*. Finished *Billy the Kid,* Michael Ondaatje.

To studio: 'Flanking Movement'. Tried to write music for Marstall 'Lied', but words very clunky. Gardening. Scrubbed shower.

The girls naming their dolls: Irial comes up with names like Barasiwa, or Sharamooshala, or Ilazia Ha, all of which have very obscure pronunciations, whereas Darla's are carefully considered permutations of Flower, Love, Heart and Beauty (such as Heart Love, Beauty Flower, Beauty Love Flower etc.).

Copy music for Joan Ashworth, animation dept, 4th floor / Install software on kids' computer /To Wembley: get DAT and mike, nail piece /Make dentist's appointment /Call Roger / Bike /Start Marstall work /Child's software shop? /Assemble computer at Bron /A. collect from Harrow Road /driving school (?Drew?)/DATs

Not v. productive. Visiting Wembley. Discovered that the new Performa can read my old Toshiba disc. Some of those *Squelchy Life* era poems read very well now. Also W.O.W. — which I think I mostly wrote on trains to Woodbridge.

Lou Reed, Lenny Henry and Bowie all called. Enjoying Tricky CD. He didn't call.

David's opening tonight.

Hardly slept last night (after sausages?). Made bread in middle of night. Smothering dreams.

More Marstall work on Sound Tools. Compiled animation tape – 'Manila

Envelope' with Fripp sounds fabulous. How about blending the poems from 1990 with that music? Drew should learn Akai.

Celebrity evening – to David's show (didn't see him). Then to meet Lou Reed at Dave Stewart's studio – we three had dinner together. Dave Stewart is a completely alluring man – full of stamina and enthusiasm. He wants me to be involved in a Paul Allen-produced film about 'Inspiration' – how ideas come into being.

On to Wembley, which Lou really enjoyed – and it was just as Anthea described it – light-hearted but lovely too. Nice seeing it through his eyes – going round it in the right order like a visitor made me think that the choreography (by Sko and Michael) was a very important part of it.

In the car afterwards, Lou said, 'You did something that no one else has ever done, something that will change the world. I can hardly describe the magnitude of this achievement' and so on for some minutes. 'Whatever could that be?' I thought. 'You got *Wired* to pay you for an interview! I've been trying to get paid for interviews for 30 years!'

We went for a drink at Mama Rouge and talked about equipment and sound. His *Metal Machine Music* was released the same week – twenty years ago – as *Discreet Music*. *Discreet Music* soft, calm, melodic and reassuringly repetitive, without a single sound other than tape hiss above about 1,500 Hz, whereas *MMM* is as abrasive and unmelodic as possible, with almost nothing below – and yet they occupy two ends of what was at the time a pretty new axis – music as immersion, as a sonic experience in which you float. The roots of Ambient.

Lou has something of Dave Stewart – boyish anything-is-possible and life-is-fun enthusiasm. Wry, complex humour with tannic hints. Talking about the crap that works – how crumby pieces of equipment make magic. I said this was a model of popular culture – where 'base' materials (doo-wop, hula hoops) keep getting transmuted into something magical and powerful.

Things to fix at Self-Storage:
  tapes playing slow
  reshape mound
  water earth in dog room

20 APRIL

Paul Mayhew to look at garden 9.30.

To work early.

To Stewart:

Last night I went to an opening of an exhibition by David Bowie. It's bizarre trying to look at the work of someone you know as though you didn't know them. Some of the work was interesting, some was poor, and I wonder if he knows the difference. Of course the critics have come out against it – but for completely the wrong reasons, in my opinion. What they hate is the idea that a pop star can hire a gallery and hang his own work in it (they've criticized it as a 'vanity exhibition'). This is because artists are supposed to sit in their garrets until a professional galleryist turns up and says, 'You're a swan', whereupon the artist looks in the mirror with wide eyes and says, 'Yes – I *am* a swan.' Why shouldn't people hire galleries? Why shouldn't people publish their own books? This kind of stupidity clouds the issue entirely.

What's more to the point (I think) is deciding, 'Yes, actually anyone can do anything – Ronald Reagan can be a post-modernist sculptor if he wants, Madonna can be a film director, Brian Eno can write a historical novel. Now, having agreed on that, let's just let everyone do their thing and ignore the ones that don't interest us.' The worst thing is this pathetic English reaction 'HE HAS NO RIGHT TO DO THAT.' It just puts the argument in the wrong place.

Wired piece out – good but truncated (though Kevin tells me this is the longest piece they've ever run). Tidied studio. Listening to JAMES tapes – I find myself not able to think about music.

A. cooked nice vegetable dinner and we talked about the War Child fashion show for hours.

Irial's new curses: 'H!' (pronounced 'Aitch!'), 'Oh Nappy!' (now going out of fashion), 'Pancakes!'

Sometimes I'm so sick of music. All I want to hear is noise that I might imagine music into. When music occupies so much cultural space, you yearn for any noise that wasn't meant to be music, that is fresh and complicated and free from aesthetic intention (and therefore available for aesthetic invention).

21 APRIL

Reheard Donnie Elbert's 'Where Did Our Love Go?'. Fabulous. Different, more pushed, 'blacker' timing than the Supremes' version: 'Baby BABY baby . . .' – the second 'baby' is pushed, falling on a triplet.

This morning I jogged (well, sort of walked fast round the garden) and had a healthy breakfast (fruit and carrot juice, melon). I felt good after that. I went to the new office and wondered exactly what I'm going to do there, with all that space. Is this another red herring – red salmon; red killer whale?

I worked on some Greenaway *Pillow Book* stuff on Sound Tools – thinking of overlay systems: creating overlapping edit patterns to make dense webs of music out of the initial improvisations.*

Greenaway cancelled his visit again. What's with this guy? Anyway, I was pleased because it meant I could have the rest of the day to myself. My e-mail conversation about death (with Patty) continues. It's so deeply moving for me – makes me realize I've a lot to deal with there. Tears at the terminal.

Carol McN. called re V&A piece – we'll use the speaker flowers! Nice solution – cheap, attractive, easy.

* Peter Greenaway had approached me to make some music for his film based on *The Pillow Book of Sei Shonago* – the tenth-century Japanese classic. We used this idea as an inspiration for some of the U2/Eno improvisations which subsequently became the album *Passengers*.

Felt good today – concentrated and productive. Drew mended my bike and I enjoyed the ride back. Played with the girls in the blossom-full garden.

Working on more 'Unwelcome Jazz' (so-called because no one else seems to like it much). Fast, angular, irrational melodies over strong, dense grooves. Emotionally they are both gleeful (Idiot Glee) and cold – real brow-furrowers. If I had a beard I'd probably suck it.

A neck breather. Piece called 'Databurst'.

Since we now have 'trial by media' why not also have punishment by media? Instead of reintroducing death penalties (since Bill Clinton says he'll seek that for the Oklahoma bombers – who now appear to be nice white boys rather than rabid Muslims), why not have the PoMo stocks? People subject to public disgrace, odium, humiliation? Then, adjacent to your Court TV channels, you could have your Punishment TV channels: 'THIS TV COURT FINDS YOU GUILTY AND SENTENCES YOU TO THREE MONTHS' PUBLIC HUMILIATION ON CHANNEL 63.' People would tune in to their favourite victim.

22 APRIL

Nick Lacey 11.00.

Darla, dancing for me this morning at breakfast, stops and says, 'I'm not called Darla. I'm called [long, long space to think] – Flower Heart.'

Meeting with Nick Lacey and Nigel Osborne. I didn't realize it was Nigel *Osborne* until I'd almost embarrassed myself ('Have you ever been there?' I asked about Yugoslavia, where he has of course been hundreds of times). Nice plan, nice meeting, nice guy. Decided to go to Mostar myself next week.

To Kilburn with kids in afternoon – got mad with Irial, who hid under the table and cried. I felt so bad and apologized – she showered me with tearful hot kisses. But she is getting naughty sometimes, especially re parity with Darla. Everything has to be 'fair', instantly.

Cooked a nice dinner with heaps of purple broccoli in oyster sauce and chopped garlic.

If I were a government I would probably want crimes such as Oklahoma to serve double duty by pinning them on people I wanted to target anyway while quickly and discreetly dispatching the real culprits.

Things that used to be rare are now commonplace: strawberries/roast chicken/ceanothus/celebrity columns/showers.

Things that used to be commonplace are now rare: long evenings working alone/listening to the World Service in the darkroom.

Early to bed.

23 APRIL

And early to rise, makes a man run round the garden.

In no order: Rolf visited, Indian food, Marstall and Swarovski discussions. To studio early in morning for Photoshopping. Worked in garden.

Music for Joan Ashworth's animation students / Cally 8.30 / Dave Bates / Helen.

Morning run. Cycling with headphones: Little Richard and the Byrds out-takes (Quine's compilation).

Good reviews for Self-Storage.

Anthea was telling me about an incident in the garden involving a dog. Irial was very curious and wanted to know all about it: 'I want to rewind so I can see that dog.'

Attention is what creates value. Artworks are made as well by how people interact with them – and therefore by what quality of interaction they can inspire. So how do we assess an artist who we suspect is dreadful but who manages to inspire the right storm of attention, and whose audience seems to swoon in the appropriate way? We say, 'Well done.'

The question is: 'Is the act of getting attention a sufficient act for an artist?

Or is that in fact the job description?'

Perhaps the art of the future will be indistinguishable. [See page 374: Miraculous cures and the canonization of Basquiat.]

24 APRIL

No entry.

25 APRIL

Beautiful day – morning run, then cycled in. More stuff for Marstall – crickets and rumbles and New York thunder.

Kids' computer installed at home.

Lately hooked on vegs cooked in oyster sauce and chopped garlic (added late so as not to fry).

Rereading my 'Generating Variety' essay – so stuffy but very clever. Twenty years old now. Pity nobody ever read it.

Mirella Freni, *La Traviata*

26 APRIL

Took Darla to school, playing snakes and whales and dolphins again. She has the loveliest chuckle when you tickle her: sort of 'Stop it – but don't' (the chuckle men dream of?). To RCA after long walk – met Helen and James Parks, who was very nice and pleased to see me. To studio – wrote report to A. Today I started helping with Fun Wear. Great meeting with Mark Edwards, who was crackling with ideas – what a fast mind!

At home later I worked with the kids on KidPix and then spoke to Joan at great length on the phone. She's always good value – full of original and sharp insights, full of the joy of discovery. I hope I'm like that at 70. Then, only a moment later, David called, in equally great spirits, and suggested a rubber-walled changing room for Pagan Fun Wear – elbows and tits poking out so the audience could see. Wow – what a dayful!

Interview with Tim Cooper (*Evening Standard*) re Pagan Fun Wear. Talking authoritatively about things that don't yet exist – hoping to make them come into being by a pure act of faith.

New (explosive) pieces for Marstall: 'Rocket Attack with Large Brass Section' (distortion created by overloading H3000 inputs). Such a bizarrely original piece. Bet they don't use it.

Back to pick up Irial and walk home with her on a lovely sunny afternoon. Fleeting glimpse of my own comings-home from school – skipping in low sun.

At home, we played with KidPix. Irial's very comfortable with it and makes nice pictures. Why aren't there things like this for grown-ups? Or rather, why aren't programmes for grown-ups made with the same assumptions: viz. people are impatient, want results quickly, prefer good rapport to endless options, are more concerned about easy usability than high fidelity.

Harvesting herbs from the window-sill – kids giggling and eating bits. Irial sorting out my socks – 'This one hasn't got a partner' – sounded very grown-up.

I called Mum and talked to her a bit about her time in Germany. She told me that a farmer used to slip an egg through the fence of the camp for her.*

Bowie called and played an amazing Scott Walker song from *Tilt* down the phone – in awe of his singing, but relieved that the record's in a different territory from ours.

* During the war my mother was in a labour camp in Germany.

To Mostar today.

Irial, very worried, said I should keep one eye looking in front and one behind – 'so the gunners don't shoot you'. Poor thing was in tears – me too – to think I'd be in danger. I can't imagine I ever thought such things at five years old. Shows also that she's understood some things about the world since A. went there five months ago.

On the plane with ultra-reserved Nick – me reading *The Language Instinct*. Explaining my theory that the photofit picture of the Oklahoma suspect that the FBI circulated was in fact a composited 'average' face which would enable them to arrest almost anyone. Then at Zurich airport we saw a man who looked *exactly* like the picture, and there was another on the plane.

A short visit into Zagreb – full of be-denimed youngsters and crashing bells. Open squares with big cafés – St Mark's Venice-style. Lovely ambience outside the cathedral.

In Split (after flight over Adriatic islands) Jim Kennedy from War Child met us – a one-time professional East End gambler with a heart of gold. Small, hunchbacked, 50s, cracked smile, sparkly eyes, black Brylcreemed hair. He apparently has a rare disease that could kill him without warning. I like him very much. The city in Diocletian's palace – beautiful, organic, labyrinthine. After dinner went for a walk – huge, teeming crowds of young people. No parents, no kids, just 18–24-year-olds in huge clumps. The language is lovely in a pouty French way. Club life during wartime.

In the taxi from the airport, once again Donny Elbert's 'Where Did Our Love Go?'.

Kazuo Ishiguro in the *Herald Tribune* says he never does journalism because he doesn't want to manufacture passions about things that don't really interest him.

29 APRIL

Split morning. All architects should visit here. An example of what many people – uncoordinated, spread out over time – can achieve. The city as culture and history embodied.

Stomach slightly dubious about last night's beer/wine/black risotto and antipasto dinner. Fish market (how can there ever be this many fish in the world?). Girls with stylishly pre-holed stockings. Roman walls – huge blocks cut to a strict angle of about 80 degrees, the walls garnished with snapdragons and yuccas, and grasses bursting out of the cracks. Little traffic – but ferocious buses. A peaceful, complex, intricate city. Amazing morning market – honey- and propolis-sellers, nut-sellers, fruit-and vegetable-sellers, battery-sellers, plumbing-fixture-sellers, asparagus-sellers: all in vague and overlapping areas (for example, some tables have flowers and small electrical tools on them, others mix plumbing fittings with asparagus). Lots of fresh, good-looking food. Bought nuts and dried fruit. Smell of sweat (good, honest) and pricey perfumes and fresh apples – unusual mixtures. Strutty soldiers.

The city reflects all its erstwhile owners – Romans, Venetians, Dalmatians. Isn't this living post-modernism? Another nice thing: extreme rabbit-warren density against big, open, empty squares, rather than homogeneous spatial distribution. What is private is condensed and intricate, whereas what is public is expansive and open.

Bought a black suede jacket with Deutschmarks.

To airport to meet Susan, Keith and Nigel. On the journey we talked about fame and music. He reminds me of somewhere on the line between John Tilbury and Bill Kelsey. Susan full of life – a natural encourager. Along the coast, no signs whatever of war.

Then into Bosnia – collapsed buildings, little houses that once held life and families casually blown over by tanks. 'Let's destroy their homes.' No crueller statement. A beautiful and sad journey. At Jim's house, this amazing, good-looking, huge-breasted 22-year-old comes out – his girl-friend! Eccentric; very nice. To old school to see site for centre. Just a shell now: great heaps of debris from heavy shelling. A giant there – the man who cleared the place out for us to see must be nearly 7 ft tall. Shook his hand, and felt Lilliputian. To dinner (very meaty) and then on to Hamid's house via a late-night tour of the bridge.

We sat up late talking and drinking rakija (he says they drink it to get to sleep, so they don't dream). Hamid is a soil agronomist, in charge of food supply throughout the year the Croats were shelling from across the river. He has a natural sweetness about him – incredibly deep smile lines – that he is reluctantly surrendering in favour of the toughness that his situation demands.

30 APRIL

Early up and took Oxa, Hamid's funny little dog, for a walk by the river Neretva. Shrapnel scars everywhere; molten splashes in the road – captured moments like those high-speed photos of a droplet hitting a bowl of milk. How are those splashes made? Does the shrapnel melt the tar, or just gouge it away? Does the shrapnel leave the shell in a molten state?

A sunny Sunday-morning atmosphere. Then with Hamid to the radio station (after breakfast – a spoon of honey, some tea and rakija – and brief filming with Nick and Nigel at school) for mind-numbing interview in tiny smoke-filled room. No tea. No sympathy (well, some). This put me in a bad and gloomy mood ('Why the fuck am I doing this?' – the question that always precedes something worthwhile). Grumbling, mumbling on to a no-lunch situation (but I had my nuts!) until I ended up in a room with Nick Lacey and the world's tallest architect (6 ft 9 in?) eating ham and cheese.

The presentation was good – I spoke generally, Nigel spoke visionarily (in Serbo-Croat), and Nick spoke architecturally. After an adjournment, questions. Colin Kaiser from Unesco delivered a snotty, cynical and nasty speech. Basic theme: 'What right do these outsiders have to come in here and tell you what you should be building?' He was so unpleasant, with a horribly drawling, faggy, disdainful way of talking, but his attack, far from hurting us, served instead to galvanize everyone else into complete agreement against him. The head of the council, a war hero who'd been in a Serb concentration camp, stood up to say that, since Unesco had actually done almost nothing for them except talk, he thought it a bit rich that they should criticize us, who'd got this far on our own steam. Speaker after speaker gave wholehearted support, and some made useful suggestions about things we should bear in mind.

Afterwards an endless lunch, which I left at 5.20 to walk past the bursting, heartbreaking cemeteries ('Amira Kustovic 15.3.91–22.12.93', 'Mohammed Slavij 4.5.71–1.5.93' – the horrible eloquence of those dates to a parent) – then on to our school for a TV interview with the erstwhile radio interviewers. I have to forgive them – they're all operating under duress, trying to make something – but it was a yawn: basic rock 'n' roll questions. Shell splatters everywhere. But no metal. Then we shifted some stones so we could see the courtyard space, and then went on to the orphanage.

Beautiful young Aida – so bright and full of life could have been 15 or 30 (actually was 16) – and those young guitarists. 'That which doesn't kill us strengthens us' – Nietzsche.

Hamid is a very sweet man. The orphanage pulls out extreme emotions. The kids' paintings on the school-house walls are full of explosions and fires and death, but with all the bright gaiety and naivety of kids' drawings anywhere. The combination is harrowing.

Over to Danielle's (she's a French lady with some sort of aid connections who lives here and interrupts a lot; full of life and quite funny), and then to eat delicious kebabs. Surprisingly, they have grass here (someone told me that the difference between the Croats and the Muslims was the difference between crack and marijuana – their respective drugs of choice).

Cease-fire ends tonight. Nigel earnestly hoping that shelling wouldn't resume. Very slender crescent moon, silvered clouds over a silhouetted mountain range. Distant, muffled explosions.

1 MAY

So many conflicting thoughts and impressions. Do I have any idea what I'm getting involved with here? Our experiments with the kids were moderately successful – awkward, too classical, and a flute-player thrown in. Nigel a dynamo of energy, good with kids but, like me, tense. One is conscious of one's outsideness – of coming from the lap of luxury to people who've been sitting in hell for three years. You don't want to insult them by being patronizing ('Yes – I know how you must feel' – I don't have a fucking clue). But the kids had a nice time in the end. But what exactly are we hoping for here?

Then the chilling visit to West Mostar – the Croat section. Drove through the old front line, past those front-line East Mostar buildings so ruthlessly, hatefully, hacked by shell holes that you couldn't put down a single hand without touching one.

In the Croat radio station the fish-faced woman with dead eyes questioned me about rock and roll etc. and then, as I started talking about the Centre, suddenly, said, 'That's all', and motioned to the guy at the tape recorder to switch off. 'But,' I mentioned politely, 'I would like to add something – that what we are doing is available for all the people of Mostar, not just those on the East.' She replied coldly, 'We do not want to hear that.'

This is the first time I think I've seen the face of fascism close up. 'We do not want to know this' – we do not want to know anything that might erode the pristine hardness and simplicity of our picture of the world.

Must be careful not to become indignant on someone else's behalf.

After the three terrifying thunderclaps in the rainy café (everyone dived under the tables), Nick and I left for Split. A long, late journey through several checkpoints. In the car Nick and I talked about prisons. He's spent time in two – in Cuba and in Morocco – without actually committing any crimes. In Cuba Nick lost his faith in Castro's revolution which I retained for another 20 years (and still do to some extent).

2 MAY

Met Darco and photog at Zagreb airport. He had hoped to take us into Zagreb and spend the day with us, but I wanted to get home. So I said, 'Why not do your interview right here?' He didn't have any machinery, but fortunately I had my microcassette, that sturdy witness to the history of modern music. We did the interview while Nick watched and listened. I left him there – on A.'s advice I took an earlier plane.

Home and took Darla to intensely fragrant Holland Park. Then discovered shelling had started on Zagreb – just at the moment I took off.

Disturbing things: Why here? Why now? (i.e. why has my roulette wheel stopped here? Why not Rwanda, Cambodia, Angola?)

'We are so full of soul'; the fish woman's dead eyes.

'Music as therapy' – do I actually believe in this concept? Once I found myself saying, 'Music is a force for bringing people together', or some similar duck-billed platitude, while in the back of my mind a voice was murmuring, 'Don't be such a twat. It's no such thing. It can just as easily keep them apart.' This a few days after Arkan, the Serb thug, had married that beautiful Serbian nationalist folksinger (thus proving that beauty, talent, social authority and intelligence also bear no necessary relation to anything useful).

Noticing myself suddenly thinking I see fascism in the tightness in people's faces – signs of the beginning of racism.

Talked to U2 (*en group*) on phone about next recording sessions.

3 MAY

To Stewart:

I just returned from Bosnia last night – a few days in East Mostar. It's the (now) Muslim half of a quite small town – perhaps 60,000 people total. It was once one of the most beautiful towns in Europe – the old, eastern, half, that is – and now hardly a single undamaged structure survives. The Serbs and the Croats (in turn, but it was mostly the Croats) specifically destroyed everything historical or in any way associated with Muslims. This is very hard to look at – 15th-century mosques just smashed to bits; all the bridges gone, including the famous and spectacular Stari Most bridge that once arced over the river.

Some parts of the front line have received so much shell fire that you could not put your palm anywhere on the surface of a three-storey building without touching a bullet hole or shrapnel scar. In the months of the fighting there were almost no hospital facilities. The Croats sniped the river, the only source of water, and cut off the electricity. 1,800 people died and over 10,000 were injured (in E. Mostar, this is). The Muslims had few weapons (the damage on the Croat side is relatively light). It's hard to convey the impression of total hate you feel when you see the extent of this damage. It's all small arms and light artillery, so the 'job' of smashing up East Mostar must have been a systematic, trudging, workaday piece of demolition – just day after day of murder.

I mention all this in response to your comment about the Oklahoma bombing. That's also a shocking thing, but in a different way. You feel (I feel) that the lunacy is confined and identifiable. In Bosnia you don't feel that. Instead you feel this hatred radiating out from the Croat population towards the Muslims – not just a few nutters at work, but an entrenched rage.

Oklahoma is very suspicious to me. I am completely unconvinced by the current arrests, and I think it quite likely that this is a Birmingham Six story – remember them? A bunch of Irishmen jailed for many years for a bombing they probably didn't do. Same evidence – 'traces of explosives on their clothes'. Later revealed that the surface of playing-cards, for example, will yield 'traces of explosives', as will several other materials. No, my feeling is that the government had to get someone quick, and that these were good targets. Am I too cynical? I don't of course mean that the govt planned it – but that these suspects are just too ideal for them to turn down. They 'want' it to be those guys, and they'll try to make it that way.

The alternative – Middle East terrorists – is too disruptive to contemplate. People would demand that US bombs the whole region.

Dreadful event, whatever the source. Brings a new poignancy to my developing dystopian theory that terror and security issues are the limiting factor on social development.

Invited Anton to come and try Photoshop.

Long conversation with Dave Bates re JAMES. Also talked to Nick at length about his Zagreb day. He was driving back into Zagreb when the rockets hit – and they saw plumes of smoke rising from the centre, but also from the airport behind them. Nonetheless, in his unflappable manner, he spent a pleasant day in Zagreb taking in a few buildings and galleries.

Rather wasted day for me – spent hours on Soundtooling a U2/Eno track – taking a little fragment of an impro and looping it. It died under the anaesthetic. Sinking feeling of nearly total pointlessness, but then lots of laughter with Anthea at dinner.

4 MAY

Listening to the U2/Eno improvisations again, trying to see what I might have missed other times round. Notating the tapes (21 hours' worth!).

Letter to Darco.

Anton over from 10.00, playing with Photoshop. I like showing him how that works. We did some new versions of Kate Moss and Johnny Cash.

5 MAY

Through market on way to studio. Joan Ashworth called to say she'd lost the tape! Made her another copy (two hours). Also transferred one-minute sections from 44 of the U2 pieces on to a single quick-access DAT.

A day sitting in a chair.

6 MAY

Walked round Portobello with Walkman and Paul Gorman's compilation tape. Rather blissful. Listening to Acacia on this perfect day.

In the market, saw the ultimate domina – 5ft 11-ish, long black hair, black jeans and huge wide arse. Very long legs, very high spikes. So gorgeously parodically *Skin 2* that you almost had to laugh.

For dinner made a West African composite with roast chicken and peanut butter sauce.

7 MAY

New piece of music in morning – lyrical, heterophonic, with rare chord changes. How difficult or discouraged are changes when working with sequencers! The effect of computer sequencing is to split music into vertical blocks with sheer edges. The whole feeling of the dynamic between 'locked' and 'unlocked' – so important in played music – is thus sacrificed in favour of 'always locked'. The result is literary linearity rather than musical all-at-onceness.

Afternoon to Wembley to meet Michael – he with three kids. Show looked good, but now just starting to fall apart. Graffiti, but nothing yet nicked! Lovely weather. Drinks in French lady's garden. Later Georgie and I stiffly limbo-ing in the garden (to the bafflement of local kids).

8 MAY

To Dublin/VE Day.

My studio desperately needing reorganization: tool area; 'paper in' zone – or better 'DON'T LET PAPER IN' zone – events board near door (so I see it on the way out).

On the way to the airport a limo (carrying princes?) sweeps by escorted by four police riders. Nearby a broken old van ('Afro Caribbean Centre') sits conked out in a lay-by.

Questions for U2: 'What record would you like to make – i.e. how would you like this to be read? How would you like to get there? Does it bother you if the result is 'undemocratic'? How much cheating is allowed? How much me?' Lincoln's axe: 'This is Lincoln's original axe. The head has been replaced three times and the handle twice.'

Categories: full songs, semi songs, soundtrack.

Further lost recordings:
    Erotic songs to older women: 'Smother Me, Mother Me', 'Clouds of Love'
    The sonic histories
    Imagined ethnic music

Out of Turkey
those ancient farmers
turning land into flesh

9 MAY

What I love about Ireland is that it brings out the best in me – maybe it's U2, who do that with everyone. Fascinating to see that, after all this time, there is still such courtesy, understanding and love between them.

Yesterday's meeting: listening, selecting, Pavarotti phoning into the lovely new studio. Infallible touch: it's just the right place for them. Bono as wildly ambitious as usual – within moments he inflates the Pavarotti/Modena project into an enormous balloon carrying half the world's artists. Such visions – to make everything happen all at once, to tie together all his current ideas in the current proposal (even when that proposal is a 15 second soundtrack) are his talent. Larry, the realist, pricks the balloon to deflate it slightly and it descends somewhat – at least back into a possible atmosphere.

At Bono's house (slowly growing in beauty and intricacy) we sat and talked and smoked and drank red wine until 1.30. In The Folly I read the Kostabi book. I love his pictures, and his 'factory' is an interesting challenge to the Fine Art Economy. Do they like him, I wonder? If so, how do they rationalize it?

Something about that place is so focusing: I wish my home felt like this (i.e. like someone else's). Kostabi reminds me to invent a body of 'lost' work.

10 MAY

Awful infuriating day – so many bitty things to do before I go away. Is there still such a thing as 'my own work'? If so, what is it?

In evening with Bill, David and A. for poor £156 meal at First Floor. I'm sick of restaurants, and more sick of what they cost. Decided to take a more creative approach to eating from now on. Four clues: (1) less, (2) cheaper, (3) faster, (4) more portable.

To Stewart:

Yesterday, before the meeting with U2, I took the precaution of putting tiny sections of each of the 44 pieces of music we have in hand on to a single tape. All this means is that when somebody says 'Drum Loop 14' and someone else says 'Which one was that?' I can readily go to it without having to change tapes (which takes only a few more seconds but is annoying). This little precaution (which however took me nearly three hours to put together beforehand) expedited the whole thing so much, and changed the whole quality of the decisions being made. I tend to spend more and more of my time thinking how to set up situations so that they work – so that they can actually take less and less time. My ideal is probably based on that story I heard years ago of how the Japanese calligraphers used to work – a whole day spent grinding inks and preparing brushes and paper, and then, as the sun begins to go down, a single burst of fast and inspired action.

That cultural image – which you find throughout Japanese culture from Sumo to Sushi – is very interesting and quite different from ours. We admire people who stick at it doggedly and evenly (I also admire them) and put in the right amount of hours. But more and more I want to try that Japanese model: to get everything in place (including your mind, of course) first, and then to just give yourself one chance. It seems thrilling.

11 MAY

Working at studio on U2 stuff all day. Richard Rogers called re Stewart.*
What a conundrum this will be.

Good, solid day's work.

Mixed paint for Pembridge this morning. Too pink? You need so little. I love mixing paint – so calm and gently enlightening. Formula = 1 tube red, 1 tsp black, 4 tsps(?) yellow in four huge 10 gallon pots of white.

To Stewart:

Records made 'at one sitting' sound so fresh now – because the rate of discovery and the emotional tempo match those of the listener. What's infuriating, though, is how fragile those fabrics are. I've noticed that, trying to work on improvisations that have 'something', they very quickly dissolve into nothing the more attention they get. It's almost like trying to reconstruct a very funny dinner party – you had to be there, and it's impossible to isolate the chemistry of what really made it work.

* Stewart Brand's book *How Buildings Learn* contained some critical (as well as some appreciative) statements about the buildings of Richard Rogers. Rogers claimed the critical statements were defamatory and untrue, and began a legal process to have the book recalled and to have the text altered in future editions. At one point I was asked to act as a go-between in this matter, which I did (to little avail). Currently (March 1996) the book is still awaiting full publication in England and the matter is in the hands of the lawyers – which is why it is mentioned so little in this diary

Anthea's idea for a newspaper: *Yesterday's News*. This is a paper that follows up on stories which the others have dropped, and also exists as a site for letters sent to other papers. So when you write to the editor, send one also to *Yesterday's News*, which runs several pages of (mostly unpublished) readers' letters.

12 MAY

Exhausting-o-rama. Meeting with Mark Edwards and Cally to do Pagan music list. Those guys are fireworks. Sent tape to Bono of U2 order.

Bought two slices of 'dolphin fish' (Titi calls it dorade) from the shop on Golborne. Marinated in black bean sauce, tabasco and garlic. Let it sit in a broth of vegetable stock and anchovy paste and lemon, and eat it with Alex Haas – still one of the nicest, most balanced people I know. The kids like him a lot (always a good sign), and so does A. – who returned late and we all had a good laugh about Iggy Pop's penis sheaths for PFW ('just your basic party penis sheath' as his letter described it).

13 MAY

To Wembley for embarrassingly empty sale of show leftovers. Ride back with two guys from Manchester and Birmingham.

To Crab and Ambulance park with girls. Afternoon walk round Portobello sort of wishing – mysteriously – that I was in an altered state, and trying to imagine myself into it.

Kevin Kelly came over and we talked about things: paranoia, militias, O. J., reasons for doing art, the evolution of English. I took him to eat fish and chips in Kilburn.

Almost finished Joan's *Cataclysm*. Starting to really worry about Pagan Fun Wear. What a mammoth task to have taken on!

14 MAY

Timeline map of empires to run round studio walls.

A. and I. and D. made my birthday cake for today, since we're all home together. In a quiet way, one of the happiest birthdays of my life. Pity I'm 47. My father's age in 1963 – when I was buying my first Beatles and Stones records.

Gardening, reading, cooking.

15 MAY

Page-a-day? / 'In the future' self-defence story /Arto tape / Elvis Costello?

From a letter to Joan:

Today I am 47 – Christ, that does seem old to me. I went out this morning to an optician and got myself tested and fitted up with some spectacles – my first pair. Time just seems to slip away, with nothing much getting done in the meanwhile. I'm sure you'll scoff at my ambition – that there is something to be done – or at my disappointment that I don't do enough, when objectively it would seem that I'm always busy. But I'm always feeling that I've spent most of my life getting ready for something, honing skills and sensibilities for. . . what? I don't mean to convey a sense of hopelessness here – I'm certainly not depressed or anything like that – but there is a feeling that things could just drift on and on like this: me being quite successful and accruing the respect of sheer inertia – being praised for still being there, while somehow not exploring the extent of my interests and intellect.

There's such an easy momentum to success – after a couple of ideas you really don't have to do anything else except coast along. In fact everybody is generally overjoyed if you don't do anything else – people like to know where they stand with you and 'what you do'. This is one of the reasons, I suppose, I value your friendship – because you don't stand in awe of 'my work' (as indeed I don't) and thus sometimes push me into other directions by rearranging my sense of the relative value of things.

Part of the difficulty is never taking enough time on my own, being used to the possibility of easy distraction whenever I feel like it. The few times I've got away from that I've always discovered something else, and a new energy with which to pursue it. Sometimes I console myself with something some Indian chap said once: 'The fruit ripens slowly, but falls quickly.' Perhaps I'm a slow-ripening fruit. The horror is imagining that I might not be that, but just a slowly fading flower. Ah, where's the Prozac when you need it?

Really nasty article in *Guardian* about Laurie.

Letter to Jenny Turner:
Your article about Laurie Anderson in the *Guardian* was a case-study in bitterness and envy masquerading (as usual) as bold journalism. The number of times in the article you 'felt like saying' something or other to her, compared to what one supposes was the reality of the situation – you sitting politely with your tape recorder while she talked – is a kind of metaphor for spinelessness. It's the old formula – be smarmy, get the goods, then retreat to a safe distance and stick the knife in.

If you'd at least had the nerve to say directly to her just one of the things you claim to have been thinking, one might forgive your nastiness. But you didn't, apparently: so to envy and bitterness one must add cowardice.

16 MAY

Letter to Dave Stewart re 'scenius' concept. [See page 363: Letter to Dave Stewart.] Letter to Rita and Paul.

Catwalk check and music check at Saatchi.

17 MAY

Listening to Wobble stuff.˙ It's getting better, but   * *Spinner.*
there isn't enough me (i.e. the more me there is in
the balance, the more I like it).

Letter to Dominic re Wob's Glitterbug remixes. [See page 427: Wobbly letter.]

War Child at Island reception in evening. Interesting company, Island: still a family feeling and somehow welcoming – people you like talking to, are not trying to escape from. No doubt this sense of 'we're doing it because we like it' trickles down from Chris Blackwell, the ultimate gentleman of pleasure in the music biz. Saw Richard Williams, Chris Salewicz and a woman with the most astonishing bust. All eyes on stalks.

115

Lovely evening with Anthea.

18 MAY

Westside.

With the U2/Eno stuff you can finish it by putting more into it, but also by putting more round it. That's what makes the idea of film music attractive – it builds context and thus gives the music 'reach'. It invites the listener to start constructing a visual and narrative space of the music. It 'grows' the music. So the approach might be to develop the imaginary context – by telling a story or threading voices – bits of invented dialogue – or ambient sound – bits of situations – through it all. [See page 368: Letter to U2.]

Realized today I've spent three years gazing at computer screens and it has got me not very far. In my next studio, as an experiment, I'll have no computer set-up. The thought of going in in the morning and not switching on is thrilling and daunting. Notice a strong anti-computer feeling around – e.g. in *Wired:* my piece, Clifford Stoll's book, Sven Bircker's piece and then the *Star* saying CD-Rom doesn't work . . . that whole dream is waking up.

Mark Edwards came over. I showed him some Bliss work done to old Jarman music. Dull. Trouble is you don't know what to do while watching. You think, 'It's fine, but what am I for?' 'Interactive' is meant to solve this problem, but the paucity of the level of interaction is usually such that you just find yourself saying, 'It's fine, but what's all the rest of me for?'

19 MAY

Westside.

One circuit of the communal garden is 600 paces – each pace being 40–42 inches = about 666 yards. So three circuits is a mile! Should get some of those weights to carry. I prefer fast walking over jogging, which makes my brain rattle uncomfortably.

Irial said to me this evening – as I was cooking my fish – 'I don't like my face, Dad.' I asked why. She said, 'Because it doesn't suit me.' How touching that one so young should think something like this. I wonder what made her say that?

Another interview about Ambient today.

20 MAY

To market with girls – didgeridoo player, steel-drum player, small orchestra (accordion, double bass, guitar) into African shop. What a place to grow up! To studio: 'Disciplinary Action', and 'Working Men's Jacket' on Photoshop. Met Anton for lunch – talked about difference between putting stuff in the music and putting stuff *around* it. Must take atmospheres, dialogues, etc. to Dublin.

Record evening birds at Blenheim.

21 MAY

Highly oral.

Anthea at Roland Gardens all day, sorting out names for Pagan Fun Wear. Went swimming in the kids' pool (lots of lovely motherly bottoms) and then to studio, where they were both very good.

22 MAY

War Child presentation of Mostar Centre model in evening – film too long; lots of talking. Me trying to chat up sheikhs. To L'Altro with Hamid. During day, faxes to U2 and Danton. Making atmospheres; massage with Leigh.

23 MAY

For Ireland: DX7 prog list, multi-track notes, folder / Dolores 9.30 / The Sudan? / scarf of speakers

Irial came down and piped, 'Alexander said he really loved me today. He did really! I thought he was going to have a wedding with me!' Alexander is six, she five.

At the Ivors,* Dave Stewart sat down next to me –   * Ivor Novello Awards
having flown in from the South of France – and
then turned out to be my prize-presenter! I got a special award for 'Innovation'. Phil Manzanera came over to say hello. Elvis Costello and Lonnie Donegan made funny speeches.

24 MAY

Out to Dublin, looking forward to a couple of weeks in The Folly. Caught thumb in lethal studio door but otherwise a very good day working on 'Tenterhook'.

Bono starts to form the idea that this could be a song about being besieged, people trying to carry on doing ordinary things (playing piano, buying shoes) while their city is being shelled. Interesting evolution of a vocal idea: he starts with a line that goes, 'Is there time for cutting hair?', this gradually moving into 'Is there time for this and that and the other?', in his new list-making style of writing. Then I suggest that other voices do the first half of each line – I'm thinking Motown – so Edge and I (now known as the E-Notes) sing, 'Is there a time . . .' and Bono responds with the rest of the line. We do it again, alternating 'Is there a time' and 'a time' so ending up with 'Is there a time . . . a time . . . is there a time . . . a time' but on each second stanza the last line becomes just 'Is there time?' Of course, Bono, being a natural-born singer, ends up filling every available space and singing over our bits as well, which I keep saying doesn't sound so good, but which he just can't help doing. It doesn't sound so bad either. Singers are like Arabs: they abhor a vacuum. And a vacuum is defined as 'when I'm not singing'.

But the result is really charmed – a misty, melancholy bitter-sweetness undercut by the sharpness of the setting: the Miss Sarajevo Beauty

118

Contest (where a group of Bosnian artists and their girlfriends put on an elaborately kitsch beauty pageant while the Serbs were shelling Sarajevo). It's so straightforward working with them like this – no ego decisions, no politics. We think this may be the song for Pavarotti (who phoned again).

Meanwhile in the control room (while it's playing) Bono and Edge are writing the theme song for the new Bond movie, *Golden Eye*. They seem to flourish with too much to do at once – producing spurts of stamina and enthusiasm and making everyone believe in everything (sometimes sufficiently to pull it off!).

Left studio at 11.30, and then Edge and Bono and myself to a late pub on the way home, chatting about people. Black and tan.

25 MAY

Fabulous morning swim – ten lengths and some back-floating in sparkling morning sun (Bono says, 'In Ireland we have summer in the morning') which left me feeling young and clean and healthy. On the way in, talking with Huge about the social benefits of pedestrian centres.

Working today on 'Tenterhook' again. Tried strings in morning before anyone else came in, but the little organ part works best. Song takes shape and Bono does Pavarotti impersonation – very well – and we then called his voice teacher to ask her whether in fact Pav could sing this. She said yes, but the long high B (I think) would raise his blood pressure a little.

Song structure settled, although at present Pavarotti seems to me the least necessary part of it (though it has been built round the idea of his voice). Song currently seven minutes long. Edge thinks more drama needed in the words; I think fewer words needed.

Long day's work (10.30a.m.–11.30p.m.) punctuated by gorgeous dinner and lots of talk about drugs and their uses and abuses. Edge's exploding-

119

head story; Bono's friend morphing into a dog, him trying not to laugh. Bono left ill at about 10. Edge and I went on to Tosca. Ali as absolutely delightful and lovely as ever, Guggi as gaunt and glamorously possessed as ever. We talked about censorship, and I told my old idea of insisting that film-makers be asked to show not less but more violence. If they want to show violence at all, they are required to show it in detail: close-ups of wounds, accurate recordings of people dying, effects on homes and spouses and parents and children, etc.

These people know so much about how to live and have fun, and it doesn't seem to have much to do with money: they would live like this in a slum or in a palace. The difference wouldn't be in the choices they made but in how often they were able to make them.

Rediscovered 'Rainforest Premaster' (from the installation I did for Anita Contini at the World Financial Center some years back) – could've been a great Ambient hit! It easily outcircles The Orb.

26 MAY

Fascinating day. 'Fleet Click' – revealed to have some amazing overdubs from the London sessions I did with Holger Zschenderlein. Immediately great, but much time spent on trying to fix Bono's original guitar (which is the only instrument suggesting chordal movement) and then deciding to use it and edit the track round it. The extraordinary development was that a strange and wonderful song appeared – suddenly, after six minutes of music. Did backing vocals. Everyone helping – cooperation at its best. (Des came up with a gorgeous sample – from 'Love is Blindness'.)

At lunch discussing comparative philosophical systems. Bono maintains Judaeo-Christianity shows good results. I say it's a question of what number and type of casualties you're willing to tolerate (arrange various philosophies along such axes). Some systems produce only total losers and flat-out winners – the banana-republic model – while others attempt a 'spread it evenly' approach – welfare-stately. Is 'scapegoatism' – a big feature of many 'primitive' societies – a way of trying to visit all current psychological distress on to just one person? And, if so, how do we feel about that kind of deal – where one person suffers enormously in lieu of everyone else? Is this the basis of torture and The Ordeals?

Great risotto for dinner. Adam asked me which philosophers I was most interested in. I talked about Rorty a bit. Later he drove me to Bono's, where there was a birthday party for Marc Coleman. Funny that Adam still gets lost on the journey. Such a nice atmosphere – real delight in each other's company. Bono's speech about Marc Coleman – sentimental but just exactly right. Marc and Anna glowing with their new child. We all chose its name by writing down our choices on bits of paper which were drawn from a hat: the result was an 'interesting' Italo-Irish pancake – 'Paolo Jack Milo Ruben Mary Coleman'. I said anyone with a name like that would have an 'interesting' life. Shortly I made to slink off to bed. Ali tried to persuade me to stay. What a persuader she is. I went, nonetheless, down to The Folly and sat there rather abjectly writing this –

27 MAY

– until Marc Coleman turned up to suggest again that I come back and join in. Which I did.

That was an interesting evening. I went back up to the party, which was very friendly – a tender feeling but lots of laughing too. Bono and Edge and I talked about our (quite long now) relationship to date, and how we'd sort of overlooked telling each other how much we'd all enjoyed the ride. Bono said they'd learned so much from me, but I said I felt I'd done better out of the deal, being able to watch them working and getting on with each other. Edge later put his arm round me and said, 'Brian, you've got such a young spirit. I always love to see you and look forward to your visits. You are a really sweet man.' I was very touched by this. I guess I don't really expect to be liked.

121

Slept, not for long, and then swam 20 lengths that felt fabulous. Into studio feeling like warm jelly and did a rough mix of 'Tenterhook' ('Is there a time . . .'). And then went back to Killiney with Adam, enjoying the ride with him. At The Folly, walked on the beach and sat in a chair reading. Then went for sausages and mash at the house. To bed at 10.

28 MAY

Woke at 4.30. Funny thing – in Ireland I rarely get an erection (though I was swimming nude the other morning, fully erect, and that was tremendous – almost non-sexual: like enjoying a muscle being flexed). It must be something to do with all that Catholicism in the air. The morning light – low sun, grey-blue overcast – is beautiful and melancholy. Would be a very sad morning in another frame of mind, but now it is soft and tender.

Sat reading, walked on beach collecting stones, then went through gorse-golden hills to Paul's for lunch. I so wanted my day to continue undisturbed. Adam driving me in one of his weird specialist cars – 2 mm above the ground and bumpy as hell. Of course we got lost, but the beauty of the day and the pleasure of Adam's conversation made that irrelevant. He was talking about Naomi, and I admired the lack of any acrimony or covertness or self-aggrandizement at her expense. He's a very balanced person.

Conversation with Joan Fredericks about semen retention.

Back to Temple Hill at 5.30. Pizza for dinner (set off unbearably loud fire-alarm with the smoke from it, and, unable to find out how to switch it off, sat eating the bloody pizza with huge kitchen-paper plugs jammed into my ears until dear Hugh called to see what was up). Listening to work tapes, reading. Then watched *The Night Porter* on TV.

Perhaps people who feel their own lives unfulfilled are inclined to lavish more time on their children's.

29 MAY

Into Dublin on the DART. Worked on 'Drum Loop Slow' in morning, using the Dimension Box. A day when everyone was at their best – though it started very Monday-morning-ish. We put up 'Isn't It White' and I got a nice organ sound. Bono heard a tune I'd played in passing and sung it into his machine. Edge then came in and took over the organ (I couldn't play the bloody thing — too many black notes) and came up with a tune himself. I checked Bono's tape – it was exactly the same tune. Then we redid guitar. Then Adam did a gorgeous bass – he's really good these days, with authority and economy in his playing. Then Bono and Edge and I sang. A song was starting to happen. Oh yes – in between I wrote a new part as a bridge. Now Larry put on new drums – great sound by Danton. As far as I can recall, nothing went wrong all day – no backtracks.

Then dinner with Ossie Kilkenny – a man who enjoys his stomach: the sculptural achievement of a decade of good food.

Back to work to add tambourine and new vocal and – BANG! – a great song ('Your Blue Room'). Energy curve rose throughout the day. In the car home B. and I fixed up the melody, singing as we courted death in his Bristol. Bono drives with the sort of abandon that suggests he really believes in an afterlife. This is the kind of driving you see in Thailand and Greece.

30 MAY

Slow day. Long swim; DART in.

We started work on 'Turning into Violins', which, from a brilliant beginning, turned out as a rather normal song. (Picasso: 'Nothing's worse than a brilliant beginning.') Overdubs: bass, timpani, three crossing vocal lines (The Supremes), at the end amazing rhythm guitar. Pitch slightly queered by a bridge I put in early on. Song ended up sounding very song-y, normal, even Beatle-ish. The way of working was what was so old-fashioned: as soon as we thought 'This is going to be a song', all the old habits about structure and positioning and energy flow came

123

back into the picture. Avoid trying to make songs: create them when you're not looking. In fact, avoid trying to make music. This one not for this record.

Marius arrived and worked well on 'New Wave Pulse'.

Took the DART home. Very dreary at night – fluorescent lights with green paint is a bad combo. Walking along the beach in the dark, the lighter stones somehow radiant.

Bono said, 'I suddenly realized I'm halfway through a good life.'

31 MAY

A slightly annoying day. My train was late and so was I – plus I felt somewhat sluggish. Then no one arrived for ages at the studio (though I had said we'd expect them after lunch), and when they did their attention was all over the place – phones, faxes, visitors, etc. Meanwhile I was working – very single-handedly – on 'Drum Loop 14'.

Edge was very late, which meant I had to have a meeting with them at just the wrong time – about 4.00. Anyway, the meeting was good and we realized we had more than enough stuff for a 'late night' record, which I'm pleased about because it means we can leave off a lot of the problem pieces (the closer to normal rock music they sound, the more people want to fix them up to normal standards).

I did crowds of voices on 'Loop 14', and then a vocal proper ('. . . out of mind, out of light') which worked well. Bono heard some playing at the end he liked, so we dumped that over (several hours' work – can't just snip on digital tape). Marius made a very groovy but somewhat 'by-the-yard' version of 'Military Jam'. Larry very friendly these days – he's a good atmosphere in the room.

Marius and I did a crossword together and I lost £20 betting him that 519 was prime (it's divisible by 3!). But almost no sustained attention today. Hard work and very long hours.

Edge gave me a ride home. He said they employ about 25 people full time.

Reading Rorty on the train this morning – it makes more and different sense each time.

1 JUNE

The usual swim repairs a rather wrecked early-morning spirit. If there's one luxury in the world I'd like it's a swimming-pool, I realize. It seems to energize me for the whole day. Perhaps a cold shower would substitute.

Into Dublin on the DART, witnessed the arrival of Prince Charles before a crowd of fat-legged housewives and scruffy urchins, them waving, mystified, at streaking allegedly royal cars. It struck me as a totally medieval scene – the royal hunt sweeps through the village. All traffic stopped, of course. A few shouts of 'GO HOME, GO HOME', with which I found myself suddenly sympathetic.

In the studio, chaos like yesterday. No one was there when Paul Barrett arrived, and, since it hadn't been my idea to invite him, I didn't know how to direct him. He stuck some trom2bone and euphonium on a couple of tracks. I was feeling not very enthusiastic and annoyed, especially when Edge and Bono came in to say 'It should be more dreamy' when P. B. had played an acre of dreamy in the hour before they arrived. But I shouldn't complain: they are generally sweethearts, and of course this is their home town – with all its distractions. But later, at dinner, I did complain anyway (over a truffle risotto – not as nice as the cep one) and said I hoped for better attention in future.

After dinner (after a stab at Marius's dense version of 'Military Jam') we went to Laurie Anderson's show, which was entirely devastating. Such attention to detail, and amazing to see one (small) person holding an audience spellbound for two hours. The video material was incredibly strong (using a three-square-screen format as I did in Hamburg and Madrid: the return of symmetry). After the show (eight ovations) we went upstairs to see her. She's always courteous and generous to all comers, even the ones that must secretly drive her mad. I can never disguise my impatience.

Grumbling. This is what I do a lot of. Is it my dissatisfied Suffolk genes coming through? Does it piss people off as much as it sometimes does me?

2 JUNE

System failing more each day. Morning writing then swim and miraculous refreshment. My body and mind in good shape. Got a wet foot picking up a lovely green palm-sized stroking-stone from the ocean.

To studio – nice mix of 'Military Jam': voice and ambience, in style of Edge's ditto. Thereafter another disturbed day working on MJ – Bono trying to develop a song: 'Heaven's (this), Heaven's (that), how wide are the gates of (something)'. Something about it doesn't grab me – too bluesy and minor; too 'known' a feeling; not complex enough emotionally. It just sounds like more music. I have no better ideas, so my only contribution is to try to derail the whole train. Anyway, it trundled on for the rest of the day.

With Marius. He sits in a little corner outside the control room, the place he's made home, with computer and sequencer and sampler. He chops up music we give him (things we're having problems with) and sequences them — rearranging them into other things. This is like giving someone a painting and saying, 'Cut this up and collage it – preferably into a masterpiece.' On the one hand I think, 'How amazing that you can make something from such fragments', but on the other I find the results emotionally lightweight. Perhaps you can't make a silk purse out of a sow's ear after all. Perhaps he just needs better information from us up front, a stronger ideological line.

The only value of ideology is to stop things becoming showbiz.

Went home with Bono and we sat upstairs listening to Nina Simone and drinking Vosne-Romanée. Then on to our record – Paul's suggested title now: *Music for Films 4.*

126

Bono suggested I go out on tour with them – a sort of surprise act with Howie B. (He said, 'It would only take about four months – then another four in Europe.' I said, 'That's a long time when you're 47.')

3 JUNE

I got up feeling about 92 and discovered Hugh wasn't home, so I had to get a cab skin-of-the-teeth and to London and Dave Stewart's. I sat playing the piano in the front room while they got ready, but all I was waiting for was Anthea and the girls, who arrived and were so pleased to see me. We went out into Dave's garden – an enchanted corner in the middle of London.

Delicious Thai lunch (courtesy of Thai housekeeper) and a chaotic afternoon with lots of interruptions. Dave asked me to do this BT thing with him. He spreads himself wide. Megan arrived, and A. and I both instantly, chemically, disliked her. She apparently dislikes everyone, in turn. I've never heard anyone talk badly of so many people in such a short time. I don't know what this film thing is about, but I don't want to be involved.

4 JUNE

'Antarctica' / 'Ito Okashi'.

We went swimming this morning. Irial got some goggles and is very good at swimming under water. She would stay in there all day if she could.

Rather reluctantly leaving the girls to go back to Dublin, and into the studio feeling not too well, to look at some music (Danton, Rob and me). It's hard working when Sunday-afternoon light is streaming in through the windows. Not very enthused; left at 8.00 to go back to Killiney. Danton drove me – beautiful sunset on the sea.

Murnau weighted his actor's shoes with lead to give him more presence. 'I talk to an actor of what he should be thinking rather than what he should be doing' – F. W. Murnau.
Zip-a-Dee-Doo-Dah.

5 JUNE

Names for books.

'Noticing what you notice.'

Piece in *Whole Earth Review* by Anne Lamott about the death of her five-month-old boy. She allowed her three-year-old son to see the body, etc. Americans are so experimental.

Another furious studio day. I felt stiff and sneezy; worked on trying to make something of the Marius pieces but I turned them to sludge. There's a condition of sound just like that colour that Plasticine always used to go – and I reached it. No one turned up till 4.00 – Adam and Larry, who explained that E. and B. had still been stagging (it was Edge's brother's stag night) at 7.00 a.m. this morning. So, understood. Mixed 'Slow Sitar' (moving single vocal line forward into part of the song which was intact, adding MSG insects* to cover distortion).

Also made ambient mixes of 'Davidoff' and 'No Wave Pulse'.

Walking home along the beach (from the station to the temple at Killiney): deep-blue sky, still able to see stones at 11.00. I looked up and saw two seals breaking the water just yards away.

Got home and sat naked with the balcony door open, smoking a cigarette, under a half moon. Smoking is fabulous sometimes. Distant fires on the beach, bright-faced people clustered round them, smoking.

* This is a recording I made several years ago in Tenkawa, Japan, of a small forest there, inhabited by a type of insect that has a chirp that makes everything sound better – wh is what led Michael Brook to christen them MSG insects, after the universal flavour-enhancer in Chinese cooking monosodium glutamate. I've used the tape often.

Violence in movies: perhaps this whole thing about kids becoming immune to violence is wrong – what they're becoming immune to are media. They know they're just watching a film (a detachment I can't make).

Maybe in the long term this is a series of experiments about our susceptibility to media and the useful limits of our empathy – certainly we don't want too little, but too much is equally crippling.

6 JUNE

Played through existing material. I suggested dropping 'Heaven' and 'Theremin'. No need to spend time on the stragglers (but, as usual, it's the stragglers that get all the time!).

So the list is this	which need
'Fleet Click'	Editing; lyric divisions
'Your Blue Room'	Lyric decisions; backing vocals
'Miss Sarajevo'	Finalize lyrics; Pavarotti?
'Tokyo Drift'	String parts?
'Tokyo Glacier'	Trombone sorting out
'Seibu (Late Entry)'	Tidy up
'Davidoff'	
'No Wave Pulse'	
'Loop 14 (Out)'	Lyric; backing vocals
'Antarctica'	Chop front
'Ito Okashi'	
'Slow Sitar'	

7 JUNE

Back to London and to Bron. Tons of e-mail, mostly unsolicited (and me increasingly uninterested – why is it so hard to pay attention to anything on a screen?). I feel no difficulty whatsoever in ignoring most of it.

Worked with my new superfast computer on Photoshop to generate Swarovski images – geometry.

Picked up Irial from school.

We all went to see Peter Gabriel in evening at his enormous new/semi-derelict house in Holland Park. What a project to embark upon! He's a born DIY-er, but on a sort of cosmic scale. Texas Cosmos Care. His interesting qualities are vision and stubbornness in about equal mixture – he's so tenacious to his ideas. I give them up as soon as there's the least resistance, and try to find another way. He's like an army, unstoppable; I'm a guerrilla, avoiding the main roads and looking for a good spot to snipe from.

We went for a coffee, and I asked him for a dress for Pagan Fun Wear. He had the idea to make something like a table worn as a dress, with gold cutlery, plates and serviettes on it – a meal served. Great idea, but very hard to get made in the time (especially since he wants to approve it first).

Spoke to Laurie, Christabel.

To Stewart:

Have you read Huizinga's *The Waning of the Middle Ages*? That's a lovely book. As also is Freidrich Herr's *The Middle Ages* (I think that's the title – a great book, and impossible to find). I think what's interesting about that period is its similarity to ours. I always feel the Renaissance was a sort of singularity in human affairs – a period when things seemed pretty much all worked out, or at least all workable out. This wasn't the feeling of the Middle Ages, straddling magic and science – rather more like we seem to be now (though our sense of magic has actually come at us through science in the form of complexity theory and evolution theory and through culture in the understanding that value is not intrinsic but something we confer – all magical processes that are self-sustaining).

8 JUNE

A comment in the paper this morning that the Danes are using fish as fuel in power stations. What strikes one as awful is that all the embodied intelligence of a living organism should be turned to such miserable account. Perhaps that's what offends about the waste of life in general – apart from the misery of, for example, ethnic cleansing, there is the squandering of a resource: human intelligence and experience.

In Munich – possibly the most dreadful city in Europe – to work on this almost incomprehensible play. André Wilms smokes at least ten cigarettes an hour and shakes like a leaf. But he really cracks me up too. At this moment no one seems to know what they're doing – no bold strokes.

Everything shades of grey. I sit there with a heap of DAT tapes slipping things in, and there's this nice French chap – Xavier Garcia – who is the live synth operator. His job consists in holding down one note – this deep rumble that André likes (and so do I).

Twenty years ago today Fripp and I played at the London Palladium – the only performance I ever did that my parents attended: in the dressing-room after, my Dad smiling and saying, 'Cor! That was loud, boy.'

9 JUNE

Rented a DX7 and made some new music in the actual theatre with Xavier. Interesting to work exactly *in situ*. The two of us jamming – he's as familiar and comfortable with his one piece of equipment as I am with mine. Good man to work with. My enthusiasm (when it's there) can keep things afloat long enough for someone else to start believing too. And then I can relax and adopt the critical 'Yes, but it could be better' role. We made an hour of stuff – probably ten usable minutes.

10 JUNE

Last day at Marstall. Rolf trying desparately not to fall asleep during my Soundtooling. Poor sod: he's doing about 20 shows for Mercedes all at once. Made him lie down and sleep. Put all music together and, to my complete surprise, the play looked pretty good on our run-through. I realize I am completely incapable of extrapolating a play from its rehearsal, or a film from its rough cut. Still completely incomprehensible to me, however. Albert Ostermaier, the author, drove me to the airport. Young, pleasant, passionately leftist in a non-ironic way that I can't imagine anyone English being now. I find myself always mentally saying 'Well yes, but . . .'

Disappointment: no sex shops. That's the best thing about German airports. One of the frustrations of life is never finding precisely the pornography you want. Extraordinary that sex fun is so hard to get. I mean, you should be able to advertise 'Man seeks position as sofa for large lady' and get lots of sensible replies, for example.

People I know who've died: Pepper, my father, Uncle Douglas, Uncle Carl, Anya Phillips, Jack Bolton, Klaus Nomi, Lawrence Brennan, Alan Grey, Jane Mackay, Derek Jarman, Peter Schmidt (funny I didn't think of him sooner). So few.

This evening 30 years ago was the great poetry festival at the Albert Hall – with Ferlinghetti, Ginsberg and (most memorably for me) Ernst Jandl, barrel-chested Austrian phonetic poet. I went with Sarah – the first time we ever went anywhere together.

11 JUNE

Swim with kids. Lunch: recycled rice with sunflower seeds fried in black bean sauce.

To studio in afternoon: Photoshopping and Well.

In evening, just eating and talking about Pagan Fun Wear. That's been our main conversation for weeks. I feel terror. This is a big gamble. How does Anthea stay so cool through things like this? Will be glad when it's over.

Reading *Prisoner's Dilemma*. Fascinating, that immediate postwar period. The power of certain individuals to change history: Francis Matthews, Bertrand Russell. The open letter – a now underused device.

So much to sort out. Paper pouring in through every hole – requests, invitations, reminders, theses, suggestions, ideas, demands. Piles everywhere.

12 JUNE

Garden Committee.

Early swim. Book idea: *Strategies for Artists*:
 (1) Inside the work, outside the work.
 (2) What you know is what you hear.
 (3) Preparation: where you choose to spend your time.
 (4) Where's the edge?

Talked to Jay Jopling about Damien Hirst's possible involvement in Pagan Fun Wear, Bill Woodrow (briefly), William Palmer, Hamish McAlpine, Jibby Beane (who can inspire the horn), Nick Serota (quite a politician), Stuart Morgan (who's now totally bald).

Did many Swarowski grids in Photoshop.

To RCA for business seminar, questioned by David Blarney (natural chat-show host) – good presentation, talking about 'inside' and 'outside' the work: about what you consider to be the edge of your artwork (and what you do there). Expanded on the theory 'Luck is being ready.'

To the Tate in the evening for 'Rites of Passage'. The show left me quite cold. Very cold. (After last year's 'Faces of the Gods' in New York, and the visit to Guggenheim, most art just looks like more art.) These big shows all now have to have a curatorial conceit – as though all the work is unified by some important 'issues'. This is a ragbag with an issue thrown over it.

13 JUNE

Meeting at Richard Rogers's office: slightly gruelling, but not too bad (though Frank Duffy was uncomfortable – seemed a bit *Yes, Minister* to me).

There are many futures and only one status quo. This is why conservatives mostly agree and radicals always argue. R. R. and S. B. – two people who are, in some way or the other, trying to make the future, but disagreeing about how it should be done.

14 JUNE

Meeting with Wobble. Placed myself in the hands of Jah – what a strong, bright face he has. For once I'll see what it's like to be the 'I'm just the channel' type of artist.

Letter from Roger (I had written asking him for tapes of some music he did for Tintin to propose them for another project):

Dear Bwine,

I don't know whether or not. I may as well stop there. Isn't it marvellous how clear it seems sometimes? Anyway, I went through the Tin-tinnery and found that all, apart from the theme (here enclosed in the first inst and notwithstanding the past participle as undersigned), were very particular to the original project (without gainsay regarding the Third Man). Therefore (henceforth and to wit) I thought it best to make available to you (not taken that any pyjama should be named in future rebates) tunes that may be of better use (understanding being three parts of the agreed settlement).

So I have sent you seven pantries that may or may not be (according to clause 5, paragraph 17) of some (and here 'some' is a digit regarding the weight of the produce or measure of porkwash) accidental necessity.

I find it easier to talk Greek with several bananas in my mouth than compile a tape of things that I have faith in. This is what comes of being a latent lawyer.*   *This isn't the real reason.

Hope you're doing aareet –

Roger

15 JUNE

Loading Fun Wear music into Sound Tools. Swarovski-ing on Photoshop.

Playing in garden in the evening – on the slide with Irial and Darla. Alarmed to find myself almost completely happy, watching little girls on a slide. Began writing 'Being an Artist' (that should fix it). [See page 384: On being an artist.]

Called Matthew Flowers re suggestions for PFW painters.

New 'swearword': 'Dungarees!' (Irial).
'I writ it down in my head' (Irial).
'Amilums' (for 'animals' – Darla).

Finished Sebastian Faulks's *Birdsong* in the studio – sitting there in floods of tears when the doorbell rang – a handsome young black man in skintight fluorescent cycling gear delivering Iggy Pop's 3-ft-long 'Basic Party Penis Sheath', which he had strapped across his handlebars. It's from moments like this that accusations of eccentricity are born, I thought, as I watched a neighbour witness this bizarre scene through her lace curtain. (Rewrite this as seen by her.)

Later Rolf and André Heller and Jasmin appeared and she nicely flashed me a few times, possibly because I was sitting there absent-mindedly playing with Iggy's enormous sheath. André is so proudly and ironically Jewish – so proud of those schmutter-ish affectations that make him so endearing. He loves playing the old Viennese Jew – shoulders tight, head retracted into body, eyes wide and beady, hands fondling each other. Asked me to be involved in his London theatre project.

Called Mum – she was croaking with fun, having lost her voice with a cold and being sort of delighted at this strange voice coming out of her.

Felt slightly useless re Pagan Fun Wear.

Called Maggie Hambling re PFW and left a long message.

Home early and took girls to market for a walk. Bought a whoopee cushion that had Darla in tears of aching laughter – rolling on the floor. Did the 'Daddy coming home from work' and 'Here's a nice seat for you' routine about 20 times – Darla falling over in uncontrollable chuckling holding her nose each time. Later I crept up to find the two of them with about sixteen enormous fluffy toys in our bed. I went in and said sternly, 'This is not funny!' But it was, and I burst out laughing.

17 JUNE

To Woodbridge on remarkably undelayed 9.30 train to visit croaking Mum. Actually a nice visit – bumped into Pat Crisp as I got off the train and we chatted – about death, basically – for ten minutes. He runs a security firm now. Then to Roger's – he's getting a job in music therapy again. Mum said in 1948 Dad earned £7 10s a week, of which £10s went on rent and the same on coal. I can remember the red-letter day when his wages went up to £20 a week – I think I was about 12.

Anthea says D. B.'s record sounds great ('brave') and sends him fax to same effect.

Reading Braudel, *Civilization and Capitalism* and *Art Forum*.

Installation: using pieces of found wood, a floor-to-ceiling column with speakers in the spaces between.

Lately getting a sense of how an art aristocracy evolves and coheres. Mutual attendances, good causes, 'We've stayed the course' and suddenly a certain group are being invited everywhere together. Interesting to plot this constellation.

I'm a member of the prat pack! *Daily Telegraph* – official.

18 JUNE

Listened to D. B. disc (after swimming and park and lunch). Strong, muddy, prolix, gritty, Garsonic, modern (self-consciously, ironically so). Every rhythm section superb (even mine). Some acceptable complexity merging into not-so-acceptable muddle; several really beautiful songs ('Motel', 'Oxford Town', 'Strangers', others). The only thing missing: space – the nerve to be very simple. But an indisputably 'outside' record. I wish it was shorter. I wish nearly all records were shorter.

Spoke to Damien Hirst. He will give some pics to PFW. He mentioned rolling in the gutter and barking with Gilbert and George, as though it was just another ordinary evening out.

19 JUNE

Patrick Hughes has also agreed to do some live pictures for us – how you value, at times like this, a simple, sweet 'Yes, of course.'

20 JUNE

In studio at 4.30 a.m. Finish Michael Stipe's trousers. Music compilation. Anthea under lots of pressure.

21 JUNE

Pagan Fun Wear. For Damien's piece:
    gloves
    drawing-pins
    newspaper (or polythene sheet)
    sheets of card
    Spraymount
    trestle
    bottles
    Tape for coat (High Twinks)
    Fell off bike! Hurt ribs
    Damien couldn't make it.

Diana was wearing a dress with a huge bustle. Great! I hope this catches on. Colin Fournier and Doris came!

Bowie called the gallery in the afternoon to wish us luck and spoke at some length – as usual very funny and enthusiastic. Asked about U2 album – would it conflict with his? I said no – we're releasing later, and it's different.

Dinner at PFW: Adam, Kevin, Regine, Paolozzi, Shar(?), Dave Stewart, Siobhan; also, briefly, Vanessa Devereux, Anthony Fawcett.

The catwalk show was fabulous, miraculous (given the complete chaos behind the stage). My coat and pants brilliantly modelled by a black musician called Austin, and two guys circling him with hand-held spots.

David's outfit ('Victim Fashion') stunning. Philip Treacy's amazing hats – a snip: should have sold for much more. Jarvis Cocker with his funny shoes – should have had him on earlier.

Lynne Franks said this was 'the most stylish charity event I've ever been to – and I've been to a few'. So many people to thank.

Anthea said, 'Never again' – but high on the success.

Late at night, an awful discovery . . .

22 JUNE

To Stewart:

Pagan Fun Wear went brilliantly – certainly one of the all-time weird events in London's recent cultural history – just the right balance between gorgeously stylish and improbably improvised. Lots of people came and they all seemed to have had a really good time. Anthea and I worked for two days and nights almost continuously without sleep in the run-up to this – so much to do and so many people to organize (35 artists and designers, 45 makers of garments and shoes, 30 models, then catering, music, permissions from 17 record companies for usages, ticket sales, table placements, lighting, publicity, interviews, etc., etc., etc.). So it was a tremendous relief at the end of the evening, at 12.30, when it was all successfully over and time to go home. I took one last walk round the various huge rooms of the pristine Saatchi Gallery (where it was held) to make sure no one had left anything behind. I was feeling fine.

I'd specially pleaded with the staff at the Saatchi Gallery to use a room they don't normally let out – a particularly beautiful space. I'd promised them faithfully that there'd be no damage and they shouldn't worry and my word was my bond, etc, etc. 'There won't be any mess at all, I promise you that.' The walls and floor of the room had been squirted with huge jets of black, red, green and yellow paint. It turned out that some youngsters who worked for one of the record companies had got drunk and run amok. My heart dropped a thousand miles – and I set about scraping the whole mess off the walls (it was poster paint, so it couldn't just be painted over – it would have mixed with the white paint).

Thankyou letters:
  Patrick Hughes
  Anton
  Cally
  Jarvis
  Paul Gambaccini
  Matthew Flowers
  Damien

At present, I can't evaluate the thing. The things I made were OK (the guys modelling them made them look fantastic!), but the bloody effort! And there is also the question of the enormous wastefulness (all that uneaten Fruitopian fruit, for example) of this event.

Garden picnic – all mothers and children plus me, at last relaxed. Lovely dappled light; soft warmth.

23 JUNE

Anthea not well (long-deferred exhaustion from organizing PFW). Downstairs with girls, full of life and laughter and singing. Took them to school and went on to studio.

Back home to play with Darla at 1.30. Inflated horse for her pool. Ate juneberries together.

Went swimming and for fish and then to pick up Irial. She said, 'I love you, Daddy. I always loved you even before I was born, when I was in Mummy's tummy. Even before Mummy knew you were going to be our daddy. That's why I went in her tummy.'

Spoke to Quine, who's in London.

Knees very stiff – as though bandaged. Also pain under arm. Steve Lyttleton found a copy of 'If I Only Had Time' for me.

24 JUNE

The time is right for my installations. The music is right, the *Zeit* is right, the drugs are right. Unfortunately the curators are wrong.

Memory is a collection of very brief moments, snapshots: painting that gate and drive in Cemetery Lane; my Belgian grandmother's big bowls of tepid coffee; school testimonials and the dread significance of their colour; early morning on a bus in Battersea, smoky top deck, with an irritable woman (Maria, I'd met her in the Speakeasy and slept with her) and her child; with my dad lying on the stones at Shingle Street after we cycled there together; delivering papers to Hasketon on an autumn evening with a low red sun through smoke from smouldering stubble.

At Wattens, in the Swarovski museum: the room I have to work in is so *small* and not at all mysterious. Went back to hotel early, cold and tired and with my knee badly swollen; fell asleep in the bath. Evening dinner with Rolf and Maria – she as always very funny. Rolf now a granddad!

Reading *The Leopard*.

25 JUNE

Ideas worth questioning: 'Being an artist is a job for life.'

Today started working with 'wedge' slides – which lock better with the perimeter shapes (and incidentally look more crystalline). Heller arrived and liked it (a lot, it seems). At dinner he raised his old-socks schnapps and said, 'It was one of the better days of my life when Rolf introduced me to you.' Huge Austrian meal with masses of chanterelles slightly ruined by too many onions.

Dreadful weather: grey, wet, cold. Mud everywhere.

Heller said Jasmin – his 'fiery Serb' – had seen me on MTV: that I was 'extremely good-looking, and full of wit'. How nice! But I wonder why? Perhaps I do look better at the moment – hair very short for the first time in my adult life, which makes my ears look nice: they stick out well.

26 JUNE

Swim, then walking. Innsbruck for art supplies, knee bandages, mirrors.

To Wattens by 11.00. Slower day at work – programming so tedious, and nothing to actually watch. Tilted one chevron in another dimension – more 3D effect. Will do with others. Lunch (with Liebstockel) and new idea for back of room (ever-smaller stars). Making slides with anything that comes to hand – paper, glue, dirt, holes – Roland (Blum) fell into a hole and hurt his leg. Now two cripples!

Depressed to think I go home for just three days after this and then away again for a week. But this thing should look good.

Perhaps make the music on site. Or at least some sonic experiments. Everyone in the hospital variously crippled – one after another, at least 20 people hobbled in. It was like candid camera till it suddenly clicked: Innsbruck = skiing.

Office and studio move to new premises today.

NEW PENCIL (very fat)

27 JUNE

Moved over to another hotel (Tyrol Europa), though I'm not sure why – sitting in the Scandic Crown this morning, watching the sun on the mountains and reading *The Leopard* after my swim in the totally deserted pool seemed just fine to me. I think Heller thought this was not up to 'my standards', and therefore had me moved.

The morning started badly – still nothing to see despite hours of programming on fucking Dataton. Then things started to pick up as I began moving the shapes in three dimensions and finding a sequence among them. Heller came in and was very impressed, which helped a lot. He talked about doing a non-religious church together. We got our outside office today (like a Portaloo with desks in it), and there was a delicious warm wind blowing from somewhere – probably Italy. I wondered what it would be like just to walk down that long, deep valley through those endless meadows.

141

28 JUNE

Mint dental floss. Moved back to Scandic Crown.

People should be trained in lying from a young age. That way you become healthily sceptical (and also train yourself to imagine what things would be like if something else was true).

29 JUNE

Worked all day in increasing Datatonic frustration. Finally, last thing at night, we slowed the programme to half-speed (which you *can* do, after all). Everything looked twice as good, of course.

Verandah meal at the Schwan, courtesy Heller. Colin Fournier and Doris arrived from Paris to Vienna via Innsbruck. Susannah Schmoegner arrived. I love saying the word 'Schmoegner' and keep rolling it over my protruding lower lip ('oe' as in a flattened form of 'bird'). She has rather beautiful slightly 'lazy' eyes.

30 JUNE

At Innsbruck airport – one of the nicest in Europe. A flat valley between impressive mountains and an outdoor café from which to watch. Gliders drifting up just below the tops of the mountains. The planes roll in just a few yards away. I sat there thinking I'd rarely been so happy in my whole life. Combination of 'legal' (i.e. non-guilt-making) time off and being near transport – realize I've always liked docks, stations, airports. There with Rolf and Sigi, waiting for Maria, who arrived in typically bizarre outfit bearing photos from Egypt.

Then home to Irial's sports day. Faintly irritating, being surrounded by all those really awful parents of other kids, offering each other novels and TV documentaries and executive directorships in between screaming at their kids to 'WIN, WIN, WIN!'

To Stewart:

You asked what we did for relaxation after the Pagan evening. Well,

I went straight off to Innsbruck to start working on my room in the Swarovski museum. This is why I haven't been online for the week. So I went from working and worrying 16 hours a day to worrying and working 14 hours a day. Actually it wasn't that worrying: the thing I've made is extremely beautiful (I think) and I really enjoyed doing it – apart from the incredibly clumsy computer program involved in running all those slide projectors. This program (Dataton Trax) is Swedish-designed and has all the worst aspects of computer culture and Swedish rationalism in one small package. Its limitations as a program would actually make a superb window through which to look at Northern European culture. The things it allows you to do (and, more importantly, the things that it leaves extremely hard to do, such as improvise) are a prime example of the non-Africanized technical mind at its most hubristic(?) and limited.

Just to give one small, and to me very important, example: I like to run these shows (as everything else) using a small number of slides but organizing it so they keep permutating in different ways (there are 12 projectors involved, so this yields the possibility of really dense overlays). But to do this you need that things should be able to move in their own cycles – that these cycles are independent. This is impossible on Trax, where everything is tied to just one clock. There is absolutely no way (so far discovered) of defeating this – the machine is not capable of doing something, therefore, that you haven't precisely specified. This makes it hopeless as a complexity generator. So my solution now is to have two or three versions running at once – more expensive and clumsy.

(By the way, did you see that snotty article about complexity and the Santa Fe Institute in *Scientific American*? I got a strong aroma of sour grapes from it – but I do slightly sympathize with him as I myself crash repeatedly into the brick walls of computer culture, and realize more and more that the hype is somewhat premature. As long as the software is nerdified, and major conceptual limitations are built right into the systems at that level, then it cannot get far. This is a philosophical question: when people program – i.e. decide on which set of possible options they should make available – they express a philosophy about what operations are important in the world. If the philosophy they express is on anything like the level of breathtaking stupidity that the games they play and the Internet conversations they have are, then we are completely sunk. We are victims of their limitations. It's as though we're using a language that has lots of words like 'cool' and 'surf' but not one for 'organism' or 'evolve' or 'synergy'. I really am heartily sick of the juvenility of it all.)

1 JULY

The Blenheim/Elgin sports day and party. Fancy dress – the three blind mice and their farmer's-wife mother, hysterically chasing with black wellingtons and a huge 'psycho' knife. It was rather brilliant and frightening. And the party was good – Hannah, Andrew and Julian came. Hannah bought me Derek Jarman's garden book – lovely and very touching. Somehow I felt the great intensity and pleasure and poignancy that must invade a slowly dying person (or, at least, one who accepts that he is slowly dying). I wonder how many people have discovered themselves through Aids (article: 'The Good Side of Aids'). The kids, very excited by the party, went to bed at 11.00 – their latest yet.

Met John Thornley from Radio 3, who offered me a programme – I suggested 'The Human Voice'.

2 JULY

Swimming with girls.

Thought the Wattens show should use symmetrical cut-outs, allowing the angle differences between the projectors to distort the symmetry.

To Stewart:

My projection things can take so many overlays because individual slides are rarely full – usually single colours, in fact, and usually only a

144

part of the slide's surface. Sometimes a slide will just contain tiny yellow dots which fall like stars over a field of intensely deep-blue scribble, which in turn is interrupted by soft white circles – but each element on a different slide, fading in and out at a different point, so that you see complicated pictures emerging and changing all the time. It doesn't sound too wonderful in description but is really grippingly hypnotic in reality. It's hard to leave the room. When we were working in Wattens I'd say, 'Can I just check that region around 15 minutes into the programme' and then find myself sitting there gazing for another 30 minutes, oblivious to what it was I'd wanted to see in the first place.

The question about features in a program is a very good one. I think you can have as many features as you like, provided you think of clever ways of organizing them into hierarchies. What that means is making sure that the features you most often need to use should be presented readily and straightforwardly. Then there should be different levels of 'hiddenness' for more obscure features. And it should be possible to say that one of those hidden features, of particular interest to you, should become 'unhidden' and thereafter be presented as a main feature.

Now this sounds idealistic, but I mention it because there is a piece of equipment – the Eventide H3000 Harmonizer series – that is designed exactly in this way. As soon as you switch it on, it works. As soon as you change the value (on a simple knob) of any of the displayed parameters (which are the ones you're most likely to want to change, it responds and tells you what new value you have set. If you like what you've thus created, you can save it – it will choose a vacant site to do this. If you want to delve further into the machine, it has a control called 'Expert'. This enables you to start playing with the basic architecture of the machine. And there is a third, very deep, level. The point about this sequence of levels is that you are seduced through them, while all the time getting good and encouraging results on the way:

And do you know why it's like this? Because it was designed by musicians (who know what kinds of things might be relevant) for musicians (who are extremely impatient with manuals). I used mine successfully for months before using the manual, and of course when I did it was a thrill to overturn some new stones in a garden in which I already felt quite comfortable. If it had been designed by nerds, I guarantee there would be the usual muddle of ill-considered and ill-matched features, described in a language that no humans speak, accessed by labyrinthine techniques that bear no relation functionally to the process of which they are supposed to be a part – making music.

You see, I've become more and more convinced that the actual physical activity of using equipment has to be commensurate with other physical activities in the same realm. Musical computers that require you to constantly use a typewriter put your whole mind into a different mode – one which doesn't necessarily preclude the making of music, but does strongly bias towards a particular type of music. Just as your handling of those stones in Avignon, feeling their weight and shape and solidity, would lead you to make a different kind of building with them than if you were dealing with virtual stonelike lumps in your computer, however wonderfully 3D they were. It's what your body (the body is the large brain) is having to do that determines much of the result – that does much of the thinking. This is entirely overlooked by most nerds, who are in fact dis-embodied humans.

You're right that other people are cottoning on to this. I see it a lot now. Unfortunately the complaints get hijacked by the Luddites, who insist that this supports their idea that computers are really no good at all – which of course I have no time for. But I think users should really start showing their support for things that work for them, and strenuously rejecting things that don't. (In fact I wrote a very congratulatory letter to Eventide some years ago, and they later informed me that their chief designer kept it framed above his desk. So people do value some feedback, it seems.) I keep showing people KidPix as the epitome of what I mean: how it produces total delight in almost everyone almost straightaway is a miracle of design.

3 JULY

To Dublin. Tired on arrival; met by Danton and Hugh.

Getting back into it. My thoughts not quite gathered. As we listen through, Bono comes up with melodic (song) ideas for every piece! The guy can't help singing – songs shooting out of every orifice! Microcassettes smoking. Then to work on 'Fleet Click', which Bono feels is flat, featureless and lacking any kind of signature/hook (which of course puts it right up my *Strasse* – like NEU! circa 1976. We always argue about this, though when the hook finally appears I'm readily caught), and so he tries several melodic approaches – including Black Sabbath's 'Paranoid' (!) – but it ends up still in no man's land.

Dinner, Bono's haircut (so shocking I almost failed to recognize him) and then 'Seibu/Slug', which starts to sound better. Lovely song appearing inexorably.

Back at 1.10 a.m.

4 JULY

The nostalgia of gooseberry jam on white bread – fruit-picking as a child.

Strange dreams and fantasies. My father returns from the grave: smiling, normal, joking and punning as always, but very short. He's wearing a black leather jacket, his hands in the pockets. During our chat I clap him on the shoulder, causing his arm to drop off inside his sleeve. He glances at it as one would a bike whose chain has come off: 'Yes, this is the problem you see.'

Long, long, long day – visit to a bookshop after ride in with Mark and Bono. ('Instinct is the compass of intellect' – Bono. 'Good results follow from the attempt to match intellect to emotion' – me. Discussion of Tom Paulin's essay on Van Morrison). Them on the way to discuss builder problems with their hotel. Jesus! – who in their right mind would actually want to own a hotel?

147

Worked on 'Seibu/Slug', which got finished despite Bono's complete deconstruction of the mix (which he was quite right about, though I was pissed off at first). Then on to 'Tokyo Drift', which really started to wear thin after 87 or so hearings. But I have faith in it – somehow it needs some other energy source: something to undermine its glib pastorality.

Edge has a very feminine sense of kindness/thoughtfulness.

5 JULY

Fax from Anthea saying I've been asked to present the Turner Prize this year. She thinks I should do it.

Those cars – all new – so small – down there – from here – so high – we drive – we fly (die) – with twilight breaking through – a different kind of blue – Those lights – blue signs – all gold – all light –

Arrived at studio with complete idea (above, written on the DART) and did it effortlessly – Vocoder on a string sound, doubled voice with whispers. I was pretty pleased with it, but the band, who arrived in several instalments, were not as impressed as me. I got antsy when they started throwing in ideas when I felt I was in the middle of something, and yelled at Adam, who didn't deserve it. Bono is useful because he quickly spots good ideas and supports them, and then makes sensible changes (like improving my hasty lyrics).

Bro-in-law Julian and Adrian, two passing gynaecologists, arrived fresh from a medical conference, and we moved on to 'Blue Room', which is really heavenly (and they really liked it, which helped). Bono and Adam so kind and hospitable to J. and A., going out of their way to make them feel comfortable and welcome – even I notice myself more courteous here.

Later Carole King joined us for dinner (and Julian, Adrian and the developer Harry Crosbie). Bono drove me home early and I went for a swim with a glass of wine at 11.00 p.m. Strange lights in the sky on the southern horizon.

A dictionary of unfamous artists. Artists I find undisappointing (Stella, Paladino, Clemente, Salle, Diebenkorn, Kounellis, Koons, Kostabi).

Book proposal: *The Bumper Book of Penis Torture*. Coffee-table.

Song: 'How Much Do I Owe Him?'

6 JULY

'Davidoff' today? / Call Dave Stewart / Set Des up with ST. / Photoshop / (follow 'Time' melody).

Those parasitic worms that cause their hosts to expose themselves to predators (so that the worm can species-jump to another host): are there ideas like that – ideas that make you stick your neck out and set yourself up for demolition?

Worked and failed on 'Davidoff ' – just ambient slurry. I put on some vocals and a bass, but in the end abandoned ship. It's emotionally empty. Then moved on to 'Tokyo Glacier' and found some simple, spacious drum feelings. Soon all hell broke loose and suddenly there was Adam playing DX7 bass, Edge playing guitar, me treating it, Bono singing, Howie B. scratching away on a record-player, and Larry on DX7. All of us in the control room, hanging from lights, under tables. Poor Danton. What a mess – but so exciting.

After occupying all 48 tracks, on to the Chocolate Club to see Gavin Friday, who gave a truly Weimar performance – both tragic and comic. What a great performance artist. *Tout le monde:* Michael Hutchence and Paula Yates (who kept looking down at her new breasts – understandably); Ali looking beautifully French with her new cut; a tall, strong girl who rather took my fancy. But I left as soon as Gavin finished, out into the warm evening air, spotted Ossie Kilkenny scurrying in Dickensian haste, and DARTed home to look through the telescope at a group of golden-faced youngsters sitting round a small fire on the beach, and at the crystalline half moon, which I so wanted the girls to see.

149

7 JULY

Possible album titles:
  Frames
  Blue Films
  Late Movie
  Cinema

Not sleeping well this week – waking more tired than when I went to bed. But the pool still helps.

2.45 a.m. What a nutty day – Pavarotti on the phone (twice); Bono trying to persuade all to play at Modena (Paul very against the whole idea, on the basis that it's all Mafia and none of the money will ever get to War Child; Larry and Adam think it a complete intrusion) but finally settling for Edge, himself and me. One of Bono's reasons for wanting to do it: 'We got so much flak from the English music press for the Sarajevo linkup (in *Zoo TV*) and they ought to know they didn't scare us off.'

Meanwhile (as we talk) me making possible album covers on Photoshop (*In Camera*, *Blue Music*) while also mixing two forms of 'Tokyo Glacier'; Howie B. buzzing away, 'It's fookin wikkud, fookin mud'; Donal Lunny et al. discussing a 'Jamaica meets Ireland' record with Adam; Shanty and Ad's bro Sebastian visiting; Dave from reception playing sax (on 'Tokyo Glacier': he's good); Miss Sarajevo; Edge squeezing in guerrilla overdubs . . .

Then on to a Japanese restaurant 'just for ten minutes' (multiplied by the Irish irrational number this comes out as 1½ hours), then all home to jump in the pool. Morleigh doing back-flips. Some interesting semi-flirting. To find someone desirable, to express it, to have it reciprocated, and to go no further. Now *that* is progress, and something my generation (or class?) never knew. Perhaps it's my non-Latin Victorian nation that never knew it. Ali's stamina is incredible – she's tipsy and lively at 3.00 a.m. and still up for more – plus she's going to Nice first thing tomorrow. In the pool: Edge, Morleigh, Ali, Guggi, Reggie and Siobhan. Bono prowling the pool-edge, DJ-ing: Placido Domingo, Paul Simon. (I always love that

150

record when I hear it, though I was so bitchy about it when it came out. Pure envy – he discovered my secret beach, and built a nice house there.) Great evening.

8 JULY

Trying to mend the pool cover with Hughie this morning and playing with Eve – a fascinating, quixotic and self-possessed child. (Edge told me that at her third birthday party when people sang 'Happy Birthday' she ran from the room saying, 'That's a horrible thing to do to somebody') Interesting seeing how she inherits from Bono and Ali (my favourite lovers, by the way).

Hughie drove me into Dalkey – a sweet little town just like Woodbridge. I bought Dawkins's *River Out of Eden* and read it on the DART. In the studio I worked on some covers. Edge then Adam then Bono then Larry appeared. I showed Howie some songs, trying to choose something for him to work on.

The life: Adam was at a wedding till 5.00 a.m., Bono up till 8.00.

We worked – not much – on 'Miss Sarajevo', which is lovely. Drove home with Bono, who dropped me at the house, and then went out. I walked on the beach collecting stones with a single white line of crystal through them – to join them up and make a long white line. For dinner I had Linda McCartney sausages and watched TV. *Rock 'n' Roll Histories* was about Deep Purple and had me in stitches, actually rolling about on the floor choking on my sausages. The way they edged people out of the band – such tactlessness. Reminded me of the sergeant-major joke.*

Then *Saturday Night Armistice* – Armando Iannucci's new show. So funny – the first comedy show where I've wanted to take notes. I love the

* *Scene 1*: Brigadier calls sergeant-major into office. 'Just received notification that Private Jones's parents have been killed in a car crash. You'll have to break it to him, Sar'nt-Major, but please be a little delicate about it this time, will you?' *Scene 2*: On the parade-ground. Sergeant-major to troops: 'All those with living parents one step forward!. . . Where d'you think you're going, Jones?'

151

idea of 'hunt the old woman' – a walk-on character who invades and parasitizes other TV shows.

As we left the studio, some young Italian fans were staring into Bono's parked car. The prettiest girl asked for a kiss, which he gave, and then said, 'Can I have one more?'

9 JULY

I can see the use and value of religion, just as I can see the use of mud-wrestling, yoga, astronomy and sadomasochism. But I reject the idea that you can't be a 'deep' human being without it or any of them. So are they all 'of equal value'? Well, some are more universal than others, which means there's more conversation about them to share, which means that they present themselves with more ready-made meanings and resonances. But 'more' isn't necessarily better – for some meanings 'switch off' others. So 'more' can mean 'overspecified' and 'rigid', which is why someone might want to base a spiritual life round motorbikes rather than Catholicism. It's open territory, with all the freedoms and improvisations that implies. The act of conferring value belongs to you.

Make a critical study of my own work to date – as if it's someone else's.

The difference between hardware and software in human abilities.

Culture crucibles: Vienna 1890–1935; Berlin 1920–35; New York 1950–80; San Francisco 1960–75; 1980–present.

To Adam's in evening – met Elvis Costello (phenomenal memory), Cait (his wife), Karen (Magnet Arts); then a long evening of talking, laughing and consuming. Bono has a great appetite for everything, but just gets funnier and funnier – boozily singing 'Drinking in the Day' in the hot tub with Suzanne (marvellously Ingres-style back and derrière) and Adam (shockingly well-toned body).

Adam has a fabulous Basquiat picture – all black and blue and very African-looking.

I often think it would be nice to make a proper presentation about evolution theory, complexity theory, etc. – to them, so that I could return the favour of good company

Remembered song: 'My Tulpa'.

10 JULY

In early (with the cleaners) to work on cover and 'Slow Sitar' ('Time') which we finished – fortunately Bono remembered a better mix, and we ended up using that with me overdubbing (doubling the piano part) to it. Then Howie arrived with mixes, which left me a bit tepid. At this stage it's more hope and faith than reality. Perhaps the sense of people's listening capacity is changed – to me these things sound empty, but I guess with the right mind they'd sound electric.

Pavarotti and crowd (including Nicoletta, a young woman with a perfect skirt) appeared with camera crew. He was actually very sweet and gentle (and gentlemanly!) and we underwent a slightly hesitant interview together – Edge, Bono, Pav, me. Bono pointed out after, 'Now they've got us on film we have to do Modena.'

After they all left, we went on to 'Loop 14 (Out)', whose song I quite quickly lost faith in, but we put on a great DX7 bass triggered from the kick-drum (pure sine wave distorting through mike channel) and it then became a whole new thing: 'Always Forever Now' (from the Damien Hirst pic), recorded with Bono doing a lead vocal, E-Notes close behind. That piece is too long by half.

Editing 'Seibu', covers – today I felt I was trying to do everything. I was a bit angry with the band for being unfocused, but the evening (AFN) was very successful.

11 JULY

An astonishingly chaotic day: in the morning working with Photoshop on some Anton Japan pics (cover idea), then back into 'Always Forever Now' until Bono wanted a 'signature' motif: so three hours of Edge valiantly overdubbing, me unable to give any useful advice. Too many cooks – I went next door. Bono meanwhile doing an interview for Irish TV, a film test for Jim Sheridan, and writing a song out in the studio with Carole King; long phone calls, Howie B. rushing in with chaotic mixes of 'Fleet Click' (he lost most of last night's work to a technical problem), Larry listening to the mixes of the Emmylou Harris record he played on (though he did put some fast congas and bongos on song), Anton arriving.

Danton and Rob working very long days – regularly 14 hours. Engineers and assistants get the hardest job – because they can't take breaks whenever they feel like it and have to be available from the first to the last.

Serbs overran Srebrenica today, I heard in the taxi home.

12 JULY

Another day of chaos – comings and goings interrupted by Anton's photoshoot (me as waiter, etc.) which was nonetheless fun. Meanwhile worrying about 'Miss Sarajevo' and Larry and Adam concerned about direction of album. I wore make-up for the shoot and thought it looked good.

Disappointed hearing 'Tokyo Drift' again – finding myself embarrassed by my voice. So English and analytical – like Radio 3.

In the evening, Bono et al. went to see Howie at The Kitchen. I went home, double knackered.

Howie's mixes: baffling – some completely uninteresting (to me), then the occasional perfect gem. I think he has a completely different concept of what a record should be – for him a snapshot, for us a painting; for him a magazine article, for us a novel. A lot seems to hang on when you will listen, and how often – is it for life or is it a one-night stand? If it's a one-night stand, then you need maximum glamour and drama. If it's a relationship, you want emotional depth. Perhaps this requires partitioning the record.

13 JULY

Drove in with Bono and Edge this morning – at 10.00. This after Bono was reportedly up til 4.00 a.m. boxing and dancing with Björk. He looked fresh as a daisy in his shiny black John Rocha suit. In the car Mark Coleman explaining about the hotel – huge sums of money involved. The builders want a lot more money. Bono expounded his theory that 'being serious' is what kills you. For sure this hotel is going to make him serious if he's not careful.

Worked on sequencing and cover, editing 'Miss Sarajevo' and so on.

At night to Björk's show, where I met Acacia's manager, who's attractive in a Nana Mouskouri way. Björk was good (her hand movements are just like her melodies – sharp, angular), but I thought the show poorly organized – a sequence which didn't get enough steam up. Audience didn't agree . . .

14 JULY

Writing this late on Saturday evening by the pool. What happened? – meetings, editing, putting together, picking up A. and kids (who've come for a visit), back to studio. Home at 3.15.

15 JULY

A. and I watching Live Aid (ten years old today) on TV tonight. I sort of finally got the point. It wrapped the world. Christo's Reichstag is quite minor by comparison – the Reichstag took 20 years to organize, Band Aid 10 weeks. The achievement, for me, is not the money that was raised but the idea that it might be possible to (temporarily) bind a large part of the globe together around one issue. I'm surprised I feel so strongly about this – and thrilled (as often) to find myself to have been wrong. Are pop musicians the only people who can address the world as though it is one place? Or was that the last gasp of unrealistic, pre-post-modern idealism? Contrast it with the indifference about Bosnia (Serbs in Srebrenica, rape, starvation, ethnic cleansing – it's all 'over there').

The failure of Band Aid is that poor Geldof ('Good old Bob,' said Anthea after the programme) was expected – by me too – to know what to do with all the money. It's so obvious that the momentum he created should have been harnessed by people who already knew that, who were good at that. Why don't people do what they're good at and get others to do the rest?

Lovely day with the family at Killiney, swimming, walking on beach.

16 JULY

Wet but nice. Walking with the girls on Killiney beach. We sat down and Darla rested her head in my lap in the sweetest way. Collecting 'interesting' stones till my pockets are bursting and I start discreetly returning them to the beach.

17 JULY

I talked to Adam on the phone today (while cleaning up the cat-shit in The Folly) about Band Aid. If you see it as a global ceremony, a get-together, a great global party, it takes on a whole new significance. It could be (or 'have been') the first of such a series, where people celebrate their commonality rather than their differences. As such it is an antidote to nationalism, to ethnic division. OK, it's also meaningless feel-good-ism, but actually that isn't so meaningless. What else but such acts of faith can make us feel cooperative? Just emergencies.

Heard a beautiful violin solo on the radio by Chial Ni Chris or some such name.

Lovely to be home again with the girls, to whom I told two long made-up stories – the friendly wolf and the man who wanted to go to the moon (and ended up on a desert island thinking he was there, singing, 'Oh, I'm the only person on the moon/ I've been here a long long time/ And all those silly people back on earth/ Don't realize that the moon's all mine'). Also a request from Laurie Fierstein – of the 'Celebration of Female Muscle' event – who'd read my *Wired* piece and wants me to be 'involved' with them. The pulse quickens! Perhaps we could début the U2 album there!

Pondering the idea of an Anti-Fascist Day for Bosnia. A strike! How would you organize that? I had this idea: to go to Trafalgar Square alone and stand there with a sign. I'd organize some media attention, and then declare on TV that I would be there every night for the next week, and invite people to join me. Would work better if I had a big name with me. David? Tom Stoppard? Who would I dare ask?

G. K. Chesterton (on seeing an array of dazzling American billboards): 'You might think you were in heaven if you were unable to read.'

18 JULY

To Stewart:

Had a great time in Dublin – such a cultural beehive right now, with elaborate waggle dances going on everywhere. Somehow the good humour and instinctive surrealism of the Irish equips them wonderfully to deal with post-modern culture. In a sense they've always been there (think of Joyce and Beckett) waiting for us to catch up.

Now I'm in the dumps about the Bosnia situation. I can't understand how the rest of us – me too – are unable to do anything at all about this, aside from being regularly humiliated by the Serbs. This is such a bad message for the future: 'Hey, if you're a small democratic country with a powerful, aggressive neighbour – bad luck. But if on the other hand you're prepared to rape and murder and pillage in pursuit of some nationalistic ideal, just go right ahead – no one's going to get in your way.'

I'm hearing the most atrocious stories from there – acts of such staggering brutality that they keep me awake at night.

And the other day there was a long long programme to celebrate the tenth anniversary of Band Aid, Bob Geldof's huge benefit concert for Ethiopia. I remember being very sniffy about that at the time, thinking that he hadn't thought it out well, that the resultant aid was just as likely to hurt as to help, etc., etc. But seeing this programme (and having now had my own modest experiences of trying to organize much smaller-scale 'charity' events) I have absolutely nothing but admiration for the guy. The programme dealt with the sheer logistics of the thing: it was conceived and put together in ten weeks and involved tens of thousands of people all working for costs or less. It was seen by an estimated 2 billion people. And hardly anything went wrong!

Was it the last gasp of sixties idealism – 'We can change the world'? The programme was both inspiring and depresssing, not least because there seems to have been an almost total failure on the part of conventional organizations – governments, international agencies – to capitalize on this wave of feeling that the concert generated. Lots of people (me too) criticized Geldof for what happened to the money after (wrangles, confusions, corruption, misspending as well as some genuinely useful projects), but watching this I thought, 'Jesus Christ! – the poor guy is just a musician. He put this whole thing together and raised the money – why should we have expected him to also be an expert on Third World economics, agriculture and politics? Someone else should have done those things.'

It left me feeling a thrill to have recognized I was wrong about all that. Funny feeling that – I have felt it a few times when my mind has been changed: the distinct sense of crossing a threshold of understanding. [See page 312: Celebrities and aid-giving.]

Music: 'Cold Jazz Piano Scape'.

A proposal that car-horns be tunable by their owners. Interesting to see what social harmony or discord would then develop. Also that there should be a car-horn that says 'Thank you' or 'You first' or 'I'm sorry'. Surely if horns were tunable – more like an extension of the voice – then a basic language could quickly develop. Even just two tones – high and low, plus volume.

Basic horn terms:
High, short, quiet: EXCUSE ME!

High short, low long, medium: YOU DONKEY (affectionate)
Repeating short high, loud: WATCH YOURSELF! (I can see a danger
that you haven't spotted)
Low short repeated, medium: HERE I COME, CLOSING IN!
Alternating high/low, very loud: MAKE WAY! LABOUR IN
PROGRESS IN BACK SEAT!
Low, long: FUCK YOU, ASSHOLE! ('An Arnold')
Low, very long, very loud: I HAVE A TINY PENIS!

19 JULY

A 5,000-year-old man was discovered in an Austrian glacier. Because he'd
been frozen, he was still in good shape, and the scientists thought that
his sperm might still be viable. Apparently 25 Austrian women have contacted the lab asking to have his child. What is this? A search for genetic
purity? [See page 411: Sperm auction.]

The reason conservatives cohere and radicals fight: everyone agrees about
fears, no one about visions.

20 JULY

Cally re covers. David Toop interview about Ambient (for his book). Gerry
and Matthew visit. To Pembridge, *Options* interview. Tried to hire multi-
standard TV.

21 JULY

Uninspired day in studio. Beautiful weather, and the last thing I want to
do is make a piece of music for the Swarovski museum.

22 JULY

We drove down to Woodbridge in lovely sunny weather. Saw Mum, Arlette
and John, Roger. Problem with keys, but house looks nice. In evening,
walked to Sun Wharf with Roger. So many stars.

Found a wasp's nest in the pit: superwasps.

New Oblique Strategy: 'Steal a solution.'

23 JULY

Wasps – drank one in the garden of a pub (quickly spat it out before damage), got stung by another (on the foot – very painful), and discovered a third sitting next to me on the train.

To Shingle Street. The shape of the beach has changed a lot in a year – deep dunes of flint. Pit picnic and photograph of Mum with four grandgirls.

Train back to London – brief dip into *Bridge over the Drina*. What makes descriptions of torture so alluring? Why can one not stop torturing oneself with such descriptions? In the end I put it away, never to reopen it.

24 JULY

To work early. Good piece started. Also cut-outs for Wattens.

The guy in Kilburn bookshop said, 'Most women I know think you're very fanciable' – apropos of what I don't know. Thanks anyway.

Drinks at neighbour's. Anthea extremely emotional about Bosnia (Pat saying that it's no business of ours and they're all as bad as each other, etc.). A. left in tears.

25 JULY

Hannah's birthday.
Cranberries visit to studio. Office/studio warming party.
'Synthetic Forest' piece.

Dolores has a rather startling clarity of intention about how she wants to record. I suggested some alternative working strategies, but she quite firmly said she knew exactly how she wanted to work (which was not like that).

26 JULY

More Synthetic Forests for Swarovski; now mixed with 'Ikebukuro'. Bit of a soup.

Paul McGuinness explodes on phone to Anthea, who had approved a press release sent by his office about the album: 'How dare you take it upon yourself to announce the release of a U2 album! THE BAND IS FURIOUS!' A. very upset (it's a collaborative album). I call Edge. He hadn't heard about it, and seemed reliably unruffled.

Jameos told me later that throughout Paul's call there was an enormous electric storm which ended when he hung up.

To new studio to work out storage/soundproofing. Idea: use the storage as the soundproofing.

A delicious risotto: basmati rice first fried in butter and onions, ½ cup white wine added and evaporated, ½ cube veg stock, 1 cup ceps (canned), saffron and grated cheese, chopped garlic, all into rice cooker. Leave to cook on 'warm' a bit longer.

Reading *Darwin's Dangerous Idea*, Daniel Dennett.

27 JULY

No entry.

28 JULY

In Wattens. Birkenstock sandals (à la Logan). Carmen the architect visited and liked the pictures of Andrew Logan's pieces. Early swim in sick-stained pool with two extraordinarily fat ladies. I imagined being in a small steam-room with the pair of them.

Slow work but good culmination. I spent most of the day carefully numbering and cataloguing slides and their positions in the carousels. The calming monotony of this activity gives me a lot of thinking space. I love routine work.

Frau Steinlechner, my taxi-driver, in buoyant mood.

Is there anyone on earth less funny than Jay Leno? The possibility should not be completely dismissed.

29 JULY

Colin Fournier called at breakfast.

Essay idea: 'The Memes That Made Me'. Also show the ancestors of *those* memes:
Life (John Conway):
von Neumann's cellular automata:
Turing
fading out beyond my comprehension.
(Transvestite version: 'The Memes That Made Me Mimi'.)

Cage's realization: that 'composing' could consist simply of creating occasions for the act of listening.

What would 'replication' in music look like?
What would evolutionary replication look like?

Imagine if you could release a record in a million randomly different forms (or just four!). Then imagine that, after first release, those are deleted. Anyone wanting the record thereafter specifies which version she wants, and is then given a random variant of *that*. But there has to be some feedback regarding which properties of the chosen version led to the choice. And there has to be a 'master' retained. This could be done with collections (anthologies) more easily. Actually, this is what *is* done with anthologies: the fit survive. Late again!

Carefully, systematically, writing down what every slide looks like ('mauve psy slab', 'big red scribble') and its position in its carousel, making a big chart so I know where each of the 13 projectors is at any moment. I love neat work.

30 JULY

Dear Frau Steinlechner asked me a favour. She told me she was going to ask me a favour, and I told her I knew what it would be, and indeed I did. Would I meet her daughter, a singer-to-be in the Whitney Houston style, when she's in London? I said, with uncharacteristically grumpy frankness, 'What for?' 'She wants someone to write songs for her.' I explained how my songs are absurd and unsingable and never mention 'I', 'You' or 'Love', and sang a verse from 'Miss Shapiro' to prove it.* That finished that idea off.

At dinner – the Fourniers, Carmen, Philip – talking about autism and its value. Strange remote restaurant run by an extremely gay Austrian and with lots of 'little touches'. Good food, but how does he find enough customers so far out in the sticks?

31 JULY

To Stewart:

Interesting synchronicity in what you're saying about wanting cops, and great ones. I've been developing this idea over the last few weeks that what we should be moving towards now is a type of consensus that does not claim to derive its legitimacy from moral or political or historical argument but entirely from the fact that it is a consensus. So I want an end to this morass of philosophy which keeps assuring us that one day there will be a final and unarguable

* DALAI LAMA LAMA PUSS PUSS

STELLA MARIS MISSA NOBIS

MISS A DINNER MISS SHAPIRO

SHAMPOOS POT POT PINKIES PAMPERED

MOVEMENT HAMPERED LIKE AT CHRISTMAS

HAHA ISN'T LIFE A CIRCUS

ROUND IN CIRCLES LIKE THE ARCHERS

ALWAYS STIFF AND ALWAYS STARCHY

YES IT'S HAPPENING AND IT'S FATTENING

AND IT'S ALL THAT WE CAN FIT INTO THE SHOW

basis upon which we will be able to organize and judge our actions –
3,000 years of that has yielded very mixed results indeed – and I want
to embrace a future where all that matters is that we have made certain
agreements between each other about what kind of place we want to live
in – and we will defend that world and defend others who have joined
us in the consensus.

For example, being a clever chap with words, I could probably mount
a philosophically convincing defence of child labour, or slavery, or
the subjugation of women. Of course I could also mount an attack on
each of them too. That I can do the former (even without conviction)
indicates to me that anyone else could too – and some with conviction.
But my point is that none of us want to keep arguing about these things
if that continuing argument allows them to persist. Let's say we want
a world without slavery, let's get rid of slavery as much as we can, and
then let's argue about it.

The discussion about Bosnia is so muddled by the failure to
distinguish between moral and legal arguments. What the Serbs are
doing is illegal, and recognized as such in international law. THAT
IS ALL WE NEED TO KNOW. We don't have to go into great
arguments about whether they should be allowed to continue because
they have historical grievances (any more than we would stand round
and watch a child being abused because we knew the parent to be a
victim of abuse). Our first priority should be to enforce law, to respect
the consensus that we have subscribed to. After that we can talk, find
out where our sympathies are.

What I am saying is that where there is law there is no need for moral
discussion. It may be that we sometimes want to revise law, and that is
the time for such discussion. All of us implicitly accept such consensus-
binding in every part of our lives, and we understand that this is how
societies stay together and are able to cooperate with each other. None
of us feel oppressed by the consensus that we can't just walk into stores
and take stuff off the shelves (not many of us anyway), and we would

all recognize why tolerating such behaviour leads to social chaos and dysfunction. So it should be internationally: if we aren't prepared to enforce our agreements and understandings, then we shouldn't be surprised when they fall apart at the merest hint of trouble. Such a waste – those relationships take such a long while to make.

My current hope is for the War Crimes Commission, which I see as the impartial expression of international disapproval of what the Serbs (and not just them) have done in Yugoslavia. I want to raise people's consciousness of the importance of that pursuit – a sign which says, 'We will find you and we will punish you.'

1 AUGUST

All day with David in London – three good interviews, unveiling the new idea: 'Forget judgements based on politics, moral arguments and history – respect agreements (even though they may be arguably arbitrary or even foundationless).' We make a good tag team: between Pete and Dud and the Firing Line.

I also had the idea to produce a set of flashcards – 100 'roles' for musicians – such as the ones we used in Montreux. [See page 395: Roles and game-playing.]

At the photo session the make-up girl (quite inadvertently) gave me a weird all-day horn. Very sweet face, nice eyes and magnificent bottom – its glorious, wobbling, kissable softness entirely undisguised by the loose long dress, her attempt not to appear ravishingly rude.

2 AUGUST

Interviews – early one first with Shavon Moldavi from Israel, who is now going to send me his tape, and then with Paul Schütze from *The Wire*, whose identity I was unaware of until he gave me a batch of CDs at the end of the thing. Bit of a smart alec – but then so am I, so we got on pretty well. Must get all these bits of interview together. Photo session also.

165

Got everyone out by 1.00 and then worked on 'Swarovski Bell Hum', a new piece for the Innsbruck show, which developed well through the day. (I left Bron for the new studio at 4.00 p.m., then went home for dinner and went back to Bron at 9.00, for three more hours. Home at 1.00 a.m.)

Overhearing Anthea on the phone: 'Hi No Yeah Yeah OK OK OK OK OK Bye.'

This bell piece for Swarovski – very simple, pretty, clear, it's tonal pattern just dissonant enough to not be soppily pastoral. Also made a four-channel version (2x2).

Try to make things that can become better in other people's minds than they were in yours.

3 AUGUST

To Stewart:

The arms embargo, lifting of, is a very hard subject for me. I don't think I agree with it pragmatically – since I think it is a way of saying to the Serbs, 'OK, it's now a fair fight so pull out all the stops', which they could do to devastating effect, wiping Bosnia off the map in months. On the other hand, the Bosnians have nothing else to live for at present, and my strong impression (from talking to Bosnians) is that they'd rather go down fighting than in this totally ignominious fashion that is slowly eroding them away at the moment.

I think your Congress, like most Western governments, has at some level assessed the situation and said, 'Well, Bosnia doesn't stand much of a chance whatever we do, so we might as well find the most painless way of losing it.' Croatia has strong support from Germany and the US, Serbia from Russia and (tacitly) France and England, but no one really minds too much what happens to Bosnia. It isn't Muslim enough for Muslims to really rally to it (and it refuses to become fundamentalist, despite the temptations of aid that have been offered predicated on its declaring itself a Muslim state), so my picture of the future is of a peace settlement being negotiated between a bigger Serbia and a bigger Croatia, with both of them expanded at the expense of Bosnia.

And it seems obvious to me that governments have been giving every help to these two groups of crypto-fascists – Croats and Serbs – about how to achieve that end. 'WHATEVER YOU DO DON'T ATTACK GORAŽDE!' then (wink wink, nudge nudge), but we won't do anything if you knock out Srebrenica and Bihać and Tuzla and Žepa. 'THE SAFETY OF OUR TROOPS IS PARAMOUNT!' (nudge nudge): take 12 of them hostage and we won't use planes on you any more. It's embarrassing seeing this going on – a sort of guide to how to win the war in a way that would be acceptable to the West.

Incidentally, has it ever struck you as odd that you are always hearing about Muslim Bosnia, but never about CATHOLIC Croatia or ORTHODOX Serbia? And did you know that, while there are bishops and priests and primates at the highest levels of both those governments, there is not a mullah to be seen anywhere in the Bosnian government?

Muslim Bosnia is a media myth: the truth is that they are the only ones NOT fighting a fundamentalist religious war.

So, lifting the arms embargo for me is part of this long-term strategy to wave bye-bye to Bosnia, and as such I disagree with it. What I want to see is the international community vigorously pursuing war crimes cases against Milošević, Karadžić, Mladić, Tudjman, etc., and sending in crack teams to arrest those people and get them out. Mad scheme – if only anyone had the balls to try it. This is a job for the Israelis (who ought to be helping out more, since Bosnia has been a traditional refuge for the Jews since Ferdinand and Isabella).

To the BBC for Paul Gambaccini's show. Mari Wilson (a strong, upright, attractive woman), my co-star, introduced herself in the lobby and gave me a tape. On the programme, I played Velvet Underground's 'Jesus' and Donna Summer's 'State of Independence', which latter had me holding back tears. Intensely moving, both in itself and, now, looking back, for its context. Idea for Paul Gambaccini programme: use music as a way of talking about social and historical movements. The rhythm track on 'State of Independence' is astonishingly clunky and poor. In fact it's one of the worst-made great records ever.

Doing treatments of the CD of *Always Forever Now.** Starting to feel that album isn't properly finished – especially the title song, which seems like a real missed opportunity for an uplifting anthemic 'State of Independence'.

* An earlier title for the album that came out as *Original Soundtracks 1: Passengers*.

In the evening A. and I sat on the balcony talking about God (her elegant theory: that God co-evolved along with humans; but me saying, 'Why do we need the idea of God at all? What does it help us do?) and the possibility of other life in the universe, about her mother, and about 'permission to be an artist'. We drank my bottle of 1954 Viña Real, which was paralysingly good and, judging by the conversation, pretty cosmic.

Bought a record-player.

4 AUGUST

More sound treating in the morning. Also essay for *Spin* about 'Games for Musicians' [see page 395: Roles and games-playing] and letter to Paul Gambaccini re programme suggestion.

Howie B. turned up at the studio with all his gear (to my surprise – I'd just imagined a chat). Fortunate that he did, because we made some nice things together. His skills with a record deck are astonishing. We played for a couple of hours. It would be fun to say, 'This is an album – all we have to do is find it.'

On to GLR for a record review programme. Lin Anderson — very funny comedienne – the other guest. We cracked up about hoovering and front bottoms. A drink after, and then home to make fish and rice for Andrew Logan, who was out on the balcony painting my eyes (four pairs).

Michael (Davis) turned up and we shot the art breeze for several hours –
until 11.30 in fact.

5 AUGUST

Darla's birthday and party. Obscene heaps of presents. Ira, Oleg, Russell,
Rolf, Hannah, Camilla. Barbecue. Me, feeling time evaporate, wishing I
was sitting alone in my studio. A. bought a tent, which I put up in the
communal garden for the children.

'Sisyrinchium striatum' drawn by Darla on her birthday.

To Stewart:

Replying to your reported media perceptions about Bosnia. I'm afraid
it does seem to be a pretty one-sided fight – by and large the Serbs have
been the aggressors, intent on 'pure blood' and greater Serbia and all
those wonderful ideas from the Third Reich, and the Muslims their
victims. The Muslims (though, as I keep saying, they're a completely
mixed-up bunch who we conveniently label Muslim) really just wanted
to be left alone and be multi-ethnic. They, as opposed to the Serbs, revel
in their multiculturalism.

As for the Croats – well, they're not the sweetest angels. Unfortunately
the best organized among them when the war started were an ultra-
right-wing military group called HOS, which, armed by neo-Nazi
groups in America, Britain and Germany, really were the main line of
defence against the Serbs. This strengthened their position within the
Croat hierarchy and they have now become a major political force there.
They are about as fundamentalist as the Serbs – unashamed Nazis who
dream of a racially pure Croatia.

The role of religion in all this is sickening: goading these fascists on
with fairy tales about destiny. All that said, the civilian population of
Croatia seems to be less brainwashed than that of Serbia, and Tudjman
is walking a line between HOS and a lot of people who want to see
a democratic Croatia. Perhaps there are a lot of Serbs who want a

democratic Serbia, but control of the media is so strong there you'd have no way of knowing.

Yes, Europe has failed. If we can't even try to honour and enforce our international agreements we may as well not make them in the first place. The only thing that can hold Europe together is an honour system backed by your 'good cops' and my 'good courts'. But there were so many secret agendas in all this: a lot of the British left – the people you'd expect to sympathize with Bosnia – actually back the Serbs, because Serbia is a traditional ally of Russia, because Serbia was anti-fascist (i.e. anti-Croat) in WW2, and because certain parts of the left think that any friend of America (which Bosnia has been) must be an enemy of the left – so, ridiculously, that translates into support for Serbia. As a result of all this, Blair has said nothing whatsoever that would reveal even the beginning of a policy line on this. He's so anxious to get elected he can't actually say anything about anything – and doesn't. Very disappointed with him lately – not just about this, but about his lack of fibre. Is this what it takes to get elected these days?

6 AUGUST

Afternoon to Trafalgar Square demo supporting Bosnia. Not huge attendance. Michael Foot spoke clearly and well, as did David Wilson. Too many speakers, too complicated. And because the Croats have now started kicking Serbs out of Krajina they get hailed as heroes and comrades in arms. Lin Jones – brilliant speaker, thrust forward chin, assertive, bustling – tries to get me dancing to Djembe drummers before 500 people. Rather enjoyed her persuasions. Bill and Michelle gave me a lift home.

To Stewart:

The Croat attack is welcome only because it temporarily prevents the Serbs mopping up more of Bosnia. I don't trust the Croats an inch. In fact there has just been an extraordinary revelation in the English papers. Apparently Tudjman was at a dinner in London and (foolishly) drew on the back of the menu his idea of what Bosnia would look like in ten years' time. He drew a big line through the middle of what we now call Bosnia. On one side of the line was Croatia (including Sarajevo, by the way) and on the other Serbia. No Bosnia at all. This diagram was revealed by Paddy Ashdown, leader of the Lib-Dems here, and possibly one of the few politicans who commands respect for his convictions (perhaps possible because he doesn't have a chance of getting elected – yet). But the diagram exactly confirms my own fears about the long-term strategy, which, as I supposed before, is being colluded with by the major powers.

The other effect of the Croat attack is to have concentrated Serb forces in Bosnia. In the long term these become a huge army of occupation. The hopeful sign is this split between Karadžić (who is truly mad) and Mladić (who is about 85% mad), though I suspect this too is part of a long-term strategy by Milošević to say, 'Of course, it was that crazy Karadžić all along – we real Serbs (not those mad Bosnian Serbs) are respectable lovers of human rights, true democrats and generally wonderful human beings.' Such an interpretation would suit the world community perfectly – appeasement ahoy!

Silajdžić – who I know – of course wants to lift the arms embargo. So would I, perhaps, in his position. Like everyone there, he feels totally humiliated by being forbidden to defend his country in the face of one of the world's largest armies. I think Silajdžić will resign soon, tired of living in a cellar. He approached me (via David Phillips) to see if I could get anyone interested in a script he has written based on his diaries of the last few years in Sarajevo. What a project! Any ideas for backers for this (which I guess would be a docu-drama) very welcome.

Last thing: of course the people who are suffering most in the Croat attack are Serb peasants – just as blameless as the Croat peasants and the Bosnian peasants who've suffered before them. I take no joy in their discomfort.

7 AUGUST

Working all morning on self-fading High Twinks (using three auto-panners cascaded). Slow, pleasant, focused work. Thoroughly enjoyable.

Bought *An Improbable Marriage* and portable CD-player for A. to take on holiday. Made her a tiny hi-fi, all connections clearly labelled.
So often I get a song in my head, tantalized by its beauty, can't place it, and then recall that it's from *Laid*.

8 AUGUST

Edge's birthday.

A., Pippa (her niece) and kids to France. Now some time alone here.

To Metropolis for editing etc. Chap from GLVC brings in a valve equalizer for me to try out. Brian May and Dave Richards come in from next door to hear it – sounds very good, but is expensive. Edge calls at 5.00 (just as I'm about to start compiling) with new edit ideas.

Tried an ambitious version of 'Fleet Click' – a sandwich form of me, Howie, me – which is sure to raise eyebrows.

Home starving at 9.15 for interview on phone with Mark Rowland from US. Burnt mouth badly trying to eat and do interview at the same time.

9 AUGUST

New Oblique Strategies:
    'Describe the landscape in which this belongs.'
    'What else is this like?'
    'List the qualities it has. List those you'd like.'
    'Instead of changing the thing, change the world around it.'
    'What would make this really successful?'
    'Who would make this really successful?'
    'How would you explain this to your parents?'
    'Try faking it' (from Stewart).

List everything you are. I am:
a mammal
a father
a European
a heterosexual
an artist
a son
an inventor
an Anglo-Saxon
an uncle
a celebrity
a masturbator
a cook
a gardener
an improviser
a husband
a musician
a company director
an employer
a teacher
a wine-lover
a cyclist
a non-driver
a pragmatist
a producer
a writer
a computer user
a Caucasian
an interviewee
a grumbler
a 'drifting clarifier' (Stewart's phrase)
Now award points for how good you are at each . . .

Russell (Mills) opening. His best pictures yet. Bought one. Paul McGuinness called to ask if Cally would not go along to France for the band meeting. Chris Blackwell and P. McG. nervous about the record 'confusing U2 fans'. I get a slight feeling they'd be happy if it just faded away gracefully.

Burton's using 'Spinning Away' for an ad: £30,000.

To dinner with Jenny (Todd) at L'Altro. She thinks I should do Turner Prize speech – as does A.

Discovered old/new U2 piece on U2 Sound Tools tape from 1991. An edit I did of 'Zoo Station'.

10 AUGUST

Full moon.

The exact basis on which the Turner Prize is awarded is one of those enduring mysteries – like the selection of a new pope. There is a pretence about democracy in the original nominations, but nobody takes this seriously. It is understandable, but, in my view, unnecessary. We shouldn't need to pretend that the selection of a winner for this prize reflects popular taste, but somehow we need this alibi. I wonder why? Anthea thinks it's because there are so few prizes (compared to the music biz) so there's a pressure to generalize the selection base of this one. I mean, if the English awarded 20 or 200 prizes a year instead of just half a dozen we might feel happier about accepting that the selected winners were the result of bias, quixotic, variable in quality and, in the end, arbitrary. If there were enough prizes to go round . . .

Working with Cally at Bron. He talked me out of the *Always Forever Now* bull's-eye cover and explained that Island were nervous about the record confusing U2's public profile. I resisted to the last, for a whole ten minutes, and said I thought everyone was being bloody cowards: 'Isn't this the sort of liberty that that kind of success is meant to earn you?' But I see the point: one doesn't want to sell things 'under false pretences' – especially

174

to an audience that might not be in a position to just write off an unwelcome record to 'experience'. Instead we came up with the 'Passengers' idea (actually based on one of Anton's airport lounge photos) and also with the idea of inventing films to which these were the soundtracks. Went out to Kilburn bookshop to buy *Halliwell's Film Guide* to get the style right. But when I phoned Anthea about it (no individual artist names on cover, but group name 'Passengers') she was slightly apprehensive. 'Don't hide your light under a bushel . . .'

Customs confiscated a video I ordered from America (*Muscle Up* – female body-builders) on grounds of 'indecency'.

To Stewart:

But don't you think that the only point of an international community (if we're going to pretend that such exists) is to establish norms of behaviour and then properly police them? Otherwise we are all of us at the mercy of anyone who can collect enough weapons and soldiers. What happened to all the thrill of smart weapons, of pinpoint bombing, of satellite surveillance? Where is it when we need it? How come we can attack Gaddafi (and kill one of his kids) but not even disturb the blow wave on Karadžić's head? No, for me the answer is clear – the West tacitly accepted that the situation there was chronically unstable, that the stronger powers had to finally win, and that the best thing, therefore, was to ease Bosnia into oblivion, preferably with as little bloodshed as possible. They failed on the last part, that's all.

Having said this, I don't mean that there was a big conspiracy – just good old Realpolitik of the Kissinger variety. What was the alternative? Up to which point could this have been averted? An academic question now, but worth thinking about for the future.

11 AUGUST

Mission Impossible music request / Call: office (re address in Bordeaux), Stewart, Roger, Andrew B., Mum.

175

Haris Silajdžić's voice on 'Plot 180'?

Future evolution from *Passengers* – a series of curated records posing as film music. The stills from the films. Fragments of the films. Films made to fit their prior descriptions (e.g. *White Nigger* by Jeff Koons).

Flew down to Nice.

Expounded 'Passengers' concept to the band – which went down well, Bono getting straight behind it. We all think that a U2/Eno record couldn't be discreetly released – would be hyped by stores as 'the next U2 record'. Also listened to the CD – which sounded really good – and looked at the female body-builder tape while listening to 'Always Forever Now' – great combination: erotic and futuristic (futurotic). Also the new 'Wanderer' (an old edit I'd found among my tapes) was an immediate success – Bono wanted it as a song on their next record. Also played another found piece from those sessions – 'Zoo Station' edit with a very loud farting noise from my synth. We'll call that one 'Bottoms' (from the Italian TV show *Show Us Your Bottom*).

'Passengers' reverted to being group name as a tag for a shifting corporate membership. I suggested this could include completely other artists (curatorship).

In the evening we ate at La Polpetta in Monte Carlo and then on to a casino. I've never been in one before. Bono and I, playing as a team, won about 3,000 francs. My style careful and consistent (many small wins in a row), Bono's wild and inspired (two big wins). Afterwards, Bono split the win with me (it was his money we were playing with). Then on to Jimmy's disco – possibly one of the most hateful places I've ever been. All those rich young people – so chic, and thin as two planks. A vodka? £34. A Heineken? £24. I wanted to throw a grenade in there. Just one, please.

Home (with Jim Sheridan and Anne-Louise and Naomi) at 4.15.

Such a short night. I woke up to a very complex sexual fantasy and then went to breakfast, baffled by detail.

Drawing and talking with Eve, who I find completely charming. To lunch in the hills round Nice at the Colombe d'Or – a perfectly placed restaurant where we ate truffles. James Lingwood and Jane Hamlyn were there. The whole place was filled with paintings – Utrillo, Picasso, Braque, Manzoni, Léger, Miró, Calder, Tinguely, Rouault, and Tal-Coat (I love Tal-Coat). We talked about the relevance of 'door-openers' – Dylan, The Velvet Underground – and Bono explained what he saw as U2's project: like Nicaragua, to unite flesh and spirit, sex and faith. Isn't this tantra?

After, we went (this was just Bono, Scorch, Lian, me) to the enclosed courtyard/pool and Lian and I swam naked (well, her with tiny white panties) under the rather bewildered gaze of several guests. Water like green velvet – like rainwater.

Driving to the airport, Bono, while gliding gracefully out of yet another 150 m.p.h. near-death situation, said (with leprechaun raised eyebrows, sparkling eyes and exaggerated Irishness), 'Sure now, it's lucky I'm on a mission from God.' We nearly died laughing – very nearly.

Also to the Maeght Museum (Freud, Bacon, Lettuce and Tomato). They all leave me a little *froid*. I sort of admire them for their obvious agony of effort, but it doesn't move me much.

It makes me think of Russian academic painting, the kind of stuff produced by the Artists' Union members, or 'Left Bank'-ery. The glorious struggle of the artist . . .

Plane and then taxi to Cap Ferret to meet up with A. and the kids. Nice house, lovely sitting outside looking out on to the quiet beach (but too much smoking). Anthea suggests credits as: 'These Passengers are . . ', then list of names.

13 AUGUST

Irial (who'd climbed in bed with me during the night) woke and, kissing me fondly, told me how much she loved me. Hard not to get up after 15 minutes of that.

Walking on the beach, counting huge washed-up jellyfish. Very hot sun later. Lovely lunch – cheese and such sweet tiny tomatoes and perfect bread. And how I prefer butter.

Listened to Eno/Wobble. Right now I like the last (unmentioned) track best. Now I wonder if I wasted it putting it there, where no one will find it (Peter Schmidt: 'Put it where it will be found').

Bono's new idea for lyric-writing: ask others to suggest new things that songs could be about, and then write to assignment. 'I tried to paint a picture – but I couldn't get it right, the colours were too bright . . .' and other reasons. 'The president's wife' (about Mrs Milošević), 'When they make me president', Borrow some gospel titles: 'I want to live the life I sing about', 'How I got over', 'Will the circle be unbroken', 'I can see everybody's mother, but I can't see mine.'

14 AUGUST

I wish I had a whole album of that strange new kind of music (last track on *Spinner*) – my 'Unwelcome Jazz'. Contacted Haris Silajdžić re lyrics for song, also Paul Gorman for conspiracy help.

Scattered thoughts. Anger with children for always interrupting.

Anger with Anthea for being bossy. Anger with myself for being a cunt. Rented three bikes and rode round the garden. Ate paella in the evening.

15 AUGUST

Send Swarovski details to Rolf.

Up early to catch the sunrise. Echoes (now dim) of feelings of self-improvement, meditations, the few silences in my life. Far, far down the beach one other man probably hearing the same echoes.

Cycled (all of us – baby seats on bikes) to Le Mirador, which was lovely and nostalgic – I think it reminded me of a ride through Tangham Forest or Broome Heath, that sandy, coniferous, isobornyl-acetate feeling. The gentle silence of a bicycle on a warm country day.

On the beach watching topless French ladies with huge wobbling sousaphones of bumfat, wishing I could hear them fart. Saw a hermit crab. Caught a wasp and made it tipsy.

Oblique Strategy: 'Define the problem in words. Now think of a context in which the problem would be an asset.'

16 AUGUST

'Culture is everything we don't have to do.' This is the first sentence of a book which will wander through cultural space – that is, the space that includes my appreciation of wobbling sousaphone buttocks on scant French ladies but does not include those buttocks themselves (unless they have been artificially inflated or wobbled according to a stylistic agenda). [See page 332: Culture.]

John Rawls's idea of a designed society: one where all its would-be members agree on the design without knowing what their place in it will finally be (from Dennett). Like the Hutterite system: where the community builds a clone of itself and divides, but no one knows who's going to which half until the day of moving.

In the evening to L'Escale restaurant for a huge assiette of snails and cockles and crabs and shrimps. Fiddly but interesting – like eating a miniature zoo. Home, with Irial on the bike for a late-night (stormy sky) swim – which she chickened out of! Then lying with her on the beach looking at the sky. So gentle and pleasant, thinking of her future memories. Then sitting out with Anthea under the stars.

17 AUGUST

Stewart's suggested essay title: 'Things I Got Wrong'. Geldof and Live Aid; Nam June Paik; The Walkman; David Salle; the value of law; Graceland; Cuba?

The space we call culture includes all the things we do that we don't have to do, and their cultural 'meaning' resides in the stylistic aspects of them. Style is the name for the way in which something is done – a way chosen not for 'functional' reasons (as easier, more efficient or some such) but for a type of aesthetic satisfaction (nicer, cooler, more acceptable, less acceptable).

Cycled to the Atlantic beach today. Such a glorious, clean place. Total nudity mixed with topless mixed with full costumes. Curious. Laying out later under the stars again with Irial, she said, 'Is the universe the biggest thing?' I asked her how many stars she thought there were. '102 billion thousand.' At night, smoking furiously, trying to calculate with a hopeless calculator relative distances earth–moon–sun–nearest star.

18 AUGUST

Made a model of the solar system in the sand for the girls. The earth was a tiny little glass bead, the sun a big drain cover about 75 metres up the beach, the nearest other star somewhere way beyond Arcachon.

All out to the lovely big Atlantic beach, where we stayed all afternoon. Seeing the variety of humankind (undisguised by their clothes) gives you a warm, sympathetic feeling for people. One of the tremendous shocks of going to a nudist colony must be meeting people nude and then seeing them put on clothes and become what they choose to project themselves as – 'I had no idea that's who you thought you were.' It's like when you meet someone you've only ever seen in uniform.

Another reason for arbitrary charity work: gaining some understanding of what a real-life crisis is like (any one will do!) and what is involved in trying to deal with it. Understanding the complexity and intransigence of real life. All charity work should be followed by careful appraisals of results – in many different terms – at least to differentiate between the probably quite helpful and the probably catastrophic courses of action. Also assessments in different time-terms: Dennett points out that Three Mile Island, a disaster when it happened, was a great success (in the longer term) for the anti-nuclear movement.

Opposite example: boreholes in the Sahel.

19 AUGUST

Up to get *Herald Tribune* and croissants. Lovely mild, sparkling morning, sitting outside eating croissants and honey with Irial and Darla – delightful.

Wines classified according to their effects: Beaunes and burgundies such as Aloxe-Corton make you laugh uncontrollably. This is good quality laughter.

Bordeaux is responsible for the decline in French literary and philo-sophical thinking, because it makes you talk a lot and – worse – makes you think that what you're saying is important. It has the same inversion effect as marijuana – the more tangled the web you find yourself weaving, the more deep you think it is. Like most drugs, it's fatal for any serious work.

Barolo also makes you talk intensely, especially about art, but fortu-nately you have absolutely no recollection of any of the conversation (other than that you know it was brilliant).

Otoñal is good for making pornographic drawings.

Friuli wines can lead to very hot feet.

20 AUGUST

New Oblique Strategy: 'What were the "branch points" in the evolution of this entity?'
New Oblique Strategy: 'Back up a few steps. What else could you have done?'

A night of long rambling dreams. Escaping from the Nazis, I get U2 together to beg their help. Yes! they agree. Intense relief, but immediately a phone call comes through for Bono – he gestures that he'll be off the phone soon, but they're after me so I have to get on with it. I can hear them coming. Meanwhile Larry has to leave to talk to Anne-Louise. I have to run (grenades; things smashing through walls) and I hide. I get back, but Edge has now gone. Just Adam, seemingly distracted, thinking about something else. Agonizing feeling of trying to get everyone together.

Cross-fade into another dream: in a pub with a bunch of politicians and Patrick Hughes, in his pink check suit, who is discussing the price of visas and who invites us all back to his house – a precarious sub-sub-sub-basement harbour-type place with water lapping up the furniture legs and boats darkly clunking nearby. We've come to see the film that Francesco Clemente has made about me. The film is all done in pastels, and I'm not in it. Patrick's house is full of weird thirties mechanical fairground gadgets, such as a rather sinister ventriloquist's dummy which sprays perfume at you as you pass, and another that offers you a cigarette.

Lovely misty morning; distant gulls. It feels like a Sunday.

Lovely rides on the bike with the girls through that delightful little fishing village. Darla needs more practice speaking – she's hesistant, always searching for words. Tries to speak too fast, to keep up with Irial's endless babbling brook. Told 'Pome and Peel' (from the Calvino book) again.

What makes complexity theory interesting is the idea that 'intelligence' arises out of the concatenation of simplicities: that therefore it doesn't have to come from somewhere else. This has fascinated me for a long time – the idea that there are equilibrating rule-sets which give rise to 'intelligent' – i.e. self-organizing, self-making – entities. This is the thread that connects 'Life', 'Stained Glass', 'The Great Learning', 'Aka-Muru-Ko',* 'It's Gonna Rain', 'Self-generating Porno Stories', *Music for Airports, Discreet Music,* the *Tiger Mountain* cover, music-generating machines, cybernetics, campanological lyrics, 'seed-planting', earnings from

* An invented sequence-generating system that yields long self-similar strings of elements. These often have a 'melodic' logic.

182

royalties. What are the threads? Evolution through iteration; rules cascaded, simple rules yielding unpredictably complex outcomes; things set in
place and left to generate for long periods, and the necessary conditions
for that to work. [See page 339: *The Great Learning.*]

21 AUGUST

Back to London after a sweet, soft, misty morning and a walk in the shal-
low bay with Irial, watching lots of crabs. Left A. and girls there on holiday.
Taxi to Bordeaux, my energy feels good. To Gatwick, to office – Drew
has built so many fantastic things. He's really good. On Well for a long
time, catching up with discussions about Bosnia and Clock Library – had
idea to make it as a theme park. This is very appealing, because it ties
everything together (and everyone).

In the evening to Emma's for dinner – also there John Brown and Claudia. John is v. funny – the king of the one-worder. When I mention the
new Bowie album he screws up his eyebrow and looks penetratingly at
me: 'Belter?' And when I say 'I think so' he asks, 'Singles?' Steve quoted
from the Deepak Chopra book: 'You don't grow old; you stop growing and
become old.' I wish I had sufficient faith in the mutability of my organism
to believe this idea.

Glad to be home.

Flying in over England, everything dull brown except the rivers and estu-
aries – virulent green with algae.

22 AUGUST

It's interesting that, while we witness the final evaporation of any kind
of vision in politics, the vacuum is filled by people outside government –
people who don't rely on their popularity with journalists, or tomorrow's
opinion poll.

In the studio to master the Pavarotti stuff. While waiting for the others to
arrive I pulled out an overlooked jam from the same tape reel and made

something good out of it – which I'll send on to Michael Mann for possible *Heat* use. Michael Woolcock (Pav's producer from Decca) and later Edge, Bono and Gavin (plus Nick Angel). We (in the end) did some useful work. Bono remembering good bits of Pav's singing (very accurate and precise memory) which Woolcock had forgotten about. But I still have problems with this voice. For me at the moment it makes the song interesting but not better. Pav's voice is weak after Bono's – so thin. It needs its context – support. I tried a few pathetic synth things, but then suggested that strings might do it. Contact Craig Armstrong re. arranging.

Bono doing a new vocal, fine-tuning.

Finian came with Dolce & Gabbana clothes for us to try – they're offering them as a contribution for the concert. Great suits.

Me running up out of toilet with 'Mecca' line.

Bono: 'Don't let people who like your music mix your records.'

23 AUGUST

New New Oblique Strategy: 'When is it for? Who is it for?' Meeting about future interviews with James and Michelle, where I too explosively explained that I get too much press already, that the balance between output and promotion is all wrong. Of course I could say to myself that talking ideas is actually what I *do*, my job, and that the records are the promotion for it.

Spoke to Craig about strings on Pav piece.

24 AUGUST

A slightly wasted day, but the studio feels nice. Writing a complex semi-pornographic story, mathematically based. Was going to Woodbridge, but Titi said there was a train strike (there wasn't – it was a tube strike). At lunchtime her granddaughter Jaydee, a sweet little child, came and ate some of my balcony tomatoes. She calls Titi 'Mummy'. Ridiculous video scene – put in *Big Bodacious Babes* and couldn't watch it (wrong connectors) or eject it. Ended up taking machine to bits.

Listened to my version of 'Ring of Fire'. Such a clear, good vocal. That song could be nice with good musicians (keep the vocal).

Realized (listening to some unused pieces from *Wrong Way Up*) that I currently lack a sympathetic listener – someone like Quine (without whom there would not have been *On Land*).

Strangely nostalgic too sorting out all those videos of rooftops and clouds and the portraits of friends from New York. Fifteen years ago.

Evening: *Die Hard with a Vengeance* at the Electric – I really enjoyed it.

25 AUGUST

How miserable I sometimes feel as day after day passes and I don't grow anywhere. Static. Too much static. Much too static. Half-awake. No one to spend time with. No one listening. (Clue: make something people want to listen to!)

Ruined by the diversion of faint success.

Self-generating poems:

STATIC STATIC STATIC STATIC
TOO MUCH MUCH TOO MUCH MUCH TOO MUCH

'Static' is at both ends of the movement continuum – things that are very fast and things that are very slow are both seen as static. Similarly with sound.

In Woodbridge, lunch with Mum and then to see Rog and Bee. Little Cissy's so captivating, and Lotty has the sweetest, most trusting, smile.

On the train, brought to tears by the final act of Tom Stoppard's *Arcadia*.

A version of 'Life' which records the generation number and the population at any given generation. Also would be great to be able to make a graph of the population.

What you have to remember is that even the luckiest people in Bosnia – the ones who haven't been maimed or raped or killed or displaced – have effectively been living in prison for the last three years. Just think about your last three years – now erase it. What's it like just to lose a big chunk of your life like that?

26 AUGUST

Why do I always find athletic events so emotional? Seeing Moses Kiptanui (whose *name* I love) winning by 100 metres – and eight Kenyans behind him. Underlining and CAPITALS – sure signs of approaching madness. So exciting that all these African athletes are coming on form – Mozambicans, Burundians, Kenyans, Moroccans.

Pissed into an empty wine bottle so I could continue watching *Monty Python,* and suddenly thought, 'I've never tasted my own piss', so I drank a little. It looked just like Orvieto Classico and tasted of nearly nothing.

Recording strings for 'Miss Sarajevo' at Olympic. Finished with six seconds to spare, me in advanced Hitler mode whipping things along (it would have cost an extra £2,000 if we'd gone into overtime). Loved watching Craig working with the (20) players.

27 AUGUST

New Oblique Strategy: 'What do you do? Now, do what you do best?'

To studio in morning, editing 'Sarajevo'. What a spectacular song! Edge and Bono came over to studio – aghast at lovely space – then we went back (Bono and Edge carrying the shopping; me on my bike) to house for lunch (their breakfast). Nellee Hooper's assistant Jane came round – 'English in all the best ways', as Bono said. He's a brilliant and inspired flirt, and makes her respond well – a talent he has with people. After, in the carnival, the four of us in fluorescent feather boas, Edge said I looked like a very kind flower. Nice compliment. Bono's funny way with fans: someone approaches and asks for an autograph, so he – green boa, orange hair, shades, ginger check suit – puts his finger to his lips: 'Sh – I'm keeping a low profile.'

During the carnival a guy started taking photos of us – very obtrusively, as if to deliberately make a point of drawing attention. Bono was nice to him

186

at first – posed for him to get a couple of pictures – but the guy wouldn't leave us alone, and was always somewhere off in the middle distance with a long lens, standing up on walls or hanging off lampposts. Finally I went and asked him if he could now stop. He said, 'But it's my job', and didn't. Bono went over, held the guy's head and stuck his thumbs in his ears – a sort of natural-bouncer move, and said something to the effect of 'How would you like that long lens stuck up your arse?'

The carnival was riotous and loud. Great to be able to show something in London that has real life and character, something you don't have to apologize for. A great feast of wild good-feeling.

'Ah, sweet mystery of life. What a gift – huh? Ain't you lucky you got in?' – Rubin Levine, violinist in *Conversations in Taxis*. I love that 'you got in' – as though it were a crowded theatre, a hot show that everyone wanted to see.

28 AUGUST

Three interviews, all done with reluctance (the bloody carnival's on!). Steve whatsit who asked about Negativland. I got mad. Such boring subjects. Yawns all round.

Carnival again. The bottom is the large brain. I am become truly invisible. People hold intimate conversations and transact drug deals mere inches from me. I am no longer here. To what use can I put this?

At the studio, some lackadaisical music, but always the question 'What for?'

Nice cycling through the crowds, drifting along at very slow speed.

A population growth formula: $x_{next} = r \times (1-x)$

If there was a proliferation of prizes with all sorts of different more or less arbitrary premisses – 'Best painting of a whale', 'Best painting in shades of grey' (the Major Prize), etc. – then the pressure would be off the Turner Prize. But there isn't, so it is expected to stand for all those absent prizes and possible reasons for giving prizes. It's like having only one event at the

Olympics – 6,500 athletes, boxers, sprinters line up to do the high jump. It can't possibly satisfy most people.

'Best picture with God in it.' 'Best lesbian painting.' 'Best picture of a footballer.' 'Best picture done in the dark.'

29 AUGUST

Finish Silajdžić proposal / Write Aida/ Call Anne-Louise re Sarajevo / Call Renata for tomorrow / Get Oblique Strats from Bron (or rewrite) / Call Phil? re interview / Drew: swing; set up video; check phones / Get essay from Lin (chase recent interview) / Alexander Centre / Call Bill and David / Egypt letter / Iteration programmes.

And I did all those things (well, nearly)! Went to Bron and noticed case missing. Panic and suspicion, which abated when Drew found it in the heating cupboard.

Lots of little editing jobs – 'Miss Sarajevo' in its multiple forms. Bloody couriers everywhere – about 70 quid a time – several a day. U2's office obviously used to much bigger revenues than our operation.

Watching tape of *The Day Today* – what I'm interested in is the state of the art, whatever the art is.

Big piece in *Time Out*. I'm in favour. It won't last beyond Christmas.

The major change in thinking, the change from which all others proceed, is from Time's Arrow to the field of events.

30 AUGUST

More bloody editing after a bad night. (Got up to drink some milk at 4.00 – bad idea. Am I slightly allergic to milk?)

Oblique Strategizing – I have far too many (about 145).

To long *Help* photo session with various young popsters – Tim from the Charlatans, Terry Hall, Marijne from Salad, a Chemical Brother.

Spoke to David Phillips.

Reading Levy's *Artificial Life* again.

Talking politics to the guy from *Melody Maker*. I was very clear, I thought.

Ate alone at L'Altro, reading furiously. The waitress there has fabulous eyes – very unlikely. She's Chinese-Irish! (Chinish)

UN military action in Bosnia – at last. But what does it mean?

Kanita Focak – beautiful Sarajevan widow.

'For war you need one. For peace you need two' – Haris Silajdžić.

The most aggressive piece of TV questioning ever on *Newsnight* (Danielle Sremac, Bosnian Serb spokeswoman *v. Newsnight* lady). Sremac maintained that the Serb positions round Sarajevo were defensive, that they'd been 'forced into' everything. The *Newsnight* lady cut her to ribbons.

31 AUGUST

A. and girls back from France (she having booked me into a hotel for a visit later).

To Stewart:

A by-the-by: I've noticed that all these complex systems generators (such as 'Life' and 'Boids' (the flocking one) and 'The Great Learning') have something in common – just three rules for each. And these three rules seem to share a certain similarity of relationship: one rule generates, another reduces, another maintains. I suppose it's obvious, really, but perhaps it's not trivial to wonder if those three conditions are all you need to specify in order to create a complex system generator (and then to wonder how those are actually being expressed in complex systems we see around us).

1 SEPTEMBER

To Brighton for War Child presentation re *Help* release.
Kids to studio. Drew built swings for them.

Daniel Hillis: 'All philosophy is just a matter of science that hasn't been done yet.' Discuss.

The three rules for complex systems:

a rule of generation

a rule of reduction

a rule of maintenance (or a tendency to persist)

2 SEPTEMBER

To Stewart:

I've been writing a proposal, by the way, for another type of synthesizer altogether, which would be based on the idea of self-evolving programmes. I may have told you this before, but I might tell it better now. The problem with designing synthesizers is that there is a tension between the number of options a designer could make available and the number that any user could be expected to understand and have access to. What this means is that synths are always less interesting (sonically) than they could be, for reasons that I generally applaud – if the machine is going to be usable, it has to not be infinitely complex.

But what if the synthesizer just 'grew' programs? If you pressed a 'randomize' button which then set any of the several thousand 'black-box' parameters to various values, and gave you sixteen variations. You listen to each of those, and then press on one or two of them – your favourite choices. Immediately the machine generates 16 more variations based on the 'parents' you've selected. You choose again. And so on.

There would also be some simple controls – for instance 'constrain mutation' – so that when you are getting close to an area you like you can focus more finely. And there could be a few typical synth controls – ways of subtracting individual elements from the mix; ways of applying overall filters and treatments.

The attraction of this idea is that one could navigate through very large design spaces without necessarily having any idea at all of how any of these things were being made. At present, synth design requires you to build from first principles (well, almost) – as though you asked someone to make a tomato by building it up from individual molecules. What I'm proposing would be much more like hybridizing – find something that's pointing in the right direction and then improve on it.

This might sound pie-in-the-sky, but remember that the machine would have the capacity to store 'successful' programs that could then become the basis (or one of the parents) of new programs – so serious long-term evolution could be applied.

I want to get some synth manufacturer interested in this. They are not too bright, in my opinion, so this might take a long time. But I think it's important as a model for other, perhaps more serious, 'self-evolving' machines. And I was very spurred to get on with this project (which has been kicking round in my mind for some time now) by Danny Hillis's piece in the Brockman book.

'I must live until I die' – J. Conrad.

3 SEPTEMBER

I go into the studio early because when I wake up I can't go back to sleep.

Things that keep me awake at night:

The mathematics of ageing. My ancestors seem to have made it to about their mid to late seventies on average. I am 47. This makes me two-thirds of the way through life.

Unsolvable minor problems: I still owe Rosetta, the Sicilian girl who taught me French in Paris in 1983, 150 francs (for example).

The bloke I was rude to at Pagan Fun Wear.

Elaborate ideas for new and never-before-imagined forms of art.

Questions and doubts about the use of art.

What I should have done, what I should have said – replays.

Discomfort in my shoulder.

The horn.

Farting.

4 SEPTEMBER

GBN meeting.

This is the day of the *Help* sessions.* Apparently everyone who said they would did.

Me in studio with Massive Attack (Mushroom, Grant and the keyboardist, Michael), mixing 'Fake the Aroma'. Pleasant, forthright guys.

Irial: 'I counted up to a billion.'

Me: 'You couldn't have done it – it would take too long.'

Irial: 'Actually, I skipped from 59 to a billion.'

5 SEPTEMBER

All day (9–7) working on finishing *Help* record at the Townhouse. Tapes appearing from everywhere, me trying to keep some mental track of it. Everything that comes in sounds good: no duds. The Radiohead song is meltingly beautiful. Andy Macdonald, Terry Hall and Tony Crean (who've done all the serious work) calmly sweating as the clock ticks on. Planes and helicopters and couriers standing by. We have to reach the planes with the tapes – which are being sent to Hamburg, Blackburn and somewhere in Holland – or else the records, CDs and cassettes will not be pressed in time for a Saturday release, which means it'll be held over till next week – when Blur are releasing. So Blur will get the number-one spot – which we would like, thank you. Enjoyable panic, but I went into Hitler mode in the last few minutes.

6 SEPTEMBER

Frantic antics. On Net to Stewart, Peter Schwartz, Paul Saffo, Rich Burdon (long correspondence about self-evolving music), then into editing stuff

* The *Help* album was recorded on this one day, and released the following Saturday. It sold over 70,000 copies on the day of release, becoming the fastest selling album in British music history. All the artists involved waived their royalties, as did the record company, Go! Discs and the artists' publishers. As a result almost all the money goes directly to War Child (it has so far raised over £1.25 million). It is also a great record and with tracks by, among others, Oasis, Blur, Radiohead, Orbital, The Stone Roses and Portishead, it serves as a unique snapshot of the current British music scene.

for *Passengers*. Cally over re cover; me editing at the same time as meeting with him, and well into the evening.

7 SEPTEMBER

Koestler Prize / Andrew Logan tapes / Tape to Cheryl.

In studio at 4.30 a.m. Editing 'Plot 180' with Haris Silajdžić bit added, also doing music for Andrew Logan's Manchester show (endless tapes). Then home to take Irial and Darla to school (Darla's first day at 'big school' – proud as punch in her uniform, dancing and singing and full of glee. A. thought she'd be less likely to cry if I took her.)

Then on to Koestler Trust Awards ceremony at Whiteley's.* Judge Tumm is such a genuinely sweet man – kind, eccentric, sharp-witted. One of the few public servants who really did what was required – served the public. My speech – off the cuff – was crap. I wanted to say that artists specialize in inventing worlds for themselves, and thus the activity is especially relevant to people who've had their world taken away from them. I did say it, but not very well. There was a guy – looked like a local-paper type – right in front of me taking notes, in an 'I suppose I'd better write down what this prat says' kind of way. His complete uninterest threw me off a bit. I shouldn't do things like that without a bit more practice – it's a different art. I'm good at press conferences and interviews – both conversational, both allowing development of an idea in some relationship to what you sense the listener is after – less so at formal lectures; really bad at very short things. The Koestler exhibition looked really strong – a mishmash, crowdedly hung, but good and sometimes poignant.

*The Koestler Award Trust exists to support art, craft, music, prose and other creative activities by prison inmates and patients in special hospitals. The scheme's Annual Competition and Exhibition was introduced into British prisons and the special hospitals by Arthur Koestler in 1961. The scheme operates on a shoestring, and produces amazing and poignant results.

Over the past few years there has been a consistent erosion of such 'soft' initiatives in prisons. Budgets for programmes like this have been almost destroyed in favour of more draconian 'punishment' regimes.

Then on to the *Help* press conference, which went well, with Tony Crean, Andy Macdonald and David Wilson. Sensed a lot of goodwill there – especially from Channel 1 woman (who in fact I mostly addressed myself to). Then home to meet the girls from school. Me: 'Did you have a lovely day at school?' Darla: 'Not a really lovely day.' But she seemed very happy nonetheless. Then a massage (pains in shoulder). The lady suggested osteopathy.

Then to CNN with David Wilson for *Help* interview — a scene of frantic and tatty disorganization, for a typically American-style piece of shit ('a Rrrock Rrrapid Rrreaction Force' – they love alliteration on American news shows). The organization of the place was completely bizarre – the 'director' wanted to alter the lighting and contacted Atlanta for permission! Noel Gallagher from Oasis was due to come, but arrived a few minutes late; anyway, they said, we couldn't have three guests in the studio. I thought, 'CNN – you're on your way out.'

Back home, then A. and I to Chelsea Arts Club for dinner with Patrick Hughes. Also there: Damien Hirst, Nigel Greenwood, Gordon Burn, etc.

BPI problems — they don't want to accept *Help* for the album charts, saying it's a compilation and should therefore go in that chart. We contend that the compilation charts exist to deal with anthologies of previously released stuff – whereas our record is all new. That probably means a few hundred thousand sales less to us.

8 SEPTEMBER

Finished Oblique Strategies for Peter Norton. Finally.

So exhilarated by the *Help* process, which has just run so smoothly. Huge sum of money expected to dwarf our Opaline efforts, but it was probably those that helped set this possibility up.

Musical eras:
 1. Mid fifties ('54–'57): Doo-wop, rock 'n' roll
 2. Late fifties ('58–'62): Girl groups, Tamla

194

3. Mid sixties ('64–'68): Liverpool, beat, psychedelic
4. Late sixties ('69–'72): Prog, bubble gum
5. Early seventies ('72–'75): Glam
6. Late seventies ('76–'78): Punk, new wave, no wave, disco
7. Early eighties ('79–'83): Synth pop, 4th world
8. Mid eighties ('84–'87): House, techno, world
9. Late eighties ('88–'91): Ambient, scratch
10. Early nineties ('91–'95): See '64-'68; add '76–'78
11. Mid nineties ('96–'98): Early generative, new irrationalist

Generative: the tenth generation.

New Oblique Strategy: 'First work alone, then work in unusual pairs.'

NOISE: In science, noise is random behaviour, or behaviour so complex that we cannot predict it. A signal sent through a medium interacts with it in complex ways and some of the information being sent breaks up into – noise. Noise is unreadable, inscrutable. Noise is not silence but it is also not loudness. It is the absence of coherence.

In music, noise is the signature of unpredictability, outsideness, uncontrolledness. The 'purest' (technically, the 'least noisy') instruments are also those traditionally used to evoke feelings of innocence, tranquillity, dreaminess and so on. Think of the impotent flute, the (literally) emasculated castrato. Then think of the instruments that always are used to evoke something-else-about-to-happen, something-about-to-enter-from-outside – the drums, the cymbals, the gongs and the shimmering high frequencies of strings.

One history of music would chart the evolution and triumph of noise over purity in music. The Renaissance looked for clear, pure tones and coherent, stackable voices. Since then it has been outside all the way, with composer after composer looking for more raspy and complicated timbres. Indeed, if one measured noisiness of instrumentation on a scale of 100, the classical palette would stop at about 50, but the rock palette wouldn't even start until about 30 (and would then continue all the way

195

out to about 90 – a figure constantly rising).

Distortion and complexity are the sources of noise. Rock music is built on distortion: on the idea that things are enriched, not degraded, by noise. To allow something to become noisy is to allow it to support multiple readings. It is a way of multiplying resonances.

It is also a way of 'making the medium fail' – thus giving the impression that what you are doing is bursting out of the material: 'I'm too big for this medium.'

Returned Quine's *very noisy* Yardbirds fuzzbox: for his collection.

9 SEPTEMBER

Nonna here. Swimming early with girls. Had to go out with Nonna to get some money from her bank to get Anthea's present.

All to Whiteley's for lunch and to see the prisoners' show. Bought four pictures! Two triangular paintings of Caribbean postage stamps – each about 3 ft on a side. Suddenly made me feel what it must be like to be in an English prison and get a postcard with a stamp full of sun and sea and tropical fish. So full of life – makes the Turner Prize seem even more recherché.

After morning garden interview (from surprise knock at door), I appear on the afternoon news re *Help*. Meanwhile trying to trace a private eye. At dinner, decided (finally) against doing Turner Prize. Incredible relief! Now all I have to do is tell Nick Serota.

Georgie Paget gave me the Institute of Social Inventions book – *Best Ideas*[*] I got the office to order me ten copies. Thrilling – at last the good news! * Nicholas Albery (ed.), *Best Ideas: A Compendium of Social Innovations*

10 SEPTEMBER

Early to rise (5.45), but at 6.30 the girls came down, both crying, 'We don't want you to go away.' At the airport I met Regine, Fintan, Naseem, then

Lewis Kovac, who manages Cranberries and Meatloaf, then Simon Le Bon, then Ben Fenner.

Spectacular dinner at Pavarotti's restaurant outside Modena (the sign of a good restaurant in Italy is how many kitsch paintings they have on the wall – this one was covered from floor to ceiling), at table with Paul McGuinness, Edge's parents and Bono's dad. (Interesting to wonder what he thinks seeing his son so flourishing – I remember my father's mixed feelings.) Rehearsal good, and for some reason I feel no nerves at all. The Simon Le Bon/Dolores song ('Linger') is quite lovely.

Last night A. and I thinking of a new game: a variation of decalynx. A huge pack of counter cards, each with an idea on it: my uncle, relativity, the golden mean, the National Debt, Tony Benn; *Les Demoiselles d'Avignon*. Cards are drawn and placed on a grid of connections (different numbers of connection paths?) with awards for meaningful links. Or organized as a set of cards with images. Cards are laid out on a grid. A player can choose any pair to connect, and make up to ten connections, then lays a coin or counter to that value on that connection. Each player can play each connection once, except when, by scoring ten, she gets another go at an existing pair.

Consider using existing institutions (schools, prisons) as places for making beautiful things. Wallpaper and textiles by children. Secondary school think-tanks.

Daily random act of kindness (Anne Herbert).

New Oblique Strategy: 'What most recently impressed you? How is it similar? What can you learn from it? What could you take from it?'

11 SEPTEMBER

In Bologna with Naseem. Bought a nose-hair clipper. Crowds round the hotel. Lots of sneezing – I've got a bloody cold. Meeting at hotel: Bono, Edge, Anne-Louise, P. McG., me. Long discussion in smoky room about whether to use Haris Silajdžić on disc. Is it good for him? Is it good for War Child? Is it good for us? Does it make sense musically? Then interviews at venue: Bono recounting good-natured arm-wrestling sessions on the phone with Pavarotti – Pav: 'I am a rich man because I am in love, because I have the music in me, because the music has given me so much – but you! You make me feel like a poor man, begging you to come to Modena.' Quite interesting hours hanging about listening to people rehearse.

Pavarotti, on hearing I have a cold, leads me to his doctor, who rifles through pockets and cases and gives me about 18 different drugs: 'This one under the tongue twice a day, this one every six hours, this before you go to bed, this one always with that one, this one just in the morning, this one whenever you like it.'

In the morning the dread call to Nick Serota to say I couldn't do the Turner speech, but he was in meetings – Sandy Nairn called back and wouldn't let me off the hook. I kept saying no, but he kept saying yes – 'You shouldn't expect to change the world in a two-minute speech.' What else should I expect? What other payoff is there? Bugger: I thought it was over!

Dolores has a nasal sexiness, a firmness that is very appealing.

Craig's nervous about how 'Miss Sarajevo' is sounding – says the contour of the orchestra's climax isn't right (too much too soon, and in the end not enough). He's co-conducting from the piano. The musicians are completely committed, cooperative and charming (14 hours' work today – would this happen with an English orchestra?).

Bono told me Dolores said to him, 'I thought you a beautiful boy in those early videos', in that lovely accent he mimics so well. We were talking about that line in one of her songs: 'My father, my father, he liked me.' We were both moved by the delicacy of that word choice – such a stronger word than 'loved'. She is apparently the one girl in a family of 11! This may explain her singular confidence around men.

On the way out of the hotel with Bono and Edge, a huge crowd of Italian fans. Bono was as usual very kind to them, and I became customarily grumpy, saying, 'I hate fandom. I hate seeing people humiliating themselves in this way. I've never been a fan.' Bono said, 'Oh – well, I've always been a fan.'

Thinking about Bosnia, and the morale benefits of them knowing that at least someone has noticed, I realize how totally wretched the Jews must have felt in WW2, when no one did a bloody thing. The utter desolation of being quietly, efficiently wiped out.

I asked Craig what I should be listening to for innovative orchestral music: he went out and bought me a Ligeti record!

'The way of the Wobble – probing the fields of plenty.'

12 SEPTEMBER

Modena. Frantic morning shoe-search with Fintan. Bought two pairs – 20,000L and 40,000L (i.e. discounted rubbish). Wanted to buy some ladies' gold platform heels, but Fintan sensibly restrained me.

Tense rehearsal with Kamen/Craig semi confrontation and me in Philistine-as-mediator role. Rehearsal good, but Pav went for (and got) the big note, turned slightly purple, and we all thought he might blow it for the evening. My cold gone thanks to the Pav snake-oil cabinet – Feldene Fast (piroxicam 20 mg), Pfizer Fluimucil 600 (acetylcysteine 600 mg) and 'Coryfin'-Bayer were the ones I used in the end). Well, if anyone has it sorted out, it should be him.

Before the show we were running through 'One' and 'Miss Sarajevo' in the dressing-room. Edge looked a bit down, thoughtful; Bono was worried about the words, which of course he had changed and added to (in Serbo-Croatian – never one for an easy life); but I felt no nerves at all (just a brief flutter immediately before). Easy for me: all I had to do was sing.

On stage in 'One' I felt an altered state – transported, 'angelic, luminous' (Anthea's descriptions from the audience). What a beautiful song! The whole audience sang with us; the orchestra gave me shivers. Funny looking out on to that crowd. To the right all the VIPs in suits and seats, Princess Di at the fore. To the left 15,000 kids dancing and shouting. Of course everyone sang to the left, where the most action was. Bono calls home after each song: asks Ali (who is watching on satellite) how she thinks it went. After the show I found myself being photographed with all those gorgeous string players from the orchestra.

Princess Di in the dressing-room, a funny little clutch at the door – her, Mo Sacirbey, Bono, Edge's father and myself. I got Pav and the others (after Bono reminded me of the time – sweet man) to sing 'Happy Birthday' for Anthea. Pav was so sweet – held her hand and gazed into her eyes while he sang – and she so gracious. She's magnificent at accepting compliments or gifts – a great and rare talent. Unexpected reformation of the three tenors: Edge's dad and Bono's dad (both tenors themselves) joined in the singing – Bob, Garvin and Luciano – plus all the rest of us, of course. At the enormous formal dinner afterwards, a glitzy and glamorous Sicilian lady came on joke-flirting with me in front of her husband, who told me how much each limb would cost me.

Botero's daughter (Lana?) one of the most radiant women I've ever seen. Like being in the sun.

13 SEPTEMBER

Breakfast *Passengers* credit discussion with Bono. Anthea's presents. Phoned Ariel Bruce, the detective who's tracing Anthea's schoolfriend (her birthday present from me). She tells me that sometimes her job is nice – as when she found the 70-year-old sweetheart of a 73-year-old man. They had been sweethearts 50 years earlier. The woman was thrilled to hear from him, and they married four weeks later. The lady confided to Ariel, 'Of course, in my day you didn't go to bed with people. But I'll tell you something, dearie – when we met again we were in bed together within four hours.'

To lunch with Wingy. Delightful afternoon walking round Bologna and in bed with Anthea (so long since we've had a day together). Fax from Jeff Koons, happy to take part in our deceit on the *Passengers* cover, but cautionary about the incendiary title. In evening, out for a quick shopping spree: three shirts, a black sweater, a red sleeveless, a white shirt, and a pair of shoes. Multi lire.

There are two schools of thought – first that humans are born innocent and that society corrupts, and second that humans are born wild and society tames. Lately I believe more in the latter – that society is the projection, the summation of our understanding, and that through it we learn to think in terms of longer nows and bigger heres. What is the sense in which both these theories are correct? Joan, for example, who rejects 'normal' society, adheres strongly to a certain society of mind. This is all a rephrasing of the *free enterprise* ↔ *state control* axis. Perhaps there are societies of atavism, societies of empathy.

Discussing with Anthea dysfunctionalism along the axis *extreme autism* ↔ *extreme empathy*. Is there a name for the latter?

A. missing girls, so won't be coming on to Amsterdam.

14 SEPTEMBER

Amsterdam. War Child party and *Help* launch – first project of War Child Dutch office. Rem and Petra there.

Wild night dancing with Wilhelmina, Michelle and Anton (who dances like a stick insect on LSD) and several beautiful women. To Stedelijk at 3.00 a.m. Riktur from Sarajevo — the band that made us dance – Ineke (tall and cool), Lillian, Sonya (lovely stomach).

But the presentation was terrible. Endless video, making people feel bad (these are the people who've already paid a lot to be here, and have thus shown that they don't need further persuading). Random artists offering their shrieking services for nothing. Awful woman with screamed poem, then a terrible, terrible American singing some shit about 'The sound of children dying'.

Interview with Bert van de Kamp. Rem seemed to be asking me if I would mind him becoming a Visiting Prof. at the RCA. Why would he think I might mind? I'd be delighted.

15 SEPTEMBER

Serious interview in morning (with whom now escapes me). Home, into office quickly, then to meet girls from school; in taxi to Golborne Road. Went to buy fish with them, the fishmen proudly showing them live lobsters. I find it difficult to justify meat-eating to kids. There's a gap in my grasp of things. Many gaps, many things.

16 SEPTEMBER

We went to Fulham, to the pool with the wave machine and the slide. I felt chilly – like a cold was coming. Had to get back fast to send tape to U2 (in South of France) by courier.

17 SEPTEMBER

Cirque Surreal. Not surreal. Sick of acrobats. But the cyclist (who Anthea thought must sleep with his bicycle) was dementedly brilliant.

Whenever I go to Chalk Farm it's raining. Is it a microclimate? All that chalk soaks it up?

18 SEPTEMBER

This evening Anthea went out with Jameos and returned chattering ten to the dozen. A whole new you. I like it. She started telling me a very long story, which got tangled in tangents, and I said, 'I have no idea what you're talking about! Get to the verb!' – at which we both collapsed laughing.

202

Even in bed she talked non-stop. She has an interesting relationship with alcohol.

To Selina Scott show. Richard Dawkins in hospitality lounge with wife, Lalla. We talked briefly, and then Selina Scott asked me about him. I replied at length and supportively – saying that evolution theory was the best theory on the table. Selina also asked me if I was an atheist, and, when I said yes, asked me how then I thought it all started. I don't know, do I? But the fact that I don't know doesn't make me say 'therefore it must have been divine'. I also don't know how Anthea's car started.

Built a tent house for the girls in their bedroom. Darla: 'Now you be the daddy and I'll be the mummy and you be the big bad wolf. No. I be the mummy and Irial be the little baby . . ', etc. Her establishing all the relationships is actually the game. Nothing much else happens – we just sort out the kinship rules. Must be a deep tribal gene manifesting.

19 SEPTEMBER

Walked the girls to school via the Crab and Ambulance park. Two little darlings in their school uniforms, both with socks stylishly rolled down (Irial's idea). I hate going away from them – and they always try to persuade me not to, with increasing success.

Quick cover for *Klar*. Enjoyed working there with Anthea sitting alongside. We've had some nice days together lately.

In Cap Ferret (after a wasteful *club-class* journey on a plane with only six passengers) the weather dreadful – or, more kindly, nostalgically miserable. Torrential rain – too wet to walk in.

20 SEPTEMBER

Lots of walking today. Finished *Midnight in the Garden of Good and Evil*, though I wanted to know more about Minerva. Out to beach twice – second time for a long walk. Very few people anywhere – ghost town. No thoughts.

Started Rushdie book in a fish restaurant. Bad idea: when I hit 'What shall we do with the Shrunken Tailor' I burst out laughing and sprayed the place with fish soup. Aside from everything else, Rushdie is very funny – something that people rarely mention about him.

An open-air show of those spinning signs – 81 of them in a field.

21 SEPTEMBER

More walking, and a very nice day. Lying in the sun on a bench; reading Rushdie's great book; back to the BeDe's and a very pleasant afternoon.

In the evening I went out to the Atlantic coast, arriving in time to see the sun set right at the end of the path. Perhaps the only night of the year it would do that. It was lovely up there, on the highest sand dune, watching the light deepen to violet red. Left at 8.45 to Calhoc to eat.

Got plane times today, but decided to stay two more days – will return Sunday. My mind – empty.

Huge object on the beach – like a small rowing-boat wrecked and turned over. It was a dead sea-turtle, the shell perhaps 5 ft long.

22 SEPTEMBER

Early to the beach (Atlantic side). Absolutely alone – not a single other person. Near vertigo to see so much emptiness. Nude, enjoying the gorgeous sensuality of the sun. The beach was huge – deep and long. Little silver fish round my feet.

Coming back into town, at 2.30, complete silence and not a soul. Like a strange science-fiction scene. Hotel proprietor lent me bike. To the point for sunset (on bicycle). The ride back was magical – through purple forests, sailing along, a smell of pines.

A late (5.15) coffee made me feel nauseous, then spaced, then sleepless.

Ages in days (at 24.9.95):
Me: 17,298

Anthea: 15,351
Irial: 2,068 (2,222 will be 27 May 1996)
Darla: 1,501
Hannah: 10,288
Petra: 14,784 (15,000 will be 19 April 1996)
Bill: 29,217 (on his 80th birthday)
New reasons for celebrating: You are 5,000 today!

Make 'concept' cards for a connectionist approach to writing: SOFTWARE/ LONG ARM/ROBOT/WET/ INVISIBLE BOMB.

23 SEPTEMBER

To the beach again, after a very poor night's sleep (heart thumping from late-afternoon coffee). Light-headed, heavy-legged. Again, a completely empty beach (well, one very distant figure). The scale does something strange to your eyes. I lay down and moved into a few hours of total sensual bliss. I think I didn't have a single serious thought all day, just drifting in this warm semi-conscious sleep. I left, walking in slow motion, when the clouds began gathering. I keep extending my stay: something about this emptying out on the beach seems useful, refreshing.

Nearly 18,000 days
Jumping from ship to ship
sometimes at the helm
sometimes in the blind hold
with vague direction
like a civil servant
a safe pair of hands
but always someone else's craft

24 SEPTEMBER

There's been no response from David re my 'shares' letter [see page 404: Sharing music]. What is he thinking? Has he even received it? I never know what gets through to him.

Noticed my hair is quite grey-silver in the sun. I like it more than that indistinct muddy colour that it was before. It shines.

'Oui' is often pronounced 'Way' or 'Ouais'.

Suppose you made a mediocre record and it went to the top of the charts. How would you feel?

It rained today.

Pleased to announce the unexpected return of Idiot Glee. I wonder what gave rise to that? The day didn't start well – in fact I felt half-dead (perhaps from so much sleep) – but I went for a bleary ride in the newly discovered fragrant forest, including a cathartic cemetery experience, wondering where all that deep sadness comes from (one gravestone had a rather naive engraving of a runner in shorts and holding a torch, full of life). All the lives that pass without trace. Then for a nice outdoor croissant with the *Daily Telegraph,* and bought two rolls, which I ate at the hotel. After lying on my bed in the sun (and dozing *again*) I went out to the beach, enjoying the cycling enormously, enjoying the strain in my legs. On the beach it was very windy, and my mood suddenly lifted into joy when a big wave crashed over the dunette and soaked my jeans. But it was on the ride home I realized I'd gone nuts – doing idiot singing and mouth exercises. 'What are those animals?' I kept singing.

There's a man sitting facing me at dinner who is so awful looking: I'm sure he's a murderer. I don't mean by that that he's stuck a knife in someone, but that he will kill someone – his wife, his kids – with his awful, sneering disdain. This is not a recognized crime, but worth bearing in mind when you read that blacks have a high homicide rate. What you get found out for are crimes of passion. But there are also crimes of passionlessness. This man lacks the balls and spontaneity to stick a knife in someone – instead he'd just slowly grind them to nothing, over years.

Decided to stop smoking. My 'one or two a day' of legend has become more like three or four, which is more than I want to smoke.

Masturbation: hanging on to the only thing you can rely on.

Last cycle rides before home journey (the lost passenger and disembarkment).

Anthea has also stopped smoking (synchronously and separately).

Bowie called A. – says, 'Yes there is something amiss there' and will propose solution on Wednesday. Time to take back my misgivings and quietly choke on humble pie.

Paul McCartney called A. to speak to me.

Is *Death of Yugoslavia* the best thing I've ever seen on TV? How did they get hold of all that incredibly incriminating footage?

Went to get notebook for Roger, but none in stock. Rainy. Walk to studio. Computer fuck-up – one faulty connector = £500 damage. Sight going.

Into studio *Leather and Lace* tapes arrived from HM Customs. Boring.

Massage with Leigh (gift from A.).

Heat work in studio. Made a very strong new piece: harsh, tight snare snapping through thick, dangerous, overhead-cable drone. Asymmetric, chromatic, clanging motif with ungainly movement ('Unwelcome Jazz' starting to pay off) over top. But the film is dodgy – the male-bonding scene makes me feel a bit ill.

Talked to Bowie re *Outside* splits on phone (he in New York). His straightforwardness in matters like this always agreeably surprises me.

Drew got seven projectors for £200 each at auction. Nell visited studio – D'Cuckoo sent gifts from SF.

Computers down, printer jammed. Fuck the lot!

Music: 'Cold Jazz for Heat', 'Heat Beat'.

Bartley Gorman V – King of the Gypsies, bare-knuckle fighter.

Don't hang up.

28 SEPTEMBER

In early (after Irial and Darla cuddling in bed) to arrange various objects on studio floor. Then McCartney called: talked for half an hour, then said he has a demo of a song he'd written for War Child ('may be a bit cornball') he wants me to listen to. Really nice bloke.

Music: 'Cold Jazz 2' – with ridiculously athletic chromatic piano runs.

Evening to Robert Wilson's 'HG' with Michael Morris. Great show – Michael is an inspiration to everyone. He was telling me about Topper – a mercenary-cum-security-guard. Dinner in Peruvian restaurant.

The best rooms in the show? Looking up there's a hole in the floor to a little chair (6 ft high) a hanging cloud of cotton wool (2 ft 6 in long) and above that a world (2 ft diameter). Sound of footsteps back and forth. That was so emotionally strong, sinister, impenetrable. Room with columns and arrows. Completely beautiful and somehow very sad! Why?

'HG' cost £130,000 – space owned by Railtrack.

Serota's visit re Turner Prize presentation. He very diplomatic and gener-ous, and concerned I shouldn't be under pressure, suggested a video instead of a speech. I worked on that idea using Bliss as a generator. Results so-so. More time lost, good time chasing bad. Bollocks! It's still on.

29 SEPTEMBER

In early to work on 'Cold Jazz 2 and 3' and then a little on Bliss. Note to Stewart re computers being the geodesic domes of our time.

Anthea has 20-day headache and goes to doctor. I have long-term shoul-der ache.

Rushing in to Lin and James to get them to listen to 'Cold Jazz 2'. Nice to have kind ears so close.

Met girls from school with a picnic which we took to the Crab and Ambulance. Four amazing little Irish girls – Sinead (seven), Chelsea (six), Kiley (six) and Lauren (five) – adopted I. and D., who were at first a bit sniffy and intimidated by this hurricane of chirping good humour and energy. Those girls (especially Sinead) were so brimming with physical confidence. I thought, 'This is what you don't get at smart private schools.' But they all got on very well in the end.

Bowie called to say Zysblat has it all in hand and is apportioning shares.

To dinner at L'Altro with David Phillips, David Wilson, Amy, A. and me. D. P. said that the discovery of oil in the Caspian Sea was leading hostile countries to try to make peace in order to benefit from a thru pipeline. It occurred to me that world peace might be secured by such linkages – split the pipeline and send it through all turbulent territories and thus give them a common interest which they would not want to threaten by war. This is an interesting inversion of my 'greater density of interconnection = creating fragility and vulnerability' worry.

David Wilson and Amy talking about the Frankfurt School; D. W. telling of being under fire in Bosnia (Jim Kennedy looked out of the window and said 'What's that flame coming towards us?' – then the building next door was hit).

I've noticed I'll eat anything black. Tonight ink risotto.

30 SEPTEMBER

Irial: 'Dad, how does a world get made?'

Dad: Long explanation.

Irial: 'Is that really true? Let me look into the bottom of my heart and see.' (Looks down T-shirt.)

Later, looking at a map, 'How do they know where everything is?'

Bumped into Sacirbey and Mabel at Frankfurt airport – he fresh from the peace talks in New York. He said the Serbs had suggested international compensation for all displaced persons. Good idea, I said, but I'm not sure he thinks so. Mentioned *Death in Yugoslavia* series. He singled out MacKenzie, the one-time UN commander, as one of the 'old villains'.

Sacirbey: 'I'm a Muslim, as you know'. I wonder why he told me that. Anthea and I thought of several possible answers to such statements (i.e. by people who feel they have to declare their faith).

Saturday night in Innsbruck – the usual three TV programmes about Nazism, lots of irresistible old footage. It is the abyss, our deepest fears about ourselves, and we can't resist looking in. We want to be good (but if we're going to be evil, this is how bad it could get).

Difference between Russian and American propaganda: the Russians never believed any of it.

1 OCTOBER

In Innsbruck. Sauna with girls and then jumped shrieking into freezing-cold pool. They have a commendable appetite for weird experiences.

To Wattens, my room full of errors (red light stuck on, blue light purple, slide holds for hours, emergency lights too bright, sound too loud, etc., etc.). Heller has sped everything up and filled every silence, which makes it all a bit kitsch – as if trying too hard to please. Desperate attempt to make sure no one is ever disorientated, even momentarily: 'PLEASE! Everything's really all right . . .' But maybe he's right – people won't come here to see just my work (that's probably the last thing they've come to see), so you have to design it so that even the 20-second wurst-muncher sees *something*. All the same, made several frantic pre-opening changes, with cabinet ministers and officials wandering in and out.

Back for lunch and quick change into ceremonial clothes – Frau Steinlechner plays me her daughter's tape in the taxi, so I gave her a genuine critique: a voice as obedient as this – obeying all the rules of good MOR singing – depends entirely on its material; the more individual the voice, the less material matters (witness the Blues). The Frau: 'But she is only 16.' Me: 'But you did ask.'

At the grand opening, presidents, ministers, labour leaders, priests, bishops all being ushered around by Heller as the imperial artist. In pouring rain, an 80-piece brass band punctuated the numerous speeches: from ministers, priests, rabbis (the Protestant, Catholic and Jewish meanings of 'crystal') and for ever on. Heller basking in praise, but trying hard to control it.

Gabriella and Christiana and Arturo Stalteri came from Venice. I got tired trying to hold conversations over all that heavy metal music, and the delightful Frau Ebner drove us back to the Scandic Crown.

Calvino's literary values (quoted by Philip Hensher in the *Spectator*): 'lightness, quickness, exactitude, visibility and multiplicity'. What does this mean?

2 OCTOBER

Had an idea this morning to invite Robert Wyatt to write lyrics/songs over my rhythmic landscapes. How to overcome his enormous modesty to persuade him? Or rather, how not to put him on a spot (where he felt he couldn't say no)?

Flew back from Innsbruck over knife-edge mountain ridges – girls very impressed. Into the studio for a couple of hours. Saw Bill Kelsey *en route*.

Realized I like the *Herald Tribune* because it is so un-English – none of that cynical sniping, none of the clever-clever sarcasm, and no whingeing columnists. But then I remember A. saying that the only thing Napoleon was frightened of was the English press. Perhaps we should rent it out to the opponents of tyrannies.

Bought a radio battery – big decision.

3 OCTOBER

Ask Ben about 'guitar' Midi device.

In early; working on music and Bliss. Ben arrived and showed me how to use Galaxy Randomizer. Then Tim Cole and John Pettigrew from Koan arrived. Worked with the system, trying to see what it could do. Days spent on computers – so dull.

Nick Serota called: God, how long can this go on? Vanessa Devereux said, 'Why don't you just stand up there and be spontaneous?' Easier said than done, in two minutes and on TV. But now I wonder if I'm making too big a fuss – and they've got me in a corner, because I can't say I just don't want to be part of that world.

Saw Marlon on the way home. Suddenly he is a big, tough bloke, working in Nu-Line. The lady in the corner shop told me how to prepare red beans island-style.

Bowie called from a distant American hotel room to relay the O. J. verdict to me as it was delivered, describing the scene in court etc. Then it was on our TV too, so we were watching it together. I don't know what city he was in – Detroit, I think. Incredible tension, with Ito slowly going over all the rules. Then the verdict – and the beautiful sad face of Marcia Clark, outwitted by shysters. I am now even more convinced (by his reaction at the news) that Simpson was guilty and that he knew he was going to be acquitted. Somehow it was a fix. As David said, 'It's down to investigative journalism now.'

Hannah said (on the phone) a clever thing: 'Have you ever met an American who was unprepared?' She's right: they always seem so rehearsed – with a TV-acquired degree in how to look happy, how to look sad, how to look contrite, how to look triumphant (this came about from Cochrane's drama-school jubilation at the O. J. result) and how to make you feel all those things (the LA A&R guy who said to me, buddy-buddy-flatter-ingly, 'Do you work out?', as if that was remotely likely).

Stewart's fax: 'Richard Rogers hit the fan.'

212

4 OCTOBER

Koan – what a sod of a program! Gnash gnash.

More work on Turner Prize. Unbelievable – never has so much time been spent on so little time.

David Sylvester's Gilbert and George review fills the whole of Pseud's Corner this week. Art-writing is too easy a target – could fill a daily pseud's corner with it.

Ben at studio fiddling with computer. On Music Shop – a new piece with a stunningly dark, long-legged, loping bass line.

Talking about rich grunge-mums with Anthea.

5 OCTOBER

Current Affairs.

Roger called early – Mum into hospital after severe heart palpitations. To Ipswich to visit her. I was unaccountably nervous before going in, but she was, as ever, in great spirits. Brave woman: someone who has faced death before and isn't so terrified. I bet my generation is going to wriggle when its time comes. The Southgates visited and were very sweet – joking and just the right amount of concern.

Roger drove me to the station – I gave him the Satie book. He called later to say Mum was OK and moved to another ward.

Girls did 'Get well' pictures for Mum – glued together with great gobs of lurid pink nail-varnish.

Seamus Heaney gets Nobel Prize.

Predicted rehabilitation of word 'pretentious' finally happening [see page 394: Pretension].

Why do some turds float?

213

6 OCTOBER

Serota accepts A.'s idea that I just hand the thing over – no talking.

To Whitechapel with Hannah darling for African art show. Very poor (except for the South Africans) – as though they'd all been told, 'Play the Africa card.' Funny how people suddenly turn out crap when they decide they're doing Art. Just as scientists allow themselves to torture rats 'for Science', 20 artists allow themselves to torture us 'for Art'. Compare with 'Faces of the Gods' in NY. Compare also with Koestler Trust show. Heretical thought: perhaps we stole and successfully developed that territory. Perhaps Picasso (or Basquiat) was actually the best African artist and the Rolling Stones are actually the best R&B band. Tim and Jon (SSEYO) visited. I'm slowly getting to grips with the program. It's not such a pig. Jeremy Silver and Declan came to see it too.

Cooked for me and Nonna – hake in coconut and ginger sauce with spring cabbage in oyster sauce and balsamic vinegar; basmati rice with garlic. Talking about Roman wine.

Bought Paradox Box for girls.

7 OCTOBER

Darla and I to studio (Irial to party). She plays so quietly alone, making little houses for my china dogs, doing pictures.

Kelsey and Ingrid over. He told me how in hospital his name had been changed to Melsey and his birth date to 29.1.33 (from 21.9.38) and how the consultant recommended he just accept the changes – it would be easier than confusing everyone. Interesting idea of having one's identity moulded entirely by official errors.

Evening interview with Susan Nickalls for *Country Life*.

Cooked chicken (garlic- and cayenne-covered), green beans in oyster sauce and balsam vinegar, lentils with garlic, potatoes.

What are the principles of leverage? Looking at books with Anthea about the six simple machines (and this somehow led on to a conversation about Pompeii).

Joke from Roger. In a western saloon – Sheriff: 'I'm looking for the Paper Bag Kid . . .' Bartender: 'What does he look like?' Sheriff: 'He's got a paper-bag coat and a paper-bag hat and paper-bag boots, and he rides a paper-bag horse.' Bartender: 'What's he wanted for?' Sheriff: 'Rustling . . .'

8 OCTOBER

Beautiful warm, sunny day. Called Rita – she has a new job – and then Mum (Rita had already called and is thinking of coming over). Swimming with Irial and Darla. Hannah and Andrew over, and we went to studio with Irial. Georgie called while I was dense in chicken oil, in a cooking trance.

Alan Yentob on *Desert Island Discs* – an OBN to Sue Lawley.

Mr Apology dead at 50 (Allan S. Bridge). John Brown brought over the magazine.

Starting to think that all the world's major problems can be solved with either oyster sauce or backing vocals.

Complicated but mediocre chicken soup, consigned to the freezer for the customary three-month rest before it goes to the dustbin.

Anthea and the camera (looking into the lens rather than the eyepiece – her and Georgie in tears laughing).

9 OCTOBER

Into studio at 5.15, writing. Then back home for breakfast with kids. I felt utterly poisoned – dizzy and unattached (could be dodgy-chicken-soup syndrome). Went back to bed for half an hour, but Darla came to sit beside me playing 'Everyone who likes flowers put your hands up', 'Everyone who likes bunnies put your hands up', then 'Everyone who likes poo put your hands up' (she throws one of those in now and again to make sure I'm paying attention).

215

Back to work – gorgeous warm day – started on 'Select-a-bonk' piece. Long conversation with Paul McCartney re his War Child song 'Cello in the Ruins'. Said I'd try an edit.

Visited Ding Dong re stiff shoulder. Then to Cromwell Hospital for X-ray (£105!). Dreadful place – where you feel they're all laughing at you for being a sucker.

Talked with A. about Bowie's songs and U2 work etc. *Spinner* in charts at 71. And *Outside* down to 19 (I predicted 21).

Playing 'shopping' in balmy garden with kids and Georgie.

Talking business tonight, Anthea reminded me that Virgin have never paid me any royalties on Devo – which I produced at my risk and with my money, not theirs.

10 OCTOBER

Another night of Irial coughing and interrupted sleep. I was awake at 2.00 and immediately my mind is away on dreadful subjects – how old I am, how little I've done, what am I looking forward to. I should drink more.

Dave Stewart called, inviting me over at 12.00 to meet some people from Thames and Hudson. They are inviting ideas for *Gesamtkunstwerk* books. I proposed *The Book of Flemish Noses,* but this was not immediately taken up. Dave Stewart's place full of new art and tiny monitors.

Bought amazing book of George Grosz drawings (*Ecce Homo*).

Block construction in studio. Drew made me two columns of breeze blocks, 5 ft 3 in high (approximate height of my parents). Plan: a speaker in each: one with a recording of my mother speaking and the other with my father speaking. The two recordings from different times, not synchronized, not connected.

Listening to tape of kids on A.'s 40th birthday in Tuscany two years ago.

Started two new pieces – one in Koan and one in Music Shop ('Drift' and 'Velveeta Pulsewar').

Bowie called from St Louis – 'No drift, just a chat' – and said how hard the band had become, how Mozza had better watch out. Also said 'Heart's Filthy Lesson' didn't get a single radio play in England.

Mandy and Joan called. A. and I talking about McCartney, telephones, Bowie, Karen Christie story: slave-trader. So many artists have shit managers.

11 OCTOBER

Another bad night – now my left shoulder hurts! Into studio early and started work on a new piece (development of 'Velveeta'). Turns out rather stately and gorgeous.

To Aero for Andrew Logan's present.

Drew making pyramids. Interview with Cally. Holi came round. Ben Fenner showing me Akai – which I now realize I will sell – so ugly the way it works.

Request to use 'The River' for Porkchop film. Tempting ($30,000) but refused – too many Uzis, and Anthea sensitive that it was the song I wrote for Irial when she was born. Must be the 15th movie this year basically about shooting. The legacy of Reservoir Dogs. The shooting scenes occupy progressively more time and attention and special effects – like endless come-shots.

Beautiful soft peach evening, freewheeled all the way home, right down Portobello. The pleasure of cycling.

This new piece today is the first emotional rhythm piece.

Clock Library letter from Stewart.

Andrew's 50th birthday party – a sort of tribute from all the people who love him and realize he is a one-of-a-kind free spirit who merits their love. I bought him a red vase, Anthea arranged to have flowers delivered to it every month for a year. Maggie Hambling gave great leg-up performance (from *Salad Days*), Andrew's mother (84) and her six eccentric offspring, Janet Street-Porter, Keith of Smile, Patrick and Di Hughes, Duggie Fields.

12 OCTOBER

Call Joan / Sing more.

Received reply to message in bottle.

Marcus Berkmann in *Spectator*: good review of *Outside* – 'Bowie best when at his most pretentious' (told you so).

David Blarney called.

Sing more? That means multi-track. My contribution may turn out to be vocal.

Rereading *Flash of the Spirit*. Interesting he lists 'call and response' as an African idea – i.e. backing vocals.

Went for X-rays – normal – and osteopath. Not much change yet.

Set up pyramids in studio with just three lights. Magically beautiful. Hung triangular paintings. Studio starting to feel good. Letter to Stewart.

Anthea's headache still there. This is worrying. I don't want to go away.

Brief experience sitting on the doctor's steps. Closed my eyes – felt that feeling of glory, of everything to live for, almost instantly extinguished by 'But I'm 47.' My feeling of glory is all to do with a certain colour of light (late-afternoon peach) falling on my eyelids.

After taking the girls to school I returned home.

'There's nothing wrong with him – he just takes up too much time' – Anthea about someone.

13 OCTOBER

Lovely autumn day – so soft and mild.

Tim Cole 9.30 (crash expert). Nieman, David Blarney re Derby show. South African man visits re installations and 'master-classes' there.

Unsettled, loose-endy, walked to Queensway, met Olivia.

I always feel I'm not getting enough of life. This lovely weather – and I didn't use it. I should recognize that sitting in Hyde Park is as useful as sitting in front of a computer. Now I'm looking forward to the remakes of the 'Little Pieces' for Derby.

Anthea traced Miss Sarajevo, now living in Amsterdam.

Any Questions: what a mealy-mouthed bunch. Oh for someone to say, 'Actually, I'm not in the least patriotic – in fact, I feel more loyalty to Cuba than England. Also I think taking drugs is a marvellous eye-opener, pornography is a fun method of self-enlightenment, and I would like to see religions taxed heavily' (all in a horsy upper-class 'Camilla' voice).

Back to studio at 10.30 p.m. Returned home at 1.30 a.m.

Tommy Cooper finds a painting and a violin in the attic; takes them to an expert who says, 'You've got a Stradivarius and a Rembrandt. Unfortunately Stradivarius was a terrible painter and Rembrandt made awful violins.' Cooper on meeting the Queen: 'Do you like football?' 'No.' 'Then can I have your tickets for the FA Cup?'

14 OCTOBER

Call Holger Zschenderlein / Do Clare's lesson on fractals / Rolf here.

Met Howie B. in street with daughter Chilli. Beautiful silver-haired woman in Wild Oats. Irial to swimming-pool party. Into studio for Koan work. Cooked chicken. Rolf and Elizabeth (and Valentina) for dinner. Thirty-eight hours' labour!

Group story-telling – Irial six paragraphs; Darla two very significant words.

Seamus Heaney, asked how he'll handle Nobel fame: 'In Ireland everybody is famous from birth and they become skilful in handling these matters.'

My diary: a book?

219

Koan work. The computer crashes so regularly, taking with it all the work since the last crash, that I have to find a way of reminding myself to save all the time. I do this by balancing a book on my head while I'm working. It falls off so often that I remember to save. Interesting spin-off – in order to keep the book there at all I have to sit well, and move my eyes more than my head. Now I'm starting to think this is the way to always use a computer.

Nice solo organ piece on Koan – like someone noodling ambiently in a church as the congregation comes in.

Art Troitsky to studio. He's colour-blind (deltonic in Russian). Indian dinner. Conversation about VR, now reminded of my early evangelism for it. But I guess it's all right to be wrong if you're wrong before anyone else.

For writing, it would be so nice to have a way of writing and then having it read back to you in your own or other people's voices – 'Let me hear Tom Stoppard saying that. Now run me that as a rap.'

Uninspired morning in studio, so I went to the RA Africa show. Memo: don't go to shows if you're feeling uninspired. It looked pretty dull to me – but I think it was me being pretty dull. In fact I enjoyed it more in the taxi home, especially thinking about that Mimmo Palladino-style piece – the Christian door with two figures carved from it. Makes me realize two things: (1) that I like my Africa cut with something else (either Islam or Christianity) and (2) that people do much better when they don't think they're being artists (contrast this with the Whitechapel show, which gave me nothing to think about in the taxi). But this show I must see again, when I have the mental stamina to deal with it.

In the bookshop I bought the big book of Tom Phillips (who curated much of the Africa show). I can see how he (like Kitaj) has been the victim of that English suspicion of people who are too clever for their own good. Some of his pictures are so extraordinarily beautiful – even without the whole cosmology of text and context with which he surrounds them (and which I really like). But that cosmology actually stops people being able to see the work: they are perhaps frightened to react to it sensually since it seems to demand intellect instead. Another riser above his station.

Back at the ranch I put together a new Koan piece which worked very well: it's a pulsed piece with complex melodic constructions which happen in a very convincingly musical way. It sounds rather like Skemptonesque minimalism, except it occasionally throws twists that no composer with good taste would be prepared to allow. And those turns get reincorporated into the piece – like the echidna's funny toes.

At home after dinner Anthea and I somehow got on to the subject of singularities. I cited the question in *New Scientist* from a reader who'd found a very odd ice-formation – like an inverted funnel – in a saucer he'd left outside overnight. He wrote in to ask if anyone had an explanation as to how this might have been formed. Anthea immediately suspected a hoax, but I argued for the possibility of once-in-the-history-of-the-universe concatenations of forces and conditions which might give rise to such things. She thought this unlikely. While we were talking about it, there was suddenly a strange whistling noise from the kitchen – a quavering, windy whistle: quite loud, and about two octaves lower than a fire alarm. We had no idea what it was, and it stopped when I went into the kitchen, but not before I was sure of its source – the cowling over the stove. Anthea said she thought it very spooky – this noise we'd never heard before. I said, 'It's not spooky. It's a singularity!'

I also asked Anthea how many mature oaks she thought it would have taken to build a top-of-the-line ship in Nelson's day. She guessed ten. The astonishing answer (from *Brewer's*) is about 3,500 – 900 acres of oak forest. She said, 'I wonder what we're doing now that's as wasteful as that.' I said it's still called Defence. [See page 327: Defence.]

221

New type of central-heating controller: analogue sliders to demarcate parts of the day; digital readout or speakout to tell you what you've done ('Heat on from 6.00 a.m. to 10.30 a.m., Monday to Friday . . .'). This should be a guiding principle for lots of controllers: analogue controllers (knobs, faders, things that relate to your fingers and muscles) are natural for inputting information, whereas digital displays (in the form of intelligent readouts, things that relate to your eyes and ears) are natural for showing you what you're doing.

Camille Paglia says that government and socialization are what civilizes us, not what robs us of pure instinct (as Rousseau supposed), and I find myself wanting government to take more seriously its 'civilizing' function – to establish and defend a set of international behavioural standards. So today's real anarchists are the Oklahoma bombers, the mad Serbs, the survivalists, the far-right laissez-fairies, the free-marketeers.

Libertarianism rests on the assumption that things left to themselves will pretty much sort themselves out. This may be true in some cosmic, entropic, sense (how could you know?), but there's no reason to assume that we or our interests would survive this sorting out.

The other part of the libertarian assumption is that 'interference' is almost always a mistake, and therefore we'd do best to leave everything alone. The failure of understanding there is that *even just noticing* is an 'interfering' act.

17 OCTOBER

Worked on Koan until it was time to go to the new osteopath for my shoulder pain. He's a nice man, but he talks like a hairdresser – non-stop, and about things that don't really interest me. Strange for someone in that profession, who you would imagine would be keen to have you relax and contemplate. Osteopathy is pretty minimalistic – a couple of cracks and a lift and you're off, several quid lighter.

Then on to the RCA, where I lunched with the Interactive Media students and Dan Fern. Then an open seminar where Dan and Jon Wozencroft asked questions and I extemporized. Bright and focused bunch of students. One of the first questions: 'What is particular about this moment at the end of the millennium?' Subjects covered: the decline of political ideology at the end of the 20th century; the interface problem (increase rapport, not options); CD-Roms and what's the use of them; collaboration; inside the work/outside the work; etc., etc. Dan said this was the first year that female admissions had exceeded male – and this without a quota system.

Dave Stewart called re the project with Paul Allen. Billboards as artsites (artsites/artistes). I told him of my plan from years ago – to buy billboard space and just 'donate' fields of gorgeous colour to the public, with a small message saying 'This colour donated by . . .' He said, 'Benetton.' Of course – what a great campaign for them. We should approach them. He offered me a job as 'Curator of the Billboard'.

Cooked lamb in cabbage leaves, Mongolian-style.

Arthur Miller in *Meridian* interview: 'It's the right that has become revolutionary and it's the left that is trying to conserve government as a liberal force . . . They were looking for the dream – and the dream was elsewhere' (of people in the thirties, who would meet each other going to opposite coasts and say, 'Don't go that way!').

18 OCTOBER

Of course big chunks of my day are now taken up transcribing this diary, creating a sort of fractal pattern in time where I write about writing about writing. This could have me heading towards real literature – the kind no one wants to read.

In very early (3.30) to work on Koan again. Now I'm getting results that surprise me, that sound like a music I hadn't imagined before. Getting my light-boxes working – and tons of new computer equipment arrives. Of course none of it works properly and it requires numerous calls to manufacturers and suppliers and the bloke next door who happens to have one himself. Thank God Drew is doing that.

Bloke came to repair Duo, so I can get talking to Stew again.

Called Bono re their next record and talked about Larry, who is just a father and is about to have a back operation then on to convalesce in NY until Xmas – thus not being around for the original recordings. It gives me a bad feeling, him being out of the picture. I think it's a mistake, and suggested that they set up a process where he could take part – Tascams and time-code and Sammy zipping back and forth with tapes.

Back home earlier to bake a cake with the girls, as promised. We made drop scones with eclectic ingredients – cinnamon, peanut butter, vanilla, pumpkin seeds, sultanas, poppy seeds – which I then fried to their delight. They came out pretty soggy (too much butter), but the girls devoured them with great pleasure and self-satisfaction.

Later we danced: 'Duke of Earl', Robert's 'Internationale', 'Return to Sender'. Then I played the JAMES *Laid* album (which is so beautiful, and was sadly a bit overlooked here).

19 OCTOBER

Letter from Roger, addressed to 'Douglas Pantry and his Seven', saying he managed to appear in the background of a John Selwyn Gummer broadcast as a limping leper. Interesting idea: undermine the credibility of politicians by always surrounding them with retards – thus making obvious what is probably true anyway.

To New York, taking advantage of Virgin's masseuses etc. Think of extending the service on airlines into new areas. [See page 304: Black marks.]

Boarding the plane I heard one of Roger's pieces, which sounded really lovely. I tried to find out the title from the stewardess, but she told me it was by Dave Stewart. I couldn't really tell her why I knew that was not the case: 'No – it's by my brother.' I can't remember which piece it is.

Reading Boorstin's *The Creators*: what a bastard Beethoven sounds – arrogant, paranoid, disagreeable. Why am I still surprised when people turn out to be not at all like their work? A suspicion of the idea that art is the place where you become what you'd like to be – Peter Schmidt's 'more desirable reality' – rather than what you already are?

At the hotel, a message from Julian Schnabel, who invited us to his twins' second birthday party on Saturday. He's so unexpectedly cordial, chatty.

Out with David Wilson and Bill Leeson to my old Thai restaurant in the evening (down by the Tombs at Bayard and Baxter), where to my surprise everyone recognized me and came and shook my hand. It must be ten years since I was last there. We were discussing whether some of the people we're in contact with have intelligence connections. Then I wondered whether the 'Intelligence community' in fact comprises a whole spectrum of interests, from the Bay of Pigs nutcases to idealist Democrats who saw the agency as the best means to change the world. I really could understand someone thinking that America was the best of all *available* (if not *possible*) worlds, and that it was therefore a service to humanity to spread its word. So the question becomes 'If they have, does it matter?'

In the restaurant, in keeping with Anthea's dictum that I never go anywhere without bumping into someone I know, I saw Renzo, the Italian promoter who still owes us money. I didn't mention it.

20 OCTOBER

I was out shopping at 5.40 a.m., to Duane Reade's to marvel at the 326 different kinds of shampoo, the 68 different aspirins, the endless canisters of shaving-foam, but also to marvel at the homogeneity of the market: among all those hundreds of shampoos, there was not one in a small-size bottle (e.g. for someone nearly bald and expecting to stay only a week). So I ended up with half an ocean of something, of which I'll use perhaps an ounce.

This is an American characteristic – hundreds of attempts to hit exactly the same target: a consumer tropics. It runs through from culture to cosmetics to politics to Hollywood, as though the only audience worth trying for is the biggest one. It's either that or it's the really specialized niche market, such as the weird cable-TV shows. They haven't gone as far as they could in that direction. [See page 390: Personal profile.]

Speaking of which, on morning TV there was *The Stallone Solution,* where Sly's intentionally witchlike (velvet, purple, black, glitz) mother offers her wisdom to the world's losers, calling in to her at very high rates. Dreadful crap, unless I flip into post-modern mode and see it all as part of the rich fabric of attempts to create meaning – the modern oracle. (But, as Bono said that time we were watching Lenny Kravitz's Jimi-Hendrix-lookalike video, 'Isn't this taking post-modernism a bit too far?')

At breakfast David W. and Bill L. and I were discussing mine-clearing – how to get rid of the approx. 100 million land-mines round the world. They are very cheap to make, very easy to forget, and very expensive to remove – about $2,000 per mine. In Angola there are mines sitting round which were laid 20 years ago. Jim Kennedy and Bill L. came up with an interesting tongue-in-cheek solution: goats! Just breed enormous herds of them and let them wander round till they've blown up all the mines (and Bill pointed out that this would constitute an Integrated Aid Programme, because it would produce goat chops as a spin-off).

Another solution would be to design cheap and dirty 'thumper' robots which just jump round all over the place quite randomly until they get blown up. It might not be expensive to make a robot which doesn't have to do anything other than behave erratically – doesn't have to get anywhere in particular, doesn't have to be able to sense anything, has no goals, no controls. I remember a thing I made once – it was a hollow plastic ball about 5 ft across containing a little motor and battery. The spindle of the motor carried a cam with an off-centre weight so that, as the motor turned, the eccentric weight forced the ball into complex and erratic motion, and it rolled about quite unpredictably until the battery finally ran out.

Later that morning, the very early press conference about the *Help* record. Not too many people turned up, but the conference was good. Surprised to find myself cast as MC, but I think I did all right. Actually Tony Crean and I made a good team: he's funny and self-deprecating and all soul, and I can handle the information part. After some questions, we played the video of 'Miss Sarajevo', which ends with those long slo-mo shots of her beautiful, proud and mischievous face. When I went back to the podium to say thanks-and-goodbye, I noticed that half the room was in tears.

The model of the music centre (£5,800) was completely smashed in the journey over here. It had been packed by nutters, and obviously something very heavy had been dropped on top of it and we ended up with bags full of splinters. Very glum.

Took Bill L. and David W. down to SoHo. Walking along on a lovely Indian summer day, David W (who's never been here before) thought this must be the nicest city in the world and decided he might want to live here (thus precisely mirroring my reaction when I came here one beautiful April day in 1978 and stayed for five years).

We went to the Guggenheim downtown and saw the Dan Flavin show. I hadn't high hopes for it, but it was amazing – so economical and clear in its intentions and results. The whole show consisted of a number of neon tubes in various colours – nothing else. Bill L. was ecstatic, and we stayed for a good hour, walking round and round. This is the argument for the artist who tills one field for ever and keeps increasing its yield. Leaving, I bumped into Roselee Goldberg, and then went down to a somewhat incomprehensible show at Sean Kelly's gallery down Mercer Street. He 'explained' it to me – it was, of course, about 'issues of race and gender', those twin columns that have supported so much mystifying art over the past twenty years.

There's a whole world of fine art that I just don't get. Is it me or is it it? (And are there any other seven-word sentences with only 14 letters?)

Anthea and the girls arrived from England about 6.00 p.m., full of excitement.

21 OCTOBER

Took Anthea and the girls down to the Flavin show, which looked just as good today. I told the girls (to sell the idea) that we were going to a kind of palace. Torrential rain started just as we left, and got worse on the way back to the hotel. Waterfalls down the fronts of buildings.

Back at the hotel we met David Phillips for lunch. Then to Julian S.'s for the party. All of Julian's five (three by previous marriage) there, plus Olatz of the endlessly long legs and Rosemary and her little boy. Julian talking at length to me about David's record – great heart but lack of space. Conversation started with him playing me an early version of 'Small Plot of Land' which he wants to use in the film. 'Much better than what went on the record,' he said. It turned out to be my original mix, where I left out everything except voice and strings, so it became a sort of orchestral piece with this beautiful sung poem over it. It did sound good – the voice so prominent. Julian said, 'It's so strange that people who have a real ability so often try to cover it up.' I said I thought this was because people don't trust what comes easily to them. (Oblique Strategy: 'Don't be afraid of using your own ideas.')

In his vast studio he played me some of his songs. The singing is frail and even awkward, but the will is strong. Is that enough? Can the formula be applied to music? There were three enormous paintings on the wall – rather beautiful ones in purple and deep red and shellac: a series. I was surprised how much I liked them. And Irial in her party dress was dancing to the music, just gliding in front of them, enjoying the space. Julian was meanwhile telling me a story about a photograph of Olatz, aged nine, on a Basque beach. As he talked, Irial turned into the young Olatz of his story.

In the evening Anthea and the girls went to bed early, and I went down to Greenwich Village for a dinner party at the many-booked apartment of Julie Peters, a professor at Columbia. (Collective noun: an insulation of books.) Among the other guests: David Phillips, Constance, a large-eyed and attractive pianist, a smart and serious German called Alfred (Prince Alfred von Liechtenstein) and his girlfriend Iwe. The way intellectual

Americans talk to each other: passionate about ideas in a way that I wish we could be, but also something of the polished flipness of the talk show – everyone's always on *Letterman.*

The question, in the end: 'Is the world getting better?' I argued that it was, but was supported only by Alfred and Iwe. The others argued that the present generation was in a mess (I said, 'What else would you expect? Would you trust them if they weren't?'), and were soon celebrating the sixties as a time of certainty and consensus. I was saying that the sixties were flawed by a dichotomy – the contrast between the idea that, on the one hand, we could reinvent ourselves and, on the other, all the metaphysical stuff which claimed that we were fundamentally predestined beings. I said this was a paralysing collision, and that things were better now – what they were calling 'lack of deep conviction' I saw as a liberating pragmatism, a possibility for action that didn't need the backing of ideology. I said that the reach of our empathy had extended – that we were willing to include more people (and other beings) in the word 'us' and that this constituted a change for the better. 'Well, I just can't go along with that old Hegelian paradigm,' said one of the guests.

On empathy increase: of course we still belong to all those local and tribal identities that we did before, but now we add to them more universal identities. The point is to stress and glamorize those new ones, to make a balance of identity pulls (psychological cold war) rather than an overwhelming subscription to one. I recognize that increasing complexity is both more richness and more vulnerability.

After that dinner there was another party to go to, but I just walked with everyone to the building (talking to Constance the pianist) and then went on back to the hotel.

22 OCTOBER

Crystal morning. To Duane Reade's and Gem Grocers for morning dew. Then out to Dutchess County with David Phillips and Lin O'Shea, the

229

Republican chair of something. She kept asking very big questions, such as 'Tell me about Culture' and 'Will there be peace in our time?' She asked me if I'd ever read Edward T. Hall, and I said yes, I'd read *Beyond Culture*, and she said, 'Well, you two must talk. I'll call him right away. You'll get on really well.' Now this really frightened me, the prospect of a phone call beginning 'Hi – I read one of your books about fifteen years ago . . ', and I discouraged her. A wrong assumption: I like your work, therefore you'll find me interesting.

But I can see how someone like her is a real catalyst in thinking meetings. She has no inhibitions at all to try to make things happen – even when there is a chance she'll come out of it badly. She's a real chancer: I'd invite her to any meeting.

Out in Dutchess County things were beautiful – all the colours of an up-state autumn. Irial found a dead vole and wanted to bring it home to show her friends at school. I felt mean trying to tell her to ignore her natural enthusiasm for things by saying that it would be a bundle of maggots by next Monday week.

Retroherence: the tendency of clusters of events to be logically connectable after they've happened ('He gave a retroherent account of events, but we all knew things didn't look that way at the time'). Retrohesive: pertaining to events that were disconnected when they happened but now cannot be separated from each other.

23 OCTOBER

To Egghead Software. *Nothing* that I wanted to buy. What a tremendous disappointment the computer revolution is. When I got the kids their computer I imagined there would be a host of great programs for kids. Wrong: there's only KidPix.

To Central Park Zoo with Alex Haas. His brightness and *joie de vivre* are infectious. The kids love him too. The zoo is lovely – they've concentrated on making a nice ambience and then putting a few animals in it:

unlike London Zoo, which is just cage after cage after horrible cage of depressed-looking beings. This American approach – probably the result of soul-searching about species-rights etc. – is far superior. Seals, polar bears, tiny frogs and tamarins (which have very serious thoughtful faces, like shrunken heads that have remained alive). The zoo, like many things in America, is a triumph for political correctness, which I am more and more inclined to defend and support. (List: 'Good results of political correctness.)

At the War Child thing at David Phillips's house, Pavarotti turned up during my speech with a perfectly timed, cheerily theatrical 'Hello' from the front door. Everyone burst out laughing, and I said, 'I suppose it's acceptable to be upstaged by him.' Karin Berg came, plus Laurie and Lou. Lots of White House people there. I wonder what they want, or are they just straighforwardly interested? Am I too sceptical, or a realist?

Mohammed Sacirbey invited me to sit in with the Bosnian delegation at the UN tomorrow during Izetbegović's speech. Very nice, but me busy tomorrow. Invitation also to visit the White House with Nancy Soderberg, Clinton's security adviser, and to meet Madeleine Albright.

Later, someone whispers to me, 'Be careful – there are a lot of people who'd like to use you.' Cynical? Sensible?

Robert Walsh and Stephani came. He gave me a photocopy of a James Hillman essay about pornography: 'Pink Madness'.

Going back to the hotel for a drink with Alex we bumped into Iman and she joined us (she'd come from the opening of the Mandela film). Great watching the ballet of her fingers while she talks.

24 OCTOBER

Interviews in morning and visit to VH1 to do a chat show with J. D. Considine and others. Everyone talks ten-to-the-dozen and has immediate and passionate opinions about absolutely everything. This is TV passion

231

– instant, intense, forgettable. I feel like a tweedy egghead snail – slow, careful.

25 OCTOBER

With girls to Guggenheim for Claes Oldenburg show and to meet Michael Chandler there. Oldenburg's earlier stuff – before he knew what he was doing – looked best. So often the case that people work best when they are stretching out over an abyss of ignorance, hanging on to a thin branch of 'what-is-still-possible', tantalized by the future.

Then we all walked across Central Park (lovely autumn day) to the Natural History Museum, where we met Anthea. I wanted the girls to see the dioramas there – which are as beautiful and still as I remember them. Their frozen silence, soft evening light. The big tree with rings going back to the Roman era. King crabs with 3 ft legspans. (Anthea told me these used to walk up the street when she was a girl in New Caledonia. Now I see why she's scared of spiders.)

To the screening of Julian's Basquiat film. Confident, interesting and involving. Trades heavily, however, on the glorious struggle of 'being an artist', which leaves me a little cold. (As struggles go, it isn't that much of one.) Funny people don't make films about the struggle of being a postman or a dentist. Bowie as Warhol: slightly reptilian, reminds me of the cold clamminess of Warhol's hand. The vortex sucks me in.

In the evening to dinner with Laurie and Lou at Barolo. Lou eulogizing Andy Warhol: 'He was just so smart! You just always were thinking, "What would Andy see? What would Andy do? What would he say?"'

Discussion about subsidies for the arts. I told them what Michael Brook's father said in defence of Canadian subsidies to artists: 'Call people unemployed and give them $15,000 a year and they'll be miserable. Call them artists and give them $5,000, and they'll be overjoyed (and might even produce something).'

'You never get enough of what you don't really want' – Eric Hoffer.

26 OCTOBER

Laraaji came over in the afternoon to see us and the children. He's like a lovely day: always original and fresh and full of laughter and new perceptions (e.g. just after Irial was born he came to visit us and said to Irial, 'Hey there, little beauty! Great to see you this side of a stomach!'). Anthea had some royalties to give him.

Saw family off to the airport in a two-acre limo with dark windows.

With Laurie to meet Michael from DIA for the New York version of 'Little Pieces', and then on to a computer art show, which was customarily disappointing. Tiny ideas writ enormous, and cheap tricks writ dazzlingly expensive. Still, someone has to do the dirty work. Best thing by far – two paintings downstairs. No connection whatever with computers.

On to Tom and Andy's studio – they jovial hi-tech hired hands – and to eat with them at the Savoy restaurant, where Lou joined us, having just that evening finished his album. Beautiful, tiny *maîtresse d'*.

27 OCTOBER

Lunch with Prince Alfred and Iwe, discussing his plans for a new European TV station: 'TV to change the world'.

Walking round SoHo checking out galleries with Alex Haas, we discovered a mutual admiration for the work of Kostabi. So we went round to Kostabi World on Broadway and there he was. He gave us each a copy of his ($250) *catalogue raisonné* – the fabulous book at Bono's place. I promised to send him some fabrics from London – multiple overlay ones from India.

Alex told me a story of how Kostabi berated (on camera) a collector wanting to buy one of his pictures, saying, 'You only want this because it's ridiculously expensive and you think it will impress people. You know nothing about what you're buying. You're only getting this because you've been told to' and so on. Of course the guy bought it. No serious patron of the arts could resist that kind of humiliation.

Back to London.

28 OCTOBER

No entry.

29 OCTOBER

A. and kids to Chorleywood for the day, so I went up to the studio to work on Koan and do some writing. James Putnam and Ikio came over in the evening to look at my pyramids with a view to presenting them in the Turin show. I asked if there was any knowledge about what sorts of musical scales would have been used in Egypt.

Anthea showed me the correspondence between her and Paul McG.

30 OCTOBER

Up at 3.10 – must write to U2 today. I'm thinking a lot of confused things. I want to spend some time on my own work – whatever that is becoming. I'm trying to think out an idea – but I need to jump into the abyss to get there. [See page 357: Into the abyss.] I don't do that working with other people, because enough stimulus comes from them to keep things ticking over (and because I can always spread the blame when things aren't working). I want to take full responsibility for something. We've worked together for such a long time, but a break wouldn't hurt. Since I've been a co-player (as well as producer) on the last two projects, I'm worried about becoming a distorting presence (i.e. if I'm not there they make something different than with me around).

Back to bed for an hour and then out early to the studio. On the way I reread Anthea's letter to Paul and his response. Difficulty is that I see both sides – and sort of agree.

234

Down to Westside to mix David's live version of 'The Man who Sold the World' – and what a great version. It sounds completely contemporary, both the text and the music, and could easily have been included on *Outside*. In fact I wish it had been — it has a clarity (there are very few instruments) which a lot of that record could benefit from. David's singing is quite brilliant lately – he's always discovering new nuances. He's developing this new approach which is somewhere between voice-of-future nightclub ennui and wide-eyed young-stoned-Londoner innocence. I added some backing vocals and a sonar blip and sculpted the piece a little so that there was more contour to it. Good bass player.

Andrée over for dinner.

31 OCTOBER

To Stewart:

An Englishman, appalled by the impossibility of reaching outlying African villages with information about Aids (no electricity; batteries too expensive) has invented the wind-up radio. Simple, brilliant idea – 30 seconds of winding gives you 40 minutes of radio. This means that aid agencies like War Child are very interested in these things, because they have no running costs. So, a South African company starts manufacturing the radios in a factory staffed by disabled people. Great idea: double benefit. War Child gets ready to back the project.

Yesterday I received a phone call from an insider, telling me that I should watch out – that this project is very dodgy and in fact they are getting ready to sell out to a big battery company. I called Bill at War Child, who's been dealing with them, and he told me that this is nonsense – it's all above board and Nelson Mandela is behind it, as well as our own Overseas Development Agency, etc., etc. And I'm inclined to believe him. But then why did this Deep Throat tell me this?

Lately I'm feeling that I'm in rather deeper water than before – not worried, but curious to see these big forces at work.

235

In early – 4.30. Worked in the dark with the new pyramids Drew made. Just three ordinary lights and a grid of 16 cardboard pyramids. Magical – no point on any surface identical in colour to any other. I love working early on winter's mornings – so silent. I love this new studio.

Cycling in, I stopped for a guy crossing the road. He stared at me: 'You're Brian Eno, aren't you?' And then, very disapprovingly and with some hostility, 'What the fuck are you doing out at this time of day?' The tone was indignant: 'Look here, mate, I'm supposed to be fucking working class and oppressed; you're supposed to be fucking decadent and in a limo. You stick to your job and I'll stick to mine.' Funny, because later Anthea showed me Pat Kane's article in the *Guardian* which made much of the fact that I always met my deadlines – as though no more penetrating revelation could ever be made about me.

Listening through to some DATs to try to find some things for Schnabel's film I found all these long-forgotten bits of work. Lots of them were in the category of 'Unwelcome Jazz' (or 'Jazz that no one asked for'). I started thinking again about that idea of treated spoken word over them, and then came across 'Everybody's Mother' from 1990 (from the original *My Squelchy Life*) which I wrote in Tuscany when it never stopped raining for two weeks.

CAMRRA: the Campaign for Really Romantic Artists.

Genes in the news every day.

1 NOVEMBER

In early, working on Koan pieces. Also trying out some projections on to the big pyramids. Lights look better.

David Phillips called from Istanbul and said he'd had a meeting with Haris Silajdžić on the tarmac at Kennedy, that Silajdžić sent his regards and thanks for what War Child has been doing (pass on to Go! Discs) and said he'd like to host a $1,000-a-plate-type dinner in LA, home of the stars and starinas, to coincide with Laurie's NY art show.

Dayton talks starting.

Interview with Edna Gundersen in Los Angeles. Making a picture in Photoshop while I talk on semi-automatic. She had a kind voice – the kind of kind voice that makes you wonder what kind of face is behind it.

Darla making me up with face-paint: 'Now you will look beautiful.'

Programme about the thirties: 'I got that job for two dollars a day. Right then a dollar bill looked as big as a saddle blanket' –

Mansell Milligan. In the UK, instead of government action they got royal sympathy. The Jarrow Crusade – turned down at the House of Commons. How convenient WW2 was – for everyone.

2 NOVEMBER

As the *Passengers* reviews roll in, once again that bad feeling in the stomach at the disparity between the spirit in which things are done – joy, enthusiasm, curiosity, fascination – and that in which they're so often received – cynicism, jadedness, resentment. The reviews have been generally reluctantly appreciative, and sometimes very good, but the general feeling is still one of suspicion: 'So what are they trying to pull now? Why do they have to be so fucking clever? Who do they think they are?' (The perennial English questions, as though people *have* to buy your records.) It would be so useful to know where the reviewers were actually coming from: every review should have, below the name of the critic, their ten current favourite works in the medium. That way you have some chance of seeing their prejudices (and they get some sense of what it feels like to be exposed).

I can see it's time for the triennial market correction. My star, having shone unjustifiably high and bright for the last three or so years, must now be snuffed for a while. This is healthy, if uncomfortable.

Wrote proposal for the Turin show.

Tim Cole from SSEYO visited in the morning and I played him some of the Koan pieces I've done. Several I did and forgot about immediately, but was delighted to rediscover. Second time this week I've been reminded that I can easily forget good work in the haste to do something new. I should employ someone – quality control – who keeps listening to whatever I do and files it under categories: 'NOTHING NEW', 'WORTH HEARING AGAIN', 'TRIED BUT TRUE', 'COMPLETELY INCOMPREHENSIBLE'. Jameos?

Schnabel called about music for his film. He's a chatterer on the phone, though always pretty interesting. I never feel comfortable in long phone conversations – my body too disengaged; I start playing with things and doodling and wandering round the room, then knocking things off the table and finally ripping the phone cable out of the socket when I try to catch them.

Paul McCartney rang about my fax re the Q awards. He said they hadn't planned to play there anyway. I said I wanted him to know that I wasn't trying to browbeat him. He said thanks, but now he'd like to browbeat me – into getting his song done.

In other developments, as they say, Bowie rang Anthea and talked at some length about how he was looking forward to the London shows, how 'muscular' the band is, how his voice is in form, etc. What a guy – still full of the enthusiasm and energy of his teens! Unfortunately, I suspect the shows may be met with the full sourness of people in their early thirties: 'What right does he have to enjoy himself at our expense?'

In the evening to South Africa House, to the showing of Trevor Bayliss's wind-up radio. Baroness Chalker gave a very confident and endearing speech. I looked at that little radio and thought about the potential it has, and thought, 'Bugger! – if I'd done only one thing in my life that was as clear and simple and useful as that.' But the good news is that the simple ideas haven't all been used up.

3 NOVEMBER

Good day at work, discovering yet more forgotten music. With A. to Andrew's Alternative Miss World.

Comments to Stewart:

It made me genuinely glad to be English, to see that much bizarreness and wit and kinkiness and intergender flirting. There were at least a dozen different genders there – it was a bit like being in one of those deep-space bars you always see in sci-fi films where creatures from all over the universe with weird body parts and funny ways of talking happen to end up in the same spot.

Before the show, a band called Minty came on to the stage. Minty consists of three or four transgender creatures naked except for Saran Wrap, holding gold handbags, a 'male' lead singer with pointed ears in a one-piece red catsuit, and a female singer wearing a crown, black platform shoes and nothing else except a small ring through her shaven pussy. (Can you still call it a pussy when it's fur-less?) She sang with all the fervour and directness of a Salvation Army girl. Great voice – ululating.

The Wyrd Sisters, three young middle-aged women who stand and scream in the day-wear section of the competition, then come out wearing pumpkins over their heads and body stockings covered in porridge for the evening-wear section, and finally appear stark naked for the swimwear section. Infectious good humour. Later, after the contest, the three of them come up giggling and wobbling and hug me – 'We used to trip to your music' – and leave traces of porridge on my Dolce & Gabbana suit. But there's something memorable about having all that rather plump, soft titty wobbling and pressing around you.

The winner is Jeanne d'Arc (the theme of AMW this time was 'Fire'), who is wheeled in on a bonfire with ladder by a team of seven or eight glistening nearly nude men, but who herself is gloriously clad in Indianesque finery, and has smoke and flames around her. She was a great dancer, lithe and oriental, her whole body dyed deep blue-green à la Tretchikoff.

In second place, number 19: 'The Russians', two guys who'd managed to make it all the way over from Moscow with the most enormous costumes – sort of Oskar Schlemmer meets Rodchenko at Chipperfield's Circus. They had 20-ft-long stalks coming out of their eyes, with little cups of flame at the end.

Miss Firing Line (third) was a wonderful middle-aged gay couple, the older being a ballerina (good on points!) with a huge flashing headdress. Their obvious affection was what really got them a place.

A 55-year-old woman – fat and sexy in an engagingly corrupt kind of way – takes my arm and pulls me towards her. She puts her hand on my chest and whispers in my ear, 'How can I get in touch with you?' I say, 'Drop your hand about 15 inches.'

In the toilet I stand having a piss between a 6 ft 2 in person with a beehive haircut and a full-length ballroom dress with the whole back missing and another person in leather shorts. In the queue behind us is the whole of the Galactic Federation.

A tall girl comes up to me and says, in a deep voice, 'Hi – you came to talk to us in St Martin's, but you won't remember me because I was a boy then. My name's Trudi Wooff.'

I was one of the judges (along with David Hockney, Zandra Rhodes, Norman Rosenthal (director of the Royal Academy), Anita Roddick of the Body Shop and several others.

Towards the end of the evening, Richard O'Brien said, 'And we can tell our children, and our children's children, that we were here this night.' I think he was being ironic, but I think I will.

What a fantastic night out! Confirms my feeling that Logan is one of our greatest artists – apart from doing beautiful work himself, he has the great talent of being able to make places where other people do great things. There's a desire to make it happen, to do your bit, not to be just a spectator. And, unusual for England, a complete lack of all those people who are normally there, looking for what's wrong with the whole affair. It occurred to me that Alternative Miss World itself (not Andrew, who's now ineligible and anyway would never be given it) should be a candidate for next year's Turner Prize.

Lift home with Zandra, always exploding with laughter, and Duggie Fields. I wish everyone had come to the show – especially Hannah and Bee and Arlette. Truly mind- (and body-) expanding. Edge Culture at its best. [See page 332: Edge Culture.] I kept thinking of Jon's thing: 'These are the first saints of the new religion . . .'

4 NOVEMBER

To studio too early in morning. Fell asleep on the floor. Very uncomfortable.

Compiled tape of samplable bits for Russell.

In the afternoon Mark Johnston and Christina Barchi called to enlist our support for the Saro-Wiwa appeal. Me reluctant to condemn Shell automatically. Heated argument.*

In the evening Anthea and I talked for ages and thought of a new game: each trying to guess which members of the opposite sex the other found really attractive. It took quite a long time to define the terms: I mean, should it be Spud-u-like, or Spud-u-love, or Spud-u-adore-and-settle-down-with? We finally decided it should be Spud-u'd-like-to-be-on-a-desert-island-with-for-a-week. We both ended up with very short lists. I put Matthew Evans and Arie de Geus (she doesn't know him) on hers, and she added David and then we finally setted for Laraaji, a very good choice. On mine there was Ali, Botero's daughter Lana(?). Since then I added James Neal's wife.

We were also talking about the difference in upbringing behaviour between those who see themselves as gene-transmitters and those who think they're meme-transmitters. We concluded

* In November 1995 Ken Saro-Wiwa, an activist from the Ogoni region of Nigeria, was sentenced to death by the Nigerian military government (and was subsequently hanged). There was a strong suspicion that Shell, the biggest oil producer in Nigeria, was hand in glove with the government and had failed to intervene in any way in what was widely agreed to be a miscarriage of justice. I was not automatically willing to believe this: I thought that, as multinational companies go, Shell had been rather enlightened about its relationships with the societies in which it operates. Unfortunately, I think my friends were right in this case. Further investigations have not shown Shell in a good light.

241

that the former would be inclined to have more kids and invest less in them culturally. We wondered what was the best balance.

Bono in an interview: 'A lot of English bands went to art school. We went to Brian.' Flattering to think of myself as a sort of one-man version of the art-school experience.

Overheard Unlikelihoods series: Two stout men walking along Portobello. One to the other: 'She was very impressed by me with all my knowledge of rugby.'

5 NOVEMBER

Bonfire night. Building bonfire in garden with Christobel and others. She's very clear – an attractive personality. Christine and Jamie came over with the two kids. Big firework display. Georgie made several amazing guys.

'Through food, the woman penetrates the man's body' – Mexican lady on the radio.

6 NOVEMBER

A dull day at work, not getting into anything properly. I should be finishing Anton's thing, but I can't get round to it. We mounted one of the pyramid groups on the wall, where it looks less good than on the floor. I did a tedious piece on Koan, and another tedious piece on the sequencer.

If I had a proper job (for instance, if my kids didn't get anything to eat today for me not pulling my finger out) I'd probably do a lot more.

Bought *Encyclopedia of Modern Warplanes* for camouflage patterns. Does anyone outside the defence establishment realize how many warplanes there are in the world? And what they must have cost?

7 NOVEMBER

Q awards, so I got into the studio at 4.10 a.m. to get some work done first. The tedious Koan piece I started yesterday turned into something rather beautiful – like Ligeti on a wet day. I'm starting to be able to make things with that system that have real mystery – and real personality. There are compositional turns that sound very intelligent. This is always fascinating me – that a system dispassionately set in motion will provide outputs that provoke you, as listener, into imagining compositional structures. The greatest thing, though, is that I can make music on this that I couldn't have imagined before (by making interactions between sets of rules that would not occur 'naturally' – e.g. a scale belonging to Berg crossed with a big-interval melodic style from Central Africa).

At the awards, our table seated (starting from my right) Anthea, Tom Stoppard, Iman, David, Amira, Anton Corbijn, Jameos, Andrew Logan, Liz Huhne, David Wilson and Lin. David and I received an 'Inspiration' award, which was presented by the ever-hilarious Jarvis Cocker, who introduced us as Mr Hunting-Knife and Mr Liver Salts.

Tony Blair presented an award for the *Help* album, and gave a good speech. Afterwards I was photographed with him and Tom Stoppard, at Harvey Goldsmith's behest. Then he came to our table, where David Wilson twisted his arm about coming out to Bosnia. I introduced T. B. to Andrew, and T. B. remembered that he'd defended him years before – when Andrew had been sued by the Morleys for appropriating the 'Miss World' title. On appeal, Lord Denning looked at a picture of Andrew in his half-male, half-female gear and said, 'Nobody in their senses could mistake this grotesque monstrosity for a beauty contest' and threw the case out.

Van Morrison came over to sit with me. I think it must be 15 years since we talked (that strange dinner in Sausalito with Christine Alicino). He was very friendly and relaxed. He then asked me to come to the Dorchester with them (Van, fiancée, manager – who Van calls 'Mother' – publicist, etc.) for a drink. As I was leaving, Robyn Hitchcock stopped me and asked if I remembered doing some performances at Winchester College using tapes and loops and so on. He was 14 at the time, and apparently they left an impression on him. It must have been about 1968.

At the Dorchester the conversation was as liquid and mercurial as Irish conversations usually are – everyone talking at once, threads crossing and tangling, lots of laughter. Being a Brit in such a conversation is like being a honky on a Harlem dance-floor.

The usual delightful long evening conversation with Anthea – this time about what to do with all the other production and collaboration requests I get now. It's very flattering and nice, and could probably make me exceedingly rich, but all I really want to do right now is piddle about in my studio. Alone. We thought that maybe I should treat 'outside work' as a kind of job – do maybe one week in six on short, focused projects. After all these years, we still enjoy talking together. It never gets dull or workaday: it's as though our two perspectives intersect in just the right way to create sparks. I guess like David and I.

8 NOVEMBER

Working on Koan early in the morning – getting some really musical results now: things I can enjoy listening to for hours on end, with just the right balance of consistency and surprise. (Oblique Strategy: 'Balance the consistency principle with the inconsistency principle'.)

Then on to Chelsea College of Art for a lecture. Talked mostly about self-organizing systems. Surprised by my ability to navigate a relatively coherent path through a quite tangled territory (which in this case included Cornelius Cardew and *The Great Learning*, the Scratch Orchestra, concepts of economy, self-regulation, homeorhesis, cybernetics, evolution theory, Bowie's lyric-writing strategies, intellectual property and copyright laws, CD-Rom usage in the future, the failure of the digital revolution, the blurring of package into contents, inside and outside the work, and the future of music, among others) without any notes at all. Well, I did have a green index card with 'Ambient Music' and 'Inside/Outside' written on it – in case I went completely blank. Noel Forster, my dear professor of old, was there and took vigorous and copious notes. Strange lecturing to someone who was once your teacher. Afterwards a scrum of very nice students. Must send some examples of Koan for them to hear.

Tim Cole and his brother over in the afternoon. Perhaps we can make my new evolutionary synthesizer together – they've been working along similar lines themselves (again). I also showed them some of the Bliss and Stained Glass work. If someone could approach those visual generators with the same sensitivity that they've shown for their musical generator, that someone would be finger-on-the-pulse for the future.

In the evening to the premiere of Paul McCartney's short film about the Grateful Dead. The original material was 140 B&W stills of the band that Linda took at the end of the sixties, and Paul scanned them with a rostrum camera and performed various video effects on them. The morphing was the hit – one photo morphs into another of the same person, producing in between a weird rubbery ghost face of someone who never existed. I think this is a clever innovation – to make films out of things that weren't filmed. Imagining the moments between the photos, or what happened next. The slow scans of the crowd at the outdoor festival, close-ups of grainy faces, put one in mind of assassinations and conspiracy theories and so on – so much the mood of the sixties: the nagging, dark, seductive undertow of the great liberalization.

Chatting with Elvis Costello before the film. I like him. Kate Bush in the theatre: very kind words about War Child.

Reading *Lords of the Rim*, about the overseas Chinese and their history.

9 NOVEMBER

Anton over for his preface. Looked a bit underthrilled when he read it. Or is that just Dutch? I know it isn't incandescent yet.

Bill and Andrée over for dinner – Bill's 80th birthday, and both full of life, leaving next week for another waterfall visit. Looking up the highest waterfalls in my various reference books, none of which agree on the rankings.

10 NOVEMBER

Bill over to the studio in the morning, looking at my computers and chatting. He seems very happy.

Letter to Van Morrison suggesting we try working like this: send me the tapes; I'll fiddle and send them back.

Passengers getting a complete range of reviews – suitably controversial. But there is a good buzz about it. I wonder now whether U2 will adopt it as one of their own, rather than holding it at arm's length and blaming it on me!

Elvis Costello called re working on something for *The X Files*. Told me at length about his weekend in St Petersburg with a group of repulsive Anglos gloating over the chaotic collapse of Communism.

Paul Simon called: 'I thought it long past time that we were in touch.' He's working on a musical about a fifties Puerto Rican gang murderer and his subsequent life in jail.

Bowie rang full of excitement about his concerts. Says he wants to work with Tricky and P. J. Harvey.

To Stewart:

Rorty is very controversial because he is seen as the smiling face of moral relativism. People think that Rorty's pragmatism (i.e. we can't make absolutist arguments for any position, so therefore the positions we take are never going to be *ultimately* defensible) is a cover for a precipitous sloughing off of all moral values and responsibilities – because they don't read the follow-on (i.e. nevertheless we have to act, and consensus is a better basis on which to do that than The Word of God).

The other thing this journo criticized me for was always bringing in my projects and productions on time – a sure sign of a non-artist, as you'll agree. It seems the thrust of his attack – which received two whole pages apropos of nothing in the *Guardian*, our leftist *Village Voice*-like national daily – was that I am a dehumanizing organization man, a covert underminer of artistic values (i.e. romantic ideas about what artists ought to be like) and a cynical manipulator of the media. The article ends by pointing out that everything I've ever done with anyone else has been purely self-serving. Another dreadful crime – to have benefited from one's own efforts.

11 NOVEMBER

Pop culture is a benign growth taking over everything it touches. Poetry next (the rebirth of the spoken word).

To Woodbridge with family and Georgie's daughter Clara. Darla not well at first – so we stopped at the South Mimms Cholesterol Centre for a few plates of fat. Delicious chicken in Schlemmertopf (cooked with white wine, celery, onion, carrot and mustard).

12 NOVEMBER

Walk in morning – clear childhood autumn smells.

Saw Auntie Freda – 90 next year. She tells me she's fed up with hearing about who's died and what new illnesses everyone's got. Bumped into Grace, who told me about her problems with Jeff – another woman (aged 23 to his 51). So Grace, when she knows he's going to see her, feeds him lots of beans and vegetables so he farts all evening, or makes sure there are no clean socks.

13 NOVEMBER

Boring day, not getting into much. Made up a cassette of the Koan music for the students at Chelsea. Visited health club to enrol, but it's very expensive. One advantage – everyone I saw there was female.

Reading Francis Fukuyama's *Trust*. Interesting that this idea – the one I espoused in my little talk to the London Stock Exchange in 1990 – should now underpin a whole book. Also retackling Rorty's *Consequences of Pragmatism*.

Half the afternoon assembling chair from kit. Beware of kits made by hippies.

14 NOVEMBER

Call Mark Edwards re new baby.

15 NOVEMBER

Everything feels awry today. We went to the Bowie concert last night. It was good, and D. B. was in great form, but I felt there were too many people playing too much of the time. Whenever there was an arrangement (an arrangement is when someone stops playing) it sounded good – as on 'Spaceboy', 'Niteflights'.

Stuart Maconie came over and I showed him Koan. In the evening A. and I talked at length about all sorts of things and watched the Ogoni tape. Although very prejudiced (beginning with the words 'The land of the Ogonis has been destroyed by Shell'), it nonetheless gave one the impression that there were forces at work within Nigeria which felt absolutely no fear of rebuttal, and to whom Shell was sympathetic.

16 NOVEMBER

Dreamed I was taken to meet a man 'who had seen his own death image' – the image that would be before his eyes at the moment he died – and would be able to show me mine. It was Jarvis Cocker, who explained that I had to stare into a dish of iron filings in water until they formed into the image. He also promised to find out my 'death number'. It was all very cheerful.

April and Lucy visited the studio in the morning for breakfast. April said Aunt Romy had had to retake her driving test at 86 years old (April: 'We knew no driving instructor would have the nerve to fail her') and she passed, making her the oldest person in England ever to pass the test. She was featured in all the local papers, but unfortunately the glow was slightly tarnished by her calling out the police to trace her stolen car, which turned out to be in the car park where she'd left it.

Ten RCA students over to look at Koan and screensavers. I gave them all a talk (which Edwin filmed) about self-generating systems and the end of the era of reproduction – imagining a time in the future when kids say to their grandparents, 'So you mean you actually listened to exactly the same thing over and over again?' Interesting loop: from unique live performances (30,000 BC to 1898) to repeatable recordings (1898–) and then back to – what? Living media? Live media? Live systems?

In the evening to Club Disobey in Islington with Lin and Russell Mills. Lots of people in various shades of black: mostly men, mostly short-haired – in fact much like me, but somewhat younger. Nice feeling, but nothing much happened. One had the sense that everyone was waiting for something – not just at that moment and in that place, but that this waiting was symptomatic of a long cultural waiting.

17 NOVEMBER

Sludgy days at work, these last few. I can't get into it properly. I need someone like me to boss me about.

Enrolled at health club.

18 NOVEMBER

Market early. Crisp, clear morning. Irial feeling sick. To the studio with the girls in the afternoon, until Anthea came to take them to the Moscow Circus.

Sorting out CDs. I have so many, and no idea where most of them came from. It's so easy to make 'sonic landscapes' now – and there are just millions of people at it. A whole technology exists for it, leading to the thought that by the time a whole technology exists for something it probably isn't the most interesting thing to be doing.

I want messages. I can't believe I hear myself saying that, but I do. I want to be told something, to have my intellectual attention engaged. Three routes to this: the use of words, the use of history-resonant sounds ('This is a recording of the gunshot that killed President Kennedy' etc. – so that all the sounds in the 'sonic landscape' are laden with meaning), strong context-linking (framing).

Of course rap is the first course of action – but it mostly doesn't take me anywhere (except Me'Shell Ndegeocello, which I realize I've listened to more than anything else this year). The poets I saw on MTV – that might be a kind of future. Who do I know who makes words? Well, David of course.

I realize the reason I like playing records (as opposed to CDs) is that they're short: they stop after 20 minutes. I want less music.

19 NOVEMBER

Assessment at health club: 'You're in good shape for your age.' I wish I could just be 'in good shape'.

In studio with girls and Clara, the endless talker. She's so great with the girls – only seven, but thoughtful and big-sisterly. Scanning found autumn leaves into Photoshop, then turning them blue, purple and pink to shrieks of amazement.

Now that artists, comedians, writers, poets, architects, newsreaders, religious leaders, politicians, industrialists, fashion designers and scientists are all acting like pop stars, there's nothing left for pop stars to do but award them all prizes.

20 NOVEMBER

In to work at 7.30. Logged on to long conversation about the Clock Library.

In the evening, Princess Di being *Panorama*-ed. First time I've ever seen Anthea say 'Sh!' very forcefully when I tried to speak over the TV. Di going on about duty and the nation and the man in the street – all concepts outside the range of my understanding. *Why* should one feel duty? *What* is 'The Nation'? Who is the man in the street? My sympathy goes out to her for the shitbag scum journos she has to deal with – imagine meeting those vile, smarmy ferrets wherever you went. But she has been too carefully tutored – one suspects her sincerity because it is too perfect. Anthea imagining Camilla Parker-Bowles's undoubtedly upcoming programme. Her projected version of Camilla: all jolly and horsy and full of fun – 'Oh well, of course, silly old me. It's all my fault. Should have trusted my instincts, but I thought he wanted to marry a princess-type. HA HA HA! Jolly daft of me. Might've known that love would win in the end or something soppy like that. HA HA HA!'

Lenny Henry called.

Howie B.'s *Skylab* record uses a loop from 'Baby's on Fire'.

21 NOVEMBER

My first Photoshop dream. I dreamed I was erasing my past in Photoshop, but it turned out that I was using the 'clone tool' so instead of erasing I was just copying chunks of the past into the future. (Consider the inverse: that you think you're using the clone tool – reclaiming memories – when in fact you're using the eraser.)

Jeff Koons asked me to write a catalogue note for his next big show.

Early to work, doing something on Koan, which crashed and destroyed an hour of work. Then upstairs to log on.

Clock Library heating up. Fred Hapgood, subterranean-living theorist, joining in.

To health club to learn some exercises – a near-death experience.

Power Mac hard drive crashed.

Back to studio, managed a couple of weird mixes ('Ambient Savage' and 'bbbbbb' and then had a meeting with Matthew Evans. He told me that

251

Pulp Fiction, the script, had sold something like 200,000 copies, that kids went to the cinema with it and doubled the dialogue, *Rocky Horror*-style, and that Quentin Tarantino had visited them for dinner and talked about nothing but films – until four in the morning. Interesting, the *Rocky Horror* connection – confirms my feeling that the whole thing is somehow just camp for its audience.

Rob Partridge came over. Whenever I show Koan to someone I get excited about it all over again. I'm finding something increasingly unsatisfactory about putting a record on – knowing that someone else knows exactly what's going to happen next. It's the kind of pointlessness you feel when you catch yourself doing a crossword, when you know that someone already has answers to all these questions and you're basically adding nothing whatsoever to the sum total of the world's knowledge or pleasure. Actually, I feel that way about those exercise bikes at the health club: all that furious pedalling just to throw away energy. Surely you could get a significant power output from health clubs all over the country? (And, as an incentive, you are told that a nearby old people's home or orphanage is entirely powered from the club. If you stop pedalling, they go cold.)*

*Further ideas for health clubs 'pay' people for the energy they produce: insert a smartcard into the machine before you start – it registers your usage, and this is deducted from your membership charge for the following year.

Or: Every day you visit the club, £1 of your subscription fee is sent to a particular child in an impoverished part of the world, so that your attendance at the club is largely responsible for this child's welfare.

Or: A health target is set and your subscription (which is reassessed monthly) is tied to it, so that when (for example) you put on a pound it costs you an extra £1 a day. A pound for a pound.

Jon Savage sent me over *No New York,* which I'd asked him if he could find for me. Good old boy, he did. It looks now nostalgically exciting – like something from a very strange time indeed (does it always seem that the past was a very strange time, with people experimenting with their very lives?).

Yardbirds thing on TV – how rock history becomes more and more watchable and interesting.

Peter Grant to a threatening promoter: 'I very much doubt if you're going to shoot me for $1,000 – don't be so fucking cheap.' Keith Relf, beneficiary and then victim of electricity.

To Stewart:

Of course, the real can o'worms opens up with the new stuff I'm doing – the self-generating stuff. What is the status of a piece of its output? Recently I sold a couple of pieces as film-music compositions (a minor triumph, and an indication of how convincing the material is becoming). I just set up some likely rules and let the thing run until it played a bit I thought sounded right! But of course the film-makers could also have done this – they could have bought my little floppy (for thus it will be) containing the 'seeds' for those pieces, and grown the plants themselves. Then what would the relationship be between me and those pieces? There is, as far as I know, no copyright in the 'rules' by which something is made – which is what I specify in making these seed-programs.

For me, this is becoming a stronger body of work every day. Having now had the chance to try out some of the work on lots of different people (even without telling them how it is being made), I am convinced of its musical worth. Then the fact of its infinite self-genesis comes as an incredible bonus. So I will be very happy if, at the end of it all, I get recognition as a pioneer in this area. That in itself (given the way things have worked for me in the past) will also turn out to pay the bills. It's something to do with what Esther Dyson was saying about servicing an idea: if I let the idea free, then I get paid for servicing it – extending it, updating it, extrapolating from it.

The end of the era of reproduction.

22 NOVEMBER

All day (from 10 a.m. to 2.00 a.m.) in the studio with Elvis Costello. Man, he can talk – Dublin must be dense with three-legged donkeys. But he's very entertaining and literate, so you don't mind.

He'd described today's session as an 'adventure' for him – to go into a studio without much prepared and try to make something from scratch: something I'm good at, something he said he's never done. But in fact he turned up with a completely (and minutely) written piece – even with manuscript paper and notation. He had every musical detail of the piece already in his mind, so all I could do was to create space by leaving things out and contributing a nice sonic landscape. I was miffed at first – I kept thinking, 'So what am I here for?' I estimate I spent less than half an hour on my contributions to the piece – doing things quickly while he was out on the phone (at one point I told him to go and call his wife so I could get a few moments to work), or fitting them in while he was doing overdubs (while, of course, still paying attention to what he was overdubbing). In fact the result was very good – unlike typical B. E. or E. C. I suppose if we described the whole thing as 'me producing an Elvis Costello song' it was a very successful day.

One very interesting thing about the piece: his orchestral approach. So a bass that only plays about five notes in the whole song — something no bass player would do spontaneously. I've only ever seen one other person who had the piece so minutely organized in his head – Scott Walker. I was very impressed then too, and felt equally semi-superfluous.

Terrible sore throat and hacking cough.

23 NOVEMBER

Swim and some exercises. Felt like a dog.

On Koan again, completely hooked. Dan Lanois came over and I played him some of my new things – the 'Unwelcomes', and the strange mixes I did of some of them. They sounded very good through his ears, and he, as usual, offered a lot of good ideas. I enjoy the 'stretched' space of those pieces – that AD 2008 club feeling we got on the *Outside* sessions. He played me an astonishing new guitar piece – more music from one single instrument in one performance than I've heard for a long time. Amazing sonic detail. Dan also very interested in the Koan work – we think to use the process on a new soundtrack piece he's doing. So I send him Koan seeds and he works over them.

I had this fantasy of doing film music simply by constructing rule-sets and then inviting the director over to listen to the system extrapolate them: 'I'm off out for a couple of hours – just take whichever bits you like and settle up with my office on the way out. . .'

Picked up girls from school and brought them up to the studio, Darla building elaborate little houses for my china dogs, Irial working on Photoshop. Darla the architect, Irial the painter.

24 NOVEMBER

Lying in bed ill this morning I wrote my Turner Prize speech. My favourite subject: the conversation of culture (and why the fine arts aren't talking). But two minutes is too short.

25 NOVEMBER

What a dreadful cold! Taking decongestants, which make me feel zingy and speedy in a not very nice way, and always thinking, in the back of my mind, about the awful prospect of the Turner speech.

26 NOVEMBER

Bill's 80th birthday party, beautifully organized by Anthea, at Cliveden. Odd feeling, being at a clan meeting of that sort, where people who haven't seen each other for decades come together again, or where relatives who've never met do so for the first time. A slight sadness too, as many of the older people said goodbye to each other. I thought, 'They must realize they'll probably never meet again', and then I thought this must have been a much more common experience in earlier times – people saying goodbye for good. What must it have been like, your young son leaving to seek his fortune in Australia?

255

I suppose we had some of that feeling when Rita left for Seattle. I think I felt I would probably never see her again. What a sad, brave ride that was, from Woodbridge to Heathrow airport in Dad's car, all three of us chattering too brightly to conceal our heavy hearts. I never considered before how heartbreaking that must have been for Dad, who loved Rita – his stepdaughter – so much, and for Mum, who didn't even make the journey, because Arlette had just been born – another daughter appearing as one left. That was in 1961.

27 NOVEMBER

TV programme about smell – I switched it on and the first person I saw was Maurice Roussel from QUEST in Paris. Theory: that molecular vibration, not shape, is the thing that enables us to identify smells. Neat experiment with left- and right-handed carvone: one smells of mint, the other of caraway, though structurally identical. The discovery is that one of them – the mint-smelling one – fits into the receptor in the nose in such a way as to mask one of the molecular vibrations. If you recreate that vibration by adding a molecule which vibrates at that particular frequency (acetone!) the smell is not mint plus acetone but caraway. No trace of acetone smell left.

I simply can't sleep. It's really pathetic that my mind makes such a fuss about this bloody Turner Prize speech. It's because I see it as poised on a knife-edge: if I get it wrong, it will live with me for a long time. A bit like one of those penalty shoot-outs at the end of a World Cup game – you could play well through the whole game, but all people would remember is that you missed. So many people have said to me it's a no-win situation. I could do something trivial or joke-y (not take the shot), but that's a cop-out. But I will never, never, never, never, never, never agree to something like this again.

The knife-edge: I don't want to stand there saying 'This is all bullshit', because it isn't, and because any such acrimony raises the question 'So why are you up there?' But I don't want to do the usual 'Well, isn't this a wonderful evening for British art.' God, I shall be glad when this is all over.

28 NOVEMBER

At the afternoon run-through – for the TV people, to make sure I wasn't going to be naughty – I looked at the work. Strange: 'Mother and Child' brought tears to my eyes. Sandy Nairn helpful as I ran through speech.

At the dinner table, Waldemar Januszczak and his wife, Yumi; Georgina Starr, a refreshingly opinionated installation artist; Richard Sherdan, writer about Bloomsbury circle; Janet Street-Porter, still growing and full of life; Neil Tennant, talking to Anthea; Colin Tweedie, who runs something called Business for Arts.

At the next table there was Damien and his crowd. I was pleased he got the prize actually, but I'm not a total fan. I sort of suspect the people he hangs out with – there's a certain arrogance about thinking yourselves so hip. Perhaps it's not dissimilar to the early John Lydon scene. I remember him coming up to me in Iggy Pop's dressing-room after a Rainbow concert in about 1978(?) and sitting down at my feet, cross-legged in his big boots, in a faux-disciple way, looking up at me and saying, 'Still making that hippy music then?' His currency was in being deliberately cheeky, in out-hipping you. And he was good at it too. About a year later I saw him slumping in an alley on Notting Hill Gate, looking truly dreadful, as though all his spiky wit had left him.

Anthea looked lovely – very colourful regal dress and beehive hairdo. Me so nervous.

The speech:
The Turner Prize is justly celebrated for raising all sorts of questions in the public mind about art and its place in our lives. Unfortunately, however, the intellectual climate surrounding the fine arts is so vaporous and self-satisfied that few of these questions are ever actually addressed, let alone answered.

257

Why is it that all of us here – presumably members of the arts community – probably know more about the currents of thought in contemporary science than those in contemporary art? Why have the sciences yielded great explainers like Richard Dawkins and Stephen Gould, while the arts routinely produce some of the loosest thinking and worst writing known to history? Why has the art world been unable to articulate any kind of useful paradigm for what it is doing now?

I'm not saying that artists should have to 'explain' their work, or that writers exist to explain it for them, but that there could and should be a comprehensible public discussion about what art does for us, what is being learned from it, what it might enable us to do or think or feel that we couldn't before.

Most of the public criticism of the arts is really an attempt to ask exactly such questions, and, instead of just priding ourselves on creating controversy by raising them, trying to answer a few might not be such a bad idea. The sciences rose to this challenge, and the book sales those authors enjoy indicate a surprising public appetite for complex issues, the result of which has been a broadening social dialogue about the power and beauty and limits of science. There's been almost no equivalent in the arts. The making of new culture is, given our performance in the fine and popular arts, just about our only growth industry aside from heritage cream teas and land-mines, but the lack of a clear connection between all that creative activity and the intellectual life of the society leaves the whole project poorly understood, poorly supported and poorly exploited.

If we're going to expect people to help fund the arts, whether through taxation or lotteries, then surely we owe them an attempt at an explanation of what value we think the arts might be to them.

And if I had another two minutes of your time I'd have a go.

And so glad that it's over, though some people called for me to continue. I thought I'd made a complete balls of it. (Those at my table kindly disagreed.)

Various people looked at me like I was Satan, or with obvious pity. Richard Rogers shook my hand. Vanessa Devereux said something like, 'There – I knew you could do it!'

Also met there: Bryan Ferry, Matthew and Angela Flowers, Camilla Braka, William Palmer, Simon Wilson (from the Tate), Kate Chertavian.

It's funny that when artists decide to act like rock stars they always choose Black Sabbath or Ozzy Osbourne as their model.

29 NOVEMBER

Lots of responses to Turner speech. Even stopped in the street: 'It was the only good thing in the programme.' A mixed compliment.

30 NOVEMBER

Pop musicians have forged tremendous breakthroughs from their lack of ideology and their indecisiveness. The only reason you need multi-tracks is because you can't make up your mind in the first place, but multi-tracks have then engendered a whole new form of music — ways of painting with sound. This is empirical composing: a method that is characteristic of improvised music, but was never before possible with music of structural complexity.

1 DECEMBER

Note from Elvis C. asking if I knew of an artist who worked with glass boxes making 'tiny theatre sets' with 'leaves and natural objects'. I thought of Cornell, but when I asked Jenny and Tony at the Todd Gallery they suggested Jane England, who's had several group shows called 'Art in Boxes'. Sent the catalogues to him. Lunch with Jenny.

Working all day on Koan pieces. It's a different kind of work now – since I am trying to replicate *Discreet Music* as accurately as possible (in order to make a 'Discreet Mutating Music'). This is actually very hard – trying to duplicate the complicated analogue conditions of the original: a synth that

259

never stayed properly in tune, variable waveform mixes and pulse-widths, variable filter frequency and Q, plus probably something like 30 audible generations of long-delay repeat, with all the interesting sonic degradation that introduced. Digital is too deterministic. At the purely electronic level, there are very few molecules involved, and their behaviour is amplified. The closer you get to 'real' instruments – including physical devices such as tapeheads, tape, loudspeaker cones, old echo units, analogue synths – the more molecules are involved, and the closer you get to a 'probabilistic' condition. This is an argument for strapping a lot of old junk on to the end of your digital signal path – valves, amplifiers, weird speakers, distortion units, old compressors, EQs, etc. – in the hope that you reintroduce some of the sonic complexity of 'real' instruments. There's nothing wrong with the pristine formica surfaces of digital: it's just that one would like to be able to use other textures as well. Think Haim Steinbach.

Anyway, my attempts to replicate *Discreet Music* result in interesting failure after interesting failure. On the route to it I get diverted. What comes out instead is another good piece of music that isn't actually anything like *Discreet Music*. This is a kind of argument for life-drawing and other academic pursuits: the act of trying to make something in reference to an external standard makes you attempt things with the medium that you wouldn't have thought to otherwise. Perhaps it's also an argument for the trainspotterish Photoshoppers trying to make their glistening photographic daffodils . . .

2 DECEMBER

To Stewart:

Developments in Bosnia are mystifying me a little right now. What is in it, I ask, for the US? I mean, it could be that they genuinely take seriously the role of global policeman, in which case I bow in humility to such responsibility. But it interests me that Dole is also now behind it – makes me think that there's been some realization that all this serves another, bigger, more long-term set of aims. What could they be?

Then there's the question of Milošević. If anyone started and fomented this war, it's him. He is a very nasty piece of work, and he is an ace survivor. To me, making this settlement with him is analogous to the Allies having managed to stop the war in, say, 1942 and then asking the Czechs and the Poles and the Belgians and so on to sit down and make peace with Adolf Hitler, now coming on as the great statesman/man of peace. Milošević is just not credible as a peacemaker: I am sure that this is just a sidestep for him on the route to a Greater Serbia. And my darkest fears are that America knows that too, and has made a deal with him – to let happen slowly and discreetly what was previously happening with great violence. I really hope that isn't the case.

On brighter news, we have just started building the centre in East Mostar! The architect and engineer and various others are out there now taking the first steps. I think this architect (Nick Lacey) is someone you'd like and respect. I detect no arrogance whatsoever in him – if you make a suggestion, he is ready to take it very seriously and make changes in the light of it, or tell you rationally why he thinks his original idea might be better. I've had only good experiences with him. Plus he's completely committed to this project.

Back to Bosnia – my overwhelming feeling (despite my dark fears) is 'ALL HAIL TO THE CHIEF!' America did something, made a difference, where we dithered and argued, and, whatever the long-term intentions, I can't argue with the short term effect. As things settle down, we're starting to hear more of what actually happened during the war. The level of atavistic brutality (particularly against the Muslims) was really sickening. I wish I had any grasp on the psychology of situations like that. What makes someone want to hack off a prisoner's arm and then hammer nails into his eyes? How do you actually go through with that? It isn't the action of a moment (one can understand rage), but a slow, gruesome process. How do you so completely ignore or suppress your own empathy towards another's suffering?

Anthea and I possibly the last remaining mammals not to have bought a lottery ticket. She hates the idea of giving cash to Camelot. I hate the predictability of the beneficiaries. [See page 370: Lottery ideas.]

3 DECEMBER

To the studio with the girls all day. To amuse myself (since I couldn't get into anything very concentrated with them here) I made some album covers in Photoshop, working from the black and white Polaroid that someone left here on Thursday. One album was called: *How Hip is Your Hat? Unwelcome Jazz from the Heart of London's Unwelcome Jazz Scene* and another was *Brian Eno – Kind of Beige*. Meanwhile they made stars with spiders on them, watched *Cinderella,* and played climbing games on the spiral stairs. Irial is so kind to Darla – helping and encouraging her, saying things in her excited hodgepodge cool talk like 'Oh man, Dad – I just showed Darla how to draw a Christmas tree once and she did it all on herself! That makes me crazy to death!'

Flatulent dish: 20 cloves of roasted garlic turned into a paste, mixed with puréed carrots and pumpkin oil, served with artichokes and kohl-rabi. Look forward to a day of fragrant farting.

The Beatles Anthology in the evening. Music on the cusp of irony.

4 DECEMBER

Long conversation with Adam – as always, emotionally dependable. I'd been thinking about calling him: he called me.

I told him I now realize that the music isn't the only important thing: that there is another objective – to maintain the solidarity of the group. I said I thought they should use this time when Larry's out of action to develop new material and then record it (Olde Fashioned Style — a band in front of some mikes) when he gets back. The emphasis then falls on questions of *performance* (rather than solving compositional problems).

Schnabel called wanting the original mix DAT of 'Small Plot of Land'. I

262

can't find it among all my Bowie DATs, but (as usual) found two other overlooked and great things. Roselee Goldberg called re film 'about people who use words to serve another purpose than narrative' (I think). Spoke to Chris Watson about his presentation here.

Idea about 'investing in bright kids': you invest in very young kids by giving the parents money towards their future education, and then you get e.g. 2% of everything they earn between the age of 25 and 35. The gamble is that they don't earn much. The possibility is that your money will help the parents get them started. The plus and minus spin-off is that the child would have more people interested in its future, more people who wanted it to do well.

Story proposal: market-places with poor people thrusting resigned urchins towards you, waving IQ reports (or with IQ scores tacked on to their chests) – 'She's a clever one, sir. She was readin' when she was two and a half.' 'All 'e needs is a little help and 'e'll become a great entrepreneur. 'E's already selling sweets to other children at 55% mark-up.' 'This is the one for you, sir! For $5,000 you can have 20% of her!' 'I know 'e's not much to look at right now, but you should see the little blighter's drawings. 'E's a buddin' bleedin' Pikarso.'

And very rich kids – those born with silver spoons – would of course be blue chip and heavily over-invested (with a very high price-to-earnings ratio).

Reminds me of that market in insurance policies of still-living People-with-Aids: they sell their policies, thus collecting something while they're alive. The buyer banks on them dying in time for him to make a profit on their investment. Sounds awful, but who loses?

To Stewart:
    The Bosnia peace agreement is starting to become clearer as I pick up bits and pieces from the papers. It is not very favourable to Bosnia, but it's quite possible that it would be unrealistic to have proposed

263

anything that was: after all, the realpolitik of the situation is that Bosnia is hemmed in by two very powerful and greedy neighbours, so the game is one of trying to create a balance between them – with Bosnia as the movable counterweight. The really good news (I think) is that Sarajevo, with its long (and still unbroken) tradition of pluralism is remaining united, although I did read about a Serb plan to use 'children and grannies' to fight for independence of the suburbs that currently have Serb majorities. (They did this before – old ladies lying down in front of aid convoys to stop them getting into Bosnia. It works: no one is going to crush a granny.)

I admire the Americans tremendously for taking this whole thing seriously and apparently deciding to do it well. To our current government, this is a completely unknown strategy. We muddle half-assed into things and fuck them up, and then muddle out again. Although Britain has this history as a great imperial power, in fact our secret history is of repeatedly going through this process. Think of the Crimea, Mafeking, Gallipoli, Dunkirk, Suez, Cyprus and many others I've forgotten. It's what Charles Hampden Turner was going on about in his book (*The Seven Cultures of Capitalism*). The British are so liable to retreat into 'safe-pair-of-hands'-type laissez-fairy tales.

A very interesting book, which I must have mentioned to you before, is Sir John Colville's diary of the Second World War. He was Winston Churchill's private sec. One of the standout impressions is the completely arbitrary basis upon which ministers and key figures were chosen: this one was at school with that one, so let's make him minister of supply, and that other one is the nephew of the Duke of Norfolk, so he'll be a good naval secretary. No concept whatsoever of merit – just an assumption that the most important thing was shared cultural assumptions.

But this is all reinforced by another British trend – towards secrecy and cavalier government. I always tell Americans that they have a Freedom of Information Act – an act empowering people to read confidential material – where we have an Official Secrets Act – to forbid precisely that. The whole assumption of British government is that 'they (the governed) wouldn't understand anyhow', and so there is a continuous attempt to actually seal the inner workings of goverment off from the possibility of social scrutiny and intervention.

5 DECEMBER

First snow of the winter. To club for some exercises. Found myself wanting to stay there all day in the unoccupied pool.

David Wilson came over in the evening to talk about War Child direction in America. Anthea out late at the War Child think-tank (held in studio).

Twenty years ago today I released Gavin Bryars's *Sinking of the Titanic, New & Rediscovered Musical Instruments* and *Ensemble Pieces* and my *Discreet Music* as the first four Obscure Records.

To Stewart (who's been at the Pentagon):

Assassins, of course, are sort of unbeatable. All normal assumptions about war assume that the enemy will finally give up at a certain level of attrition. Of course this isn't true of afterlife-promised fundamentalists, who are only too pleased to fight for glory. The same was so with the Japanese in WW2 (and that's the basis on which van der Post justifies the use of atomic weapons – otherwise they just would never have stopped fighting). The mujahidin in Bosnia are a threat, though, because they provide Serbs and Croats with an easy ideological target: 'You see – we told you these Bosnians were fundamentalists.'

One of the interesting and not-much-remarked aspects of this war has been the use by all three governments of paramilitaries and militias. The Serbs, of course, were using the Bosnian Serbs in this way – which is why Milošević has been able to keep his distance and come on as Mr Peace by disowning them. Even within the Bosnian Serbs, the most ruthless fighting groups (which, in turn, the 'official' Bosnian Serbs shrug their shoulders about) have been the private militias – such as

265

Arkan's Tigers. The Croats have HOS, an extreme-nationalist neo-Nazi fighting force funded by Aryan-nation types around the world, and then the Bosnians have the mujahidin. For each army, these zealots are the best trained, the most fearless and the most ruthless. And it is impossible, as you can understand, for each army not to use them.

I wonder if this is another aspect of the future of 'low-intensity conflicts': the deployment of semi-official 'pit-bull' units that do the really dirty work while the 'officials' sit round wringing their hands: 'We just can't keep them under control. . .'

Interestingly, low-intensity war is in some sense a return to medieval warfare. I read once that Richard the Lionheart, who led the English army for 18 years (I think from the age of 14 till his death at 32!) fought only three major 'proper' battles. Armies avoided set-piece battles, because they were unpredictable and very expensive, and could lead to the breakup of a force that may have taken years to assemble. Instead they favoured seige, terrorism, looting, raping and pillaging – the usual stuff – in the hope of forcing surrender. The army as a fighting force was just a back-stop.

On another subject not-quite entirely: I may have mentioned that one of the things that War Child is looking at now is clearance of land-mines – one of the most pernicious outcomes of low-intensity conflict. There are estimated to be 100 million lying around now – and their victims are disproportionately children, who tend to wander where others haven't. So we've been looking at the whole technology, and one of the most depressing aspects is the total imbalance between the ease of sowing the mines (for which, of course, all sorts of clever high-tech machines exist) and the near-impossibility of ever finding them again.

Most mines now are non-metallic, small, easily concealed – and the only way of getting rid of them is either by manual search or with these elephantine earth-thrashers: basically tanks with huge flails that beat the earth and set off the mines. Both these methods are expensive and fallible – estimates are that clearance costs about $2,000 per mine.

Well, the problem is all to do with finding the things. Now, the point of all this! Recently there has been proposed a new theory of how smell works. I won't go into it in detail, but suffice it to say that it is a 'vibration' theory (rather than a 'shape' theory). We respond, it seems to molecular vibrations. Now, it looks possible that, on this basis, it might be feasible to construct smelling-machines that are capable of extremely high-resolution searching for explosives, and these might not have to be very expensive. If this could work, it's a huge breakthrough. I wonder if any of your Pentagon-ists know anything about this?

6 DECEMBER

The paradox of modern painting: the message, again and again, is 'Hey look – anyone can do it!' But the market of course depends on exactly the opposite message: 'Hey look – this is special.' [See page 330: Duchamp's *Fountain*.] It is literally true to say that I could make a Damien Hirst painting – in fact I did make 250 of them in an afternoon for Pagan Fun Wear (which Damien signed) – and so could almost anyone else. Or they could get someone to do it for them. So why pay Damien however much it costs for his? I don't mean people shouldn't, but I wonder exactly why they do.

Possible reasons:

Reliquary – *this* is the one touched by Him and therefore has a special intrinsic value, an unquantifiable something that will improve me. The St Anthony's Scrotum syndrome.

Currency – this is an item of currency in exactly the way that a particular piece of paper with a picture of the queen and the right watermark is. An item of currency is defined as something which we agree doesn't have intrinsic value (a £100 note is only a piece of paper) but which has conferred value. It has the value of our confidence in it. That means that the partners in the transaction have constructed a set of cultural agreements that allow them to agree that this thing can be used as a value-symbol. I give it to you for £100 of goods, and you accept it because you know you can pass it on to someone else within the same set of cultural understandings.

267

None of us actually holds the thing up to aesthetic scrutiny: 'Er, sorry – I don't really like the design on that one: I can only give you £36 for it.' The difference with this form of currency, of course, is that it is very negotiable – *you can change its value.*

History – this is the one that was there at the time, the first of its kind! This is the Magna Carta of modern dot painting, the Lincoln's axe of dissected-beast sculpture. Look at it and think: it all started here. Closely related to reliquary, but without the metaphysical overtones of contained value. The value is in the event of which this is the remaining physical evidence.

Psychology – investing this much money in such a thing is good for me. It will make me think about the future. It is an investment in new thinking.

Philanthropy – I think art is a Good Thing and I register my commitment to it by supporting this artist.

Society – I would like to be part of the community of people who buy pictures.

Howie B. came over in the afternoon. We talked about the new U2 record. There's a lot of chefs in that kitchen – he, Flood, Nellee, and the band.

I predicted a possible future: that all the bright beginnings would get submerged in overdubs and then have to be rediscovered in the resulting Irish stew. I suggested that he keeps a separate, covert, version of the record – the Howie B. version, consisting of anything he likes as it happens – which, during some dark night of the soul, he can pull out and play to them – something clear, bright and bold. The thing they want from Howie is his weird sense of space, his ability to leave things alone and let the listener do the work.

We did some jamming together, him playing the H3000 in a way nobody else would – using the input-level control as a distortion unit, for instance. His openness and ability to completely immerse are impressive.

Dinner in evening with Peter and Joyce Rudge, Dave Bates and Amira, his Bosnian fiancée, at La Famiglia. Talking about JAMES, their next record.

Jim and Dave have been doing some good work, trying to push the envelope. The problem is that they have made a music that doesn't necessarily include Tim: it's good stuff, but hard for a singer. There's rhythmic and sonic drama, but little *harmonic* drama for him to respond to. What singers like are shifts of harmonic gravity which they can either float above or succumb to. There's two different polar types of singer: floaters and divers. Tim tends to be a floater – some of his best effects happen when there's a strong vortex set up in the music and he manages to stay in the same place. Gospel singers tend to be divers – sucked down and thrown back up by the music, or engaged in great passions of will and surrender with it. But for either of these you need something other than a harmonic plateau.

The other part of my conversation concerned other vocals. I said I thought that we had learned three things from African music. The first was pushed rhythm, which doesn't occur in traditional Western music much; the second was flattened scales; and the third was call-and-response.

Unfortunately people don't recognize the importance of call-and-response. This is because most songs are now written by the people who plan to sing them, and for them the picture is normally complete when they're in it (and uninteresting to them if they're not). But a listener likes more than this. The backing vocals, the response, are the voices of society: whether gossiping (as in 'Is she really going out with him?' 'I don't know – let's ask her!') or affirming (as in 'Amen!' and 'Yeah, yeah, yeah') or warning ('Foolish little girl . . .'). Even songs that are 'personal' – where one doesn't want to invoke the conspiracy implied by group singing – can use the voices of conscience or of the various alter-egos. They turn monologue into conversation. Interesting to speculate on what other roles backing vocals could play: the voice of speculation ('what would happen if . . .')? of precise measurement? of disagreement? of doubt? of alternative ways of saying something (like shadow possibilities, parallel stories)?

I would like to do a systematic study of *hit* songs over the last 30 years. I am sure that at least 80% of them have second vocals in some form or another. But I would bet that not 30% of all recorded songs use backing vocals. Asked Jameos to research this.

I suggested trying to capitalize on the work that J. and D. have done by now adding to it the band's other strength – developing things by improvisation. The best way to do this would be for the two of them to get out of the picture for a while and leave the rest of the band to start improvising against their tracks. They'd need to transfer the stuff on to eight-track, so they could take out the bass if necessary – if they needed to make a different change. A good strategy for starting improvising would be to arrange ways for people to drop in and out – instead of everyone playing all the time, which again plateau-izes.

7 DECEMBER

Carol McNicoll and Beckett came over to play with Photoshop.

Later a long meeting with JAMES, discussing strategy for their recording. Surprised to discover that they hadn't been all in the same room since the Westside sessions. They have a list with something like 30 pieces on them. I reiterated the dinner conversation. I also suggested (on the importance of backing vocals) that they start working with a Digitech Vocalist,* so perhaps Tim will have two mikes – one for his normal voice and one for creating instant harmonies via the Vocalist. Pleasant meeting, with the music playing quietly in the background as we talked – anything that caught our attention, we then talked about (a good test – music interesting enough to stop the conversation).

* An intelligent digital harmonizer which produces voices accompanying a singer.

On the e-mail this morning: a message from someone at NYU saying that Jaron had been giving a talk and had said that, though I was his dear friend, unfortunately I believed in computers like many other otherwise clever people. What can this mean, I wonder – expecially after the slamming I gave the industry in *Wired?*

Responded to Tom Sutcliffe's piece in the *Independent* about my Turner Prize speech. [See page 365: Letter to Tom Sutcliffe.]

Swordfish in a marinade of anchovy sauce and pumpkin-seed oil with cayenne, with two whole bulbs of garlic. Do I stink to everyone else?

Rationality is what we do to organize the world, to make it possible to predict. Art is the rehearsal for the inapplicability and failure of that process.

8 DECEMBER

No entry.

9 DECEMBER

No entry.

10 DECEMBER

Irial: 'What would happen if you dug out of the universe?'

Me: 'I don't know – no one's ever been there.'

Irial: 'Somebody told me that a whole new world would be there.'

Me: 'Did they tell you what would be in that world?'

Irial: 'God would be there! And bears. Just bears and God.'

Meanwhile, on the religious news this morning – which everyone should listen to if they want to glimpse the far horizons of human nuttiness – an item saying that the Iranians are now claiming that the sighting at Fatima was actually of *Fatima* – who is apparently a Muslim saint. There is now an international incident brewing because the Portuguese government is refusing visas to Arabs anxious to make pilgrimage to the place.

A beautiful porcelain sculpture, obviously hollow, completely sealed. On its base, the words 'Inside here is my darkest secret.'

11 DECEMBER

Overheard on Westbourne Grove (scene: burly traffic warden filling in ticket. Distraught-looking young lady standing beside car):
Him: 'You must be Libra.'
Her: 'Sagittarius.'

In the health club: Björk, Elvis Costello and my neighbour Tom.

Tom and I talked in the sauna about land-mines in Angola (he was just filming there).

Drew unable to travel to Turin because of plane cancellations.

To Stewart:

Very interesting piece in the *Tribune* today about the preparations US troops are making for Bosnia, and strangely similar to the things Fitzgerald mentioned in *Fire Over the Lake* (which I read 20 years ago now!). She describes how, before the Tet Offensive, the Vietcong got their men together and told them there would be deaths, showed them the coffins in which they'd be taken back to their villages. This article described a slightly dilute version of the same thing – a colonel saying to his troops, 'Hands up those who think there won't be casualties?' No hands go up, and he says, 'Right – there'll be casualties.' And so on. An interesting new sense of realism, not so confident and gung-ho as 30 years ago.

12 DECEMBER

To Turin very early in the morning. Arrived at the huge Egyptian Museum – freezing and cavernous, but the second largest collection of Egyptian artefacts in the world (after Cairo, before the British Museum). Especially impressed by the very early things – beautiful tools from the pre-Dynastic era. Slate scrapers and blades, perfectly shaped to the hand, but carved as fish and birds. I'd love to have one of those always in my pocket. Also some very early cave paintings. Completely African in feeling, and looking just like Basquiat (the most recent great cave painter).

My space was a small rock temple that had been transported in large sections from Nubia before the flooding of the valley by the Aswan project. The temple was shaped, in plan, like a squared-off shamrock – just 17 ft deep and about the same across the two bottom 'leaves'. The door, a 3-ft-deep hole in the rock, was where the stalk would be. The walls were carved, and at the back two half-formed seated figures appeared out of the stone, like mineral ghosts. Either they had not been finished or their fronts had been hacked away. The space was about 7 ft high, but the original height was more like 5 ft 6 in, I think. What an intimate, deep atmosphere! Imagine walking out of the brilliant sun into this tiny cave.

The director, Signora Donadoni – 50-ish, swept-back silver hair in a tight bun, wing glasses – affected a severe no-nonsense demeanour, but kind and hospitable. She and Luigi, a very sympathetic scientist at the museum, took me down to the deepest storerooms – years of undisturbed dust, thousands of boxes of pottery shards and embalmed things. There I found some useful bits and pieces.

I had to, because nothing I'd planned to work with (aside from the white pyramids that we brought with us) was actually there. So it was a big improvisation, in rather difficult circumstances. No electricity – the main light switch (controlling the 400 megawatts of blinding neon) located somewhere in the next city. So it was either total darkness or total blindness.

In the evening, when they kicked me out of the museum, it looked bleak. I watched some housewives stripping on cable TV in the hotel, but they were too normal (in a *Sun* page 3 way) to catch my imagination. They all had that carefully manicured pubic hair, like little goatee beards. Also watched a completely nutty religious character – a South African televangelist who could probably turn the pope to atheism.

13 DECEMBER

In at 6.45 to start work again – but the lovely Francesca, my security guard, couldn't switch any power on. But this was interesting: I had almost an hour working in early-morning gloom, and all I could concentrate on was concept and composition (it was all I could see). So this actually improved the thing a lot. I ended up using three of the early-19C models of temples set at off angles (Signora Donadoni described them rather disapprovingly as 'scenographic') and with Barcelona lamps inside them so they glowed and flickered. Behind them, powerful deep-red light, picking out the stone ghosts on the wall. A long, tapering ladder lying flat across the floor. The grid of white pyramids lit by magenta and green lights. Effect of dream-moonlight. I thought it lovely, but I'm not sure anyone else did, except Luigi and his wife (who said, 'Ah – beautiful!' and clapped her hands when she saw it).

Phoned Drew from the airport to suggest some further changes to it.

14 DECEMBER

To studio early, working on Koan and Photoshop, and then got into another variation of the arrangement of 'Hedex' for JAMES. All this going swimmingly until Jameos appears at the door to remind me that there is an interview – now. I was furious – furious with myself for having agreed to do it. Then I remembered that the rest of the day was blocked out with things to do, so no more fun. Fed up, but fortunately the first interviewer was a pleasant and bright Berliner, who apologized profusely for the few daft questions he was obliged to ask (eyes lowered: 'My publisher wants to know if Roxy Music is going to have a reunion') and otherwise asked interesting ones. Then another interview, with a very English Frenchman, Hugo Cassavetes. Also an intelligent, probing person. I felt I owed both of them a bit more time than I actually gave them.

Jameos gave me a top-30 chart where he'd marked all the songs with backing vocals. In the top 30, only three without.

Then to the club for a swim. Into the steam-room and there's Björk lying fast asleep on the bench. She woke as I came in and we sat chatting for 15 or 20 minutes about my observation that Icelanders have good diction – particularly for labial-dental fricatives. Her theory: they enjoy *hardness* – so I told her about the Alan Lomax book *Folk Song Style and Culture*. She shrieked when I told her that one of the findings was that wide-interval singers (like herself and the Bayaka pygmies) generally occurred in anarchic, nomadic, non-hierarchical social groups, whereas close-interval singers were typically found in caste-ridden societies. We thought this was because, for an anarchic singer, every note should assert independence and freedom from history, whereas the caste singer moves cautiously and subtly through the intricacies of fine distinctions, preset palettes of possibilities. Also invited me to a New Year's party in Iceland – which she says is the biggest per-capita firework consumer in the world.

Then back for another interview with *PC Format* magazine with a very pleasant Irish guy. Interesting talking within a purely technical frame like that. I felt unusually doctrinaire, and demolished nearly every new-technology daydream in less than half an hour. [See page 352: Interview with *PC Format*]

Lunch with Mark Kidel, who seems to have been covering a lot of the same ground as me for the last 20 years. He wants me to take part in a film about The-Artist-As-Shaman,* which is an interesting and provocative subject, but he wants me to talk about how this applies to rock stars, which I find hard to warm to. I bristle at the words 'rock star'. Curiously, he worked with Alan Lomax for several months – also with Robert Farris Thompson (the only white man in *Who's Who in Black America*).

Then on to see George Sluizer's film *Crimetime*, which I found bizarre, brilliant and corrupt. Strong word – but it kept coming into my mind, so I write it down. Dave Stewart – the other proposed composer – described it as 'sick'. The archness,

* In 1978 I took part in a conference in New York where I argued for the idea of the artist as a type of contemporary shaman – someone whose job it is to generate a critical mass of confidence by whatever means. Implicit there is the idea that the artist's job is to convince the audience – not herself but them. This suggests a certain detachment from the process by which she does that. This was a very unpopular idea, because artists were at that time >>

campness, of the film is very disturbing. I really don't know what to think about it, or whether I want to do it. The sets and the cast (especially Pete Postlethwaite and Karen Black) are totally brilliant.

Afterwards I met Tim Booth to go to Turnkey to check out the new Digitech Vocalizer. On the way, I tried to explain my feelings about the film. He said, 'It must be a surprise for you to find that you have not only morals but reservations.' It is a surprise, in fact.

At Turnkey we tried out the Vocalizer – an instant inspiration device. I'll get one, for sure. They should too. Also the Waldorf Wave synthesizer, which sounds completely gorgeous but costs five grand. It's a really *musical* instrument, but I'd have to think hard about it at that price. The price of something is what it costs financially multiplied by what it costs in learning time. So you have to make a calculation. And I could see myself getting lost in this one for several months.

>> supposed to be sincere and not manipulative, but it stuck with me. Or I stuck with it. The term 'confidence trick' has a bad meaning, but it shouldn't. In culture, confidence is the currency of value. Once you surrender the idea of intrinsic, objective value, you start asking the question 'If the value isn't in there, where does it come from?' It's obviously from the transaction: it's the product of the quality of a relationship between me, the observer, and something else. So how is that relationship stimulated, enriched, given value? By creating an atmosphere of confidence where I am ready to engage with and perhaps surrender to the world it suggests. [See page 374: Miraculous cures and the canonization of Basquiat.]

In the evening with Anthea to a funny party at the Belvedere in Holland Park for the Go! Discs party. Table with Bill, David, Anne and Michelle, Andy Macdonald and Renée, Roger Ames, Tony Crean and a jovial lawyer, Tony Russell. Proposed medical version of Chris Burden: at the entrance to the gallery, a huge bowl of tablets. You take one. All you know is that, among the 25,000 tablets are 50 containing E and one containing cyanide.

15 DECEMBER

E-mail link fixed. Seventy messages waiting to be answered. Groan.

To Stewart (re the creation of value):

New measures of value. Well, one of the things I think artists (and other shamanic figures) keep doing for us is charging up different areas of the world with value. Things that we thought we didn't want, or things that we didn't even notice we had, are suddenly 'charmed', and become expressive, valuable. This is an analogy to the idea of discovering 'soul' in everything – the basis of animist religions.

Think of 'distortion', for instance – all the things that technology does which we didn't want it to do. Think of how we learn to read 'distortion' as resonant with new types of meaning – so the grain of 8mm film comes to mean urgency, amateurishness, the invaluable unrehearsed moment caught. The overload of a guitar comes to connote the idea of breaking the frame of the equipment, doing something that can't be contained – and this adds a whole new side to one's expressive palette, because one can now juxtapose things that can be contained against things that 'can't' (inverted commas because of course such a usage is an artifice now – as all these usages become). And the artifice part is another interesting transition – when something moves away from being 'byproduct' or 'spin-off' or 'accidental side-effect' and becomes instead part of the available vocabulary, but still retaining some of the resonances of its accidental origins.

All of these processes add value. In fact they create value by conferring it where it has never been before. This seems to me an essentially human attempt to not take the world for granted – to try to look at everything as though it exists for purposes that we might not yet have discovered or noticed.

My friend Peter Schmidt used to talk about 'not doing the things that nobody had ever thought of not doing', which is an inverse process – where you leave out an assumption that everybody has always made and see what happens (e.g. music has to be made of intentionally produced sounds was the assumption that Cage left out). In that version of this process, you discover a value in the absence of something – in fact you

277

discover that the absence of something is the revelation of something else (Buñuel, the film-maker, said, 'Every object conceals another' – a message that I often relay in the studio when overdubbing starts).

E-mail from Tom Sutcliffe, asking if he could quote from my letter in his review of John Barrow's *The Artful Universe*. We talked for a while about theories of art and culture – he wondered about the possibility of a sentient species without anything equivalent to culture.

Letter to George Sluizer:

Thanks for the chance to see your film yesterday. I have to say that it is one of the most disturbing experiences I have ever had in a cinema. The film is brilliant in many ways: the sets and the casting particularly impress, and Karen Black is astonishing and totally compelling, and Postlethwaite is hauntingly nasty. But the feeling of the film is so dark and weird that I really don't know what to make of it. To be honest with you, I'm really not sure how much further into the psyche of these exceptionally sick people I wish to delve. Nonetheless, I will, as suggested, compile some things for you to listen to, and I'll send those off to you early next week.

At present I think somehow that Dave may be a better choice for this movie than me – his highly developed sense of irony may be closer to the mood of the film. I think I might take it all a bit too seriously. . .

Anthea out this evening with Lin. We haven't had dinner together – just the two of us – since Monday.

Comedy on TV. The Steve Coogan piece ('Natural Born Quizzers') was brilliant – modern drama at its best.

Reading *Jihad vs. McWorld* by Benjamin R. Barber. The contention: that fundamentalism and post-modern rootlessness arise from the same socio-economic forces, and that they both, in their separate ways, leave out the concept of *citizenship* – the freely entered into, not-for-profit, pragmatic conversation which is the basis of democracy.

Talked to Dave Stewart, and read the letter to him. He was also thinking about the movie – impressed, but felt it needed to be undermined by kitsch: muzak rather than music. He also thinks there are structural problems with it. I never spot things like that.

In the afternoon worked on new piece, 'Caribbean Ox Dance', then in evening to Clerkenwell to the studio of Angus Fairlie and Sarah Lucas for a performance by ABANDABANDON, who mime to loops. The show started an hour late, but in the meantime I talked at length with Marc Quinn, who is reading the John Barrow book. We talked about my Turner speech observation – that there are so few intelligible and interesting books about art as a biological activity. I said I probably had them all – and that in total they occupy about 20 inches of shelf space. I told him Morse Peckham's thesis: that art is the way in which we rehearse for uncertainty and learn to endure 'cognitive tension' – thus balancing the human drive to classification and control whatever the cost. I also told him about the thought experiment in Arthur Danto's *Transfiguration of the Commonplace*, where 12 artists of completely different ideological persuasions end up exhibiting identical square, red canvases. Nice chap – not 'arty': articulate, open.

I left there after the 'band' had done two numbers – shared a car with Georgia Byng and Marc and a guy called Jason, who said he'd found the performance really depressing. I said that while at art school I took exception to nearly all paintings, but after leaving discovered that in fact I enjoyed nearly all paintings, and this was sort of how I feel about going out – since I do it quite rarely.

On to join Anthea and David Phillips for dinner at W11. David giving us some inside on the Balkans negotiations – how Mladić had greeted the Dutch troops in his office in Srebrenica. There was a small pig sitting on the office table. Mladić took out a knife and cut its throat, and, as the blood gushed out, told the Dutch commander that this was what the Muslims could expect.

D. P. said that Milošević, negotiating at Dayton on behalf of the Bosnian Serbs, didn't show their delegation the plans for the partition of Sarajevo until 15 minutes before the deal was initialled. Upon seeing them, one of the Bosnian Serb leaders fainted.

Apparently Milošević – that crafty, disgusting fundamentalist – has made a deal with the Americans that all files connecting him to genocidal activities should be buried. This was the price of his becoming the great peacemaker. It's too disgusting: like expecting the Czechs and Poles and Jews to sit down with Hitler in 1945 and sign a deal with him (a deal where he gets most of Czechoslovakia and Poland and is entitled to 'resettle' any Jews or Gypsies he didn't succeed in frying).

D. P. was in the Balkans taking round a deputation of diplomats to study the Kosovo problem. Kosovo is almost completely ethnic Albanian, but Serbia claims (and dominates) the territory and has purged Albanians from all official or prestigious posts – teachers, doctors, etc. Conditions are terrible, and the Serbs have been increasing the pressure in the hope that the Kosovars would fight back. But their leader is what D. P. calls 'a Gandhi-style pacifist' who has held things together against all the odds, and has frustrated the Serbian plan with non-violent protest.

Found two good pieces of broken ladder in the street.

17 DECEMBER

To studio with girls for much of the day. Home for evening, watching *The Beatles Anthology* with Anthea. Interesting to notice how a lot of those quite weak songs have that ring of total authenticity now. I bought an old book about Picasso's paintings of the twenties and thirties. The text was by Tristan Tzara. There were 20 plates, and 14 of them were absolutely the worst paintings I've ever seen. The other six were among the best. And I kept looking at this book and thinking, 'Didn't he know? Or didn't he care? Which was it? Did he just think, "Oh, let other people decide. I just do it – you make of it what you like."' Or did he really not see a difference?

Or did he think that his judgement was no more reliable than anyone else's – that he had no particular basis on which to choose or dismiss a picture?

The Beatles' message was 'Look: we can do anything – and make it work!' So the work becomes cradled within (and assessed in terms of) a process of creative improvisation in which the whole culture is at that moment engaged. And improvisations are very forgiving – entered into in the spirit of 'What's to lose?'

'All You Need is Love', performed for the first global satellite link-up, must have been a great moment. Funny to think that only a few years before that we'd all clustered round the only Catholic TV in the neighbourhood to see the new pope (John XXIII). And my Auntie Rene fell to her knees before the TV.

Back to studio at 10.00 p.m. to write and work on Photoshop. It occurs to me that you could make a Koan-like visual experience – a self-guiding ride through Photoshop space, where each state on the journey is a filter-modulation from the previous state. Did a series of 48 'frames' from such a journey ('Me as a girl'), sliding in and out of figuration and abstraction. Some of the frames very economical – at 10 pixels per inch – and others monochromatic. Advantage: since nothing is being backed up, the computer can operate much faster. All it does is apply sets of rules iteratively, but not synchronously.

18 DECEMBER

No entry.

19 DECEMBER

The good news: all over Europe, in Israel, in Russia and even in America, the rabid right is losing credibility – Haider, Le Pen, Zhirinovsky, Netanyahu: are all lagging from last year. The bad news: except in England, where half-mad ideologues now form a large part of the government.

And the 'opposition': what are they actually opposing? Only the fact that they aren't the government.

Surely the most important thing now is to change the conversation — make the Liberals and Labour the two main parties (with the Tories as the third party, the outsiders). If the Libs got into second position they'd soon make it to first (so many Conservative votes would transfer to them if they were perceived as having a chance). And at least that would be an original position in my lifetime.

The only exciting thing about an election is not that Labour might win, but that the Cons might disappear and be replaced by the Liberals, and the old slanging match would change. So the important thing is for people to vote for whoever (whether Lib or Lab) is most likely to win in a given area, to force the Cons into third place. Slogan:

'CHANGE THE CONVERSATION – LEAVE OUT THE TORIES.'

Whatever you now find weird, ugly, uncomfortable and nasty about a new medium will surely become its signature. CD distortion, the jitteriness of digital video, the crap sound of 8-bit – all these will be cherished and emulated as soon as they can be avoided.

It's the sound of failure: so much of modern art is the sound of things going out of control, of a medium pushing to its limits and breaking apart. The distorted guitar is the sound of something too loud for the medium supposed to carry it. The blues singer with the cracked voice is the sound of an emotional cry too powerful for the throat that releases it. The excitement of grainy film, of bleached-out black and white, is the excitement of witnessing events too momentous for the medium assigned to record them.

Note to the artist: when the medium fails conspicuously, and especially if it fails in new ways, the listener believes something is happening beyond its limits.

Tim Cole, Jon Pettigrew, Jameos, Anthea, Rob Partridge for meeting about release of Koan. 'GENERATIVE MUSIC' name agreed.

Darla calls Melanie 'Lemony'.

20 DECEMBER

This morning I found a place selling empty capsules for making your own tablets.*

About *The Transformation of War*, which Stewart sent:

I've been reading the van Creveld book, for which enormous thanks. It is a brilliant work – I like very much his analysis of the history – from war between nobles, to total war, to low-intensity conflict. And some of his reversals of 'common sense' are immediately 'aha!'-making – for instance the idea that empires were actually sustained (not lost) because of their remoteness, because that was what made it impossible for the 'subjects' to take the conflict to the heart of the empire – which is now no longer the case.

Another point he makes which I find very telling is that low-intensity conflict is likely to arise between very unmatched opponents. A poor country can't face down a rich one on the battlefield, and therefore relocates the struggle – into the population.

And lastly (for now, though there are many others) for me it's interesting to see the failure of America in Vietnam as the result of a lack of ruthlessness – of a liberal and humanitarian conscience weakening the drive to uncompromising war. So perhaps this reflects well on the Americans, this apparent failure.

* These empty capsules are for 'Tudging Powder'. The idea for this dietary supplement comes from an article by Colin Tudge in which he discussed the diet of early humans. He pointed out that even until recently the nomads of Africa and Australia enjoyed a diet of several thousand different foodstuffs – compared to the dozen or so that they settled down to when they were 'civilized' – and his theory was that the human body evolved around that kind of diet: huge variety of items, irregular, smallish amounts of each, occasional gluts. So my idea was to pound into a coarse powder everything edible, plus some grit and dirt – and then put that into capsules. It has to be coarse so that you get uneven amounts of everything, different from day to day. Further modifications: throw dice to decide how many tablets you take in a day, or fill the tablets with different quantities of Tudging Powder – from empty to very full.

283

21 DECEMBER

Nick from Turnkey brought over the Waldorf Wave and the Digitech Vocalist. The Waldorf requires attention and patience. The Digitech is pure inspiration.

Redesign 13-amp plugs with inbuilt erasable appliance labels.

Office party.

Dancing all night with the Dutch team – Wilhelmina and Michelle and Anton (briefly), then joined by Veronica, Hannah, Andrew, Ben. Great dancing with Hannah. Everyone said we have exactly the same style. Dancing, like handwriting style, may be genetically transmitted?

Met and talked to Catherine from Unicef about their land-mine programme. Bill Leeson said that there were now land-mines disguised as child's toys. Logical: land-mines are designed to maim rather than kill (since a maimed victim is a bigger burden than a dead one), and who better to maim than kids, who thus become burdens for that much longer? David Wilson told me that there is a big research project going on at Lawrence Livermore to develop detection devices. There is a proposal for us to visit there. The problem is that any detectors are foolable by decoys – all you have to do for each explosive device you plant is spray round a few thousand other little pills designed to confuse the detectors.

Peter Gabriel came. Talked about Disneyland with A. and me.

At the party, Rob Partridge said to me, 'You gave hope to other balding men.' My new epitaph: 'Co-wrote a couple of decent songs and went bald shamelessly.'

22 DECEMBER

Good dinner-party question (to an unknown neighbour): 'What *exactly* did you do today?'

The reason for enforcing altruistic styles of social behaviour is to do them for long enough to experience their rewards.

I watched some of the best of *Have I Got News for You*, which made me ache with laughter. 'And the odd one out is so-and-so, because the other three haven't got any eyebrows.' Paul Merton: 'So what are those things above Teresa Gorman's eyes? A pair of trained caterpillars?' Paula Yates cruelly ribbed for her falsies. Made me think that if men could extend their dicks they'd be carrying them round in wheelbarrows.

A sociological movement which claims that mugging is an essential expression of soul.

23 DECEMBER

Busman's holiday: indiscriminately accept every job anyone offers you. Let your life be structured entirely by deadlines and by what people want from you.

Kids' party in the studio – 28 children, a wizard and a few parents. Studio is great for parties – lots of room for people to run around, and good lighting. Anthea organizes; I do the lighting and ambience.

Showing Hannah how to use Photoshop.

Reading *The Transformation of War*.

24 DECEMBER

Worked in the studio. Printed out the whole text of the diary to date. To neighbours for a drink.

25 DECEMBER

Great morning excitement as the girls open their gifts. A Barbie horse and carriage for Darla that takes me about two hours to put together. I imagine all over the western hemisphere disgruntled unshaven fathers doing the same thing. And then no pissing batteries (but the Indian shop was open). Anthea and I decided to postpone presents for each other, but nonetheless she bought me some gloves, a key-locator (which goes off every time Darla laughs) and a book by the BMA about drugs and medicines, and I bought her a negative-ionizer/room-perfumer, a book about vitamins and minerals, and an electric car-perfumer.

Van Creveld: war is being pushed into corners where modern weapons don't work. So the effect of more sophisticated weaponry is to remove the conduct of war further away from the terms on which we prefer to fight it. Insecticides.

26 DECEMBER

Over to Kent for lunch and evening games with A.'s family. Thirteen people round the table. 'Clumps' very successful, as always, but a new variation in 'Poetry' also worked well (players each have the same question, but a different word to incorporate).

27 DECEMBER

Set up Andrée's computer for her, trying to strip away all the unnecessary nerdery so that it can work just as a simple word processor. Ended up with a model of how computers ought to present themselves. Her workplace is terrifying – a freezing caravan in the garden, full of books about Greek military campaigns and classical Roman writing, with power cables threading between precariously balanced jugs of milk and old copies of the *Spectator*.

Julian drove me back to London (I left before A. and the girls). I asked how people set up in private practice. A room in Harley Street can be rented for about £50 a morning. So anyone could set up there: just screw a plaque on the door and wait for customers. I started thinking about a production surgery: instead of people sending me demo tapes, they'd come to my surgery and we'd talk through their 'case'. 'I'd like you to try these backing vocals for a couple of weeks, then come back and tell me how you're getting on.' Or 'Trouble is, you need a bit more fibre in your diet. I suggest a full month of Captain Beefheart.'

28 DECEMBER

Rolf and Esther (new girlfriend) came to studio with two huge bouncy balls for the girls (like those in *The Prisoner*). We played football in the studio. Curious teams: Irial, who wanted to be a team on her own; Darla, who's on my team but gets the ball and lies on it; then Esther, who has a broken leg (skiing), and 6 ft 4 in Rolf forming team 3.

Styles of feet in a culture reflect styles of dance. African big-flat-firm-on-the-ground feet, dancing styles that 'get down' and pull to earth. Ballet is pointed and keeps as tenuous as possible a connection to the ground – as though earth is something to break free from. Interesting seeing the 'rootedness' returning in rap trainers – big, fat, heavy feet. Then the paradox of heavy platforms, which rise and root at once.

Hopelessly dreadful dance prog on BBC2 in the evening. So breathtakingly, overwhelmingly awful that I couldn't stop watching for a moment. Some of the worst dancing I've ever seen (dignified by Bach drivelling on in the background). Cringing. It was unforgettable. So much of modern dance is a reaction against something that no one else cares about anyway. Probably they were breaking all sorts of balletic rules and pushing the envelope in all directions – but the message isn't in that envelope anyway. It's like watching two theologians discussing Mary's virginity: you just don't care about the whole subject.

Sometimes I think that all I want is to rid the world of artists.

Wingy for dinner. She told the story of David Carson, a designer for *Raygun* magazine, who set a whole Bryan Ferry interview in 'Dingbat' font – illegible ornaments. There was a photo of Bryan and three pages of 'Dingbat'.

29 DECEMBER

All to Woodbridge to see Mum. Went for a walk with Roger and talked about music and recording.

Message from Bono on answering-machine: did we want to go to Sarajevo with Ali and him for New Year's Eve? Leaving tomorrow from Dublin in a Cessna Citation to Split, and then driving up through Mostar. We can't both go, because no nanny. And I like spending New Year's with A. But it's once in a lifetime – this is a moment in history. I faxed, saying I was tempted.

30 DECEMBER

Freezing cold.

Emma Nicholson goes Lib-Dem. It's amazing how rarely this happens. Why aren't politicians constantly changing allegiance?

Bono called from Dublin airport at 8.00 a.m., saying that plans had changed and he now had to fly immediately to Zagreb.

Anton for dinner in evening (Anthea at theatre with Wingy). Looking through the pictures in his book, I realize you're looking at a series of stills from the 'plays' that we subjects think we're in: 'Here's another performance of the play called me.' This is what makes celebrity photography different – these are people who've spent time in front of cameras and have made some decisions about what they're doing there, and in which way they'll help the camera to lie.

When we're looking through the pictures, Anton tells me stories about the sessions, about how the pictures happened. He should publish them with the pictures, but he thinks they subtract from the mystery of the pictures, from the viewer's freedom to project into the scene. But my taste is to make things as clear as possible and then to see if they still work, or to expose the simplicity of the trick so you realize that you (the viewer) make it work.

Oblique Strategy: 'Take away as much mystery as possible. What is left?'

Soon cigarettes will only appear in hip photographs (just as swords only appear in ceremonies). Plot ratio of people smoking in real life against those smoking in photos.

31 DECEMBER

The last day of the year.

Picture frames that have to be switched on to open up – so you choose to see a picture, and it has duration.

Talking with Elvis Costello in the steam-room about the difference between scored and played music. When music is generated by a group of people playing, everyone tends to play most of the time. With scoring, you're likely to use instruments when you need them. No one feels bad about standing round for three-quarters of an hour and then going 'bong' on a timp if that's what the score demands. This is why scored music is more 'colouristic' and contoured than most pop – whole sections come and go; the dynamic and timbral ranges are very broad.

Anthea's new unthinkable future: that nuclear radiation, in small doses, will be found to be good for you (this to be discovered when, 30 years hence, the inhabitants of Mururoa atoll are all in outstandingly vigorous good health).

Tomorrow I can go to sleep without having to write this diary.

Resolutions:
REDUCE: amount of paper in house
consumption of wine
random radio listening
INCREASE: visits to cinema
reasons for having parties
evenings with friends
proper cataloguing
time alone

APPENDICES

AMBIENT MUSIC

In 1978 I released the first record which described itself as Ambient Music, a name I invented to describe an emerging musical style.

It happened like this. In the early seventies, more and more people were changing the way they were listening to music. Records and radio had been around long enough for some of the novelty to wear off, and people were wanting to make quite particular and sophisticated choices about what they played in their homes and workplaces, what kind of sonic mood they surrounded themselves with.

The manifestation of this shift was a movement away from the assumptions that still dominated record-making at the time – that people had short attention spans and wanted a lot of action and variety, clear rhythms and song structures and, most of all, voices. To the contrary, I was noticing that my friends and I were making and exchanging long cassettes of music chosen for its stillness, homogeneity, lack of surprises and, most of all, lack of variety. We wanted to use music in a different way – as part of the ambience of our lives – and we wanted it to be continuous, a surrounding.

At the same time there were other signs on the horizon. Because of the development of recording technology, a whole host of compositional possibilities that were quite new to music came into existence. Most of these had to do with two closely related new areas – the development of the texture of sound itself as a focus for compositional attention, and the ability to create with electronics virtual acoustic spaces (acoustic spaces that don't exist in nature).

When you walk into a recording studio, you see thousands of knobs and controls. Nearly all of these are different ways of doing the same job: they allow you to do things to sounds, to make them fatter or thinner or shinier or rougher or harder or smoother or punchier or more liquid or any one of a thousand other things. So a recording composer may spend a great deal of her compositional energy effectively inventing new sounds or combinations of sounds. Of course, this was already well known by the mid-sixties: psychedelia expanded not only minds but recording technologies as well. But there was still an assumption that playing with sound itself was a 'merely' technical job – something engineers and producers did – as opposed to the serious creative work of writing songs and playing instruments. With Ambient Music, I wanted to suggest that this activity was actually one of the distinguishing characteristics of new music, and could in fact become the main focus of compositional attention.

Studios have also offered composers virtual spaces. Traditional recording put a mike in front of an instrument in a nice-sounding space and recorded the result. What you heard was the instrument and its reverberation in that space. By the forties, people were getting a little more ambitious, and starting to invent technologies that could supplement these natural spaces – echo chambers, tape delay systems, etc. A lot of this work was done for radio – to be able to 'locate' characters in different virtual spaces in radio dramas – but it was popular music which really opened the subject up. Elvis and Buddy and Eddy and all the others sang with weird tape repeats on their voices – unlike anything you'd ever hear in nature. Phil Spector and Joe Meek invented their own 'sound' – by using combinations of overdubbing, home-made echo units, resonant spaces like staircases and liftshafts, changing tape-speeds and so on, they were able to make 'normal' instruments sound completely new. And all this was before synthesizers and dub reggae . . .

By the early seventies, when I started making records, it was clear that this was where a lot of the action was going to be. It interested me because it suggested moving the process of making music much closer to the process of painting (which I thought I knew something about). New sound-shaping and space-making devices appeared on the market weekly (and still do), synthesizers made their clumsy but crucial debut, and people like me just sat at home night after night fiddling around with all this stuff, amazed at what was now possible, immersed in the new sonic worlds we could create.

294

And immersion was really the point: we were making music to swim in, to float in, to get lost inside.

This became clear to me when I was confined to bed, immobilized by an accident in early 1975. My friend Judy Nylon had visited, and brought with her a record of 17th-century harp music. I asked her to put it on as she left, which she did, but it wasn't until she'd gone that I realized that the hi-fi was much too quiet and one of the speakers had given up anyway. It was raining hard outside, and I could hardly hear the music above the rain – just the loudest notes, like little crystals, sonic icebergs rising out of the storm. I couldn't get up and change it, so I just lay there waiting for my next visitor to come and sort it out, and gradually I was seduced by this listening experience. I realized that this was what I wanted music to be – a place, a feeling, an all-around tint to my sonic environment.

After that, in April or May of that year, I made *Discreet Music*, which I suppose was really my first Ambient record (though the stuff I'd done with the great guitarist Robert Fripp before that gets pretty close). This was a 31-minute piece (the longest I could get on a record at the time) which was modal, evenly textured, calm and sonically warm. At the time, it was not a record that received a very warm welcome, and I probably would have hesitated to release it without the encouragement of my friend Peter Schmidt, the painter. (In fact, it's often been painters and writers – people who use music while they work and want to make for themselves a conducive environment – who've first enjoyed and encouraged this work.)

In late 1977 I was waiting for a plane in Cologne airport. It was early on a sunny, clear morning, the place was nearly empty, and the space of the building (designed, I believe, by the father of one of the founders of Kraftwerk) was very attractive. I started to wonder what kind of music would sound good in a building like that. I thought, 'It has to be interruptible (because there'll be announcements), it has to work outside the frequencies at which people speak, and at different speeds from speech patterns (so as not to confuse communication), and it has to be able to accommodate all the noises that airports produce. And, most importantly for me, it has to have something to do with where you are and what you're there for – flying, floating and, secretly, flirting with death.' I thought, 'I want to make a kind of music that prepares you for dying – that doesn't get all bright and cheerful and pretend you're not a little apprehensive, but which makes you say to yourself, "Actually, it's not that big a deal if I die."'

Thus was born the first Ambient record – *Music for Airports* – which I released on my own label (called Ambient Records, of course). The inner sleeve of that release carried my manifesto:

AMBIENT MUSIC

The concept of music designed specifically as a background feature in the environment was pioneered by Muzak Inc. in the fifties, and has since come to be known generically by the term Muzak. The connotations that this term carries are those particularly associated with the kind of material that Muzak Inc. produces – familiar tunes arranged and orchestrated in a lightweight and derivative manner. Understandably, this has led most discerning listeners (and most composers) to dismiss entirely the concept of environmental music as an idea worthy of attention.

Over the past three years, I have become interested in the use of music as ambience, and have come to believe that it is possible to produce material that can be used thus without being in any way compromised. To create a distinction between my own experiments in this area and the products of the various purveyors of canned music, I have begun using the term Ambient Music.

An ambience is defined as an atmosphere, or a surrounding influence: a tint. My intention is to produce original pieces ostensibly (but not exclusively) for particular times and situations with a view to building up a small but versatile catalogue of environmental music suited to a wide variety of moods and atmospheres.

Whereas the extant canned-music companies proceed from the basis of regularizing environments by blanketing their acoustic and atmospheric idiosyncrasies, Ambient Music is intended to enhance these. Whereas conventional background music is produced by stripping away all sense of doubt and uncertainty (and thus all genuine interest) from the music, Ambient Music retains these qualities. And whereas their intention is to 'brighten' the environment by adding stimulus to it (thus supposedly alleviating the tedium of routine tasks and levelling out the natural ups and downs of the body rhythms), Ambient Music is intended to induce calm and a space to think.

Ambient Music must be able to accommodate many levels of listening attention without enforcing one in particular; it must be as ignorable as it is interesting.

September 1978

Like a lot of the stuff I was doing at the time, this was regarded by many English music critics as a kind of arty joke, and they had a lot of fun with it. I'm therefore pleased that the idea has stuck around so long and keeps sprouting off in all sorts of directions: it comes back round to me like Chinese Whispers – unrecognizable but intriguing. Those early seeds (there were only four releases on the original Ambient Records label – *On Land* and *Music for Airports* by me, *The Plateaux of Mirror* by Harold Budd, and *Day of Radiance* by Laraaji) have contributed to a rich forest of music.

(1996)

AXIS THINKING

> An axis is a name for a continuum of possibilities between two
> extreme positions: so the axis between black and white is a scale of
> greys.

I can illustrate this idea by applying it to the description of haircuts.

Rather than only being able to say of someone's haircut that it is, for
example, masculine or feminine, we're as likely to want to say that it's quite
masculine, or quite feminine, or unisexual – somewhere in the middle.
When we do this, we acknowledge that the sexual possibilities of haircuts
don't just fall squarely at one or another of the polar positions – masculine
or feminine – but somewhere on the wide range of hybrids between them.
In fact we would feel constrained if we couldn't make descriptions in these
fuzzy, hybrid, terms.

If you were trying to describe a particular haircut, however, you'd probably want to say more than 'It's quite feminine', or some other comment
about its gender-connotations. You might also want to locate its position along other axes – for instance along the axis *neat* ↔ *shaggy* – 'It's
slightly shaggy' or 'It's very neat.' If that then gave you enough descriptive
language to say everything you could imagine ever wanting to say about
haircuts, you could locate every example you ever met somewhere on a
two-dimensional space – like this sheet of paper. So you could make a
kind of graph – *masculine* ↔ *feminine* on one axis, *neat* ↔ *shaggy* on
the other. On this graph, which is a simple cross in 2D space, any point
represents a particular position in relation to the four polar possibilities:

masculine ↔ *feminine*   *neat* ↔ *shaggy*

I call each of these points a cultural address. I could equally well call it
a stylistic address. It is the identification of a particular point in stylistic
space, a 'possible haircut'.

Those four terms still constitute an impoverished language in which to describe most haircuts, and to describe a wide range of possible haircuts we would need several others: *natural* ↔ *contrived*, *rebel* ↔ *conformist*, *wild* ↔ *civilised*, *futuristic* ↔ *nostalgic*, *businesslike* ↔ *bohemian*. Each of these polar pairs defines another axis along which any particular haircut could be located. And each of these exists as a 'dimension' in the hair-cut space, which now becomes multidimensional and no longer easily drawable on a sheet of paper.

We shouldn't forget that each of these poles has no absolute and for-all-time meaning but is also in its own slow motion, stretching the axis of which it defines an end-point this way and that. A really natural haircut, for example, is no haircut. But when we use the term 'natural cut' we don't think of someone with shaggy locks hanging over their eyes, but of someone who went to the hairdresser and said something like, 'Can you make it look sort of natural – a bit windswept?', as opposed to someone else who said, 'Can you do me a nine-inch beehive?'

And there is another complication: the resonances are quite local culturally. A man with very short hair in East London in 1985 would be assumed potentially dangerous and 'hard'. The same man in San Francisco would be thought gay.

And if we look more closely we see that many of the things that we would consider single qualities of hair are actually themselves multi-axial spaces. To describe hair colour, for example, needs much more detail than *dark* ↔ *light*. It needs an axis of redness, an axis of greyness, an axis of colour homogeneity, an axis of shine.

What strikes you as interesting when you begin thinking about stylistic decisions (or moral or political decisions) as being locatable in a multi-axial space of this kind is the recognition that some axes don't yet exist. For example, with hairstyles, as far as I know, there is not a *dirty* ↔ *clean* axis. That's to say, your hairdresser isn't likely to ask you, 'How dirty would you like it?' It's still assumed that there is no discussion about it: the axis has not been opened up. We would all want it 'as clean as possible'.

Peter Schmidt used to talk about 'the things that nobody ever thought of not doing'. A version of this happened in clothing fashion. There was recently a style – variously described as non-fit, un-fit and anti-fit (the name didn't stabilize) – which was to do with people wearing clothes that exist at the never-before-desirable end of the newly discovered axis *well-fitted* ↔ *badly fitted*. These clothes were deliberately chosen to look completely wrong. This was way beyond baggy, which was a first timid step along that axis. Baggy implies the message 'These are my clothes, but I like to wear them loose.' Non-fit says, 'These are someone else's clothes' or 'I am insane' or 'I cannot locate myself' or 'I don't fit.'

With punk, a brand-new axis opened up: *professionally cut* ↔ *hacked about by a brainless cretin*. As often happens, this appeared (and was intended) to be an anti-style style, and was shocking because we had never previously considered the possibility that the concept 'style' and the concept 'hacked about by a brainless cretin' could overlap one another. But, as usual, the effect was not to overthrow and eliminate the idea of style but to give it new places in which to extend itself. 'Hacked about by a brainless cretin' became not the death of hair-styling but the furthest outpost of a new continuum of possible choices about how hair could look.

This is a transition from polar thinking – the kind of thinking that says, 'It's either this or it's that', or 'Everything that isn't clearly this must be that' – to axial thinking. Axial thinking doesn't deny that it could be this or that – but suggests that it's more likely to be somewhere between the two. As soon as that suggestion is in the air, it triggers an imaginative process, an attempt to locate and conceptualize the newly acknowledged grey-scale positions.

I am interested in these transitions – these moments when a stable duality dissolves into a proliferating and unstable sea of hybrids. What happens at such times is that all sorts of things become possible: there is a tremendous energy release, a great burst of experimentation. Not only do the emerging possible positions on this new-born axis have to be discovered and experienced and articulated; they have to be placed in context with other existing axes to see what new resonances appear.

A good – and undigested – example of this process is the (apparently temporary) demise of state communism in Eastern Europe. It's extraordinary that when the Berlin Wall came down everyone assumed that the whole world was about to become one big market economy running on the same set of rules. What happened instead was that the old dualism *communism* ↔ *capitalism* was revealed to conceal a host of possible hybrids. Now only the most ideological governments (England, Cuba) still retain their fundamentalist commitment to one end of the continuum: most governments are experimenting vigorously with complicated customized blendings of market forces and state intervention.

An example of such a complicated blending is defence spending, which allows a government nominally committed to 'market forces' to have at its centre a completely intact command economy within which it can direct the flow of social resources. (See page 327: Defence.)

The period of transition is marked by excitement, experimentation – and resistance. Whenever a duality starts to dissolve, those who felt trapped at one end of it suddenly feel enormous freedom – they can now redescribe themselves. But, by the same token, those who defined their identity by their allegiance to one pole of the duality (and rejection of the other) feel exposed. The walls have been taken away, and the separation between inside and outside is suddenly gone. This can create wide-scale social panic: vigorous affirmations of the essential rightness of the 'old ways', moral condemnation of the experimentalists, 'back to basics' campaigns, all the familiar signs of fundamentalism.

Essentially, cultures wish to be able to control, or at least channel, such excitements and panics, turning what could be chaotic uncertainty into a power either for revolution or for consolidation. This is normally mishandled. Hostile propaganda campaigns are good examples of fundamentalism at work: they are designed to push the concepts of friend and enemy to extreme and unambiguous positions, and to cement a complete and unvarying identification between two different axes: *us* ↔ *them*, *friend* ↔ *enemy*.

301

Zones of Pragmatic Deceit are the social and mental inventions that exist to lubricate the friction between what we claim to stand for (i.e. simple polar pictures) and what we actually have to do to make things work (i.e navigate over networks of axes). These two are often quite different, as situations change much faster than the moral constructions that are supposed to describe them.

A good example of a ZPD is the American consulate in Antigua, which has an elaborate system of deterring, or at least preconditioning, black people entering the United States by subjecting them to bizarre humiliations in theoretically routine matters such as getting a visitor's visa.

The machinery of this humiliation is highly evolved: after several hours' queueing, applicants are required to address the ever-sneering, never-interested staff through a thick glass panel which has a small hole 7 ft from the ground, and a narrow slot at the bottom, about 3 ft from the ground. Since the staff routinely feign inability to hear or understand what anyone is saying, shrugging their shoulders and making to walk away to rejoin the interminable conversation they were having before, applicants are soon forced to their knees so that they can talk up through the little slot. This induction into American society sets the right tone: instead of 'Bring us your poor, your sick . . . etc.', it's 'On your knees and beg.'

This system exists because America – like Britain, which has evolved other forms of immigrant humiliation – is committed ideologically to the concept of open borders, but is increasingly worried by the prospect of huge immigrant communities, and has no new language (other than that of failure) in which to discuss a reassessment of position. This is the difficulty with polar thought systems: they offer only two possible options. You could say that the evolution of culture is the gradual rethinking of the whole matrix of axes: the discovery of new ones, of course, but also the careful tailoring – trimming and extending – of existing ones. For instance, the axis of 'possible human relationships' used to extend from 'total slave' to 'absolute ruler'. Fewer cultures are now willing to accept either of those extreme polarities as part of their vision of civilized behaviour, so you could say that this particular axis has been effectively shortened – focused down – to a narrower range.

What characterizes fundamentalism is a set of extremely narrow axes that allow almost no movement, no experimentation. And liberalism is perhaps the attempt to keep the axes as open as possible without incurring complete social fragmentation. The importance of symbolic behaviours like art and religion and sexual fantasy is that they allow us to experiment symbolically with new and even prohibited positions on the axial matrix – experiments that may be inconvenient, dangerous and divisive in 'real life'.

(1993)

STORY: BLACK MARKS

The airliner settled comfortably at its cruising altitude, and one by one the privacy walls slid down from the ceiling. Clem pressed the hydraulic controls on his seat and adjusted it into a chaise-longue configuration. He selected a deep amber filter for the window, and the room softened to a lovely deep peach colour – just how he liked it. He relaxed back on the plush seat, enjoying his few square feet of private airspace, and began idly playing with the surround system for the hi-fi. He had the wine open ready on the coffee-table, two crystal glasses provocatively waiting.

He wondered who it would be this time. That was a large part of the thrill, of course, never being quite sure. Eurasian was generally dependable (it ought to be, after all, with Doris Kloster and Jean-Paul Goude on the selection board!) and certainly preferable to PacRim American, with its over-bright inflatable starlets (although every now and again we all flew American Bimbo – as it was universally known – while vociferously claiming we'd done so only under protest: 'Couldn't get on to Eurasian; had to fly Bimbo. Should've seen the airhead I got – must have put her on for additional buoyancy'). But Eurasian prided itself on sophisticated, somewhat older, hostesses – women who'd received their extensive training at the famous Ryuichi Sakamoto College of Advanced Air Etiquette in Kyoto, and who were capable of intelligent conversation about art, literature and business.

There was a gentle rustling of the privacy wall. A soft, dark voice with an Eastern European tint whispered, 'Are you ready for a visitor?' Clem sat up, felt his stomach turn slightly. He didn't recognize the voice. It was a new one . . .

'Do come in,' he said, and she appeared, crouching slightly as she moved through the wallflap.

'I'm Marika,' she said, with a haughty but slightly mischievous inflection. 'I understand you'd like company.'

Clem looked up at her standing there – Latvian or Estonian, he suspected, and extraordinarily good-looking, with catlike green eyes, deep olive skin and high cheekbones. She wore a white Egyptian-style robe with gold embroidery, and gold sandals. Her skin, radiantly rich against the flowing robe, had been exquisitely demelanized into butterfly and dragonfly tattoos, which gambolled and frisked over her long arms and strong shoulders. Her hair was set in a high, tapered cone, with delicate spangles and ornaments cleverly woven into it. She wore large round earrings, thin gold circles framing fine translucent violet sheets of Jovian agate.

'Must have taken bloody hours,' thought Clem as he admired how well turned-out she was, and felt pleased that Eurasian was clearly starting to take him more seriously as a passenger.

'Do sit down,' he said, 'and please join me in a drink.'

Marika joined Clem on the chaise-longue, and he poured two glasses of white wine. Marika accepted her glass and looked over it at Clem.

'So what have you been up to this week?' she asked, her tone slightly hard-edged and demanding.

'Perfect!' thought Clem. He liked this part of the game a lot, and tended to prolong it.

'On Monday I chaired an important meeting with North-Eastern Scenarios about the organ futures market. I delivered three scenarios about transplant technologies, and Harriet Worthington, my colleague, talked about the newest developments in neural cloning. It went well, and I think we may have persuaded Bombay Organ to sign up . . .'

Marika cut in: 'Did you mention the paper that was in *Nature* last week about genetically modified sheep-kidneys? I think it was by Pataudi's team from Helsinki U.'

Clem looked up at her, slightly puzzled. 'I don't think I saw that one,' he said, and she shook her head and tutted, her eyebrows raised in exaggerated surprise. 'How could you have missed it? Isn't that supposed to be your job?' Her expression had now changed to derisive bafflement.

She stopped shaking her head and looked directly into his eyes. 'I think that's the first black mark against you . . .'

Clem cast his eyes downward, as he knew he should, to avoid the mildly stimulating embarrassment of her steady gaze. He continued talking, slightly more ruffled now.

'You're right. I really don't know how I missed it. Stupid of me. Well, anyway, on Tuesday I was on a network with Matsushita and Fujitsu and ATT-Philips, trying to arbitrate in their VR standardization talks. Problem at the moment is that the ATT-Phil system is unreadable to the Fuji, and produces strange distortions on the Mat. At a pinch you could probably use it, but it's not ideal. The Mat, on the other hand, being a 60/40-based system, sort of works on the ATT-Phil, but is useless on the Fuji. But Fuji have the biggest market share, so they think they can just bully their way to being the standard, whereas ATT-Phil are claiming Fuji have been manipulating the market. It's a bloody great mess, actually.'

'Don't swear,' said Marika sternly, 'and, anyway, who exactly were you talking to at Fuji? I assume you had Tetsuji Maezawa on the Net? From what I know of him, this is exactly his sort of problem.'

'Maezawa?' snorted Clem, laughing. 'Everyone knows he was fired from Fuji two years ago. You've got it a bit wrong there, I think.' He was pleased to get one up on her, but his victory quickly dissolved as he noticed her left eyebrow raising slightly imperiously, and saw a mocking smile turn one corner of her mouth upwards.

Again she glared at him, with a hint of a sneer as she spoke: 'Yes, he was indeed fired two years ago. At least you got that bit right. However, if you'd been paying any attention at all you'd have known that Maezawa is now consulting for Fuji again, and has been for at least two months. Fuji wouldn't tell you because they're a bit embarrassed that they had to beg him to come back at about three times his original salary. But it's absolutely common knowledge – at least to anyone with half a brain.'

Clem was crestfallen. He was sure she was right, and he genuinely hadn't known about Maezawa. He'd selected his net entirely from the personnel list that Fuji had sent him, and Maezawa certainly wasn't on that. 'Sod it,' he thought – 'that could have made a big difference.' All the other Fuji personnel were such dreadful yes-men you couldn't get anywhere at all with them. Clem looked at his feet.

Marika said languidly, reflectively, suggestively, 'I think that probably deserves two more black marks.'

'Oh good,' thought Clem – 'I thought so too.' So that made three black marks, plus the three unredeemed from last week's overnighter to Amsterdam, and then another two he'd got as a promotional thing for some credit card he'd signed up for.

'That gives me eight,' he said eagerly, and Marika feigned surprise, and widened her dark eyes.

'My, you really are in trouble,' she said, and looked at him with mock pity. 'I don't see how you're going to talk your way out of this mess.'

And indeed, after asking him a few more questions, and before they'd crossed Alaska, he'd collected two more black marks.

'Well,' she said, 'That makes ten – which is quite intolerable.' She stood up and looked sternly down at him. 'I think we'll have to deal with this matter right here and now.'

She turned away from him, then stood waiting, hands on hips.

'Start at the ankles,' she said.

(1993)

307

BLISS AND SCREENSAVERS

Bliss is a computer program invented by Greg Jalbert which enables a user to construct generators of visual patterns which unfold over time on the computer screen. The program offers control over types of mark, treatments of images, positioning on screen, and colour evolution. It is the closest thing to a 'musical' approach to visual-pattern generation that I have seen.

Jean Tantra designed a screensaver called Stained Glass. Its beauty is its subtlety of colour and detail but particularly that it evolves by 'digesting' and reconfiguring bits of itself. I made hundreds of combinations of it with other screensavers – using them as seeds to be eaten by SG – and offered the set to After Dark, the company that first released Stained Glass. They expressed no interest, and, as far as I know, no longer sell Stained Glass.

Both these works were interesting to me because they showed the possibility of using the computer as a medium in which self-generating systems could be allowed to grow, rather than simply a way of moving big blocks of preformed data around. This led me to the solution of the CD-Rom problem (i.e. that they were largely based on the wrong set of ideas about what computers were useful for) – see next appendix, CD-Roms.

CD-ROMS

(1) Everyone and his auntie wants to make a CD-Rom – not necessarily because they have some compelling artistic reason, but because they think everyone else is making one.

(2) Into this aesthetic South Sea Bubble, now blow the hot air of techno-hype which says that because x million players have been sold, and x hundred thousand CD-Roms, everything must be hunky-dory and going the right way. This might seem to be the case at first glance, but –

(3) Nobody is actually happy with their entertainment CD-Roms. The average number of plays is minimal. People enjoy *Myst*, which is a game, they like *Compton's Encyclopedia* and the Robert Wilson *Life of Stalin* and the *Street Map of America*, all of which are archives. They like their databases of photographic images or type fonts or other useful tools, which are also archives. But nobody I've met, except rabid fans, thinks that the things being sold as non-game 'entertainment' are at all entertaining, and I predict that soon everyone will just stop buying those. Of course there has been a market for the first few – there was nothing much else for rock fans to buy, after all – but I can't believe that this market will persist in any of its present forms.

I have a proposal for a completely new type of CD-Rom – something based not on loading the ROM with preformed chunks of material (music, videos, texts) through which a user navigates, but instead making a series of generators of new, unpreplanned material over which the user can choose various degrees of control. I base this on my experience of cellular automata (self-evolving virtual populations such as John Conway's 'Life' and Craig Reynolds's experiments on flocking behaviour), screensavers (such as Jean Tantra's Stained Glass and Greg Jalbert's Bliss), the graphic work of William Latham and Karl Sims (both of whom have invented programs for creating complex and beautiful 3D 'organisms' in the computer), autocatalytic set theory, games such as Sim Earth and Sim City, and the experiments that David Bowie has been making with text-generating systems.*

The great advantages of this idea are as follows:

(1) The computer is dealing with manipulating small sets of rules or recipes (i.e. the instructions responsible for generating material), rather than huge blocks of data (such as premade bits of video). This immediately gets round the sluggishness associated with any current CD-Rom experience. The computer is doing what it is good at – playing with numbers – rather than what it is manifestly hopeless at – being a surrogate video-player or hi-fi system. The amounts of data that the computer needs to handle are vanishingly much smaller, and therefore more of the computer can be engaged in doing something interesting: growing the whole thing anew before your eyes. I want to do something that's like juggling seeds rather than moving mature forests.

(2) Perhaps more importantly, this gets round the biggest limitation of Roms – that quite soon you've been through the archive and seen everything you're ever going to see, and your only choice is to see it in another order. My proposed CD-Rom offers an always new experience, since it does not rely on chunks of preformed material (which, being so memory-intensive, can only be few in number), but is always generating new material – limitlessly. There is no possibility of having an identical experience twice.

(3) It dispenses with the awful tedium of 'interactivity'. What I want is something that you could, if you chose, just switch on and allow to free-run, confident that it would self-generate something worth watching. But, coupled with this, you could make the whole

---

* And of course now I would add Koan into that list – see page 335: Generative music.

computer 'live' – so that any key you touch, any mouse movement you make, will cause a reaction in the program. Again, this is easy and fruitful to do with generators and tedious to do with playback systems, which is what most CD-Roms actually are. You don't need to spell out these connections, but allow them to be discovered. It should be sufficient to know that each control-source is connected to a particular parameter in the program, and, in any given scenario, is always connected to that parameter.

CELEBRITIES AND AID-GIVING

I've also been there, pouring scorn on those egocentric compassionates who make themselves feel better by 'helping out' people about whom they know nothing. In fact at the time of Live Aid I spent a lot of time saying why I thought the whole thing had been misconceived and was likely to do much more harm than good. I sneered publicly at Jerry Dammers in the *Guardian* about his 'Free Nelson Mandela' record. Fortunately dear Robert and Alfie (Wyatt and Benge) took me vigorously to task about that. Our conversation developed into a correspondence about aid in general, and when Anthea – someone for whom kindness comes without too many ideological complications – became involved with War Child I gradually U-turned.

Since then I've noticed how attitudes like the ones I held discourage people from getting involved with things. It's safer to keep your head down and just get on with your career. A lot of people quite reasonably wouldn't want to put up with the relentless sneering that Sting has undergone for his attempts to help someone, so they decide against doing anything, or decide to do it anonymously. A few months ago Linda McCartney sent 22 tons of her vegetarian burger mix to Sarajevo – then under seige – via War Child. She was adamant that the gift should be anonymous, probably because she knew the English press would crucify her for it – which they promptly did, when they found out several days later (after thousands of Bosnians had dined on her food). The implications of the criticisms were as follows:

she only did it for the publicity;

she just wants to make herself feel better for being so rich;

she wants to convert the world to Linda-Burgers – it's just marketing;

she couldn't get rid of the stuff in Britain.

A few years ago I could have imagined myself thinking all those things.

But there are two things to consider. First, even supposing all those things were true, what difference would it actually make? Does the possibility that someone's motives may be mixed invalidate what they do? Imagine you're drowning in a river. Fortunately someone has seen you and is about to throw a lifebelt out to you. But no! – someone else is holding her back, shouting, 'I don't think your motives are pure!'

Second thing to consider: if you really believe that celebrities shouldn't be doing this kind of thing, and you're going to use your public voice to try to embarrass them for it, then perhaps you owe the would-have-been recipients of their largesse at least an explanation. And 'I've succeeded in persuading people not to help you by ridiculing them in my daily newspaper and increasing our circulation by 20,000' is probably not going to do.

If people want real scandals, they might look into the hallowed practice of trading 'aid' for defence sales, as we did in Malaysia with the Pergau dam: 'You buy weapons from us, and we'll build environmentally disastrous dams for you.' What is happening here is quite clear: we use aid to subsidize our weapons industry (and our construction industry). I suggest that people who want to get upset about mixed motives might think about those rather than Linda McCartney's. [See page 327: Defence.]

I have retained some parts of my original position, though. I think a lot of aid is ill-considered, irrelevant, dissolved in bureaucracy, too late and sometimes actually harmful (an example of the last is considered in the essay 'Ethical Considerations of Carrying Capacity' in *Managing the Commons*, by Garrett Hardin and John Baden). But if you really expect would-be donors to make a complete financial audit and an impact study before they decide to give anything then you're not going to get much giving done. Of course we must to some extent take the good sense of charities on trust, and one way the press could do something useful here is by paying proper attention to how those charities deal with the money they get – and publicizing it, so that the straightforward rip-off schemes which give a tiny percentage of their takings to charity are exposed. We need a kind of *Which?* magazine for charities.

There is no argument that I can defend which says that people have to be involved with aid (and when we wrote to musicians asking for their help with War Child events we always tried to make it very clear that they could just say no, and no one would think any the worse of them for it). People are free to do as they choose, to involve themselves with whatever causes interest them, or with none at all. They don't have to justify their decision not to be involved. But, equally, they shouldn't be made fools of if they do get involved.

(1996)

CLOCK LIBRARY

Project summary by Stewart Brand, 3 October 1995

Civilization is revving itself into a pathologically short attention span. The trend might be coming from the acceleration of technology, the short-horizon perspective of market-driven economics, the next-election perspective of democracies, or the distractions of personal multi-tasking. All are on the increase.

Some sort of balancing corrective to the short-sightedness is needed – some mechanism or myth which encourages the long view and the taking of long-term responsibility, where 'long-term' is measured at least in centuries.

Clock Library proposes both a mechanism and a myth. It began with an observation and idea by computer scientist Daniel Hillis. He wrote in 1993:

> When I was a child, people used to talk about what would happen by the year 2000. Now, thirty years later, they still talk about what will happen by the year 2000. The future has been shrinking by one year per year for my entire life.
>
> I think it is time for us to start a long-term project that gets people thinking past the mental barrier of the Millennium. I would like to propose a large (think Stonehenge) mechanical clock, powered by seasonal temperature changes. It ticks once a year, bongs once a century, and the cuckoo comes out every millennium.

Such a clock, if sufficiently impressive and well engineered, would embody deep time for people. It should be charismatic to visit, interesting to think about, and famous enough to become iconic in the public discourse. Ideally, it would do for thinking about time what the photographs of Earth from space have done for thinking about the environment. Such icons reframe the way people think.

Hillis, who invented and developed the 'massive parallel' architecture of the current generation of supercomputers, is pursuing a variety of avenues of design for the Clock. Some involved drawing energy and time-measure from a massive bimetallic lever which pulses with daily and seasonal temperature variation. Some rely for driving force on the traffic of visitors. One is a form of water clock. Another is a huge marble clock, where different-sized marbles roll excitingly at certain periods, accumulate, then trigger the next-slower marble. Hillis expects to keep proliferating design ideas for a while, soon winnow down to the most practical and thrilling candidates, protoype some of those, and then build the big one. It would be timely to have a millennial Clock working in time for a grand performance in the year 2000.

The project became the Clock Library with the realization of the need for content to go along with the long-term context provided by the Clock – a 'library of the deep future, for the deep future'. It could be used for scholarly retreats, for conferences, and for focused research in its special collections. In the fullness of time – centuries – it could become a repository for kinds of information deemed especially useful over long periods of time, such as minding extreme longitudinal scientific studies, or accumulating a 'Responsibility Roster' of policy decisions with long-term consequences.

To deliver mythic depth, the Clock Library needs to be a remarkable facility at a remarkable location. City sites can be ruled out as being far too turbulent for the long haul. High deserts are attractive for their broad horizons and high-preservation climate. Still, the site must not be too remote for easy visits from worldwide.

In addition to its mythic core facility, the Clock Library as a cultural tool may need to be widely dispersed – on the Net, in publications and distributed services, and at branch locations. The point, after all, is to explore whatever may be helpful for thinking, understanding, and acting responsibly over long periods of time. Specific manifestations of the overall project could range from fortune cookies to theme parks. Some may spin off as commercial businesses. For now, we intend to begin building an astonishing Clock and a unique Library and see what develops from there.

Who is we? The founding board of Clock Library is Daniel Hillis, Stewart Brand, Kevin Kelly, Douglas Carlston, Peter Schwartz, Brian Eno, Paul Saffo, Mitchell Kapor and Esther Dyson. Hillis created Thinking Machines Inc. and its supercomputer, the Connection Machine. Brand created the *Whole Earth Catalog* and co-founded Global Business Network. Kelly is executive editor of *Wired* magazine and author of *Out of Control.* Carlston is chairman and CEO of Broderbund Software. Schwartz is president of Global Business Network and author of *The Art of the Long View.* Eno is a British musician, music producer and artist. Saffo is spokesman for Institute for the Future. Kapor founded Lotus and co-founded the Electronic Frontier Foundation. Dyson created and runs *Release 1.0,* the leading computer industry newsletter.

The present version of the Clock Library scheme has grown from a year's online conversation among the board members. Brian Eno proposed 'the Long Now' as what we are aiming to promote. Peter Schwartz suggested 10,000 years as the appropriate time-envelope for the project – 10,000 years ago was the end of the Ice Ages and beginning of agriculture and civilization; we should develop an equal perspective into the future. Douglas Carlston noted that the organizational institution will be as much of a design challenge to last one hundred centuries as the Clock or the Library.

In the autumn of 1995 Clock Library has an office, bank account, and non-profit status. It is developing a financial framework, design of the Clock, conception of the Library and its initial services, and a location to build them.

STORY: COSMETIC PSYCHIATRY

The surgery was delightful: airy and plant-filled, and with a tinted window through which amber sunlight burst. Shirley was so happy she'd finally come.

It was her friend Sylvia who'd told her about it. She'd known Sylvia since college, and, out of inertia more than anything else, they'd occasionally meet for coffee and send each other Christmas cards, exchanging not-too-intimate details about their affairs, then their husbands, their children, and now, again, their affairs. It was an acquaintance marked by a reliable dullness, the steady drip-filtering of normal-life titbits.

Until, that is, Sylvia took the plunge into cosmetic psychiatry and emerged sparklingly neurotic, full of psychic texture, a fountain of bubbling idiosyncracies. Now she was the life and soul of the kaffee-klatsch – so much to talk about! It was hard, actually, to ever catch her at home these days, let alone arrange to meet with her, so full was her diary. Her newly scatty giggle, her wild outbursts of anger, her amusing absent-mindedness made any gathering come to life. And then, a few months later, when her estranged husband, Jeffrey (who'd always been such a drip), went under the same metaphorical knife and emerged as a conceptual artist with an engaging speech defect and mild multiple schizophrenia, their lives took a whole new turn. Jeffrey (now also bisexual) moved back in, and they fought and fucked, bellowed and threatened, and howled with manic laughter practically round the clock. Everyone wanted to visit them, to be able to say they'd attended the wacky party where Sylvia downed Jeff with a single blow of a Chablis bottle, or the one where Jeff was discovered having anal sex with Sylvia's brother, the Curate of Montreal, in the woodshed, or, most memorably, the time they dropped hallucinogens together and somehow completely exchanged personalities, Sylvia furiously arguing among herselves about decommodification and floating signifiers, while Jeff incessantly sprayed perm-set on his shining bald pate and optimistically combed the air. It was a complete riot, everyone agreed.

318

Inspiring though all this was, Shirley felt she was after something a little less dramatic. She'd been through the catalogue of nervous disorders and was attracted both to manic depression and to obsessive behaviour. It was the doctor who persuaded her that obsessive behaviour, though slightly more expensive to do, was actually very appealing and easily updated. This mattered a lot to Shirley – after all, you didn't want to get stuck with the same neurosis for ever – and then she read that Stephanie Wilson, the actress, had had one done and as a result always had to open the door with the same hand or else she got real mad. Everyone remarked on it. On the talk shows, they always arranged things so that Stephanie had to open a door with the wrong hand. It made for fabulous TV.

Shirley's mind was made up.

She opened her eyes, emerging slowly from the anaesthetic cloud. The room around her stopped wobbling and fell into place. There was some vaguely familiar soft music playing, something ambient. Outside, in the sunny gardens, young birds twittered and a lone dog barked haphazardly. The warm eyes of the doctor and nurse gazed down at her. She tried a smile.

'How are you feeling?' asked the nurse, stroking the back of her hand. And the doctor, not waiting for her reply, said, 'Everything went just fine. You were a perfect patient.'

The nurse reached behind Shirley's head and helped her into a sitting position. The room was delightful – peach and gold – except for UGH! (how on earth hadn't she noticed them before?) those absolutely dreadful curtains. Some vile sub-Laura Ashley print – completely disastrous!

'They'll have to come down immediately,' she stated flatly and incontrovertibly, her angry, trembling finger directed accusingly at the curtains. 'I hate florals at the best of times, and these are particularly disgusting.' She was shaking with rage. She thought she'd never felt so upset.

'But of course, of course,' said the nurse, breathless with apologies, 'We'll see to it right away. They'll be gone when you get back from lunch.' She

319

reached for the phone and said something to the maintenance department. As she spoke, she flashed a quick smile to the doctor, who returned it with a conspiratorial wink. The operation had worked, of course, but just to confirm it they would arrange for Sylvia's lunch to be served on a complete rose-pattern service.

(1992)

CULTURE

Let's start here: 'culture' is everything we don't have to do. We have to eat, but we don't have to have 'cuisines', Big Macs or Tournedos Rossini. We have to cover ourselves against the weather, but we don't have to be so concerned as we are about whether we put on Levi's or Yves Saint-Laurent. We have to move about the face of the globe, but we don't have to dance. These other things, we choose to do. We could survive if we chose not to.

I call the 'have-to' activities functional and the 'don't have to's stylistic. By 'stylistic' I mean that the main basis on which we make choices between them is in terms of their stylistic differences. Human activities distribute themselves on a long continuum from the functional (being born, eating, crapping and dying) to the stylistic (making abstract paintings, getting married, wearing elaborate lace underwear, melting silver foil on to our curries).

The first thing to note is that the whole bundle of stylistic activities is exactly what we would describe as 'a culture': what we use to distinguish individuals and groups from each other. We do not say of cultures 'They eat', but 'They eat very spicy foods' or 'They eat raw meat.' A culture is the sum of all the things about which humanity can choose to differ – all the things by which people can recognize each other as being voluntarily distinguished from each other.

Of course, some aspects of culture are so unquestioned that we don't think we have choices about them – until someone decides to exercise such a choice, as when Sister Rosa Parks chose to sit at the front of the bus.

But there seem to be two words involved here: culture, the package of behaviours-about-which-we-have-a-choice, and Culture, which we usually take to mean art, and which we tend to separate as an activity. I think these are connectable concepts: big-C Culture is in fact the name we reserve for one end of the *functional* ↔ *stylistic* continuum – for those parts of it that are particularly and conspicuously useless, specifically concerned with style. As the spectrum merges into usefulness, we are inclined to use the words 'craft' or 'design', and to accord them less status, and as it merges again into pure instinctual imperative we no longer use the word 'culture' at all. From now onwards, when I use the word 'culture' I am using it indiscriminately to cover the whole spectrum of activities excluding the 'imperative' end. And perhaps that gives us a better name for the axes of this spectrum: 'imperative' and 'gratuitous' – things you have to do versus things you could choose not to do.

The second thing to note is that humans spend a huge amount of their resources and energy exercising and defending and maintaining their cultural choices. Even the most materially disadvantaged groups of people manage to create things that make no obvious functional difference to their lives. Art came out of Auschwitz. Songs and dances (and a whole new musical culture) came out of the slave plantations. But, as social wealth and ease increase (or as other areas of control disappear or are circumscribed), questions of stylistic choice become increasingly central preoccupations, consuming greater and greater amounts of time.

As civilizations get older, a greater proportion of time and attention is spent on the things we don't have to do. More and more products, activities and groups of people are defined by their affiliation to particular stylistic choices. It is as though our attention, allowed to drift away from the imperative end of the continuum, increasingly explores the gratuitous one.

My question is this: 'What are we doing there?' We understand why it makes sense to create a hammer, or a ship, or even a telescope. These all make a difference to how much control over our circumstances we are able to exercise: they directly extend our physical bodies, make life more controllable. But if you ask most people, including most artists, why we do all this other stuff, you'll find it hard to get a straight answer.

People will say, 'Well, it's nice, isn't it? I like it.' OK. It is nice and I like it too, but what is actually being liked? The most obvious thing would be to say that it is the way certain things have been made, the particular organization of the lines and colours and structures of them. This supposes that we for some reason prefer some arrangements of elements over others, and obviously we do. But that doesn't get us any further. Why do we prefer some arrangements of things over others?

Is it because some arrangements are 'better' – intrinsically more satisfactory – than others? That's to say, is it nothing to do with us, but to do with the fact that those arrangements partake of some quality outside of our minds? This is what most of art history has supposed: that we respond to things as 'beautiful' because they in some sense 'contain' beauty. The beautifulness is 'out there' – which is different from saying that they arouse feelings of beauty in us. There is a very clear understanding in this theory that the beauty is already in the work, and one aspires to an appreciation of it – the very word 'appreciation' implies this: that there is something already there waiting to be appreciated. So there were numerous theories about colour combination and golden sections and magical arrangements of lines to which humans were supposed to respond – naturally, as it were – strongly. The extension of such ideas led to some absurdities: missionaries supposing, for example, that the natives could be civilized by sufficiently large doses of Bach being poured over them from gramophones.

Another theory suggests that we respond not to what things are in some intrinsic sense, but to the way in which they are different from other similar things we have seen. Thus we are engaged not in a simple act of looking at something but in the more complex act of looking at something in relation to the background of expectations that other similar things in the same medium have aroused.

It's easy to drift off the subject here, and people have been doing it for centuries. What happens to you when you engage with a piece of culture (when you look at a painting, get a haircut, go to a movie)?

What happens to you when you go to a movie? You sit in a chair, and you watch a world construct itself before you. Then you get a description of some people in that world. You watch the working out of the interactions between the people and the world they're in. What do they do? What would

I do? You are watching the collision of implied value systems within a proposed environment. This is called 'drama', and when we see that the value system is doomed to fail disastrously we call it 'tragedy'. When it fails ludicrously we call it 'comedy'. For millennia, fiction and theatre (and now film and TV) have been about this – about the proposal and description of a world and the dynamics of value-laden interactions within it.

It's interesting to note that neither the proposed world nor the value system involved in the collision needs to be 'realistic' for us to be interested, just as a chess game doesn't have to represent a realistic military conflict. We are interested in the processes of interaction between the proposed elements. We are interested in our own grasp of those processes.

We want to know the rules, and we want to rehearse our ability to extrapolate from them.

When Chekhov wrote his stories, what was revolutionary about them was his reluctance to imply a moral judgement of his characters. He portrayed a world not of free will – where people are 'good' or 'bad' because they want to be – but a world where people are more or less the results of their environment: where their choices are limited, a repertoire of possibilities derived from the grammar of their upbringing and circumstances. In this world, we try to cope with people by being sympathetic to their plight. If they hurt us, we do not call them 'evil' but instead we see them as victims too. In fact we do not believe in 'evil' as an intrinsic quality that things might have.

The *Rambo* series represents a different kind of story. In these films the world is very clearly divided into 'good guys' and 'bad guys'. There is a life-or-death struggle, where there is no time for fine judgements or discussions of how things got that way. Just as the existence of evil is a given, so is the duty to fight it. In a *Rambo* film, people 'are what they are'. They are not emergent, changing, complex or fluctuating. There is no point in trying to delve into their motives, since these are obvious: they are us and therefore good, or they are possessed of the devil and want to eradicate us. It is fashionable to regard these films as stupid, but don't they in fact depict some kind of real crisis? There could, surely, be times when we are required to act with such blunt distinctions, times when it is 'them' or 'us'. And how would we do that? Maybe Rambo knows how, where Chekhov wouldn't.

What are we watching in these films? We are seeing ideas being exercised for us, seeing how things fit together or don't, what the implications of collisions between them might be.

What about haircuts? Getting a new hairstyle is asking the question: 'What would it be like to be the kind of person who has this kind of haircut?' And what's the use of that? Well, isn't this what we do that makes us different from other animals? Isn't it the fact that we have this huge amount of cultural rehearsal in how things could otherwise be, how things could look from someone else's eyes, that enables us to understand each other and cooperate with each other?

To explain: it's usual to think that human culture starts with language, that this is the great divide. But I think it starts with empathy, and empathy is beyond language, a precondition for it. What connects us is not our ability to speak to each other: that is just one of the products (a great one) of our ability to imagine what things look like from each other's eyes.

Humans have this ability to an extraordinary degree. Hundreds of times during a day, we inhabit other minds, other worlds, other sets of assumptions. If we didn't, we'd be unable to function in society. All communication depends on finessing an already vast bundle of assumptions (about who you are and where you are speaking from) with a few sentences or gestures. People who are used to inhabiting each other's mental worlds do this with tremendous economy: the wink that's worth a thousand words, for example, or the slight shift in intonation that carries a whole paragraph within it. Language is the sharp edge of this, but it is only a door into the vast reservoir of experience of other worlds and other views that we all carry about.

And I think that when we engage in cultural acts, transactions, whatever you want to call them, we rehearse this ability to step from one set of assumptions to another, from one perspective to another. And I think we get better and better at it.

This is why I think the world could be getting better – though of course fundamentalism is the deliberate attempt to limit the scope of this ability, to say, 'We will only accept one view of the world.' Since this is strictly impossible (even when you're insulated by immense wealth), fundamentalism is always riddled with glaring internal contradictions.

As is pragmatism – but we expected that.

(Based on a series of lectures given in 1991)

DEFENCE

Suppose you're the president of a big, vaguely democratic country with all sorts of people and all sorts of ambitions. Calling it a democracy means that these people are supposed to decide what happens with their money.

Suppose also that you are a well-informed and technically literate leader who has the best possible intentions – you want to improve the lot of the people by clever, new, non-polluting technologies, for example. However, your advisers tell you (and you know from experience) that these technologies are pie in the sky right now, that it will take 15 years at least to develop them.

But the people want lots of things right now: new health plans, better housing, better roads, more police, etc. How are you going to sell them on the idea of research into noble metals, or parallel-processing computers, or arcane gene technologies – or any of the other long-term projects – when you're not even sure they'll pan out?

Well – you don't even try. You can conceal all that within defence spending. Defence is increasingly the way that governments explore new technologies. The attractive thing about it from a president's point of view is that it allows his government to command a large part of the GNP centrally, undemocratically and secretly, and to funnel it wherever it pleases. This is a wonderful tool – a socialist command economy right at the centre of 'capitalism' – and seems to be the way to get back some form of economic control over a market that could otherwise go into chaotic spins (and completely overlook long-term planning).

An example of this in action was when the American government rescued the failing Ford company in the seventies by backing Ford's 'Little David' anti-helicopter system. This system was a dog from the word go – and ended up coming in massively over budget and failing 68 of the 73 required performance criteria. It was never deployed, but saved Ford. As a weapons system it was useless, but as a bit of pragmatic socialism (to keep

23,000 people in jobs) it worked just fine – and saved the government from having to admit publicly that it occasionally needed to explore other spaces along the *capitalism* ↔ *socialism* axis. (See page 298: Axis thinking.)

The trouble is, it doesn't work. This concealed form of axis thinking – this Zone of Pragmatic Deceit – is not viable for several reasons. Not least among these is that its by-product is weapons – and some of them actually do work. And to pretend that there is no connection between the emergent trend towards low-intensity conflict and easily obtainable weaponry is crazy. It's no accident that aid packages to Third World countries are so often connected to these countries' commitment to buy weapons from the aid-'donors': because in fact the aid flow is to us, not to them. They are helping us deal with the inconsistencies and mood swings of our big economies. They are the direct victims of those economies, and our bribes to them to continue being victims are likely to rebound. Those weapons can point our way too.

Of course another reason for the failure of this as a technique of directing the economy long-term is that it requires all projects be translatable into military terms (since you aren't allowed to be socialists or *dirigistes* and admit openly that you're controlling the economy). Though great ingenuity is put into this (I knew of a man who studied dolphins for ten years on the pretext that he might come up with some new ideas about submarines for the Defense Department), it still excludes all sorts of things that we might think socially desirable but can't put a military frame round – reduction of CFCs, for instance, or maintenance of fish stocks, or aquifers, or soil quality, or combating disease, or ensuring adequate housing. Does it surprise you that these questions get so little attention? – that the annual budget of the World Health Organization, for example, is equivalent to two and a half hours' global defence spending?

The third reason for failure is that the defence industries know exactly how to exploit the dilemma of governments. They know that government needs them to move big sums of money around, to employ people, to keep things rolling. And they know how to keep the government hooked.

Popular techniques include heavily funded campaigns to depose politicians who speak out against defence spending ('She's taking your job away from you'), and ways to spread big defence projects over as many parts of the country as possible – so that you co-opt (ensnare) as many politicians as possible. This process is detailed in Nick Kotz's *Wild Blue Yonder* – a Pulitzer Prize-winning study of the development of the B1 bomber. The manufacture of that was spread over 48 states.

So even the very limited effectiveness of defence-as-economic-control is compromised by the uninterest of the defence industry in anything other than its own company results, which creates a momentum towards a particular subset of defence projects – those that pay best. The industry's interests are simple, and only glancingly compatible with those of the government, let alone the population.

So what exactly is defence defending us against?

First: democracy. Defence is circumnavigating the complications of allowing government expenditure to be subject to popular control.

Second: the admission of pragmatism. Defence spending lets us continue mouthing all this gabble about free markets while keeping a handy command economy behind our backs.

Third: globalism. Defence needs enemies, and will find them.

Fourth: thinking. We slip by with all sorts of unexamined assumptions about our place in the world, because there is no pressure to think about them. We are the aristocrats of the globe, smiling benignly at our plantation workers. We think we're here because we're so smart, but it might also be because we can keep everyone else poor – and fighting.

Fifth: very occasionally, real enemies.

All this isn't to put forward an argument against having a defence strategy and systems of defence, but to ask that we stop hiding all those other jobs behind it, and that we run it clearly and efficiently.

(Based on a letter to the *Spectator*, 1986)

DUCHAMP'S *FOUNTAIN*

The attempts to keep art special become increasingly bizarre. This was a theme of a talk I gave at the Museum of Modern Art in New York as part of the 'HIGH ART/LOW ART' exhibition.

Looking round the show during the day, I noticed that Duchamp's *Fountain* – a men's urinal basin which he signed and exhibited in 1913 as the first 'readymade' – was part of the show. I had previously seen the same piece in London and at the Biennale of Sao Paolo.

I asked someone what they thought the likely insurance premium would be for transporting this thing to New York and looking after it. A figure of $30,000 was mentioned. I don't know if this is reliable, but it is certainly credible. What interested me was why, given the attitude with which Duchamp claimed he'd made the work – in his words, 'complete aesthetic indifference' – it was necessary to cart precisely this urinal and no other round the globe. It struck me as a complete confusion of understanding: Duchamp had explicitly been saying, 'I can call any old urinal – or anything else for that matter – a piece of art', and yet curators acted as though only this particular urinal was A Work Of Art. If that wasn't the case, then why not exhibit any urinal – obtained at much lower cost from the plumber's on the corner?

Well, these important considerations aside, I've always wanted to urinate on that piece of art, to leave my small mark on art history. I thought this might be my last chance – for each time it was shown it was more heavily defended. At MoMA it was being shown behind glass, in a large display case. There was, however, a narrow slit between the two front sheets of glass. It was about three-sixteenths of an inch wide.

I went to the plumber's on the corner and obtained a couple of feet of clear plastic tubing of that thickness, along with a similar length of galvanized wire. Back in my hotel room, I inserted the wire down the tubing to stiffen it. Then I urinated into the sink and, using the tube as a pipette, managed to fill it with urine. I then inserted the whole apparatus down my trouser-leg and returned to the museum, keeping my thumb over the top end so as to ensure that the urine stayed in the tube.

At the museum, I positioned myself before the display case, concentrating intensely on its contents. There was a guard standing behind me and about 12 feet away. I opened my fly and slipped out the tube, feeding it carefully through the slot in the glass. It was a perfect fit, and slid in quite easily until its end was poised above the famous john. I released my thumb, and a small but distinct trickle of my urine splashed on to the work of art.

That evening I used this incident, illustrated with several diagrams showing from all angles exactly how it had been achieved, as the basis of my talk. Since 'decommodification' was one of the buzzwords of the day, I described my action as 're-commode-ification'.

EDGE CULTURE

Joel Garreau's book *Edge City* proposes that the life of cities has shifted from the traditional centres to the edges – so that, instead of a centre from which everything flows and to which everything is related, there are now cities which are actually strings of new, active, local centres disposed around the empty, now-dead old centre. This is clearer in America than in Europe: in America, businesses and malls locate themselves outside, and important connections run from one point on the edge to another, often missing the centre altogether. I used Garreau's perception to come up with the idea of 'Edge Culture'.

It occurred to me that what has happened in culture might be seen in the same way. The traditional 'centre' of fine-art culture – 'serious' music, drama and painting – is not the only place where the action is. Whole new cultures – suburban and vulgar and fast – have grown up round it and now refer to each other rather than to it. Meanwhile the town halls and government offices of old culture still locate themselves where no one lives any more. This is giving rise to a new idea about where we live – culturally.

The history of the history of art is really the tale of various people trying to make claims for one possible story (of culture) over all the others. In diagram form, imagine that we'll represent 'our culture' as a whole field of 'cultural events' – a field which includes Little Richard, Madonna, Vanessa del Rio, Dave Brubeck, Hokusai and Lee Perry, as well as Beethoven and Laura Ashley and Mies van der Rohe. The classical job of the art historian is that of drawing one strong, clear connecting line through that field. That line is called 'the fine arts', and is seen as being the power-centre of 'our culture'. On it would traditionally fall, for example, Chaucer, Dante, Shakespeare, Monteverdi, etc. Another art historian may make a different set of choices, or apportion emphases differently, and would argue for the validity of his line.

The point I'm making is that the activity of being an art historian has traditionally consisted of drawing a line through the whole field of culture and then claiming that the 'value' of things can be assessed by their proximity to that line. You might call this a search for an absolute centre, and you are hearing its echo whenever you hear the question 'But is it art?'

In the 20th century, the field of cultural objects has become both broader (more things from our own and other cultures were 'allowed in') and denser (more things were made and known about, more activities became sites for stylistic experimentation). Traditional art history dealt with this by *broadening* the line it was trying to draw – to include more things within it – so that you were allowed to discuss modern music with reference to Duke Ellington as well as Stravinsky. But its basic premise didn't change – there was still the idea that a *line* existed (objectively), that it could be found and defined, and that it had a direction – that it was going somewhere; that its evolution was a single narrative.

In the last two decades this idea has become seriously eroded (though you often wouldn't know it from reading art critics). Instead we see a broad and dense field of cultural objects connected very, very richly – with lines going every which way depending on who you are and where you stand and what you're looking for anyway. Thus a cultural event such as 'Picasso' can figure in many different 'stories' (a story is a non-absolutist version of a 'history' – it's a version of events that makes no claims to be 'the truth') and can have quite different values in each. The entity called Picasso has thus become of negotiable, not absolute, value.

This is the key idea. If you abandon the idea that culture has a single centre, and imagine that there is instead a network of active nodes which may or may not be included in a particular journey across the field, you also abandon the idea that those nodes have absolute value. Their value changes according to which story they're included in, and how prominently. It's a bit like modern currency: all values are now floating, and there is no longer the 'gold standard' that art history sought to provide us with.

333

When history is replaced by stories, the curator becomes a storyteller, her path an adventure through the cultural landscape, creating meaning and resonance by combination and juxtaposition. Think of modern sampling musicians like Howie B., whose work is essentially the 'curating' of his record collection – creating a new music out of the juxtapositions of existing musics.

And, back to where I started, for me the picture of Edge Culture is very clear – I see a whole mess, an urban sprawl, of culture-objects joined by the journeys we make between them, which are the stories we tell that connect them to each other. These stories are meta-objects, further nodes in the dense field.

Is there then any measure of relative importance between things? Perhaps 'the number of stories something figures in'. This, of course, will change in time and place, and things will go into eclipse as they become stale and back out again as they become recharged with resonances (think of 'Blue Velvet' in David Lynch's film, or the quoted hymns in Gavin Bryars's 'Sinking of the Titanic').

I like this Edge Culture. I like the feeling that anything can happen, any connection can be made, that anything could become suddenly important and filled with feelings and meanings. It's the closest I can get to animism.

(1992/3)

GENERATIVE MUSIC

One of my long-term interests has been the invention of 'machines' and 'systems' that could produce musical and visual experiences. Most often these 'machines' were more conceptual than physical: the point of them was to make music with materials and processes I specified, but in combinations and interactions that I did not.

My first released piece of this kind was *Discreet Music* (1975), in which two simple melodic cycles of different durations separately repeat and are allowed to overlay each other arbitrarily. (Thus, for instance, if one cycle is 29 seconds long and the other 33 seconds long, they will come back into sync every 957 (i.e. 29 × 33) seconds. Subsequently I released *Music for Airports*, *On Land*, *Thursday Afternoon*, *Neroli* and other works, all of which use variations on this and similar 'automatic' systems.

In my audio-visual installations I found another way of making ever-changing music. I distributed the pre-recorded musical elements over several (usually four to eight) audio cassettes of different lengths. These were all played back simultaneously, each cassette feeding its own amplifier and pair of speakers. It was thus possible to make music that was different at any point in space and time – or effectively so, because in fact the cassettes would have come into sync again after a few years, if any of the shows had lasted that long (e.g. five cassettes of lengths 23, 25.5, 30.2, 19.7 and 21.3 minutes would fall into sync about every 14 years).

I enjoyed these shows – especially the knowledge that the music I was hearing at any given moment was unique, and would probably never be heard in exactly that way again.

My records, however, were always recordings of the output of one or another of these combinatorial systems: though it could produce original music forever, what went on the record was a 30-minute section of its output, which would then of course be identical each time you played it. However, what I always wanted to do was to sell the system itself, so that a listener would know that the music was always unique. Since this would have involved persuading my listeners to buy four or five CD-players instead of just one, and then buy the set of four or five CDs to play on them, I didn't spend too much time on the project.

But with computer technology I began to think that there might be a way of doing it. I was inspired initially by certain screensavers – those little graphic devices that use very little computer memory but keep generating new images on the screen. I wrote several proposals based on the idea of using the computer to make music in a similar manner – not as a way of replaying huge chunks of preformed material (which was what was being done, to devastatingly miserable effect, with CD-Roms at the time) but instead as a place where compositional 'seeds' provided by the composer would be grown. I thought this made composing into a kind of genetic activity – in the sense that the compositional 'seeds' were actually interacting sets of rules and parameters rather than precise musical descriptions. I imagined the piece evolving out of the interaction of these probabilistic rule-sets – and therefore evolving differently in each 'performance'.

Since I know nothing about writing code for computers, this would probably have remained a pipedream were it not for a company called Sseyo who had been thinking on exactly the same lines.

In early 1995 I received from them a CD of music that had been made by their software program called Koan. A couple of the pieces were clearly in 'my' style (they readily acknowledged that my 'ambient' work had been part of their inspiration for the Koan system), but what surprised me was that I would have been proud of them. I contacted Tim Cole at SSEYO, and he arranged for me to get a copy of the Koan 'authoring tool' – the program by which one writes the rules for these pieces – and, after a few days of typical interface frustration, I took to it like a duck to water.

Koan works by addressing the soundcard in the computer. A soundcard is a little synthesizer sold as an optional add-on to the computer. The computer sends instructions to that soundcard and tells it what noises to produce and in what patterns. Koan is a very sophisticated way of doing this, enabling a composer to control about 150 parameters that specify things like sound-timbre and envelope, scale, harmony, rhythm, tempo, vibrato, pitch range, etc. Most of Koan's instructions are probabilistic – so that rather than saying 'Do precisely this' (which is what a musical sequencer does) they say 'Choose what to do from within this range of possibilities.' The Koan program allows that range to be more or less specific – you could, if you so chose, write absolutely precise pieces of music with it, though this would probably be its least interesting use.

Some of the works I've made with Koan sound to me as good as anything I've done. That's important: they work as music and are not – as so much computer-based art has been – just a 'neat idea'. They also symbolize to me the beginning of a new era in music. Until 100 years ago every musical event was unique: music was ephemeral and unrepeatable, and even classical scoring couldn't guarantee precise duplication. Then came the gramophone record, which captured particular performances and made it possible to hear them identically over and over again. But Koan and other recent experiments like it are the beginning of something new.

From now on there are three alternatives: live music, recorded music and generative music. Generative music enjoys some of the benefits of both its ancestors. Like live music, it is always different. Like recorded music, it is free of time-and-place limitations – you can hear it when you want and where you want. And it confers one of the other great advantages of the recorded form: it can be composed empirically. By this I mean that you can hear it as you work it out – it doesn't suffer from the long feedback loop characteristic of scored-and-performed music.

Edgar Wind, in his 1963 Reith Lectures, said: 'It might be argued that, in the last analysis, listening to a gramophone or a tape recorder, or to any of the more advanced machines of electro-acoustical engineering, is like listening to a superior kind of musical clock.' I too think it's possible that our grandchildren will look at us in wonder and say, 'You mean you used to listen to exactly the same thing over and over again?'

The idea of generative music is not original to me (though I think the name is). There have been many experiments towards it over the years, and indeed a lot of my interest was directly inspired by Steve Reich's sixties tape pieces such as *Come Out* and *It's Gonna Rain*, I think, however, that this new linkage with an increasingly commonplace technology will make this an area that many composers and listeners will want to explore.

THE GREAT LEARNING

In 1967 Cornelius Cardew wrote an epic work called *The Great Learning*. This was a piece in seven sections, based on some Confucian texts. I became intrigued by the last section of that piece – Paragraph 7 – and subsequently took part in several performances of it.

In 1976 Michael Nyman was asked to guest-edit a special contemporary-music issue of the now defunct *Studio International* and asked me to write a piece for it. I used this as an excuse to apply some of the ideas I had been picking up from Stafford Beer's books on cybernetics and general systems theory to a discussion of this and some other pieces of music.

For me the essay was important because it was my personal discovery of complexity theory – the idea that complex, self-consistent systems can derive from very simple initial conditions, and quickly assume organic richness. This is at first counter-intuitive: we're not used to the idea that something so apparently 'designed' should be able to appear without a 'designer'.

The essay was originally published under the title 'Generating and Organizing Variety in the Arts' – a misleading title – and is not wonderfully written, but I think the ideas are still good.

A musical score is a statement about organization; it is a set of devices for organizing behaviour toward producing sounds. That this observation was not so evident in classical composition indicates that organization was not then an important focus of compositional attention. Instead, the organizational unit (be it the orchestra or the string quartet or the relationship of a man to a piano) remained fairly static for two centuries while compositional attention was directed at using these given units to generate specific results by supplying them with specific instructions.

In order to give more point to the examination of experimental music that follows, I should like to detail some of the aspects and implications of the paradigm of classical organization – the orchestra. A traditional orchestra is a ranked pyramidal hierarchy of the same kind as the armies that existed contemporary to it. The hierarchy of rank is in this pattern: conductor, leader of the orchestra; section principals; section subprincipals; and, finally, rank-and-file members. Occasionally a soloist will join the upper echelons of this system; and it is implied, of course, that the composer with his intentions and aspirations has absolute, albeit temporary, control over the whole structure and its behaviour. This ranking, as does military ranking, reflects varying degrees of responsibility; conversely, it reflects varying degrees of constraint on behaviour. Ranking has another effect: like perspective in painting, it creates 'focus' and 'point of view'. A listener is given the impression that there are a foreground and a background to the music and cannot fail to notice that most of the 'high-responsibility' events take place in the foreground, to which the background is an ambiance or counterpoint.* This is to say that the number of perceptual positions available to the listener is likely to be limited. The third observation I should like to make about the ranking system in the orchestra is this: it predicates the use of trained musicians. A trained musician is, at the minimum, one who will produce a predictable sound given a specific instruction. His training teaches him to be capable of operating precisely like all the other members of his rank. It trains him, in fact, to subdue some of his own natural variety and thus to increase his reliability (predictability).

I shall be using the term *variety* frequently in this essay and I should like to attempt some definition of it now. It is a term taken from cybernetics (the science of organization) and it was originated by W. R. Ashby.† The *variety* of a system is the total range of its outputs, its total range of

---

* This ranking is most highly developed in classical Indian music, where the tamboura plays a drone role for the sitar. I think it no coincidence that Indian society reflected the same sharp definition of roles in its caste system.

† W. Ross Ashby, *An Introduction to Cybernetics* (1956; reprinted, London: University Paperbacks, 1964).

340

behaviour. All organic systems are probabilistic: they exhibit variety, and an organism's flexibility (its adaptability) is a function of the amount of variety that it can generate. Evolutionary adaptation is a result of the interaction of this probabilistic process with the demands of the environment. By producing a *range* of outputs evolution copes with a *range* of possible futures. The environment in this case is a *variety-reducer* because it 'selects' certain strains by allowing them to survive and reproduce, and filters out others. But, just as it is evident that an organism will (by its material nature) and must (for its survival) generate variety, it is also true that this variety must not be unlimited. That is to say, we require for successful evolution the transmission of *identity* as well as the transmission of *mutation*. Or conversely, in a transmission of evolutionary information, what is important is not only that you get it right but also that you get it slightly wrong, and that the deviations or mutations that are useful can be discouraged and reinforced.

My contention is that a primary focus of experimental music has been toward its own organization, and toward its own capacity to produce and control variety, and to assimilate 'natural variety' – the 'interference value' of the environment. Experimental music, unlike classical (or avant-garde) music, does not typically offer instructions toward highly specific results, and hence does not normally specify wholly repeatable configurations of sound. It is this lack of interest in the *precise* nature of the piece that has led to the (I think) misleading description of this kind of music as *indeterminate*. I hope to show that an experimental composition aims to set in motion a system or organism that will generate unique (that is, not necessarily repeatable) outputs, but that, at the same time, seeks to limit the range of these outputs. This is a tendency toward a 'class of goals' rather than a particular goal, and it is distinct from the 'goalless behaviour' (indeterminacy) idea that gained currency in the 1960s.

I should like to deal at length with a particular piece of experimental music that exemplifies this shift in orientation. The piece is Paragraph 7 of

The Great Learning by Cornelius Cardew, and I have chosen this not only because it is a compendium of organizational techniques but also because it is available on record (DGG 2538216). In general I shall restrict my references to music that has been recorded. I should point out that implicit in the score is the idea that it may be performed by *any* group of people (whether or not trained to sing). The version available on record is performed by a mixed group of musicians and art students, and my experience of the piece is based on four performances of it in which I have taken part.

Cardew's score is very simple. It is written for any group of performers (it does not require trained singers). There is a piece of text (from Confucius) which is divided into 24 separate short phrases, each of one to three words in length. Beside each phrase is a number, which specifies the number of repetitions for that line, and then another number telling you how many times that line should be sung loudly. The singing is mostly soft.

All singers use exactly the same set of instructions. They are asked to sing each line of the text the given number of times, each time for the length of a breath, and on one note. The singers start together at a signal, and each singer chooses a note for the first line randomly, staying on it until the completion of the repetitions of the line.

The singer then moves on to the next line, choosing a new note. The choice of this note is the important thing. The score says: 'Choose a note that you can hear being sung by a colleague. If there is no note, or only the note you have just been singing, or only notes that you are unable to sing, choose your note for the next line freely. Do not sing the same note on two consecutive lines. Each singer progresses through the text at his own speed.'

A cursory examination of the score will probably create the impression that the piece would differ radically from one performance to another, because the score appears to supply very few *precise* (that is, quantifiable) constraints on the nature of each performer's behaviour, and because the

---

* Each paragraph corresponds to one in the Confucian classic of the same title.

342

performers themselves (being of variable ability) are not 'reliable' in the sense that a group of trained musicians might be. The fact that this does not happen is of considerable interest, because it suggests that *somehow a set of controls that are not stipulated in the score arise in performance* and that these 'automatic' controls are the real determinants of the nature of the piece.

In order to indicate that this proposition is not illusory, I now offer a description of how the piece might develop if *only* the scored instructions affected its outcome. I hope that by doing this I shall be able to isolate a difference between this hypothetical performance and a real performance of the piece and that this difference will offer clues as to the nature of the 'automatic' controls.

Hypothetical performance. The piece begins with a rich sustained discord ('choose any note for your first note'). As the point at which singers move onto their next line and next note is governed by individual breath lengths ('sing each line for the length of a breath'), it is probable that they will be changing notes at different times. Their choice of note is affected by three instructions: 'do not sing the same note on two consecutive lines', 'sing a note that you can hear', and, if for some reason neither of these instructions can be observed, 'choose your next note freely'. Now, let's propose that there are twenty singers, and that by some chance they have all chosen different first notes. Presumably one of them reaches the end of his first line before any other singer. As he cannot repeat his own previous note, he has an absolute maximum of nineteen notes to choose from for his 'next note'. He chooses one, and reduces the 'stock' of notes available to nineteen. The next singer to change has a choice of eighteen notes. By a continuation of this procedure, one would expect a gradual reduction of different notes in the piece until such time as there were too few notes available for the piece to continue without the arbitrary introduction of new notes in accordance with the third of the three pitch instructions. With a larger number of singers this process of reduction might well last throughout the piece. So, in this hypothetical performance, the overall

343

shape of the piece would consist of a large stock of random notes thinning down to a small, even, occasionally replenished stock of equally random notes (as they are either what is left of the initial stock or the random additions to it).

Real performance. The piece begins with the same rich discord and *rapidly* (that is, before the end of the first line is reached) thins itself down to a complex but not notably dissonant chord. Soon after this, it 'settles at a particular level of variety that is much higher than that in the hypothetical performance and that tends to revolve more or less harmonically around a drone note. This level of variety is fairly closely maintained throughout the rest of the piece. It is rare that performers need to resort to the 'choose your next note freely' instruction, and, except in the case of small numbers of singers, this instruction appears to be redundant.* This is because new notes are always being introduced into the piece regardless of any intention on the part of individual performers to do so. And this observation points up the presence of a set of 'accidents' that are at work to replenish the stock of notes in the piece. The first of these has to do with the 'unreliability' of a mixed group of singers. At one extreme it is quite feasible that a tone-deaf singer would hear a note and, following the primary pitch instruction to 'sing any note that you can hear', would 'match' it with a new note. Another singer might unconsciously transpose a note into an octave in which it is easier to sing, or might sing a note that is harmonically a close relative (a third or a fifth) to it. A purely external physical event will also tend to introduce new notes: the phenomenon of beat frequency. A *beat frequency* is a new note formed when two notes close to each other in pitch are sounded. It is mathematically and not harmonically related to them. These are three of the ways by which new material is introduced.

Apart from the 'variety-reducing' clauses in the score ('sing a note that you can hear', 'do not sing the same note on two consecutive lines'), some

---

* A number of the score instructions seem redundant; all of those concerning the leader, for example, make almost no difference to the music.

others arise in performance. One of these has to do with the acoustic nature of the room in which the performance is taking place. If it is a large room (and most rooms that can accommodate performances on the scale on which this piece normally occurs are large), then it is likely to have a *resonant frequency*. This is defined as the pitch at which an enclosure resonates, and what it means in practice is this: a note sounded at a given amplitude in a room whose resonant frequency corresponds to the frequency of the note will *sound louder* than any other note at the same amplitude. Given a situation, then, where a number of notes are being sounded at fairly even amplitude, whichever one corresponds to the resonant frequency of the room will sound louder than any of the others. In Paragraph 7 this fact creates a statistical probability that the piece will drift toward being centred on an environmentally determined note. This may be the drone note to which I alluded earlier.

Another important variety reducer is preference ('taste'). Because performers are often in a position to choose between a fairly wide selection of notes, their own cultural histories and predilections will be an important factor in which 'strains' of the stock they choose to reinforce (and, by implication, which they choose to filter out). This has another aspect; it is extremely difficult unless you are tone-deaf (or a trained singer) to maintain a note that is very discordant with its surroundings. You generally adjust the note almost involuntarily so that it forms some harmonic relationship to its surroundings. This helps explain why the first dissonant chord rapidly thins out.

In summary, then, the generation, distribution, and control of notes within this piece are governed by the following: one specific instruction ('do not sing the same note on two consecutive lines'), one general instruction ('sing any note that you can hear'), two physiological factors (tone-deafness and transposition), two physical factors (beat frequencies and resonant frequency), and the cultural factor of 'preference'. Of course, there are other parameters of the piece (particularly amplitude) that are similarly controlled and submit to the same techniques of analysis,

345

and the 'breathing' aspects of the piece might well give rise to its most important characteristic – its meditative calm and tranquillity. But what I have mentioned above should be sufficient to indicate that something quite different from classical compositional technique is taking place: the composer, instead of ignoring or subduing the variety generated in performance, has constructed the piece so that this variety is really the substance of the music.

Perhaps the most concise description of this kind of composition, which characterizes much experimental music, is offered in a statement made by the cybernetician Stafford Beer. He writes: 'Instead of trying to specify it in full detail, you specify it only somewhat. You then ride on the dynamics of the system in the direction you want to go.'* In the case of the Cardew piece, the 'dynamics of the system' is its interaction with the environmental, physiological, and cultural climate surrounding its performance.

The English composer Michael Parsons provides another view on this kind of composition:

> The idea of one and the same activity being done simultaneously by a
> number of people, so that everyone does it slightly differently, 'unity'
> becoming 'multiplicity', gives one a very economical form of notation
> – it is only necessary to specify one procedure and the variety comes
> from the way everyone does it differently. This is an example of
> making use of 'hidden resources' in the sense of natural individual
> differences (rather than talents or abilities) which is completely
> neglected in classical concert music, though not in folk music.†

This movement toward using natural variety as a compositional device is exemplified in a piece by Michael Nyman called *1-100 (Obscure 6)*. In this piece, four pianists each play the same sequence of one hundred chords descending slowly down the keyboard. A player is instructed to move on

* Stafford Beer, *Brain of the Firm: The Managerial Cybernetics of Organization* (London: Allen Lane, 1972), p. 69.
† Michael Parsons, quoted in Michael Nyman, *Experimental Music-Cage and Beyond* (London: Studio Vista, 1974).

to his next chord only when he can no longer hear his last. As this judgment is dependent on a number of variables (how loud the chord was played, how good the hearing of the player is, what the piano is like, the point at which you decide that the chord is no longer audible), the four players rapidly fall out of sync with one another. What happens after this is that unique and delicate clusters of up to four different chords are formed, or rapid sequences of chords are followed by long silences. This is an elegant use of the compositional technique that Parsons has specified, not least because it, like the Cardew piece, is extremely beautiful to listen to.

Composition of this kind tends to create a perceptual shift in a listener as major as (and concomitant with) the compositional shift. It is interesting that on recordings, these two pieces both have 'fade' endings (the Cardew piece also has a fade beginning), as this implies not that the piece has finished but that it is *continuing out of earshot*. It is only rock music that has really utilized the compositional value of the fade-out: these pieces use it as a convenience in the sense that both were too long for a side of a record. But a fade-out is quite in keeping with the general quality of the pieces and indicates an important characteristic that they share with other experimental music: that the music is a section from a hypothetical continuum and that it is not especially directional: it does not exhibit strong 'progress' from one point (position, theme, statement, argument) to a resolution. To test the validity of this assumption, imagine a fade-out ending halfway through Beethoven's Ninth Symphony. Much of the energy of classical music arises from its movement from one musical idea to another – the theme and variation idea – and this movement is directional in the sense that the history and probable futures of the piece have a bearing on the perception of what one is hearing at the present.

Experimental music, however, has become concerned with the simultaneous permutation of a limited number of elements at a moment in time as well as the relations between a number of points in time. I think also that it has tended to reduce the time-spans over which compositional ideas are developed; and this has led to the use of cyclic forms such as that in Gavin Bryars's *Jesus' Blood Never Failed Me Yet*. (It is interesting that this piece, Paragraph 7, and *1–100* are all based on 'found material'; and in each case the focus of the composer's attention is toward *reorganizing* given material. There is a special compositional liberty in this situation.)

I do not wish to subscribe to the view that the history of art is a series of dramatic revolutions where one idea overthrows another. I have made some distinctions between classical and experimental compositional techniques, and between the perceptual modes that each encourages in a listener, but I do not wish to propose that the development from one to the other is a simple upward progression. I have ascribed characteristics to these two musics as though they were mutually exclusive, when virtually any example will show that aspects of *each* orientation exist in any piece. What I am arguing for is a view of musical development as a process of generating new hybrids. To give an example: one might propose a 'scale of orientations' where, on the right hand, one placed the label 'Tending to subdue variety in performance' and, on the left, 'Tending to encourage variety in performance'. It would be very difficult to find pieces that occupied the extreme polarities of this scale, and yet it is not difficult to locate distinct pieces at points along the scale. A classical sonata, if only by virtue of the shortcomings of musical notation, allows some variety in performance.* On the other (left) hand, the most random of *random music* (whatever that term meant) is constrained in its range by all sorts of factors down to the straightforward laws of physics. So we might place the Cardew piece toward the left, but not as far left as, say, a free-jazz improvisation. A scale of this kind does not tell us much about the music that we place on it, but its function is to remind us to think in terms of hybrids rather than discontinuities.

Given the above reservation about polarizing musical ideas into opposing camps, I should now like to describe two organizational structures.

---

* It is interesting to observe that the sound of a string orchestra results from minute variations of tuning, vibrato, and timbre. This is why electronic simulations of strings have not been notably successful.

My point is not that classical music is one and contemporary music the other, but that each is a group of hybrids tending toward one of the two structures. At one extreme, then, is this type of organization: a rigidly ranked, skill-oriented structure moving sequentially through an environment assumed to be passive (static) toward a resolution already defined and specified. This type of organization regards the environment (and its variety) as a set of emergencies and seeks to neutralize or disregard this variety. An observer is encouraged (both by her knowledge of the ranking system and by the differing degrees of freedom accorded to the various parts of the organization) to direct her attention at the upper echelons of the ranks. She is given an impression of a hierarchy of value. The organization has the feel of a well-functioning machine: it operates accurately and predictably for one class of tasks but it is not adaptive. It is not self-stabilizing and does not easily assimilate change or novel environmental conditions. Furthermore, it requires a particular type of instruction in order to operate. In cybernetics this kind of instruction is known as an *algorithm*. Stafford Beer's definition of the term is 'a comprehensive set of instructions for reaching a known goal'; so the prescription 'turn left at the light and walk twenty yards' is an algorithm, as is the prescription 'play a C-sharp for a quaver followed by an E for a semiquaver'.* It must be evident that such specific strategies can be devised only when a precise concept of form (or identity, or goal, or direction) already exists, and when it is taken for granted that this concept is static and singular.

Proposing an organizational structure opposite to the one described above is valueless because we would probably not accord it the name *organization*: whatever the term does connote, it must include some idea of constraint and some idea of identity. So what I shall now describe is the type of organization that typifies certain organic systems and whose most important characteristics hinge on this fact: that changing environments require adaptive organisms. Now, the relationship between an organism and its environment is a sophisticated and complex one, and this is not the

* Beer, *Brain of the Firm*, p. 305.

349

place to deal with it. Suffice it to say, however, that an adaptive organism is one that contains built-in mechanisms for monitoring (and adjusting) its own behaviour in relation to the alterations in its surroundings. This type of organism must be capable of operating from a different type of instruction, as the real coordinates of the surroundings are either too complex to specify, or are changing so unpredictably that no particular strategy (or specific plan for a particular future) is useful. The kind of instruction that is necessary here is known as an *heuristic*, and is defined as 'a set of instructions for searching out an unknown goal by exploration, which continuously or repeatedly evaluates progress according to some known criterion'.* To use Beer's example: if you wish to tell someone how to reach the top of a mountain that is shrouded in mist, the heuristic 'keep going up' will get him there. An organism operating in this way must have something more than a centralized control structure. It must have a responsive network of subsystems capable of autonomous behaviour, and it must regard the irregularities of the environment as a set of opportunities around which it will shape and adjust its own identity.

What I have tried to suggest in this essay is a technique for discussing contemporary music in terms of its functioning. I have concentrated primarily on one piece of music because I feel that the technique can thereafter quite easily be generalized to deal with other activities. I do not wish to limit the scope of this approach to music, although because music is a social art that therefore generates some explicit organizational information, it lends itself readily to such analysis. I have in the past discussed not only the fine arts but also, for example, the evolution of contemporary sporting practices and the transition from traditional to modern military tactics by asking the same kinds of questions directed at the organizational level of the activities. It does not surprise me that, at the systems level, these apparently disparate evolutions are very accurate analogues for each other.

* Ibid, p. 306.

In his book *Man's Rage for Chaos* Morse Peckham writes: 'Art is the exposure to the tensions and problems of the false world such that man may endure exposing himself to the tensions and problems of the real world.'* As the variety of the environment magnifies in both time and space and as the structures that were thought to describe the operation of the world become progressively more unworkable, other concepts of organization must become current. These concepts will base themselves on the assumption of change rather than stasis and on the assumption of probability rather than certainty. I believe that contemporary art is giving us the feel for this outlook.

Since reading this essay, Stewart Brand has pointed out a different sense of the word 'algorithm'. This may be the result of a gradual change of usage over the 25 years since Beer used it in his original text. Stewart says, 'I think that "algorithm" does NOT require a goal, as Beer stated. It is much more like the instruction or instruction set that made the pieces you describe come to life ("hold a chord till you can't hear it"). My American Heritage Dictionary defines "algorithm" as "A mechanical or recursive computational procedure."'

* Morse Peckham, *Man's Rage for Chaos* (New York: Schocken Books, 1967), p. 314.

INTERVIEW WITH GARRICK WEBSTER
FOR *PC FORMAT*

Eno: I keep saying to people, 'Screensavers are the most interesting things yet that anyone has done with computers.' For me, the whole thrust of computer development has been in completely the wrong direction. It's all a huge army marching nowhere. There are a few little things that point somewhere else, and screensavers are actually one of them. Unfortunately, even the people who market the screensavers are among the thickest people on Earth. But by pure accident they occasionally hit on a good one.

Webster: I think what they do is come up with lots of wacky things.

Eno: That's right. 'Wacky' is exactly the word for it. I hate 'wacky'. 'Wacky' is the opposite of what I want from life.

Webster: Flying toasters and fish-tanks aren't very demanding or creative.

Eno: There's one they came up with which they only included in one edition of After Dark. Of course it was so good they immediately left it out ever since. They've never used it again. It's called Stained Glass. Have you ever seen that? Well, upstairs on one of the other computers I have about 250 variations of Stained Glass that I've made. It's very much like Latham. It's a self-generating one, in the sense that it keeps looking at its own output and then building from there. It has very few rules, it's very very simple. But there's just enough probability in there for it to grow in completely different directions each time. It's absolutely spell-binding.

I think the problem is that computers have been designed by people who thought the best thing about computers was that they could move huge blocks of data around. They thought that was the interesting thing, so the important thing was to have more memory, more types of data that you could move around together, and so on. But I think that the best thing about computers is that they can grow things from seed. That's really what the Latham thing is, that's what Koan is, that's what Stained Glass is. What

352

I'm interested in is the idea that you can use this as a generator, not as a reproducer.

You know CD-Roms have been a total disaster. A complete disaster. There is not one CD-Rom I can think of that I would ever want to look at again. They are so tedious because they rely on this idea that you can move huge blocks of data around. So, your choices are 'Do I move to this block of data or do I move into that block?' So tedious! What I want to suggest is that CD-Rom is the vehicle by which you plant all these seeds in the computer and it grows them. That's very fast for a computer to do, because you're moving a few kilobytes of information instead of hundreds of megabytes.

Webster: It makes me think back to this guy from Paris I met who developed Le Louvre. They weren't very happy with it because it was linear. It all relied on you making choices. They wanted to develop an artificial intelligence that would open things up for you automatically and take you to different places and unexpected places.

Eno: Shall I tell you something? Conceptually, the whole project is wrong from the ground up. I think the whole idea that you want to sit in front of this and go to places is a bad idea. I think that's the whole principle that has dominated the thing so far. Only idiots actually want to do that with their lives. Only people who have nothing else to do actually find it interesting to go and look at bloody pictures on a computer. It's a pathetic way of looking at things.

Webster: So if I asked you, say, about multimedia your response would be negative. Predominantly multimedia has come out on CD-Roms...

Eno: No. Multimedia predominantly has come out in fairgrounds, circuses and theme parks. That's real multimedia. Multimedia is things like rock groups giving huge shows on stage that use sound and light and pictures and slides and television and everything else. That's the interesting multimedia, I think. There's a big history of that now. But the people who make CD-Roms know bugger all about history. It's like it never happened to them: they didn't connect it with what they're doing.

Webster: I think what they're doing is they just want to make reference things. What you're thinking of has a completely different purpose to theirs.

Eno: No. I believe they are wrong. I don't think there's any confusion about this – I'm not misunderstanding what they're doing as far as I'm concerned. I think they're barking up the wrong tree. If you look at the possibilities of, of let's say CD-Rom, because it stands as a kind of signal example of the failure of this whole area. Now at one end you have a thing called archive. CD-Roms are really good at that. It's a great way of storing tons of information of disparate kinds. In my opinion the best CD-Roms have been the ones that are closest to being archives, actually. For instance there's a really good one of an early Robert Wilson theatre piece in the seventies. If you haven't seen that piece, this is a very good way of finding out about it. He's got film of the performance, he's got lectures and so on. It's very, very good; it works extremely well. You probably wouldn't want to watch it more than twice, but it's a great archive.

Everything that people have tried to do that's called entertainment leans so heavily on that function that it's not very entertaining. It's something you can do for information and, great, that's lovely, we like information.

But right at the other extreme here, this area here that really very few people have looked at, is this idea of using the computer as a generator. And what have you got up there. You've got William Latham, a few screen-savers; you've got this [indicates Koan]; you've got – what's that very interesting guy? – Karl Sims; you've got these odd little dots. You've got the Sim Earth and Sim City things – they sort of belong in here as well. But, really, nobody has put a lot of attention into this. People's perception is that this part is odd and funny, but the truth is that this is where the action's going to happen. That archive job is a historical thing that will become less important in the future.

Webster: You have your own CD-Rom, Headcandy, don't you?

Eno: It's a piece of shit. That has nothing to do with me, actually. I hate that thing.

354

Webster: This was BMG. They put that out. How did it happen?

Eno: Well, I really walked into that. I was a complete sucker, to tell you the truth. The guys developing that, they had the rights to that video stuff. It's video feedback, basically. I like video feedback, and I've done quite a lot of my own stuff in that area. So they played me this and said, 'We'd love to use your music on this.' They had this on a great big screen with fantastic colour and so on, and they played some of my music with it and it looked fantastic. The music was coming through a big system, the thing was on a huge screen – it looked fantastic. Now this was before I knew a lot about CD-Roms. I said, 'That's great – I'll do you some music for that, if you want', and I made some new music. But when I saw the result it was so awful and terrible and disappointing I've never looked at it again. I looked at it for about a minute. The image is this big and it looks like shit anyway. The music sounds like tin, and every time the image changes the music stops. It was an absolute disaster.

Garrick: They also gave out the prismic glasses, which was a bit of a cop-out. The actual image was so small if you put them on and turned the lights off it would seem as if that image was glaring out everywhere.

Eno: It was awful. It's typical CD-Rom rubbish. I really apologize to people if they bought that on the strength of my name, because I tell you I did everything to get my name off there. Oh, it was embarrassing. It was absolutely terrible. It's one of the only things that I've ever been involved with that I really feel bad about.

Webster: What do you think of the idea of interactive music? Like the work Thomas Dolby's done in a game where the actual music responds to the way the player plays. If you play very aggressively the tempo picks up, and if you're more latent in your actions it becomes quieter.

Eno: Sounds pretty boring to me.

Webster: But that's a similar thing. You never get the same thing twice.

Eno: Well, I've never heard it so I really can't say. It depends entirely on how good the music is. The process itself is not that interesting or novel – there's been a long history of attempts to do that. Usually the connections between you and it are so trivial that they're not interesting to explore for long. There's no subtlety in the rapport you can have with the thing. OK, you go like that [*raises arm*] and something goes 'Bang!' You do it twice it goes 'Bang!' You do it a third time, OK, that's that trick played. They're generally so impoverished, like nearly all interactive things.

Now, I should tell you I'm a Visiting Professor of Interactive Multimedia at the Royal College of Art, and I spend all my time telling them that the area is not interesting. Really, they can't assume that there is anything to talk about yet. It's only beginning, and most of the attempts are so nauseatingly wacky, actually. You know, the sort of nerdy things that are [*wrinkles nose*] 'real neat' and 'totally cool'. Oh please. Go back to primary school. No children would play with things like this. It's only neat if you're intrinsically fascinated by computers, and I'm not. I think they're not intrinsically fascinating things any more than I think record-players are intrinsically fascinating things.

INTO THE ABYSS

After several months of work, I slowly grind down and it all starts to seem like 'my job'. I do it, and I probably don't do it too badly, but I find myself working entirely from the momentum of deadlines and commitments, as though the ideas are not springing forth but being painfully squeezed out. At the back of my mind, unadmitted to, are some nasty thoughts swimming about in the darkness. They whisper things like: 'You've had it' and 'You're out of steam.'

Experience has shown me that, when I reach this point, all the distractions I can muster are only postponements. It's time to face up to total, unmitigated despair.

I sometimes do this by going alone on a 'holiday' – though that word scarcely conveys the crashing tedium involved, for I usually choose somewhere uneventful, take nothing with me, and then rely on the horror of my own company to drive me rapidly to the edge of the abyss.

It goes like this: me thinking, 'What's it all for?/ What's the bloody point?/ I haven't done anything I like and I don't have a clue what to do next/ I'm a completely empty shell.' This lasts two days or so, and is the closest I ever get to depression. Then I suddenly notice – apropos of something very minor, like the way a plane crosses the sky, or the smell of trees, or the light in the early evening, or remembering one of my brother's jokes – that I am thoroughly enjoying myself and completely, utterly glad to be alive. Not one of the questions I asked myself has been answered. Instead, like all good philosophical questions, they've just ceased to matter.

I think the process involves reaching the point of not trying any more to dig inside, but just letting go, ceding control, saying to myself, 'I am utterly pathetic, so I might as well give up.' And at the point of giving up I'm suddenly alive again. It's like jumping resignedly into the abyss and discovering that you can just drift dreamily on air currents.

I think I got this idea from Robert Fripp. I was in New York in 1978, living in a hotel, with bronchitis, and feeling very miserable. I met up with him one day and, on the subway, told him how down I was and that I felt like a completely empty shell.

'But, Captain,' he said (he always called me this), 'don't you realize that all over North America people are shelling out enormous fortunes to feel the same way?' I nearly fell on the tracks laughing, and felt wonderful for the next six months. Peter Schmidt used to call that feeling Idiot Glee.

This feeling, of sheer mad joy at the world, is ageless. It's the fresh, clear stream at the bottom of the abyss.

Joy is energy.

(I can get there even more painfully by sitting and working alone. This is a real cruncher, as I try one old idea after another and they all look miserable and stupid and embarrassing, until finally I stop caring and, in a condition of total somnambulism, fall over something new. This is much harder, and wastes a lot of tape. It's better to do the holiday/abyss first, and then work alone.)

LETTER TO PETRA

I've had an amazing week this week. My friend Stewart Brand (who was recently the subject of a huge *LA Times* article entitled 'Is this the most influential thinker in America?') has been in town for the week, so I arranged several things for us to do together – things I've never done before. We went to see Big Ben, climbed the 300 steps into the machinery of the clock and saw how it all worked (he's interested in clocks), had our ears rattled by standing right next to the bells as they rang for 11 a.m. We went to the House of Commons and saw the stupid chaos of Prime Minister's Question Time (what a lesson in how not to take decisions). We went to see the Tom Stoppard play *Arcadia* (you must see this – it interweaves a whole body of scientific stuff about complexity theory with a really intricate and funny narrative. There can be no other playwright working at this level, I think).

But today was something else. I'd been invited by the curator of the Egyptian section of the British Museum (who it turns out is a fan of my ideas and came to my lecture at Sadler's Wells – which he remembers much more fondly than I do) to have a look round in the back rooms and the basements at the stuff they don't show. AMAZING! Suddenly you realize that all these museums are run by archaeologists for other archaeologists, so the selection of stuff on show is based on what they think is archaeologically important – not on what you or I might find beautiful or extraordinary. I saw such incredible things – so African. It made me realize that this amazing and stable civilization – which persisted for 3,000 years with only the most minute stylistic changes – was really a great flowering of *African* – that's to say, non-European – culture. I don't think it's been taken seriously enough – all those archaeologists think it's interesting, but they look to the Greeks and Romans (nice white boys) for art and inspiration and civilization, not these incomprehensible and mysterious Africans.

My curator/guide told me that many of the huge black statues we were looking at had come to England as ballast – weights to stabilize boats that had landed their cargo in Egypt and were now returning to England – and were then just dumped into fields around the port at Plymouth. Incredible, looking at these beautiful life-size sculptures of fire gods in black granite, to think that they meant so little to anyone that they were just thrown away. And, as we looked at a beautifully mummified 4,000-year-old cat – carefully wrapped in fantastically fine linen, looking like it had been done yesterday – he said that 30,000 of these had been shipped to England to be ground up into fertilizer in Liverpool. We saw so many things that the museums never show – examples of more popular, less refined, painting and decoration from millennia ago, stuff that looked more matter-of-fact (and therefore in some ways more surprising) than the High Art we usually see.

But two things were especially powerful. The first was a chair – a little wooden seat much like one you could find today in IKEA, but with superbly calculated curvature to accommodate one's shoulders and upper back, angling in at the bottom to support the lower back, the legs just the right weight, strengthened by triangular cross-braces, and with the original woven rattan seat still intact. It looked so sort of mass-produced – as though the person who made it turned out several of them a year – and this was very impressive. It said so much to me – to think that 4,000 years ago such a thing (and all the activities associated with such a thing) actually existed is utterly shocking. This was not a rough seat or a regal throne (both of which I would not have been surprised by) but an ordinary, everyday, middle-class, comfortable seat. A whole world suddenly sprang out at me – a world of sophisticated and experienced craftsmanship; a world of settled techniques, of settled life (because a chair like this only makes sense in such a life); a world with much more than just slaves and kings. Four thousand years ago.

The second thing was a hand and forearm – of a woman. The nails were beautifully manicured and hennaed, and in perfect condition, and the hand, which was quite black, was gently curved as if holding a small animal or bird. I held this hand, slipped mine into it, and felt momentarily a connection with this several-thousand-year-old woman coming to life across the ages. It was a powerful feeling, and the fact that there was no body to this arm and hand allowed one to imagine the living person, not just a skeleton. I was holding the hand of a person from so many years ago – a person who'd lived in this sophisticated and complicated society which loved pets and drank beer and went hunting with boomerangs and played games with bats and balls.

I hope you'll come to London one day and let me take you down there, through these dark passages with uninspiring green doors enclosing windowless rooms within which sit treasures from another civilization.

After that we went on to Richard Rogers's Channel 4 building (Stewart was being interviewed there), and it was funny seeing that in comparison. Where this kind of architecture completely loses it is in its sense of detail. In brief, there is no sense of detail. Big, flat, boring sheets of glass do nothing for me. Architects should be taxed on the glass they use, so that they're encouraged to come up with some other ideas. There should also be a tax on flatness of surfaces: if you want to use a whole expanse of flat, mass-produced concrete, you have to pay for it. If there is some detail and texture, the tax is correspondingly reduced. Detail and texture have a reason for existing beyond just my taste: they flatter wear and erosion. A flat block of concrete looks worse every day it exists. A carved form looks better, because the patterns of erosion it undergoes outline the carving. In between these two extremes are various degrees of texture. But glass must be stopped. How utterly stupid to make the whole west face of a building from glass! What's that like on a sunny day? Of course you're not allowed to put up curtains (and there's nowhere to hang them anyway, since glass can't be drilled into), so what do you do?

I'm enjoying working with this guy Nick Lacey (the architect doing our place in Mostar). He is really decent, thoughtful and motivated without being dogmatic. Probably most architects would find him feeble for not using enough glass or in other ways failing to subject his clients to sufficient pain, disorientation and humiliation. Speaking of this, Christopher

361

Alexander (he who wrote *Pattern Language* and others) has just published a new book called *A Foreshadowing of 21st Century Art* – a study of very early Turkish carpets. If this isn't one of the best book titles ever, I'm a Dutchman. The book is beautiful and costs £100 – I've just been given a copy by Stewart Brand. Without even reading it yet I have formed an idea of what the thesis could be – and I like it. Perhaps it's about the idea of an art that evolves; an art without heroes (or with lots of heroes – same thing); an art that is all detail, where the big forms appear slowly and without anyone ever knowing for sure how they got started – like those Egyptian things.

LETTER TO DAVE STEWART

I had hoped to get a chance to have a word with you and Paul Allen after the show, but the Bottom Line was far too busy for that. I did see you whiz by, but it didn't seem at all the right time to start talking about documentary films. But I have the beginnings of an idea which you might be interested in.

A few years ago I came up with a new word. I was fed up with the old art-history idea of genius – the notion that gifted individuals turn up out of nowhere and light the way for all the rest of us dummies to follow. I became (and still am) more and more convinced that the important changes in cultural history were actually the product of very large numbers of people and circumstances conspiring to make something new. I call this 'scenius' – it means 'the intelligence and intuition of a whole cultural scene'. It is the communal form of the concept of genius. This word is now starting to gain some currency – the philosopher James Ogilvy uses it in his most recent book.

Now I would love to be involved in making something to explore this idea – to support my thesis that new ideas come into being through a whole host of complicated circumstances, accidents, small incremental contributions made in isolation (as well as gifted individuals, of course) that in total add up to something qualitatively different: something nobody has ever seen before and which could not have been predicted from the elements that went to make it up.

One of the reasons I am attached to this idea is that it is capable of dignifying many more forms of human innovation under its umbrella than the old idea of 'genius', which exemplifies what I call the 'Big Man' theory of history – where events are changed by the occasional brilliant or terrible man, working in heroic isolation. I would prefer to believe that the world is constantly being remade by all its inhabitants: that it is a cooperative enterprise. Folk arts and popular arts have always been criticized because

363

they tend to exhibit evolutionary, incremental change – because they lack sufficient 'Big Men' making shockingly radical and unpopular steps into the future. Instead the pop scene carries much of its audience with it – something the fine arts people are inclined to distrust: the secret question is, 'How can it possibly be good if so many people like it?'

Of course it would be stupid to pretend that everyone's contribution is therefore equal to every other's, and I would never claim that. But I want to say that the reality of how culture and ideas evolve is much closer to the one we as pop musicians are liable to accept – of a continuous toing and froing of ideas and imitations and misconstruals, of things becoming thinkable because they are suddenly technically possible, of action and reaction, than the traditional fine-art model which posits an inspired individual sorting it all out for himself and then delivering it unto a largely uncomprehending and ungrateful world.

There are a few recent cultural moments where the scenius process is particularly clear: 1905–1915 in Russia; Dadaism in France; the experimental music scene in America through the late fifties and early sixties; the Anglo-American psychedelic scene of the sixties; punk in 1975–8 (the eclectic and cooperative nature of which is documented in Jon Savage's book *England's Dreaming*); and then perhaps something as specific as the evolution of 'adobe style' in South Western American architecture, or even the mid to late eighties at Goldsmiths'! It could also be interesting to include some scenes that were less specifically artistic – for instance, the history of the evolution of the Internet. In all of these sequences, there are sufficient gifted and eccentric individuals to satisfy anyone's hero-appetite, but the interesting thing is how they were fed and supported by a vigorous and diffuse cultural scene. That's the process I would like to explore.

LETTER TO TOM SUTCLIFFE

I agree with many of the points you made: in particular that there is little hope (and absolutely no point at all) in trying to codify responses to works of art. Of course the whole point of the enterprise is to make 'places' that engage the imagination of the viewer, and, once engaged, it can go where it will.

But I'm not trying to ask the question at this sort of level of detail. What I'm after is actually rather simple (you'd think). I'm probably looking for just one sentence, and not even a very big one. I've been looking for it for about 25 years. Damn! I know it's round here somewhere . . .

Imagine an alien anthropologist coming to Earth and finding here a type of being that mixes liquids together in transparent tubes and observes them closely, dissects animals, makes precise arrangements of electrons, and records things compulsively. The alien thinks, 'What on Zog are they up to?', until someone tells him, 'They want to know how things work – they're called scientists.'

The same alien now finds another group of beings. These are mixing coloured liquids together, dissecting animals, making precise and complex arrangements of electrons, and recording things compulsively. He says eagerly, 'I know what you're doing – you want to know how things work!' They look at him and say, 'Well, actually we're artists.' Slightly nonplussed, he says, 'Oh, I see. So what exactly are you doing it for then?' To which they reply brightly,

'. . .'

So, you see, the problem is not very complicated. I don't want to explain in detail all the many manifestations of human culture. All I want is a big frame within which I could be fairly confident they are located. Sometimes I think I've found that, but it's a bit clumsy. Of course, it might be in the nature of things that such a frame is undrawable – that it always wants to expand to include more things as soon as it is drawn.

I can make several attempts at answers, but they're all long-winded – which makes me think they're susceptible to a reduction I can never quite find. My long-winded answers have formed the basis of several talks I've given on the general subject 'Why do we evolve culture? Why are we so interested in style? What does it do for us?'

One suggestion is that the whole basis of human specialness is our ability to cooperate – and to cooperate you have to be able to imagine what it would be like to hold another picture of the world. You're unable to cooperate unless you can be mentally in at least two worlds at once – your own and that of the person with whom you're working. The failure to grasp other pictures of the world is what we call autism, and in its extreme form is something we regard as a severe dysfunction. Well, all animals are by our standards relatively autistic – unable to see into each other's minds, lacking empathy.

So how do we develop this ability to experience and speculate about other ways of thinking and feeling about the world? I think we do it by continually immersing ourselves in cultural experiences that rehearse us. This is obvious in films and novels – where we quite explicitly enter an imagined world and then watch imaginary characters in imaginary quandaries. In so doing we develop a lot of surrogate experience about what it is like to be someone else, somewhere else, with different assumptions.

So I can imagine culture being a kind of simulator, an empathy lab, a way of trying things out with only symbolic risks attached.

But then there's a whole other possibility too – not incompatible. This derives from the aesthetician Morse Peckham, who wrote a book called *Man's Rage for Chaos*. His theory is that art exists to rehearse us in various forms of cognitive uncertainty. He sees 'science' in its most general sense in the same way as you described it – as an attempt to make the world more comprehensible, to be able to make better generalizations and predictions about things. He says that we are good at this, but it has a price: we become overcertain of our generalizations and simply ignore the times when they don't apply. We lust for certainty so much that we ignore that which reminds us how uncertain we are.

He suggests that this is what art is for: to confront us with mysteries, things that we don't properly understand, we know we don't understand, but we nonetheless find ourselves excited and stimulated by. This linkage of uncertainty with pleasure is the key to his theory – a way of training ourselves to enjoy exploring, to act without complete information, to improvise.

LETTER TO U2

Thinking this morning about an approach to the project from here:

Edge called yesterday and said that he thought the tape sounded pretty good – I thought so too. It's much more finished-sounding when you put it all together. So I was wondering what would actually make it seem complete.

This set me thinking. We've been approaching the next stage of the work in the normal way – thinking, naturally enough, what else we could put in to the music – what types of instruments, what sorts of changes, what vocals, etc.

I thought, 'Why don't we also start thinking of what we can put round the music?' The reason we were originally interested in doing a film soundtrack is because the film supports the music – that's to say, one's awareness that this is music for a film stimulates the imagination to think pictorially and scenically, to connect the emotions of the film with the music. You stop just listening to a piece of music in the abstract and imagine the situation that it belongs to. This is why the Lynch and Tarantino soundtracks have such strength – because the music is completely reinfused with power by being placed in a strong context. The song 'Blue Velvet', for instance, is a song from my childhood (I was 13 or 14 when it came out) and I remember despising it for being so pathetically white and wimpy. But hearing it in the Lynch film completely changed it: everything that had seemed pale and restrained about it became weird and mysterious – as though the song was a kind of veil that concealed all sorts of kinky undertones. In a case like that, you can say that the film – the thing around the music – rewrote the music. 'Blue Velvet' is now a different piece of music, imbued with far more depth and ambiguity than it ever had before.

I suggest we think about how we can do the same thing with this music. It would be easy if we had a film to relate to, but it looks like we might not have. But perhaps this is an opportunity then to do something new – to create a completely imaginary 'surround' for the music. I can think of a few different ways of doing this.

First, one could suggest an imaginary film by alluding to it in the titles of the pieces – so they become called things like:

(1) 'Toller and Hermatt Wait at the Crossroads'
(2) 'Duststorm Approaching'
(3) 'Early Afternoon, South Corner of Davis and Vine'
(4) 'Winter Night, Texas', etc.

Second strategy: there could be bits of dialogue trapped in the music – just short fragments in different voices drifting through, or maybe handled more musically – sampled and repeated and worked into the music.

Third approach: use bits of other atmospheric sounds as backdrops for each piece. For instance, I have a recording of a thunderstorm which I made in New York in 1978. I have another recording of someone shooting in a forest in a volcanic crater in Japan – insects, enormous reverberation. Yesterday I did a couple of experiments in this direction – just running some atmospheres against the tracks. It sounded great. Now I've started to make some new atmospheres which are semi-real, semi-electronic. I hope to have some examples to play next week.

Fourth: do it all with the record cover: write the whole narrative and identify where the pieces of music fit. For example, 'Toller and Hermatt Wait at the Crossroads': After leaving the forest, Toller makes his way back to the road and heads out across the plateau towards the crossroads. From far across the plain, he sees Hermatt, trudging determinedly through the twirling dustclouds, occasionally disappearing from sight in them. The two men reach the crossroads at almost exactly the same moment – did they time it that way? – but say nothing to each other. They sit, back to back, and wait, their heads turned, both staring in the same direction, each refusing to look at the other.

369

LOTTERY IDEAS

The distribution of lottery money among 'good' causes is the problem. Who decides?

Idea for another distribution system: anyone can nominate a 'good cause' to which the money should be put, and then a huge list of these good causes is sent to every household in England. Everyone is told that they can allocate 'their' share of the lottery (which could be expressed as an actual sum of money) between a maximum of say ten charities. The distribution is made based on the returned lists.

Another possibility: distribute the lists with the tickets. When you buy a ticket you get a list automatically. Or you fill in the name of a good cause for each ticket you buy, and all the slips are forwarded.

How do new causes get on the big list? Perhaps a certain minimum number of supporters is required, which gets the name on the list. The position on the list is then established by the number of people who supported the initial application. New causes lobby for signatures to improve their initial ranking in the list.

When someone chooses to support a charity (by allocating their ticket share to it), this counts as a point in the listings. Thus new causes stand a chance of being visible among the established ones. The most well-supported causes are visible.

Publish results as they come in – bit by bit – so there's some feedback in the process, and people can see what's being ignored and supported. Use public 'clocks' to show what different causes are getting.

Results: people know that what gets supported represents some expression of popular interests. Good causes start making their case to the public. Opera atrophies.

The same system should apply to other forms of taxation.

It's not complicated – it's what computers are for.

THE MARSTALL PROPOSAL

To make this proposal clear I have to explain that I do not make a distinction between what are normally called 'sound effects', 'treatments' and 'music'. I see all these as being part of the province of the composer – which is the sonic design of the production. Therefore I want to suggest a 'sound presentation' for the play, based partly on the notes you have given me and adding some new ideas.

I am especially interested in three main layers of sound, which we may call ground, dialogue and atmosphere.

Ground is a lower level of very deep, almost subsonic sound which probably comes mainly from under the seating area. This may be abstract, or it may sometimes be related 'musically' to the action. You can think of this sound as the 'ground' or 'geology' of the play.

Atmosphere is a top level of very high sounds, all from small speakers driven by Walkman tape-players. There should be at least 50 and probably more like 150 of these small speakers in the space, and they could easily be designed to be movable (for example, so that they move closer to the heads of the audience during the play). Each of the cassette-players would be playing a cassette tape prepared so that certain 'sonic time-zones' could be made within the duration of the play. It is part of the nature of these small players that they can't be synchronized precisely, either with the play itself or with each other, but I believe this should be seen as an advantage. Instead of predictably synchronized sound there will be 'sound clouds' – the whole space of the theatre charged with sound, and every night slightly different. I think it will give the feeling of a living space, a space full of real sounds, sounds from the outside. I would make or supervise these tapes.

Examples: In a distant corner of the theatre, as though through an open window, we hear a dog begin barking. From another corner, another dog starts up. Gradually, the air becomes filled with barking dogs, all of them distant, but as though the walls of the building have somehow dissolved and we are now out in open space. Or rain starts falling, a drop here, a drop there, until the room is filled with these tiny metallic drips like tiny metal blades. Or a distant revolutionary song is joined by a patriotic song, then by a football song, and so on until the room is filled with a cacophonous goulash of idealistic singing.

Another use of these small speakers is to mount groups of them on trellis grids, which can be hung from the roof and dropped in and out of certain scenes. By this means it would be possible to quietly lower a grid of speakers down to within a few feet of the heads of the audience so that suddenly sounds appear very close to them. These moving panels could also be used to relay the voices of the actors – so that those voices could be brought very close to the audience sometimes.

Between the layer of 'atmosphere' and the layer of 'ground' is the layer of dialogue, which I believe can be used to create 'context derived from speech'. This play has a lot of dialogue, and it seems obvious that the discussion between Toller and Tollkirsch must be treated as the real sonic (as well as theatrical) centre of the play. So I would like to suggest building from the voices themselves – using them as the sources of sonic material which becomes part of the sonic atmosphere. This can be done by using two treatment devices (Eventide H3000 Harmonizers) equipped with my programs so that any section of either actor's performance can be amplified into a unique sonic event.

Examples: One of the actors sounds as though he is talking in a very small concrete cell, while the other is in a cathedral. Or one of the actors speaks in a babble as though a whole crowd is chattering incoherently, while the other sounds like a beautiful, harmonious choir. Or one of the actors speaks like a young girl, the other like a robot.

The fourth layer of sound is the layer most like conventional music – in the sense that it would entail distinct pieces of pre-recorded composed sound. I must say I have fewer ideas about this than anything else, perhaps because to me, at the moment, that is not such an interesting prospect, and I was wondering what you would think about the proposal of asking someone else to do this. My own feeling, from reading the play and talking to you, is that it would be somehow very elegant to avoid using much pre-composed music, but to concentrate on creating a sonic and psychological landscape from what are normally called 'sound effects' and from the voices of the actors themselves. However, there is no reason to be doctrinaire about this: if you would like to include 'ordinary music' as well I'm sure this would still work fine.

If you do wish to do this, why not think about this music as a frame for the sounds that the actors are generating with their voices (i.e. as a backing for 'Sprechstimme' songs) and for the atmospheric sounds? If you take this approach, it may be possible to generate all the 'music' that you need live – one keyboard player with a fairly small body of equipment could certainly make such frames during the performance. Therefore I'm wondering whether the solution to this part of the problem is for you to work with the keyboard player from quite early on in the rehearsal process, just as you would work with the H3000S and the voice treatments, so that from the beginning you are creating sound landscapes for the play as well as visual and theatrical ones.

MIRACULOUS CURES AND THE
CANONIZATION OF BASQUIAT

I often think about this story:

In the 18th and 19th centuries people were 'taking the waters' for a wide variety of illnesses. By this time the scientific medical establishment was quite well developed, and careful records were made of the patients' conditions, their treatments and their progress. This documentation was made by doctors of good character and reputation: their work in other areas substantiates this. They were interested to discover what special properties spa waters had, and why the cures were so often effective. They failed in this, and the search for the curative agents was gradually abandoned, on the assumption that whatever special balance of minerals the waters contained was too subtle for the instruments of the day to register.

Modern instruments are much more sensitive, but they reveal (again and again) that there is no consistent difference between spa water and other kinds of water. It's just water, exhibiting the natural variability of that substance. The effect of this non-discovery (the repeated failure to identify any special properties in spa water) diminished interest in water cures, which anyway by the late 19th century were going out of fashion. But it left unanswered a question, which seemed to be this: 'Were those doctors of the 18th and 19th century wrong in either their observation or their reporting, or was there really something in the water?'

A possible solution appeared a few years ago. It was discovered (a surprise result of space exploration) that prolonged periods of weightlessness have the effect of precipitating out heavy metals from the body. Heavy metals are mostly toxic. Space travellers return to Earth with less of them (and therefore less toxicity) in their systems. Now think back to 'taking the waters'. Remember that these cures were of very long duration: typically you might remain in the water several hours a day for several weeks or months. In water, of course, you approach weightlessness. Could it be that 'taking the waters' is a way of cleansing the body of heavy-metal toxicity?

374

I don't know if this is how it worked, but what interests me is that it could be. It's an answer that sidesteps the implied dilemma of the original question. The implication was this: if the doctors were right (that people were getting cured), then there must have been something in the water. If there isn't anything in the water, then the doctors must have been wrong (people weren't really getting cured). But now a new possibility arises: that there was actually nothing in the water, but the doctors were right. What has happened is that a new concept – depending on a property of water nothing to do with its mineral make-up – has been introduced.

Here's another story, a relative of the first:

There was a famous Indonesian shaman who cured people by dragging bloody clumps of something-or-other out of their bodies, saying that these were the source of their illness. These healing sessions were conducted in near darkness amid great ceremony and mysterious incantations. Subsequently, the shaman was investigated by a team of Western doctors, who used infra-red cameras to reveal what he was in fact doing – of course, he was pulling those sodden lumps not from out of patients' bodies, but from somewhere on his own. It was a trick. The only problem was that the trick worked: he had a very high cure rate. We might say that this doesn't count because it's all in the patients' minds: that they have been tricked into using their own will to cure themselves. We might not want to regard such a cure as scientifically acceptable, because it demands that we accommodate the complexities of the human mind into the medical equation. And even if we do accept that patients are not people who simply have things done to them until they get better, but people who are manoeuvred into a frame of mind from which a cure will proceed, can we also accept that it therefore doesn't matter if this frame of mind is created by the most outrageous fakery? How actively will we embrace 'placebo effects'?

Richard Williams is an English journalist who wrote for many years about music. There is a famous (and true) story from the early seventies about his receiving a white label (pre-release test pressing) of a new record by John Lennon and Yoko Ono. It was an exclusive. He reviewed it at length in *Melody Maker*. Side 1 had a normal enough format – five or six songs – but his attention was taken by side 2, which consisted of a 20-minute-long continuous tone – a pure sine wave. This was the kind of bold experimentation that one expected of John and Yoko, and Williams, clearly impressed, reviewed the piece favourably and at some length. It turned out to be a test tone – he didn't know that it was common practice for cutting engineers to cut a pure tone on to test pressings in order to monitor things like turntable stability and vinyl quality.

Whenever I heard this story, it was accompanied by a snigger. The feeling was that Williams had been 'caught out': that he'd shown himself foolish and gullible for mistaking a test tone, that most deliberately artless of all sounds, for a piece of real art. I felt differently about this. In fact it was perfectly possible that J. and Y. would have released such a thing. But, more importantly, why shouldn't Williams have had a musical experience with a test tone? And doesn't the fact that he obviously did tell us something about the nature of art experiences in general?

It seems to me that we find this difficult to accept because it presents us with a very similar dilemma to that posed in the 'taking the waters' story: if the critic was right (if he really did have an art experience) then there must have been something in the test tone. But we know there's nothing in test tones, so the critic must have been wrong: he obviously wasn't actually having an art experience. He just thought he was – just like the Indonesian patients felt they were better.

Now on to Robert Hughes, and something he wrote about Jean-Michel Basquiat. I like Hughes a lot – I find him a clear, intelligent thinker and articulator, and as such fairly unusual among writers about art. But I also like Basquiat, whereas Hughes doesn't get him at all. In his book *Culture of Complaint* Hughes discusses the canonization of Basquiat: how he was elevated to sainthood after undergoing a sort of fine-art-as-rock-and-roll saga – discovery, drugs, acceptance, rejection, rediscovery, more drugs and an early death. Basquiat, of course, also benefited from the added cachets of being black and being presented as though from a poor family, which wasn't actually quite true. But all in all, he was a commendably eighties figure: a victim – of implied racism and drug abuse – and a precociously charismatic outsider. Hughes looks unkindly at Basquiat's pictures and finds them childish and simplistic. His talent, Hughes says, lay not in his ability to paint as such but in his ability to project himself (and make himself projectible, if that's the word) as a media event – an art star.

There are several threads of thought here. Some are more clearly exposed than others. There is the criticism of Basquiat's painting itself, with which one can only agree or dissent. I personally like his paintings. I also think, however, that 'anyone could have done them', and that in fact a lot of other people did, in some way or another, more or less interestingly, with more or less commitment. It was a feeling of the times, and someone had to come through with it. In the vernacular world this would not be a criticism: it merely says that someone is part of a scene and that, for all sorts of reasons, a lot of people get interested in the same kinds of marks and sounds and implications of lifestyle at roughly the same time. That's what you'd expect to happen, isn't it? Yes, but the existence of such a vernacular osmosis, so perilously close to 'mere fashion', constitutes a threat to the mythology of the art world. That mythology relies on the idea of geniuses, of people so different from everyone else that their achievements must be separated off and protected and ringed round with complicated verbiage. I've always been suspicious of this – as Hughes is – but now another idea comes to mind.

Is this myth-making actually the process whereby grown-up people create valuable experiences for themselves? I mean, is this elaborate polka of romanticization and charisma-manufacture, of canonization, the way that we make for ourselves experiences that are sufficiently laden with resonance and depth and authority for us to be challenged and changed by them? Are we like the shaman's patients, cooperating with the artist in creating an atmosphere of sufficient power that a shabby piece of sleight of hand can do the trick for us? And could we still benefit if we knew how it worked? Is it necessary that we be 'believers' rather than 'sceptics' for us to have the right kind of experience? Could Richard Williams have made any use of that test tone if he'd known what it was? And what exactly is the use of the experience anyway?

Changing ourselves. Surely that must be what we're after when we look at pictures and watch movies and listen to music. It sounds more Californian than it really is. Changing ourselves includes switching on the radio when we're bored – to change from being someone who's bored to someone who's being less bored, or bored in a different way. But of course we would prefer to think that the art we venerate does more than just feed us sensations to keep us from the gloom of our everyday existence. (Why would we prefer that? What's wrong with the opposite? I remember someone saying that all human creativity is a desperate attempt to occupy the brief space or endless gap between birth and death.) We would like to think that art remakes us in some way, deepens us, makes us 'better' people. Certainly this is the unspoken thought behind the concept of subsidized public art spaces – we don't give the same high-level cultural endorsement to public skateboard spaces, or public discotheques, or red-light districts.

Then there are the criticisms implied in the suggestion that Basquiat's only real talent was for charisma-creation and self-promotion. Each of these criticisms is founded on assumptions which are not mentioned: that Basquiat was primarily operating as a painter in the sense that Hughes assumes; that the art world shouldn't conspire to create 'geniuses' for itself; and that self-creation is out of bounds as a job for artists.

Suppose some things. Stop thinking about art works as objects, and start thinking about them as triggers for experiences (Roy Ascott's phrase). That solves a lot of problems: we don't have to argue about whether photographs are art, or whether performances are art, or whether Carl Andre's bricks or Andres Serrano's piss or Little Richard's 'Long Tall Sally' are art, because we say, 'Art is something that happens, a process, not a quality, and all sorts of things can make it happen.'

Then suppose that what makes a work of art 'good' for you is not something that is already 'inside' it, but something that happens inside you – so the value of the work lies in the degree to which it can help you have the kind of experience that you call art. It is then possible, within the context of the right expectations, for a test tone to become a musical experience. It is also possible for you to have quite different experiences from me, which says nothing about the test tone and everything about our separate perceptions of it, our different expectations and cultural predispositions. What we could then agree is that there is nothing absolute about the aesthetic value or non-value of a test tone, and that we don't even have to consider the question of aesthetic value with a view to arriving at any single answer: it could have one value for you and another for me, and different ones for both of us at another time. It can change value for each of us. More interestingly, we can also say that there is nothing absolute about the aesthetic value of a Rembrandt or a Mozart or a Basquiat.

Suppose you redescribe the job 'artist' as 'a person who creates situations in which you can have art experiences'. Then you might accept the notion that an artist could be someone who convinces you, by some means or another, including outrageous fakery, that the test tone you're about to hear is in fact a piece of music.

Suppose now that these means can include the creation of 'media events', networks of spin and buzz that make you think you are in the presence of something special – the event itself is minimal, but the spin is sufficently powerful to infect you with enthusiasm, and you have a great time. Is that going too far?

Suppose that you could even think of yourself as the media event, as the experience-trigger itself, so that everything to which you simply directed your attention transmuted mysteriously into art.

And suppose that people wanted that, and wanted to believe in it, and wanted to make each other believe in it. Who is then the artist? You or them? Who is making the patient feel better? The shaman or the patient? Is the value of the art experience to be found in the 'weightlessness', the suspension of disbelief, the floating surrender, that it produces, rather than in its objective mineral properties?

(1993/4)

379

MOSTAR CHILDREN'S MUSIC CENTRE

The Mostar Children's Music Centre, planned and funded by War Child, is a new kind of institution. Its first concerns are the immediate needs of Bosnian children. But the Centre is also intended to be an institution of international stature which may serve as a model of its kind, applicable in other times and cicumstances.

On the site of a bomb-damaged primary school in the eastern and most ruined sector of Mostar, architect Nick Lacey has designed a building which maintains the original Austro-Hungarian facade but with an interior of airy spaciousness reminiscent of the city's Turkish ancestry.

The Centre will contain a music therapy unit, specialising in problems associated with the aftermath of war, alongside a broad, inclusive clinical practice, accepting children referred from the Mostar region and beyond. Nigel Osbourne, composer and Professor of Music at Edinburgh University, has already started music therapy sessions with small groups of orphans in the region. There will also be a postgraduate training course and research unit validated by the Faculties of Medicine and Music of the University of Sarajevo. In addition, a small art therapy unit will be located within the Centre.

The clinic and course will be staffed by two full-time music therapists recruited, in the first instance, internationally, a locally appointed assistant, regular visiting professors from abroad, and staff of the University of Sarajevo. The Centre will act as an educational and social resource for the region, offering wide-access musical and creative arts, including facilities for young musicians to perform and record. Since the Centre will be located in the heart of the city and since cafés are the most popular meeting places for Bosnian people, a large informal café area will be open on the street side of the building, offering a welcome to all passers-by. Furthermore, the Centre will incorporate a small but professionally equipped recording studio. This will be useful not only in therapeutic terms for war-traumatised children but also as a practical means of supporting the Centre in years to come.

At the time of writing this diary, a third of the total funding required of £3,000,000 had been raised, all from within the music industry. Further funds will always be welcome.

NEW WAYS OF SINGING

(From a letter to Tim Booth of JAMES)

I have a great deal of sympathy with the singer in an improvising situation. He has a much more difficult job, in a sense, than any other instrumentalist. These are the things that make it difficult:

- he can only make one noise at a time;
- he has to invent language as well as music;
- the options for sonic experimentation are much more limited than with most other instruments;
- whatever he does is going to be focused upon in a way that other instruments will not be.

These are the conditions under which singers labour: they just do not have the range of options available that another instrument might have. So here's a simple solution: change the conditions!

OK – the last one on the list is the hardest to change, since it's more to do with the cultural attitudes of listeners than with what you do as a singer – but even here there are choices, and particularly if you change the first three conditions.

Let's look at those.

One note at a time? There are ways of working round this – harmonizers, for instance, or long-repeat echos which layer up into dense vocal clouds. Also, you could ask other people to sing as well – just say in advance, 'This jam will have other vocals.' You could also have a sampler loaded up with vocal bits and use those to sing around. You could get those bits by sorting through existing tapes and transferring vocal selections from them or by doing new bits – Mark could help sort this out.

Sonic experimentation? Well, it can be done, but, apart from your occasional megaphone, it very rarely is. Whereas every other instrument has moved into the late 20th century by surrounding itself with sound- modifying appendages, the voice is still largely in the same position it has occupied since the 14th century. It needn't be that way. What about having an H3000 (I'd send you some of my programs, many of them specifically designed for voice and never yet used) with a mike going straight into it? Or how about the kind of processing set-up that Larry has? Or both? And a little simple mixer so that you could blend treatments together? You could always have a 'clear' mike too, which went direct to a track untreated, so you wouldn't have to commit to whatever treatment you got going. You'd immediately find yourself singing differently, I guarantee. It would allow you to use your voice as a way of making landscapes, tints, clouds of sound, as well as violent, hard-edged, jabbering, shuddering, thin, dense, babyish, feminine, distorted. It would be like having hundreds of different types of megaphone at your disposal.

The good thing about an approach like that is that it takes the pressure off the singer to always have to focus on 'words' and 'music'. It creates a three-dimensional space to work in: language and melody are the two familiar points, but now there is a new one: sonic texture, landscape, vocal atmosphere, call it what you will. Think about this. It vastly multiplies the number of roles that the voice can have, and it takes the pressure off it to always address the familiar words and music role. The voice can now be purely atmospheric, purely rhythmic (as well as any of the other mixtures).

ON BEING AN ARTIST

WHERE DO YOU WORK?

Do you work 'inside' or 'outside'?

To work inside is to deal with the internal conditions of the work – the melodies, the rhythms, the textures, the lyrics, the images: all the normal day-to-day things one imagines an artist does.

To work outside is to deal with the world surrounding the work – the thoughts, assumptions, expectations, legends, histories, economic structures, critical responses, legal issues and so on and on. You might think of these things as the frame of the work.

A frame is a way of creating a little world round something. Traditionally that little world isn't given much thought – there's almost a feeling that to invest too much time in that part of the job is to be looking in the wrong place. So a frame on a traditional painting is a standardized object, a set of approximately-all-right cultural odds and ends. If it's an old painting there's a bit of gilding and some moulding, and if it's a new picture there's likely to be hard edges and perhaps a flash of aluminium. These are just signs that act more as insulators (ways of excluding certain meanings) than attractors (ways of making meanings).

In classical music, the concert hall, the tails and the black garments are all signs to the audience that they are about to see something located within a particular set of values relating to what musicians do and what composers do and what audiences do. Like the gilded frames on old paintings, much of what they offer is insulation, reassurance, a sense of correct location. They are relatively unquestioned and neutral addenda to the work (composers do not normally specify dress style and colour in classical compositions).

But this is not true of much modern art, or of almost any popular culture, where the edges of the work are often so fluid that we don't know where they are – or they don't stay in just one place. A lot of the confusion

384

people feel when faced with new art, whether popular or fine, is the problem 'Where does it end?' – which is the same as saying, 'Where is it at?'

For example, when Madonna first appeared she was criticized because she seemed to be committing as much or more attention to the fashion and lifestyle considerations of what she was presenting as to her music. These criticisms tell you a lot about the expectations of the critics. Clearly they had in their minds a hierarchy of importance. Music should be at the centre, and then these other things should be seen as packaging, the wrapper. Like many of the things critics get heated about, this is a very old idea dressed up in cool new language. Who said music should be at the centre of the experience? Why? Why isn't it acceptable to have an artist who works on a number of fronts, one of which is music? Why not, further, accept the idea that the music could itself become the package – an interesting way of presenting a series of modern haircuts, for example?

The biggest arguments about validity are almost always about this subject: whether or not certain things are allowed to be included as suitable areas for artistic attention, and whether or not certain others can be left out. Peter Schmidt used to have a phrase: 'to omit what no one else has thought of leaving out'. In music, no one thought of leaving out the music.

So I might present a sculpture that consists of only one angled wire line, but I might tell a sufficiently interesting story about it, or about how it got like that, to create a world around it that gives it meaning. I might say, 'This line is the precise trajectory of the bullet that passed through President Kennedy's body', or 'This line is a three-dimensional graph of the relationship between the changing price of paintings in the 20th century, profits in the defence sector and the length of the average working week' or 'This piece of wire was bent this way by Joseph Beuys.' All those statements are ways of engaging a part of you other than your immediate senses and asking that part of you to take part in the appreciation of the work. You can view those statements as a frame.

Some work is almost all frame, which is to say that almost all of its power derives from what can be said about it, what it can be drawn into connection with. The great Borges story 'Pierre Menard, Author of the Quixote' is an extreme example of that idea. Arthur Danto's thought experiment (the exhibition with 12 square red paintings by different artists, for different reasons) in *The Transfiguration of the Commonplace* is another. Both of these are exercises in the conferral of value.

Is there anything in a work that is not frame, actually?

(1995, unfinished)

PAGAN FUN WEAR

'Pagan Fun Wear' took place on Midsummer's Night, 21 June. It was our second ambitious fund-raising event for War Child, following on from the 'Little Pieces by Big Stars' art show and auction in 1994.

Pagan Fun Wear was many things: a Bacchanalian feast, a fashion show, an auction, and an art event. We were very fortunate to be given use of the Saatchi Gallery – which had a show on at the time – for the evening.

THE FEAST

As with the 'Little Pieces' dinner, the feast was created by Jonathan Rutherfurd-Best and his company Urban Productions. This was as much performance art as dinner, with extraordinary table decorations and semi-naked waiters adorned with phallic rubber horns.

THE FASHION SHOW AND AUCTION

All the fashion items had been designed by musicians, and realized by students from Central St Martins and Kingston University. As with 'Little Pieces', the roll call of musicians who contributed designs was impressively eclectic: Laurie Anderson, Joan Armatrading, David Bowie, Adam Clayton, Jarvis Cocker, Phil Collins, Siobhan Fahey, Bryan Ferry, Gavin Friday, Gary Glitter, Jaron Lanier, Dolores O'Riordan, Iggy Pop, Lou Reed, John Squire, Dave Stewart, Michael Stipe, Pete Townshend, Scott Walker, Robert Wyatt and myself. Björk and Tricky, beating all other bids, enthusiastically paid a lot of money to buy each other's laundry.

Several designers – Rifat Ozbek, Zandra Rhodes, Vivienne Westwood, Thierry Mugler and Philip Treacy – also donated finished garments, so a few garments were vaguely wearable.

Probably the new fashion discovery of the evening was Jarvis Cocker. Not only did he design a rather fetching pair of transparent loafers, he also agreed to model them himself. At the auction which followed, he refused to allow the bidding to stop until it reached £5,100, and so became, overnight, one of the most expensive accessory designers in the UK.

THE ART EVENT

The music for the catwalk show was chosen from relatively new bands, all of whom seemed to be at the current cutting edge. The collection was an unusual mix, and the quality was such that it seemed obvious that it would make a good compilation album. We made an edition of 500 CDs and then 500 boxes to put them in. We put other things in the boxes too . . .

All the boxes were hand-sprayed by me at my studio, and so each was unique. David Bowie gave us 500 pieces of his Minotaur wallpaper, while Anton Corbijn took 500 Polaroids during the event, one of which went in each box. In addition, two artists – Patrick Hughes and Damien Hirst – kindly agreed to contribute 250 small paintings each, all of which were required to be made during the evening. Patrick did so, surrounded by boxes being filled, sealed and sold, raffle-ticket-sellers, fashion students and the occasional naked waiter. Unfortunately Damien was in the middle of making Blur's 'Country House' video at that time, and couldn't get to the show, so during the afternoon his assistant and I created 250 original Damien Hirsts on his spinning paint machine (it is of course quite usual for Damien to have other people physically make his work). These were then rushed over to him for signing and returned for packing during the event. The boxes were sold for £100 each, and are probably worth a lot more.

Pagan Fun Wear was ludicrously ambitious, chaotic, exhausting and a great success. It involved 21 models, 33 students, no end of helpers, and all those musicians and designers – all, of course, donating their time and services. It made more than £60,000 for War Child, and raised the charity's profile within the music business, probably helping to pave the way for the highly successful *Help* record. It took a great deal of effort from a relatively small number of people, and this seems like a good opportunity to thank them:

Anthea, James, Lin and Drew from my office, who organized the whole thing;
Rick Kirwin, who somehow created a brilliant, smooth catwalk show out of total chaos;
Cally, for all his help with the boxes;
Mark Edwards and Paul Gorman, for their excellent musical taste;
Paul Gambaccini, for hosting the evening;
Ted Owen of Bonham's as auctioneer;
Anton, Damien and Patrick for their unique works;
Sally Reeves, who did all the PR;
Greg Jakobek, for artwork and printing;
Charles Saatchi and the staff of the Saatchi Gallery;
the first-year fashion students and staff at Kingston School of Art, the second-year fashion students at Central St Martins, and the other assemblers of clothing and accessories.

STORY: PERSONAL PROFILE

Within moments of waking up, Daniel Xavier Shelton remembered: today was his 38th birthday. And what a lovely day it was: the October air felt crisp and clean, and the light had that early-winter coldness that he liked so much. He'd decided not to work but to take a day off from the network and go for a long walk instead. This was one of those days he really enjoyed being single and freelance.

As the coffee percolated, he turned on the radio. The sentimental strains of 'Oh Danny Boy' burst into the room. 'Oh God,' he thought as he spun the tuning-dial, 'I should have known.' The radio blipped and squeaked through the closely packed frequencies. He settled on a news channel, catching the end of an item about some potentially menacing new development in the North African trade wars. He listened as he warmed his miso soup.

'– and, meanwhile, local observers have claimed that heavily subsidized Libyan parallel-processing computers are now being dumped on to sub-Saharan markets. Chad has threatened to retaliate by withdrawing support from the Pan African Neural Network Agreements which she co-sponsored last year with Mali.

'And now back to London, where today it is the birthday of [a slight voice change here] *Daniel X. Shelton*. Happy birthday, *Danny*! This message comes to you from *Harvey Winger*, at your local branch of *The Gap*. He'll be looking out for you today, Danny, and has a small gift for you instore. So why not come and say hello to *Harvey* at *The Gap*?'

'Bloody hell,' thought Danny. 'They can put a man on Pluto but they still can't convincingly match the voice-bites.'

The news returned, and Danny crossed the room to open the blinds. As he did, he heard a loud fanfare from the street below. Three smiling young blondes, rather scantily dressed as pageboys, raised long trumpets festooned with heraldic red and yellow flags and blasted fanfare samples at his window. An awning over their heads proclaimed, 'THE SWEDISH TOURIST BOARD CONGRATULATES YOU, DANNY, ON YOUR HAPPY DAY. WHY NOT SPEND THE NEXT ONE WITH US? CALL FREEVIEW 0800-SWEDEHOL & WE'LL SHOW YOU JUST HOW WELCOMING WE CAN BE.'

The girls were still fluttering their eyelashes and flexing their hips as Daniel turned away. He was, he told himself, unmoved by their thinly veiled invitations. That stuff was really old hat now. But he was at the same time a little troubled by the realization that, in the eyes of the market-profilers, he now belonged to the age-and-status group that would be susceptible to such temptations. And he had to admit that the girl on the left was a bit more interesting than usual. He found himself looking out at her again. For the first time that day, he felt a little middle-aged.

In the background, the computer pinged regularly and persistently as it registered receipt of his e-mail. He relied on his code-sorter to pull out the stuff he actually needed to see, but since his software was now over eight weeks old it let a lot of the smarter stuff through. The profilers seemed to learn your codes and interests faster than your friends could these days.

From the bathroom window, as he shaved, he caught sight of the puffs of skywriting in the cloudless sky: 'DANNY! CALL MUM!' it shouted across the top of the city.

MUM, of course, was the acronym for Medical Underwriters' Management – a large health-insurance company. Well, thought Danny, you really have to give them marks for trying. And then he remembered suddenly that he had actually been thinking of extending his medical cover. Perhaps he *would* call MUM. He made a note into his hand-held.

In the early days of profile marketing, when it was still called junk-mail, people made tremendous efforts to remain invisible to the market-research companies. The whole thing was felt to be a gross invasion of privacy. There had been numerous attempts to undermine the profiling project: people moved into very poor neighbourhoods, for example, to confuse the computers that generated the profiles, or occasionally bought

391

goods that were completely inconsistent with their lifestyles. Whole universities, in revolutionary temper, invented systems where nobody ever bought anything they might use themselves, but instead engaged in complex forms of barter with one another. It never really got off the ground, because of the numerous profile-informers on campus. A lot of people made their way through college by secretly profiling their friends.

But the real problem was that personal-marketing was extremely successful. It seemed that everyone made a big fuss about the intrusion, and then went straight out and bought the goods.

And so, gradually, like all those little invasions, people grew used to it, and even came to expect it. It didn't bode well for your social prospects, for example, if you weren't routinely surrounded by a buzz of sales activity. There were even agencies which could generate false marketing activity around you so that you could appear more sought after than you actually were. Imagine the situation: you're sitting at a candlelit dinner in a theme-restaurant gazing into the eyes of a new prospective mate, when the waiter discreetly interrupts with a dusty and venerable bottle of Burgundy to which is attached a note: 'Best wishes to you both for a wonderful evening. Do call in again, Danny, at the gallery. There's a rather fabulous late Tang vase I think you'd like to see – Jeremy.'

Danny got dressed and left the apartment. The air was bracing and he waved away the offer of a limousine ride from F&R HiFi, but accepted the hand-held personal weather-forecaster from the Hampstead Garden theme park ('Where it's always sunny, Danny') and walked swiftly away from the neighbourhood.

The park was almost empty. Some ordinary-looking people walked their dogs, and the joggers continued their lonely, panting, circuits. There was still a slight frost sparkling on the grass. It felt great to be alive in this big oasis of silence. Danny looked at his new weather-forecaster. It showed a picture of clear blue skies and a slowly falling temperature. Then suddenly the tiny screen changed to a slowscan movie of the Nude Themepool at the Hampstead Garden park.

How amazing! There on the screen, smiling and radiant, and slowly lowering her gorgeous nude body into the glittering water, was the page-girl he'd caught himself admiring that morning in the SwedeHol ad. Her breathy, girlish voice emerged thinly from the tiny speaker: 'It's lovely once you're in, Danny.'

(1993)

PRETENSION

Pretension is the dismissive name given to people's attempts to be something other than what they 'really are'. It is vilified in England in particular because we are so suspicious of people trying to 'rise above their station'.

In the arts, the word 'pretentious' has a special meaning: the attempt at something that the critic thinks you have no right even to try. I'm very happy to have added my little offering to the glowing mountain of things described as 'pretentious' – I'm happy to have made claims on things that I didn't have any 'right' to, and I'm happy to have tried being someone else to see what it felt like.

I decided to turn the word 'pretentious' into a compliment. The common assumption is that there are 'real' people and there are others who are pretending to be something they're not. There is also an assumption that there's something morally wrong with pretending. My assumptions about culture as a place where you can take psychological risks without incurring physical penalties make me think that pretending is the most important thing we do. It's the way we make our thought experiments, find out what it would be like to be otherwise.

Robert Wyatt once said that we were always in the condition of children – faced with things we couldn't understand and thus with the need to guess and improvise. Pretending is what kids do all the time. It's how they learn. What makes anyone think you should sometime give it up?

ROLES AND GAME-PLAYING

During the *Outside* sessions I was trying to find some new ways of making improvisations go somewhere they wouldn't otherwise. The usual problem with improvisational work is that it is either too homogeneous (everyone settling in mutually familiar territory and droning on endlessly) or too chaotic (people making things that don't cohere in any interesting ways at all).

I had been thinking about game-playing a lot. It was an approach that Roy Ascott had pioneered at Ipswich Art School during my time there, and I had most recently seen it working with my wife's family. At Christmas and other times the whole family play quite elaborate games which allow normally retiring people to become suddenly enormously extrovert and funny. Watching them, it occurred to me that the great thing about games is that they in some sense free you from being yourself: you are 'allowed' forms of behaviour that otherwise would be gratuitous, embarrassing or completely irrational. Accordingly, I came up with these role-playing games for musicians.

In the first game I gave each musician one of these role-sheets, but no one knew what instructions the others were operating under – so that individuals were in different cultural universes. Initially people got roles that related to the instruments, but for later improvisations I swapped them round (but again covertly). It wasn't until afterwards that everyone found out where everyone else had been . . .

The second experiment, 'Notes on the vernacular music of the Acrux region', was an attempt to imagine a new musical culture, and to invent roles for musicians within it.

The idea is not that games such as this should dominate the proceedings, but simply that they should give you a different place to start. If you've managed that, you hopefully rely on the musical intelligence and curiosity of the players to explore the new territory fruitfully. Since we were a group of players for whom that was likely to be true – Reeves Gabrels, Erdal Kizilcay, Mike Garson, Sterling Campbell, David Bowie and myself – we got good very results from these.

One interesting thing here: in both these games I wrote roles for the co-producer/engineer (Dave Richards) and the assistant engineer (Dominik Tarqua), so that they were also active in the improvisations. Their contributions proved to be very important.

The roles:

1

It's 2008. You are a musician in one of the new 'Neo-Science' bands, playing in an underground club in the Afro-Chinese ghetto in Osaka, not far from the university. The whole audience is high on 'Dream-water', an auditory hallucinogen so powerful that it can be transmitted by sweat condensation alone. You are also feeling its effects, finding yourself fascinated by intricate single-note rhythm patterns, shard-like Rosetta-stone sonic hieroglyphs. You are in no particular key – making random bursts of data which you beam into the performance. You are lost in the abstracted rational beauty of a system no one else fully understands, sending out messages that can't be translated. You are a great artist, and the audience is expecting something intellectually challenging from you.

As a kid, your favourite record (in your dad's record collection) was *Trout Mask Replica*.

2

You are a player in a Neo-M-Base improvising collective. It is 1999, the eve of the millennium. The world is holding its breath, and things are tense internationally. You are playing atonal ice-like sheets of sound, which hang limpid in the air, making a shifting background tint behind the music. You think of yourself as the 'tonal geology' of the music – the harmonic underpinning from which everything else grows. When you are featured, you cascade through glacial arpeggios – incredibly slow and grand, or tumbling with intricate internal confusion. Between these cascades you fire out short staccato bursts of knotty tonality.

You love the old albums of The Mahavishnu Orchestra.

3

You are a member of an early-21st-century 'Art and Language' band. You make incantations, permutations of something between speech and singing. The language you use is mysterious and rich – and you use a mélange of several languages, since anyway most of your audience now speak a new patois which effortlessly blends English, Japanese, Spanish, Chinese and Wolof. Using on-stage computers, instant sampling techniques and long-delay echo systems, you are able to build up dense clouds of coloured words during performance. Your audience regards you as the greatest exponent of live abstract poetry.

Samuel Beckett is a big influence.

4

You are a musician at Asteroid, a space-based club (currently in orbit 180 miles above the surface of the moon) catering mainly to the shaven, tattooed and androgynous craft-maintenance staff who gather there at weekends. They are a tough crowd who like it weird and heavy, jerky and skeletal, and who dance in new, sexy, violent styles. These people have musical tastes formed during their early teens in the mid nineties.

Your big influence as a kid was The Funkadelics.

5

It's 2005. You are a musician in a Soul-Arab band in a North-African role-sex club. The clientele are rich, sophisticated and unshockable – this is to the Arab world what New York was to the US in the eighties. You play a kind of repetitive atonal funk with occasional wildly ambitious ornaments to impress your future father-in-law, the minister of networks for Siliconia, who is in the audience.

You love the recordings of Farid el Atrache.

6

You are in a suburb of Lagos, the new Silicon Valley, where the ultra-large-scale-integration industries are all located. The place is littered with weird nightclubs catering to the eclectic international community there – clubs offering 'Neo-Science' bands, 'Art and Language' bands, and 'New Afrotech'. Yours was one of the first New Afrotech bands to appear. The music you make is eclectic: it's a heavy dance music, based on influences as diverse as soul, Silicon Techno and Somadelia, but of course all with a very strong African flavour. This manifests in highly percussive and rhythmically complex orchestrations, an aggressive edge reminiscent of the great Nigerian bandleader Fela Ransome Kuti, and long pieces that open up slowly with multiple climaxes and breakdowns. You are considered one of the great 'Crack Rhythm' players on the club scene.

Your biggest early influence was Tunde Williams, the trumpet player and horn orchestrator for Fela in the mid seventies.

7

It's 2005. You are MO-tech for NAFTA's leading ForceFunk band. The job originated in the sixties and was then called 'stage technician', but, as things became increasingly complex technically, it became clear that many important musical decisions were being resolved in the technological choices made before the band ever mounted the stage. In a sea of options, the person who chooses between them helps determine the work. So the job of *modus-operandi* technician came into being. Your job is to arrange things before performances – choosing what various people should be playing, for instance, which presets on synthesizers should be engaged, which drums should be used, etc. – in such a way that the musicians are put into interestingly new and challenging positions, to notice which of these arrangements work and to encourage them, and also to notice which don't and to change them.

You are especially impressed by artists such as Aphex Twin and the Ambient school.

8

You are a leading recordist at Ground Zero studios in Hiroshima, the largest studio in the Matsui media empire. It is 1998. You are famous for your surprises – when the band listens back to the take, you will, unbeknown to them, have set up a landscape of sound within which their performance is located. You regard yourself as a 'sonic backdrop painter'. You work using treatments or existing 'environmental' sounds and triggered loops or overdubs – any way you please. You work closely with your star assistant, whose taste you frequently consult and who has a library of sound effects that you draw on.

Your favourite historical figure is Shadow Morton.

NOTES ON THE VERNACULAR MUSIC OF THE ACRUX REGION

The popular music of Sector Acrux is primarily a music of interlock and permutation. It is distinguished by its tightly webbed, interwoven motifs. The greatest musical thrill to an Acrucian listener is hearing the complex webbing and intertwining of very detailed rhythmic and melodic lines – just as we might, perhaps, enjoy the detailed patterning on a rich oriental carpet, or the rich interweave of creatures in an ecology.

Acrucian musicians are occasionally employed solely to make music, but more usually they are accompanists, scene-setters – creating and evolving 'fields' over which the Acrucian singer-poets (the 'painters') can paint their vast and elaborate stories.

The stories that come out usually surprise visitors when they first hear them. They often seem to ramble vaguely, dissolve into meaningless strings of words, collect themselves together again, head in a strong direction for several seconds as though the vocalist has suddenly remembered what he was saying, and then just as suddenly break apart, sometimes into single syllables and phonemes. Nothing thrills the Acrucian listener more than this sense of teetering on the cusp between brilliant meaning and obvious nonsense. Occasionally the painter will repeat and explore a sung motif (although very often the distinction between singing and speech is not easy to make, and it certainly is not important to the Acrucians), and this may be taken up by the players in a kind of chant. Usually these sung parts are distinguished more by their speed of delivery than by their harmonic movement – they are often enunciated much more slowly than the other parts of the vocal delivery.

Another fascinating aspect of the Acrucian singer's art is the use of ambiguous 'hinge-words'. This is akin to the Li Dynasty poetry of China, where extremely brief poems were constructed using words with multiple meanings, resulting in a cascade of possible interpretations. The Acrucian equivalent works because of the limited phonetic palette of the language (just as the Chinese depended on the relatively small number of pictographic characters) – there are relatively few sounds, but many tonal and contextual variations on them, and the job of the singer becomes that of teasing out these hidden resonances by variations in pitch and stress and placement. When this is done well, the conflict and sympathy between different meanings can create a dazzling moiré of shifting messages.

The subject-matter is often at first glance very commonplace: pieces of gossip, bits of weather reports, comments on the singer's current affairs, things read out from bits of paper handed up by the audience. It is a measure of a singer's skill and imagination that she be able to wring deep and moving resonances from apparently ephemeral trash. Visitors are often told the story of the legendary paintress Diva Wobedi who practically overthrew a whole government by the amazing and pointed sarcasm she drew out of a page of racing results.

The music of Sector Acrux, although dense and rich sounding, is structurally quite simple. There is an initial period of loose, non-rhythmic, material called 'drift'. During this period the musicians hint at and flirt with the parts that they are going to play in the first 'field' of the song-picture. There are usually two fields in a song-picture, and these alternate at intervals. The first field customarily lasts for up to a half of the total length of the song, until, at a signal from the painter, the musicians snap into the second field. From then on the alternation between fields is controlled by the painter, or by a predetermined formula. Usually there is also a section called 'The Net' or 'The Dish', where new sonic material is accepted into the piece, often captured from data transmissions or other stray electronic sources. Sometimes this material is trapped electronically and retained as a backdrop or atmosphere throughout the rest of the piece – an analogy in sound to what the painter is doing with words. The end of the piece is usually a return to the drift, but with the added elements that have been captured during the performance. At any point during the performance, the painter might call for 'Water': this translates approximately into 'Stay in this place; play with restraint and fluidity', and usually indicates a sort of suspended feature section for the vocalist.

The instruments of Acrux almost all evolved from earth instruments, although some have by now hybridized into very bizarre objects. One such is 'The Orbiting V', an oddly shaped strung instrument, always highly amplified and played with dazzling speed by young Acrucians. Fascinated as they are by ancient and obscure gadgetry, these young wizards, when they are not zipping frantically over the instrument, entertain their audiences with ringing clouds of sound that are self-perpetuating and self-mutating. The sharpest thing for such a musician is to strike the instrument rarely but to generate huge and long-lasting panoramas of sound. The eastern sector star Elvas Ge'beer has been known to perform a whole seven-hour concert with one single strike of the instrument, spending the rest of the time changing parameters on the odd assortment of archaically wired junk at his feet and holding lengthy conversations with members of the audience, even after they have clearly fallen asleep.

Another favourite instrument is an elaborate and beautifully constructed harp-like object played flat with hammers – similar to the grand piano that flourished in pre-galactic Earth, but often used now as a source of sparklingly atmospheric ostinato material. Its best contemporary player, G. Noisemark, somehow manages to blur the distinction between separate strings, producing gorgeously dissonant liquid cascades of sound.

The engine section of the band consists of the batterist and the holders of the 'grand sword'. The batterist makes rhythmic webs from all sorts of sound, and is constantly reinventing his instruments. Batterists are essentially collectors of short sounds for rhythmic use, and most of them have a closely guarded personal library consisting of thousands of these. The Was/Hington Heights player P. Maclert Singbell, for example, carries around an enormous library of recordings of fatal gunshot sounds for use as percussion elements. He is said to have the only surviving recording of the shot that struck down the legendary 20th-century dictator John Kennedy, and another of the Swiss assassin Hud Helvetica cracking his knuckles prior to the brutal murder of the diminutive expeditor (v.i.) Roni Bean.

Working closely with the batterist are the holders of the grand sword. Our closest relative to this is the bass-stick. The grand-sword players – there are normally two or three in a band – usually dictate the modal environment and pace of the song by their opening parts. The other musicians quickly adopt a position relative to this. Tradition dictates that the best grand-sword players come from the old Turko-Armenian settlements in the western zones of Acrux, and their mysterious art is passed down through families. One of the most accomplished is the extraordinary polymath Azile Clark-Idy, a player renowned for his abilities to immediately deduce which of the 4,000-plus Acrucian ragas the music is set in. The relationship between the sword players is complex and hierarchical, but the idea seems to be that they should end up sounding like one impossibly competent player, interlocking with each other in a completely indistinguishable manner. Normally this is achieved by the players operating in different registers – what we might call baritone, bass and ultra-bass. One of the notable new players of the ultra-bass grand sword is the recent immigrant Bengurt Greathewm, not Turko-Armenian but a Natovian of Finnish stock.

The 'expeditor' is the physical embodiment of the painter. Her job is to visualize the emotional content of the painter's work to the other musicians – to act as a kind of physical idea. Had she been born into a higher stratum of society, no doubt she too would have been a painter, but the expeditors are drawn exclusively from the untouchable castes. This is not to say that they lack fame and celebrity – indeed their sayings are communicated throughout society. The mythical Belgian-Irish expeditor Ann O'Brie, for example, is the source of many popular aphorisms, such as 'The most brilliant must learn from the most benighted', 'The future will be like perfume' and 'He who lives by the condom shall die by the condom.' In performance, the expeditor will assume a variety of roles – dancing to indicate different inferences appearing in the painter's verbal games, for example, or yelling urgent verbal instructions such as 'HOLD!' or 'KEEP ON!' or 'EASY DOES IT!' A popular expeditor's comments are frequently met with enormous gales of applause from the audience, and they often achieve great popularity and adulation, for they are seen as representing the voice of the people.

In the technical department of every Acrucian band is a formidable array of the most modern technology, all designed to manipulate the sound that the performers are making. The technical overseer in such a set-up is called the 'stretcher', and sees his job as that of extending the music electronically. Also in the technical department is the 'crowd-maker'. No Acrucian band likes to play without a supportive crowd, and so they all carry electronic samples of crowd noises to add to the performance if the real crowd is not loud enough. A good crowd-maker will respond to every change in the music with speed and flamboyance, whipping up an atmosphere of frenzy which quickly communicates to the audience. Recently the crowd-makers and stretchers have been assuming a more active role in the music of Acrux.

SHARING MUSIC

Since a lot of this book is about making records, and since most of my income arises from doing that, I thought it would be interesting to give an idea of how the income is actually generated and divided up. This is an extremely complex topic and I'm just skimming it: what follows should really be hedged with little clauses like 'except in the case of where . . .' But this is an overview, not a legal document.

When you buy an album, the money you spend gets divided up between a lot of people. The various people responsible for selling the record – the record company, the distributor and the retailer – all take their cuts.

The artist who recorded the record gets paid too: the record company passes on a negotiated royalty on each record (typically somehwere between 12 and 22% of the retail price). This is called the record royalty.

And of course the original composer of the music gets paid: copyright laws mandate that the composer receives a fixed royalty on each record (usually about 8% of the dealer price). This is collected by the composer's publisher, who also gets a slice (normally about 20% of what is collected).

In many cases the artist and the composer are one and the same person, who therefore collects both types of payment: perhaps about £1.60 per record.

But there is also another source of income from music. When a record is played on the radio or in a supermarket or on an aeroplane or in any public place there is theoretically a payment due to the composer of the music. The precise amount is determined by a labyrinthine set of national and international agreements which is policed by different non-profit-making societies in each country – in England it's the Performing Rights Society. Their job is to record each 'use' of a piece of music and then to charge the user and pass the money back to the composer. For instance, the owner of a café with a jukebox pays about £120 a year to the PRS, who divide that up between composers; a hotel which plays music in its foyer pays the PRS about £25 a year for every fifteen bedrooms. This is usually referred to as performance income.

Some examples:

If I recorded an album of myself singing Kate Bush songs, I would receive from the record company a record royalty of about £1.15 for each album sold. If I didn't produce this record myself, I would then have to pay my producer, who would get a royalty amounting to somewhere between 10p and 30p a disc.

Kate Bush (who need not know anything about all this) would also receive money: her publisher would collect – through the Mechanical Copyright Protection Society – about 65p for each record sold. The publisher would pass this on to Kate (minus their 20%-ish cut, so Kate probably earns more like 50p per disc).

Undoubtedly my single of Kate's 'Wuthering Heights' would soar to the top of the charts immediately. Again Kate and I would be paid — but for a single this is about 40p for me, the artist, and about 20p for Kate's publisher (therefore about 16p for her).

But big hit singles get a lot of radio play (and thus become bigger hit singles). This is where being the composer really starts to count financially, because it is the composer who earns the bulk of the direct income from airplay and other uses, not the performer or the producer. For example, the PRS is currently (October 1995) paying out around £50 per 3-minute play on Radio 1 (shared between Kate and her publisher). Local stations like Capital FM pay about £11. For a Radio 1 A-listed hit I could expect about 20 plays a week; if Capital like it they might put it on 40 times. There are radio stations all over Britain . . . So Kate would be receiving several thousand pounds a week from my version of her song. Now multiply that by the world.

Recently there has been an initiative to ensure that the performer gets some income from all this airplay. An organization called PPL exists to pay *performance* income to record companies and artists. The split is 67.5%

to the record company, 20% to the artist, and the rest to the Musicians' Union (which distributes to other players on the record). So far payments from PPL are fairly negligible.

The most you could earn from making an album? Well, if you were the composer, the artist and the producer (which is not totally unusual) then you get all these bits of income. So you could be earning, from record sales, something like £2.00 per record. If you're in the top bracket, and consequently receiving a much higher royalty, it would be more than this.

And this doesn't include all the income arising from airplay, use of the music in public places, on aeroplanes, in films, in ads, and on Teach-Yourself-Golf tapes. By far the largest proportion of that income is payable to the composer.

So perhaps that little glimpse into the labyrinth explains why most artists would prefer to write their own material.

But it also raises some interesting and vexed philosophical questions: if composing is the place where the big money is earned, then we need a definition of what 'composing' actually means. Presumably the only usable definition is 'putting into the music those elements that make it recognizably what it is, recognizably different from everything else'. Now you enter a real hornets' nest, where even given the best good will and intelligence – and I've rarely encountered less than that – agreements can become very complicated.

The old picture of what constituted a piece of music was based on the assumption that the identity of a piece of music was to be found somewhere in its melody and lyrics. Those things were seen as central, whereas others – such as interpretation, performance, production, arrangement and packaging – were regarded as 'non-compositional'. Thus the notes and lyrics that the Gershwin Brothers wrote on their scores constituted the compositional essence of the music. It's clear that this was – and still is – true for a lot of music, but it's equally clear that it is becoming less and less true for much new music.

This is because the practice of making music has changed so much over the last fifty years: composers and listeners are now routinely putting a lot of their attention into those aspects of the music which in Gershwin's day would have been seen as peripheral, as additions to the central compositional core.

I think of it like the layers of an onion: in the traditionalist view, it would be easy to identify that core of the onion and then to rank all other activities – performance, production, etc. – in terms of their apparent distance from it. But popular culture keeps confounding this picture by producing artists who decide to focus their compositional attention on a more 'peripheral' layer of the onion – and who conversely often pay very little attention to the things that copyright legislation would deem central.

Ambient Music (see page 293) is actually a good example of this, choosing as its subject-matter the sonic textures and spaces newly available as a result of electronic recording technologies. There is not really a reliable legal structure for dealing with the idea that music could be composed as a tapestry of abstract sound-textures rather than a structure of melodies and lyrics. And at another, much further remove there are bands for whom music is a carrier for style: the music is the package, and the package – hair, clothes, etc – has become the content. And why not?

The problem really arises from thinking that pop music is primarily a *musical* activity. It isn't, and never has been. This is why it has often been controversial and the rallying point of alternative cultures: would anyone care about it at all if it were *just* music? Pop has always involved a mélange of *at least* the following: melodies, sounds, language, clothes, fashions, lifestyle, attitudes to age, authority, relationships, the body and sex, dancing, visual imagery and the reassessments of value in all these things. So occasionally artists come along whose impact is not only or not much in the sound/language layer of the onion (which is the area that copyright legislation recognizes, the area traditionally called 'music'), but somewhere else.

And of course when people get excited about 'music' and buy records, what they're actually buying is this whole big mixture. They are of course

407

expecting that the traditional 'musical' elements (inasmuch as they are there at all) be at least acceptable and preferably wonderful, but they are not just buying those. They're buying into a philosophy, a look, a set of feelings about cultural life.

Since there is really no evolved structure for thinking about this, agreements end up being based either on traditional hand-me-downs that everyone recognizes have become more or less arbitrary, or on ad-hoc agreements which must be reassessed for every project. Each of these reassessments is actually a new view of how cultural value is created, where we think it comes from, and what the relationships are between different forms of it. So these are not, in the end, just trivial questions of 'How much do I get?'

Being a 'producer' – my frequent job description – introduces a whole new set of complications. First of all, no one really knows what the job description means. Is it the guy who sits in the corner of the control room grinning encouragingly and chopping cocaine, or is it Phil Spector, who writes the music, hires the musicians, grooms the vocalists, invents the sound, designs the image and then marries the lead singer? Somewhere between these extremes is a vague cloud of activities that get credited on record covers 'produced by. . .'

Traditionally, the producer was employed by the record company to shepherd studio-naive musicians through the job of getting their work onto disc – liaising with an engineer to get the sound of things right, suggesting additions to the music (as Muff Winwood used to say: 'I hear horns'), generally supervising the process from song to finished record. This job would also have involved some budgeting, hiring of extra musicians and so on. Things have changed, though: musicians are more sophisticated and the process of recording, far from being a mystery to them, is their musical palette, the set of terms within which they conceive the music. An increasing concern with the aspects of music beyond lyrics and melody characterizes the process of composing modern music, so the traditional job of 'producer' has partly been taken over by the musicians.

But the reverse has also happened: since so much of what characterizes a modern recording is exactly those aspects, what the producer does starts to merge with the job of composing: in short, the jobs traditionally called 'producing' and 'composing' have both expanded to overlap each other.

This kind of role-blur is the rule now, not the exception. More and more, creative jobs become generalized over several people, because those jobs themselves are increasingly likely to involve several layers of the cultural onion. Also the technologies we now use have tended to make creative jobs do-able by many different people: new technologies have the tendency to replace skills with judgement – it's not what you *can* do that counts, but what you *choose* to do, and this invites everyone to start crossing boundaries.

We have to think of ways of allocating the resources that arise between the people who made the work – which means deciding what 'the work' actually consists of and then making allocations on that basis. This can be very, very difficult, since it involves agreeing on judgements about the relative importance of all the different things and processes that go to make up a modern recording. Here's an example of one such situation:

Z's record had taken some months, working over and over on the same few pieces and bringing them slowly to life. It was coming together, but a sense of workmanlike routine was starting to pervade everything. It was tiring. The whole process needed a tonic, a leap out of the microcosm of details to widen the lens, to get back out to the bigger picture, grab a broad brush, and generally mix more metaphors. Accordingly I suggested a few days of improvisation, trying to do complete, whole new things instead of details, and, in a few hours of playing we came up with several substantially finished new pieces, some of which ended up on the record. I was also a player in those improvisations.

Now, how do I assess my contribution to that process, and to those songs? My authority in the situation led Z to trust me and try the experiment. But, the other way round: the fact that Z trusted me gave me that authority. My faith in the process, and the philosophical

409

frame within which I located the likely results of this way of working, added some momentum: if it seemed a somewhat obscure idea so late in the day (when we were supposed to be 'finishing' the record), I told a good enough story about it to make it seem at least worth a go.

On the other hand, the improvising process wasn't strange to Z, who'd just forgotten to do it lately. And it was Z's record, Z's studio costs, Z's reputation and credibility that were all at risk, not mine. So you could argue that the boldness was on Z's side, not mine.

But it was still my idea, and I was still a player in, and sometimes a sort of director of, the improvisations. So should I have been called a co-writer? Well, I had previously decided that my credit as 'producer' should cover whatever I did in the studio with Z, even though I knew this was an arbitrary distinction. The deal in my mind was like this: 'You call your work "song-writing", and I'll call mine "producing" – even though we both acknowledge that we overlap and do each other's jobs sometimes.'

So what I ended up suggesting there is the other way of dealing with allocations of this sort: simply to make almost arbitrary prior agreements and honour them no matter what actually happens during the process.

Of course, none of this deals at all with the completely new tangle of complexities that arise as a result of sampling – where people use bits of other people's music within their own. Currently this matter is in complete flux: on the one hand there are legal teams trying to put together structures that would describe the 'value' of a usage and try to establish payment for the samplee, and at the other end of the spectrum there are people like Negativland who believe any attempt to copyright 'intellectual property' is retrogressive – and Esther Dyson, who believes it effectively impossible anyway. I became more and more persuaded by their points of view.

STORY: SPERM AUCTION

Beryl was terribly excited. She'd been on the edge of her seat for the whole auction but hadn't bid once. She was waiting for the third-from-last lot: number 180. By the way the hall began filling up as the morning wore on, she had the feeling that many of the other women were doing the same.

The auctioneer's shrill voice cut through the hubbub. Her assistant re-emerged from a side-door carrying a large photograph of a handsome black man – Tadd Robinson, the charismatic champion surfer. In his heyday, back in the nineties, the auctioneer reminded her clients, Robinson was virtually unbeatable.

'"Brave" is too mild a word for this big, powerful man,' she said, and then added with the merest trace of a smile, 'as perhaps is "big".' The crowd tittered at the mildly sexual innuendo and then listened politely as the auctioneer opened the bidding.

'Lot 179: we have seven specimens of Tadd Robinson, all in prime condition, and all collected when he was 29 years old – in his fourth year as World Surfing Federation champion. We are directed to offer the seven specimens as one lot. May I now open the bidding at $20,000?'

There was no response from the floor. The auctioneer quickly scanned the crowd: 'Who'll start me at 15?' she said brightly. 'Come on now, ladies – you know this is an excellent price.'

From the left of the hall, a smart woman with a double-breasted suit and fashionable gold-mirror contact lenses raised her pen slightly. 'Ten,' she said, with no trace of emotion. Beryl turned to look at her – obviously an institutional buyer, probably bidding on behalf of one of the big speculative gene-banks. They often stockpiled the larger lots, keeping them stored at minus 70 until the whims of the market turned – or were changed – to their favour. Another woman, clearly professional, entered the bidding and the lot was quickly settled at $18,000.

411

The gavel fell to close the sale, and suddenly Beryl's tummy erupted in butterflies. THIS WAS REALLY IT! Now there was tangible tension in the air. The institutional buyers began filing out disdainfully, but as quickly as they left other women and couples squeezed in to take their seats. The place was completely crowded. Beryl glanced around at the others, and saw them doing the same, weighing up each other's relative wealth and prospects.

The auctioneer cleared her throat and lightly tapped the table. There was an instant hush.

'The next lot, as I'm sure you all know, is very special indeed. It is really one of a kind.'

As she spoke, the assistant raised a photograph, obviously greatly enlarged from a rather grainy original, of a genial, elderly, still handsome man. He was almost completely bald, and his clear, kind eyes squinted as though at a strong sun. His face was turned upwards away from the camera, looking into a bright future. On his great forehead there was a strange, dark birthmark.

'Mikhail Gorbachev', said the auctioneer, 'was first president of the liberated USSR. He lost that post, of course, but what he is really remembered for is his subsequent presidency of the United States. This truly remarkable man helped America rethink its place in the world – and if there is one person of whom it is possible to say "He saved the world" then it must surely be him. The nature of his disappearance is still a complete mystery, but that mystery is certainly no greater than the provenance of the sperm specimen which we are auctioning today. We simply do not know when, where or by whom it was collected. All we know is that it is genetically identical to Mikhail Gorbachev, and so we must assume that it is in fact his. Apart from the gene map, however, there is no paper on this item.'

The stirring speech generated a flurry of muttering in the hall. Beryl thought back over the past year, since the time the Gorbachev specimen had come to light. She remembered those first excited hopes, the pie-in-the-sky conversations with her husband, Robert, and his immediate attraction to the idea. Like most men of his generation, Robert was infertile, and his search for the right father for his children had taken him through all the usual choices – fighter aces, football players, Nobel Prize-winners, balding synthesizer players. But Robert was nothing if not ambitious, and when the Gorbachev specimen turned up – well, that was it. He was going for it.

'It's an investment, is how I see it,' he said, bent over a sheet of figures on the kitchen table. Beryl remembered leaning on his shoulder and watching his pencil racing up and down the columns, his calculating the odds of it taking and then the odds of it being a boy, and then the likely value of its future sperm.

'Yup,' he said, 'there's a risk factor, but the pay-off could be huge. I think we could raise it from the bank if I have a word with them. And anyway, even if it's a girl, it's still a Gorbachev!' Robert was completely convinced and wouldn't hear a word of Beryl's dutifully expressed cautions, her half-hearted can-we-really-afford-its, and ('Thank God,' she thought) ploughed right ahead.

And then her parents had offered to chip in too. 'Look, if it goes over the 250 thou, you can count on us for another hundred.' Dad, like most people of his generation, remembered Gorbachev very fondly, and obviously relished the idea of being grandfather to his child. And Mum was unusually excited, occasionally calling at odd times in the evening to say things like, 'But I really think you must teach the child Russian as a second language.'

Beryl and Robert decided not to show their new child to the media until the day after his birth. By then the whole maternity ward was swarming with teams of camera-people connected together by long cables, clustered round attractive reporters talking chirpily into their microphones.

Robert cuddled the little boy under the lights and looked proud, pointing, for the benefit of the cameras, to the dark birthmark on his neck. The whole of the town council (which had ended up contributing $100,000 to the price of the gene specimen on the grounds that it would be a great

413

profile-raiser for the city) was waiting to get in the door, while the mayor talked emotively to another camera team about the symbolism of this new beginning.

Huge clumps of exotic flowers filled every spare corner of the room, and Beryl's mother fussed over them, looking for window-sill space. A delivery girl pushed her way through the throng to hand Beryl yet another bunch. She looked at the accompanying card:

Warmest congratulations to you and your new arrival from all of us at Atlanta Gene Supplies. Oh Happy Day!

We do hope you'll get in touch with us when you're ready to discuss his future. Remember, you can count on a 'Yes' at AGS.

She put it with all the others on the bedside table. Her eyes briefly met with Robert's. They flashed triumphant smiles. They were so happy.

(1993)

UNFINISHED

The word is out, and the word is wrong. 'Interactive' is the wrong word.

Let's get one thing clear: culture, like conversation, is by definition interactive. To talk about 'interactive culture' is as redundant as to talk about 'interactive conversation'. Of course a conversation is interactive, since it involves at least two people making choices, engaging with meanings external to themselves, and responding to them. Culture is not different from this: it is an invitation to you to engage with a different world, a world of your and someone else's imagination. Without your active engagement in that invitation, nothing happens. You are never actually a passive consumer of culture, because the only sense in which the verb 'to consume' has any meaning in this context is when it means 'to agree to engage with'.

Adding a computer mouse to allow you to make some crude choices is not in essence different from giving you a remote with which to control your television, if all you're actually being offered is the chance to navigate through this huge block of preformed data rather than that.

So what is the difference between the things that people are making now as compared to what they were making before? I think it can be summed up in a better word: 'unfinished'. The idea is very clear: here is an object of culture which you must finish to be able to use it. Another way of saying that is to suggest that culture-makers are moving away from providing pure, complete experiences to providing the platforms from which people then fashion their own experiences. This is certainly not a theme confined to the arts, by the way: more and more consumers are expecting to buy into systems that they then customize for themselves. A good recent example is the new type of home hi-fi system that offers all sorts of options of sound treatment – the implication being that the machine you've bought needs to be adapted to your situation and your interests and whims, and, more fundamentally, that the record you've bought is not a finished and sacred item but is susceptible to further changes by you.

Compare this to the old era of 'high-fidelity', where the idea was that you, the consumer, should serve the music, honouring it with expensive and so-called 'accurate' equipment, and then sitting or kneeling on your chair, equidistant between your speakers, being careful not to cough or move your head.

In fact, this classical notion of how we use culture has almost disappeared, except of course in Old High Culture, which, though often the first to host the new cultural experiments, is nearly always the last to learn anything from their results. But in general we no longer feel such a sharp distinction between the culture-maker and the culture consumer. We feel that culture is there for us to use and to incorporate into our lives as we wish. We don't feel guilty about using the Fauré Requiem as background while we clean the house, and we don't feel bad wearing jeans with a Versace jacket. We mix and match. We make our own cultural statements.

This has of course affected how culture is being produced: people are starting to make things that implicitly invite 'mixing and matching' instead of presenting us with neatly finished pieces. You can see this breakdown of the singularity of the art-object most spectacularly in the remix movement in popular music. It used to be the case that a record was expected to contain the definitive and perhaps only version of a song, and that the job of the band and the producer was to create this 'ideal' object. Now this has loosened up a lot. It is very usual for a song to be released in up to 20 different forms – short mixes, long mixes, radio mixes, dance mixes, ambient mixes – and of course it can't be very long before we are routinely faced with the awesomely tedious prospect of having to mix everything ourselves at home, the artists just selling a CD-Rom 'kit of parts' which you then assemble.

The concept of 'unfinished' represents a new idea about the cultural tools we work with, about how we expect to behave both as 'artists' and as 'consumers', about how those roles increasingly overlap; but it also represents the beginning of a new philosophical landscape. Once we get used to the idea that we are no longer consumers of 'finished' works, but that we

416

are people who engage in conversations and interactions with things, we find ourselve leaving a world of 'know your own station' passivity and we start to develop a taste for active engagement. We stop regarding things as fixed and unchangeable, as preordained, and we increasingly find ourselves practising the idea that we have some control. Most importantly, perhaps, we might start to think the same way about ourselves: that we are unfinished (and unfinishable) beings whose task is constantly to re-examine and remix our ideas and our identities.

This is the most optimistic thing I can think of – that people abandon the increasingly perilous old definitions of identity, such as race and ethnicity and class and blood, and start thinking of identity as something multiple, shifting, blurred, experimental and adaptive. I think the philosophical underpinning for such a change is already sliding into place under the guise of pure entertainment.

(1994)

UNTHINKABLE FUTURES

These unthinkable futures developed out of an Internet conversation with Kevin Kelly and others. They were first published in *Whole Earth Review* in 1992.

- Ordinary people routinely employ publicists, and public relations becomes the biggest profession in wealthy countries. Life becomes an endless struggle for media attention.
- Sexual roles reverse: men wear make-up and are aggressively pursued by women in ill-fitting clothes
- Everybody becomes so completely cynical about the election process that voter turnout drops to 2% (families and friends of prospective candidates), until finally the 'democratic process' is abandoned in favour of a lottery system. Everything immediately improves.
- It turns out that nearly all the conspiracy theories you ever heard were actually true – that the world really is being run by 150 malevolent men with extremely nasty prejudices.
- Simultaneously, it begins to become clearer that there really are significant racial differences between people – that the stereotypes were right after all.
- Smoking is proven to be good exercise for the lungs.
- A new kind of holiday becomes popular: you are dropped by helicopter in an unknown place, with two weeks' supply of food and water. You are assured that you will not see anyone at all in this time. There is a panic button just in case.
- Seed companies start selling packets of unpredictable mutants produced by random genetic-engineering programmes: 'JUST PLANT 'EM AND SEE WHAT COMES UP!' Suburbia becomes covered with exotic blooms and giant cucumbers.

- Genetic research shows that it is possible to create gifted scientists, great artists, sublime linguists and supreme athletes. Everyone subsequently starves to death through lack of farmers, cooks and waiters.
- Video phones inspire a new sexual revolution where everybody sits at home doing rude things electronically with everyone else. Productivity slumps; video screens get bigger and bigger.
- Suicide becomes not only commonplace but socially acceptable and even encouraged. People choose when to die: living too long is considered selfish and old-fashioned.
- As the cult of youth fades away, plastic surgeons find a profitable new market in making people look interestingly wrinkled, wisely aged and experientially weatherbeaten. Also, as oriental aesthetics sweep the West, the traditional values of physiological symmetry and freedom from blemish are seen as naive and uninteresting. Perfect youngsters from Colorado, after years of fretful mirror-gazing, finally save enough money to get their noses put on wrong, or to have a few teeth blackened.
- Tanned skin is once again seen as a mark of the peasantry. Sunblock-wearing becomes routine. Modern beaches have UV filter domes over them.
- Mass outbreaks of allergies unexpectedly solve all major transportation problems by confining almost everyone to their sealed residences. Telecommunications stocks soar.
- Abandoned high-rise projects become the residence of choice for the urban chic, changing hands for ever-increasing sums, until finally only lawyers, stockbrokers and publicists (skilfully posing as members of dispossessed minority groups) are able to afford them. Original graffiti and piss-soaked elevators are highly prized and protected by court orders.
- AD 2010: California elects the first transsexual governor. All public toilets are redesigned at great expense.

419

- New drugs to pacify children (modern laudanum) are smilingly sold by big pharmaceutical companies. The drugs have names like 'Mr Sandman', 'Sleepytime' and 'Land of Nod'.
- A new concept of 'Global Darwinism' takes root: people argue for the right of the human species to be rid of weak specimens. Aid to developing countries ceases. Hospitals become 'viability assessment centres' and turn away or terminate poor specimens and unpromising cases.
- In reaction, a new definition of viability (based on memes – ideas – rather than genes) is invoked. People are subjected to exhaustive tests (occupying huge amounts of their time) to check the originality and scope of their ideas. A new profession, meme-inspector, comes into being.
- Schools abandon the attempt to teach the three Rs, concentrating instead on wacky and controversial 'personhood' therapies. Everyone grows up bonkers in some way or another. The whole of the next century is like the late sixties.
- A highly successful new magazine, *Ordinary People* – edited by the nonagenarian Studs Terkel – focuses only on people who have never done anything in particular to deserve attention.
- A new type of artist arises: the professional objet-trouvist (or vernacular curator) – someone whose task is to gather together existing but overlooked pieces of amateur art and, by directing public attention at them, to make them important. His taste is what is being collected.
- The first Bio-Olympics, where athletes can have anything added to or subtracted from their bodies, take place in 2004.
- 'News' is increasingly understood to be a creation of our attention and interests (rather than 'the truth'), and news shows are redesigned as 'think-tanks' where four interesting minds from different disciplines are asked the question 'So what do YOU think happened today?'

- Later, four uninteresting minds, chosen from the pages of *Ordinary People* magazine, are asked the same question.
- Pro-Lifers discover that women are 20% less likely to miscarry if confined to bed and sedated for the first trimester. Congress bows to pressure and legislates obligatory rest. Shopping in the early stages of pregnancy becomes punishable.
- The set of *Terminator 9* is wrecked by a pressure group of industrial robots who object to this stereotyping.
- Jesus returns to Earth and is discovered in flagrante delicto with a group of flagellant monks from Opus Dei. Judas is rehabilitated.
- A microbe engineered to eat oil slicks evolves a taste for rubber. Transport grinds to a halt on burst tyres. People stay home and have sex more, but condoms crumble unstoppably. World population doubles in six years.
- As scenario projections become more accurate and convincing, people become increasingly aware of the unwelcome results of their own actions. All social action becomes paralysed, bogged down in endless evaluations in purely negative terms: 'Is this course of action less harmful than that?'
- Travelling as a process enjoys a revival. People abandon the idea of 'getting from A to B' and begin to develop (or rediscover) a culture of travelling: semi-nomadism. Lots of people acquire super new faxed-and-modemed versions of the mobile home. It becomes distinctly 'lower class' to live in a fixed location. Fast forms of transport come to be viewed as fast food is now – tacky, undesirable, fake.
- Manufacturers of underwear finally realize that men's balls are not all the same size.
- Prince Charles converts to Catholicism, thus avoiding becoming king without actually abdicating (Anthea's theory).
- Television producers, impressed by the phenomenal success of the broadcast Anita Hill/Clarence Thomas hearings, regularly invent

421

and stage semi-surrogate 'hearings' where emotional issues are vented. Nobody is ever sure whether they are fixed or partially fixed or actually for real. They take the place of staged wrestling matches and roller derby for the thinking classes.

- The commonly held notion that it is correct to surround children with love, security and affection suffers a serious decline in credibility when it becomes apparent that kids thus reared are entirely unequipped for a world that is cruel, dangerous and insecure. Enlightened parents begin experimenting with new forms of toys: teddies with sharp teeth and unpredictable behaviour, building blocks with abrasive surfaces, mildly toxic crayons, unsafe play areas.

- Disabled people finally come into their own as remote operators of tele-robots. They are the only ones prepared to commit the immense amount of time necessary to learning the finesse of working within another body.

- Slavery is re-evaluated. Professional people, tired of the responsibility of controlling their own affairs, annually submit to 'slavery-vacations' where they work very hard for nothing and under strict surveillance. This becomes a secular version of taking holy orders.

- A new art form comes into existence. It attempts to recreate the first experience of old pop records etc. by complex multimedia presentations – the exact time of day, the right light, the same smells. It is especially popular among the emerging communes of old people who sit around enjoying their last 30 years in a blissful haze of pot smoke and old Rolling Stones records (Stewart's idea).

- Big changes in education: a combination of monetarism and liberalism creates a new paradigm wherein schools are expected to be run as successful business, manufacturing and research enterprises. Some results:
  - The infant think-tank, where the innocent originality of children is routinely tapped by captains of industry for large sums of money.
  - Various highly original manufacturing industries: hand-painted

wallpaper and postcards, naive sculpture and pottery, clothing design and manufacture.

– Teachers chosen (by the kids of course) on the basis of their performance record and likely profitability. They are subjected to gruelling and penetrating interviews by the kids, their employers-to-be.

– The old concept of education 'in the abstract' (i.e. unrelated to real tasks) is practised only in the most benighted outposts of the old world – England, America, etc.

– Successful children are traded between schools for huge transfer fees.

– Schools completely abandon divisions based on age. People of all ages turn up and sort themselves into effective and profitable groups.

– People with lots of money give their children small 'start-up' companies for Christmas, or endow their kids' schools with them.

(See also page 411: Sperm auction; page 390: Personal profile.)

WAR CHILD

War Child is a charity started by Bill Leeson and David Wilson, two English film-makers. They were in former Yugoslavia making a film, but felt unable to ignore what they saw going on around them; so, after completing their work (for the BBCs 'Arena' series), they put film-making on the back burner in order to do something practical in Bosnia. The charity was formed in 1992, with its main aim to focus public attention on the physical and psychological problems of children caught up in the war.

Anthea got me involved. She'd heard a radio interview about War Child in early 1993 and contacted the radio station to get a phone number. She then went to its offices (two small rooms in a Camden back street) and suggested trying to use her music-business contacts to raise money. She also suggested adding me to their list of patrons (at that stage Tom Stoppard and Juliet Stevenson). We gave them some money, and later I met David and Bill and was impressed by their attitude and dedication. I completely trusted them.

We soon formed a think-tank of interested people to generate ideas about how we could help. Like everyone else, we were getting fed up with mediocre events being put on for good causes, so our first decision was that anything we did should be of good enough quality to justify its existence regardless of its charitable intentions.

The first event we put on for War Child was an exhibition, at Flowers East gallery, of pictures and photos and objects made by musicians and people with close ties to the music business. These were all subsequently auctioned at the Royal College of Art. Naturally we were identified (in *Time Out*) as shameless self-publicists, but it all went ahead nonetheless and raised a lot of money. More importantly, perhaps, it gave the young people of Bosnia some sense that people they respected were paying some attention to what was happening to them, and it raised the profile of War Child within the music fraternity. It was altogether a great success.

During the period of this diary Anthea organized Pagan Fun Wear (see page 387), an absurdly ambitious project which nearly finished us both off, but once again added to the cachet of War Child within the music business. Two events followed this that – in financial terms – dwarfed our shows. The *Help* record, organized by the unfailingly energetic people at Go! Discs, saw 20 bands record and release an album within a week. This went to the top of the charts and has made an enormous contribution to War Child's funds. Then, just three days later, Luciano Pavarotti's huge concert with friends at Modena generated several hundred thousand pounds more.

So why did I get involved in the first place? I'd never been actively involved with any charity before, and I've been quite critical of such involvements on the part of others. But Yugoslavia (and Anthea) changed my mind. I felt that it was impossible for me not to react when a country that seemed to embody the civilized, pluralist conduct that we claimed to defend was getting mauled and tortured by crypto-fascists. It didn't help that we were all more or less lost in a complex moral/historical argument that was lovingly stirred by clever Balkans historians who wanted to be sure we understood how complex and intractable the whole situation was. But it became clearer and clearer to us, over many evenings of conversation, that two things (at least) were not complicated. The first was that most of the victims of this war – especially the children – were entirely innocent, so one need not fully decide all the imponderables before trying to help them. To do otherwise struck me as rather like seeing a man having his head bashed in with a hammer, and then listening patiently while the aggressor (still hammering) tells you what a difficult life he's had.

The second thing I realized, and which became a running theme for me throughout this year, is that there is a distinction between moral ideas and legal agreements. Legal structures come into being to describe the envelope of acceptable behaviour: they define the currently acceptable range of relationships between people, institutions and states. They are arrived at by consensus – 'this is what we've agreed to adhere to' – and, by definition, do not lay claim to absolute rightness: they are always subject to review.

They are an expression of 'what seemed best at the time, in the circumstances', but, while they remain in force, it behoves us to respect them and to defend them. Just as we would not accept someone walking into our house with a gun and saying, as they loaded our belongings into a bag, 'I don't agree with any of those laws about private property', so we ought not to accept one group invading another and saying, 'We don't agree with all those laws about territorial integrity.' In both cases, we should say, 'You are free to disagree, but this isn't the way to express such differences.'

It seemed to me that so much of the argument about Bosnia was an argument about whether the Serbs had a reasonable moral case for their attempt to annex it. I don't know the answer either, but it became clearer and clearer that this was not the time to be waiting, paralysed by indecision, for the final result of that essentially moral discussion (which already had been running for a few hundred years) before we decided to act on what was clearly a breach of our legal agreements.

This same applies, incidentally, to the Salman Rushdie affair. All the discussion about whether *The Satanic Verses* was actually blasphemous, whether writers should be allowed to write such material, whether Iran had good reason to be upset and so on, was beside the point in the face of an action that was quite clearly and transparently not legal: the exhortation (and promise of reward) by a foreign power to kill a citizen of another state. There is no moral discussion needed here: such behaviour is something that we have agreed not to do, and, finally, these agreements (and not the moral constructions that claim to underpin them) are the basis of cooperation and empathy.

WOBBLY LETTER

Dear Dominic,

My impressions on the Wobble mixes:

(1) 'Cello, Arabic Style'. Lovely, leave it as it is.

(2) 'Solo Organ'. Also fine, though bass loud (so you don't hear the original pulse well enough, which makes the bass seem a bit unanchored, I think). Nice bass part though: how about just a simple rebalance? I like reverb on basses – a touch here would be nice.

(3) 'Steam and Cello'. Perhaps because I know the original, this seems a slightly arbitrary combination to me. But I like it (but I also love the original piece, which I think could be a bit louder, or perhaps heard solo for longer, especially the part (about three-quarters of the way thru) where it grinds into that very low section).

(4) 'Thai Arpeggio'. Nice cross-fade into this piece – actually, all the cross-fades are nice and work well. The piece sounds good, and I like whatever has happened to it via the Wobbling One.

(5) 'Radiothesia'. I like the bass on this a lot, but I have problems with the 'twangs' on it – at least until later on, where he starts to do something weird with the repeat on them. I like that – making them strange features. Perhaps that should have happened more, and earlier. Otherwise they're in danger of being late-seventies funk. The melody is simplistic and happens too much for my taste. I wish it were slightly more atonal in its choice of notes, less regular in its internal timing (right now each note occupies exactly four beats). Is it really necessary to have a melody? If so, it must be more weird than this.

(6) 'Scrapy' is good. I selfishly wish the original stuff of mine was louder – its weirdness is what gives the thing a strange edge. I like very much the times when the original piano stuff breaks through – for instance when there's that gap and then the return, and you hear that

rapid piano figure. I think Wob should treat me here as one of the world's legendary soloists, now unfortunately deceased, whose secret archives he has just discovered . . .

(7) 'Space Diary'. Nice movement into this, and it's smart of him to leave it alone.

(8) 'Decentered Spinner'. This track I have some trouble with. It's just that the Wobbling One is so up and enthusiastic here, and the original music, courtesy of the Miserable One, is so darkly romantic and Moorish. They seem to be having a communication difficulty: as though the sultry and perfumed Moorish maiden, her dark eyes downcast, awaits her lover on the violet-fragranced balcony, and he swings in upside down on a bungee rope playing air guitar and wearing a red nose. But I guess these things do happen – especially to me.

(9) 'Copter/Trumpet'. This is a big improvement on a piece that had very little going for it – in fact it's really a Wob piece with some sound effects from me. A big success, but again I wonder whether the copters and trumpets might be better louder – whenever I hear them break through I like it. Maybe there are reasons for why they are discreet – but the stutteriness of them sounds great among these big washes. I think that original performance should be treated not as a sound effect but as a bizarre new solo instrument (played here by the legendary Al Orange), featured, and allowed to stutter around more conspicuously. All that said, this is still very good.

(10) 'Synth & New Piano'. I think the opening on this is so great. I almost wish it stayed in that mood for a much longer time. This is another case where I love the original piece and want to hear more of it – and I think the metal insects that Wob has added are a great contribution. Any chance of a longer section of just me and wobble insects? I think a hiatus like this would be welcome after the long and full piece before. Listening again, later, I am convinced this is a good idea. At present the bass enters at about 20 seconds into the

track. I think I could easily hear its entry (together with drums) at 47 seconds or at 1 minute 11 seconds or even later. This doesn't require replaying – even just a little mix of the new front piece to edit on to the existing mix would work.

As a bit of a lad for a funny-sounding drum kit ('The Godfather of the Drum Treatment' as the *Bolton Chronicle* once referred to me), I am perhaps unjustly judgemental when I hear other people's attempts. But I have to say it: this drum treatment seems unsympathetic. It's too – too – too ravey? Too Aren't-we-having-a-far-out-time? Too If-I-put-enough-flanging-on-this-you'll-think-it's-interesting. (I say this as a consultant to the Coalition to Prevent Unnecessary Flanging – COPUF – an interest I felt I should declare now.)

I like the music on this track where it isn't trying to be musical. Another way of saying that is that I think the main balalaika melody is close to being trite – again (like on 'Radiothesia') it has this problem of being very even in pace and rather unsurprising: the notes go pretty much where you'd expect them and have little emotional charge. It's a shame, because the rest of the music on this track – all swirling and dissonant – is really strong. Perhaps I attach too much importance to melody, but I feel it is being pushed forward rather proudly in this mix and doesn't quite live up to its pedestal.

My summing up. The first thing is that this is a big improvement (as a record) on what I'd got before, no doubt about that – so my comments should be seen as matters of detail rather than concept. The second thing is that I like it more as I hear it, presumably as I stop listening for what I originally did and start hearing the things as whole pieces. I notice on reading my comments that I frequently want to hear more of me. This is the typical bastard prat musician's response to any mix you play them where they're not the only instrument, and I'm embarrassed to find myself saying it. BUT: what I like about my stuff (in this context) is that it makes a very nice contrast: the stutters and wobbles and the peculiar harmonic

429

structures I use – these all take the stuff somewhere else, somewhere out of the ordinary. They are what I do that other people don't.

But another voice in the teeming firmament of my mind says, 'Just shut up and leave it alone for once. Let someone else decide.' And it does make an impression that people whose opinion I should respect have said they like this. It's probably harder for me to hear this objectively than anyone else, because I'm always listening through to what I know I did underneath it all. So I need advice, persuasion, sympathy, reassurance, love, bribery, compassion, slow-at-first – typical Moorish-maiden stuff.

AUTOBIOGRAPHY AND LIST OF WORKS

I was born in 1948, in Woodbridge, Suffolk, a small market town near the east coast of England. My father was a postman and my mother a Belgian immigrant.

I grew up in Woodbridge, and my mother, brother, sister, aunts, cousins, and other relatives still live there or in the area. I went to a Catholic grammar school and then to Ipswich Art School, where I studied with Roy Ascott, Anthony Benjamin, Tom Phillips, Noel Forster and others. I took a Diploma in Fine Art at Winchester School of Art with Heinz Henghes, Trevor Bell and others.

I left Winchester in 1969 and moved to London. Shortly afterwards I joined Roxy Music and began making and producing records. In the late seventies I picked up my visual art activities again and began making installations with light, video, slides and sound.

SOLO ALBUMS

1973	*Here Come the Warm Jets* (Virgin)
1974	*Taking Tiger Mountain (by Strategy)* (Virgin)
1975	*Another Green World* (Virgin)
	Discreet Music (Obscure)
1976	*Music for Films* (limited edition of 500) (Virgin)
1977	*Before and After Science* (Virgin)
1978	*Music for Films* (Virgin)
	Ambient 1: Music for Airports (Virgin)
1982	*Ambient 4: On Land* (Virgin)
1983	*Working Backwards 1983–73* (ten-album boxed-set) (Virgin)
1983	*More Music For Films* (Virgin)
1985	*Thursday Afternoon* (compact disc) (Virgin)
1986	*More Blank Than Frank* (compilation) (Virgin)
	Desert Island Selection (compilation for CD) (Virgin)

1992	*Nerve Net* (Opal/Warner Bros)
	The Shutov Assembly (Opal/Warner Bros)
1993	*Neroli* (All Saints Records)
1997	*The Drop* (All Saints)
1997	*Extracts from Music for White Cube* (Opal)
1998	*I Dormienti* (Opal)
1998	*Lightness: Music for the Marble Palace* (Opal)
1999	*Kite Stories* (Opal)
2000	*Music for Civic Recovery Centre* (Opal)
2001	*Compact Forest Proposal*
2003	*January 07003: Bell Studies for the Clock of the Long Now* (Opal)
2003	*Curiosities Volume I* (Opal)
2004	*Curiosities Volume II* (Opal)
2005	*Another Day on Earth* (Opal)
2010	*Making Space* (Opal)
2012	*LUX* (Warp)
2015	*My Squelchy Life* (Opal – Record Store Day exclusive)
2016	*The Ship* (Warp)
2017	*Reflection* (Warp)
2018	*Music for Installations* (Universal – six album box set)
2020	*Rams Original Soundtrack* (Opal – Record Store Day exclusive)
2020	*Film Music: 1976–2020* (Universal)

ALBUM PRODUCTION OR CO-PRODUCTION

1973	*Portsmouth Sinfonia Plays the Popular Classics,* Portsmouth Sinfonia (Transatlantic)
1974	*Hallelujah,* Portsmouth Sinfonia (Transatlantic)
	Fear, John Cale (Island)
1975	*The Sinking of the Titanic,* Gavin Bryars (Obscure)
	Ensemble Pieces, Christopher Hobbs/John Adams/Gavin Bryars (Obscure)

New and Rediscovered Musical Instruments, David Toop/Max
Eastley (Obscure)

Lucky Lief & the Longships, Robert Calvert (UA)

1976   Voices & Instruments, Jan Steel/John Cage (Obscure)

Decay Music, Michael Nyman (Obscure)

Music from the Penguin Café, Penguin Café Orchestra (Obscure)

1977   Ultravox, Ultravox (Island)

1978   More Songs About Buildings & Food, Talking Heads (Sire)

Q: Are We Not Men? A: We Are Devo, Devo (Virgin)

No New York, Contortions/Teenage Jesus and The Jerks/Mars/
DNA (Antilles)

Machine Music, John White/Gavin Bryars (Obscure)

Irma – An Opera, Tom Phillips/Gavin Bryars/Fred Orton (Obscure)

The Pavilion of Dreams, Harold Budd (Obscure)

1979   Fear of Music, Talking Heads (Sire)

1980   Remain in Light, Talking Heads (Sire)

Ambient 3: Day of Radiance, Laraaji (Virgin)

1981   The Pace Setters, Edikanfo (Virgin)

Fourth World Vol. 2: Dream Theory in Malaya, Jon Hassell
(Virgin)

1984   The Unforgettable Fire, U2 (Island)

1985   Hybrid, Michael Brook (Virgin)

Voices, Roger Eno (Virgin)

Africana, Theresa de Sio (Polydor)

1986   The Falling, Carmel (2 tracks) (London)

Power Spot, Jon Hassell (ECM)

1987   The Joshua Tree, U2 (Island)

The Surgeon of the Night Sky Restores Dead Things by the Power
of Sound, Jon Hassell (Intuition)

1988   Flash of the Spirit, Jon Hassell/Farafina (Intuition)

1989   Zvuki Mu, Zvuki Mu (Opal/Warner Bros.)

Words for the Dying, John Cale (Opal/Warner Bros.)

Inc, Terry Riley (Celestial Harmonies)

1990   *Exile,* Geoffrey Oryema (Real World)

1991   *Achtung Baby,* U2 (Island)

1992   *When I Was a Boy,* Jane Siberry (WEA)

       Complete Service, Yellow Magic Orchestra – live album mix
production (Alfa)

1993   *Zooropa,* U2 (Island)

       Laid, James (Phonogram)

1994   *Wah Wah,* James (Phonogram)

       Bright Red, Laurie Anderson (Warner Bros.)

1995   *Outside,* David Bowie (BMG)

1999   *Millionaires,* James, with Saul Davies, Mark Hunter & David
Baynton-Power (Mercury)

2000   *All That You Leave Behind,* U2 (with Daniel Lanois) (Island)

2008   *Viva la Vida,* Coldplay (Parlophone)

2011   *Mylo Xyloto,* Coldplay (Parlophone)

2017   *Altar,* The Gift (La Folie)

PRIMARY COLLABORATION

1972   *Virginia Plain,* Roxy Music (Virgin)

       Roxy Music, Roxy Music (Virgin)

1973   *For Your Pleasure,* Roxy Music (Virgin)

       Pyjamarama, Roxy Music (Virgin)

       No Pussyfooting, Fripp/Eno (Virgin)

1974   *June 1st 1974,* Kevin Ayers/John Cale/Eno/Nico (Island)

       Evening Star, Fripp/Eno (Virgin)

1976   *801 Live,* 801 (Virgin)

1977   *Cluster and Eno,* Cluster and Eno (Sky)

       Low, David Bowie (RCA)

       Heroes, David Bowie (RCA)

1978   *After the Heat,* Eno/Moebius/Roedelius (Sky)

1979   *Lodger,* David Bowie (RCA)

1980	*Ambient 2: The Plateaux of Mirror*, Harold Budd/Brian Eno (Virgin)
	Fourth World Vol 1: Possible Musics, Jon Hassell/Brian Eno (Virgin)
1981	*My Life in the Bush of Ghosts*, Brian Eno/David Byrne (Virgin/Sire)
1983	*Apollo – Atmospheres and Soundtracks*, Brian Eno with Daniel Lanois and Roger Eno (Virgin)
1984	*The Pearl*, Harold Budd/Brian Eno with Daniel Lanois (Virgin)
1988	*Music for Films III*, Eno with Lanois, Budd, Brook, Jones, Laraaji, Mahlin and Theremin (Opal/Warner Bros.)
	You Don't Miss Your Water (*Married to the Mob* soundtrack, USA film) (Warner Bros.)
1990	*Wrong Way Up*, Brian Eno/John Cale (Opal/Warner Bros.)
1995	*Spinner*, Brian Eno with Jah Wobble (All Saints Records)
	Original Soundtracks 1: Passengers, with U2, Pavarotti, Howie B., and Holi (Island)
1997	*Tracks & Traces*, Harmonia & Eno (Grönland)
2000	*Music For Onmyo-Ji*, Brian Eno with Peter Schwalm (Japan only) (Victor)
2001	*Drawn From Life*, Brian Eno with Peter Schwalm (Virgin)
2004	*The Equatorial Stars*, Fripp & Eno (DGM)
2006	*Beyond Even*, Fripp & Eno (DGM)
2008	*Everything That Happens Will Happen Today*, Brian Eno/David Byrne (Todo Mundo)
2010	*Small Craft on a Milk Sea*, Brian Eno with Leo Abrahams and Jon Hopkins (Warp)
2011	*Drums Between the Bells*, Brian Eno with Rick Holland (Warp)
2014	*Someday World*, Eno•Hyde (Warp)
2014	*High Life*, Eno•Hyde (Warp)
2017	*Finding Shore*, Tom Rogerson with Brian Eno (Dead Oceans)
2019	*Apollo: Atmospheres & Soundtracks Extended Edition*, Brian Eno with Daniel Lanois and Roger Eno (Universal)
2020	*Mixing Colours*, Roger and Brian Eno (Deutsche Grammophon)

INSTALLATIONS

Over the past forty-one years, I have had 173 shows of my audio/video installations in the following locations: Abu Dhabi, Adelaide, Amsterdam, Asheville, Athens, Baku, Barcelona, Bari, Beijing, Berkeley, Berlin, Bilbao, Bonn, Boston, Brighton, Brussels, Buenos Aires, Buffalo, Calgary, Cape Town, Cleveland, Cologne, Copenhagen, Dublin, Egeskov, Eindhoven, Florence, Frankfurt, Gateshead, Geneva, Grenoble, Hamburg, Hanover, Helsinki, Herefordshire, Houston, Hove, Huddinge, Istanbul, Karlsruhe, Kobe, Kristiansand, Lanzarote, Łódź, London, London Ontario, Long Beach, Lyon, Madrid, Macclesfield, Mantua, Mexico City, Miami, Milan, Minneapolis, Montreal, Munich, Naples, New York, Oxford, Palma de Mallorca, Paris, Perugia, Prague, Riga, Rio de Janeiro, Rome, St Louis, St Petersburg, San Francisco, Santa Monica, Sao Paolo, Sarajevo, Stockholm, Sydney, Tenkawa, Tokyo, Toronto, Trani, Turin, Vancouver, Venice, Vienna, Wattens, Wrocław, Zaragoza.

BIBLIOGRAPHY

(books referred to in the Diary)

Nicholas Albery (ed.), *Best Ideas: A Compendium of Social Innovations*

Christopher Alexander, *A Foreshadowing of 21st Century Art: The Color and Geometry of Very Early Turkish Carpets*

Ivo Andrić, *Bridge over the Drina*

Benjamin Barber, *Jihad vs. McWorld: How the Planet is Both Falling – Apart and Coming Together and What This Means for Democracy*

John Barrow, *The Artful Universe*

Stafford Beer, *Brain of the Firm*

John Berendt, *Midnight in the Garden of Good and Evil*

Daniel Boorstin, *The Creators*

B. A. Botkin (ed.), *Lay My Burden Down: A Folk History of Slavery*

Stewart Brand, *How Buildings Learn: What Happens After They're Built*

Fernand Braudel, *Civilization and Capitalism: The Perspective of the World*

John Brockman, *The Third Culture: Beyond the Scientific Revolution*

Italo Calvino, *Italian Folktales*

John Colville, *The Fringes of Power: Downing Street Diaries 1939–1955*

Anton Corbijn, *Star Trak*

Martin van Creveld, *The Transformation of War*

Arthur Danto, *The Transfiguration of the Commonplace*

Richard Dawkins, *River Out of Eden*

Daniel Dennett, *Darwin's Dangerous Idea: Evolution and the Meanings of Life*

G. M. Dillon (ed.), *Defence Policy Making: A Comparative Analysis*

Laurie Toby Edison and Debbie Notkin, *Women En Large: Images of Fat Nudes*

Sebastian Faulks, *Birdsong*

Francis Fukuyama, *Trust*

Joel Garreau, *Edge City*

George Grosz, *Ecce Homo*

Bill Gunston, *The Encyclopedia of Modern Warplanes*

Edward T. Hall, *Beyond Culture*

Garrett Hardin and John Baden, *Managing the Commons*

Friedrich Herr, *The Middle Ages*

James Hillman, *Going Bugs*

– *Inter Views*

Robert Hughes, *Culture of Complaint*

Johann Huizinga, *The Waning of the Middle Ages*

Will Hutton, *The State We're In*

Kevin Kelly, *Out of Control: The Rise of Neo-Biological Civilization*

Nick Kotz, *Wild Blue Yonder*

Eric Kroll, *Fetish Girls*

Giuseppe Tomasi di Lampedusa, *The Leopard*

Steven Levy, *Artificial Life*

Alan Lomax, *Folk Song Style and Culture*

A. J. McMichael, *Planetary Overload: Global Environmental Change and the Health of the Human Species*

Nicholas Negroponte, *Being Digital*

Gilles Neret, *Erotica Universalis*

Michael Nyman, *Experimental Music: Cage and Beyond*

James Ogilvy, *Living Without a Goal*

Michael Ondaatje, *Billy the Kid*

Robert E. Ornstein, *The Evolution of Consciousness*

Morse Peckham, *Art and Pornography: An Experiment in Explanation*

– *Man's Rage for Chaos: Biology, Behavior and the Arts*

Tom Phillips, *Tom Phillips: Works and Texts*

Steven Pinker, *The Language Instinct*

Karl Popper, *In Search of a Better World: Lectures and Essays from Thirty Years*

William Poundstone, *Prisoner's Dilemma*

E. Annie Proulx, *Postcards*
Richard Rorty, *Consequences of Pragmatism*
– *Contingency, Irony and Solidarity*
Salman Rushdie, *The Moor's Last Sigh*
Jon Savage, *England's Dreaming*
Sterling Seagrave, *Lords of the Rim*
Leonard Shlain, *Art and Physics: Parallel Visions in Space, Time and Light*
Sri Nisargadatta Maharaj, *I am That: Conversations with Sri Nisargadatta Maharaj*
Clifford Stoll, *Silicon Snake Oil*
Tom Stoppard, *Arcadia*
Robert Farris Thompson, *Face of the Gods*
– *Flash of the Spirit*
David Toop, *Ocean of Sound: Aether Talk, Ambient Sound and Imaginary Worlds*
Charles Hampden Turner, *The Seven Cultures of Capitalism*
Rebecca West, *Black Lamb and Grey Falcon*
Edgar Wind, *Art and Anarchy*

ABOUT THE AUTHOR

Brian Eno – musician, producer, visual artist and activist – first came to international prominence in the early seventies as a founding member of British band, Roxy Music and immediately followed by a series of influential solo albums. His visionary work as producer includes albums with Talking Heads, Devo, U2, Laurie Anderson, James and Coldplay, while his long list of collaborations include recordings with David Bowie, Jon Hassell, Harold Budd, John Cale, David Byrne, Grace Jones, Karl Hyde, James Blake and most recently with his brother Roger on *Mixing Colours*. His visual experiments with light and video continue to parallel his musical career with exhibitions and installations all over the globe. To date he has released over forty albums of his own music and exhibited extensively, as far afield as the Venice Biennale, St Petersburg's Marble Palace, Ritan Park in Beijing, Arcos de Lapa in Rio de Janiero and the sails of the Sydney Opera House. He is a founding member of the Long Now Foundation, a trustee of Client Earth and patron of Videre est Credere. His latest album, *Film Music: 1976–2020*, was released in November 2020.